The Company
They Kept

◆

LARA PUTNAM

The Company
They Kept

Migrants and the Politics
of Gender in Caribbean
Costa Rica, 1870–1960

◆

THE UNIVERSITY OF NORTH CAROLINA PRESS
CHAPEL HILL AND LONDON

© 2002 The University of North Carolina Press
All rights reserved
Manufactured in the United States of America

Designed by Heidi Perov
Set in Cycles and Stone Sans
by Tseng Information Systems

The paper in this book meets the guidelines for permanence and
durability of the Committee on Production Guidelines for Book
Longevity of the Council on Library Resources.

Library of Congress Cataloging-in-Publication Data
Putnam, Lara.
The company they kept : migrants and the politics of gender in
Caribbean Costa Rica, 1870–1960 / Lara Putnam.
p. cm.
ISBN 0-8078-2732-0 (cloth : alk. paper) —
ISBN 0-8078-5406-9 (pbk. : alk. paper)
1. Migrant agricultural laborers—Costa Rica—Puerto Limón—Social
conditions.   2. United Fruit Company—Employees—Costa Rica—Puerto
Limón—Social conditions.   3. Women—Costa Rica—Puerto Limón—
Social conditions.   4. Blacks—Costa Rica—Puerto Limón—Social
conditions.   5. Sex role—Costa Rica—Puerto Limón—History.   6. Power
(Social sciences)—Costa Rica—Puerto Limón—History.   7. Puerto Limón
(Costa Rica)—Social conditions.   8. Puerto Limón (Costa Rica)—
Economic conditions.   I. Title.
HD1531.C8 P88   2002
306.3'6'097286109034—dc21
2002001552

cloth   06 05 04 03 02   5 4 3 2 1
paper   06 05 04 03 02   5 4 3 2 1

THIS BOOK WAS DIGITALLY PRINTED.

To my parents

Contents

Appendix

Illustrations, Figures, and Maps

Illustrations

Figures

Maps

Acknowledgments

This book would not exist but for an extended family whose contributions of love, labor, money, and time made it possible to raise three small children and write a doctoral dissertation simultaneously. Natalia González, Christin Campbell, Aracelly Pérez, Elsa Pérez, Mario Pérez, Jonathan Putnam, Robert Putnam, Rosemary Putnam, Ruth Putnam, Louis Werner, and Zelda Werner each gave essential support. My parents have provided impeccable models of nurturance and intellectual integrity, and I hope that I have done them proud. Most of what I know about the complicated weave of productive and reproductive labor has been taught to me by my children, Miriam, Gabriel, and Alonso—sometimes against my will—and I am grateful for their love and resilience. To my husband, Mario, my deepest thanks are due.

Research for this project has been generously supported by the Rackham School of Graduate Studies, the Latin American and Caribbean Studies Program, the Project on Secondary Migrations in the African Diaspora of the Center for African and Afro-American Studies, and the History Department, all of the University of Michigan; the Fulbright-USIA program; the Mellon Foundation; and the Vicerrectoría de Investigación of the Universidad de Costa Rica. My research in Costa Rica would not have been possible without the help and friendship of Rina Cáceres, Elizabeth Fonseca, Héctor Pérez, and Ronny Viales of the Centro de Investigaciones Históricas de América Central; Rocío Vallecillos and the staff at the Sala de Consulta of the ANCR; my research assistants, Ileana d'Alolio and Carlos Fallas Santamaría; and Juan Carlos Vargas. Archivists at the Harvard Business School's Baker Library, the ANCR, and the Museo Nacional de Costa Rica went out of their way to track down photographs and facilitate permissions. The David Rockefeller Center for Latin American Studies at Harvard University provided a warm home during this project's conclusion.

Moji Anderson, Soili Buska, Sueann Caulfield, Frederick Cooper, Laura Gotkowitz, Lowell Gudmundson, Thomas Green, Peter Guardino, Anne Hayes, Aims McGuinness, Dunbar Moodie, Stefan Palmié, Robert Putnam, Rosemary Putnam, Rebecca Scott, Florencia Quesada, and Ronny Viales all read and commented on partial drafts of this material. Conversations with Aims McGuinness have been so central to every stage in this project that I once threatened to blame him in the acknowledgments for any errors remaining. My extraordinary dissertation committee members—Frederick Cooper, Catherine MacKinnon, and Ann Stoler—asked precisely the right hard questions. Elaine Maisner, Lowell Gudmundson, and an anonymous reader for University of North Carolina Press greatly improved the final product; Mary Reid edited the manuscript with meticulous care. Finally, Sueann Caulfield and Rebecca Scott have been exemplary advisers throughout my graduate education and beyond: models of intellectual enthusiasm, rigorous critique, and enduring support.

The Company
They Kept

◆

Certain woman call me a one-pant man

I shouldn't be in society

calling myself a calypsonian

but she say she going to run me out the country.

Me no know brother me no know

what I done this wicked woman

I only sing me sweet calypso

she say she going to run me out of the land.

She went and called the police on me

telling them I'm running contraband

when the government come down and see

they glad was to leave the calypsonian.

She went and called the authority

telling them I'm a foreigner

they come with soldiers and artillery

compelling me to show them me cédula.

—Calypso by Walter Gavitt Ferguson

of Cahuita, Costa Rica

Introduction

Sebastiana Veragua was born in 1890 in Colón, the Caribbean terminus of the French Panama Canal project gone bankrupt the year before. When her grandmother, who raised her, fell ill in 1904 she brought Sebastiana north to Port Limón, Costa Rica, and placed her as a servant in the home of Colombian lawyer Salomón Zacarías Aguilera. After two years of cleaning house and caring for Aguilera's three children for half the going wage, seventeen-year-old Sebastiana decided to heed the "words of love and affection" of Costa Rican laborer Leandro Chacón. One Sunday evening they met in the park while the military band played, and Sebastiana accompanied Leandro to his rented room. She did not return to collect her belongings from the Aguilera home until three days later, the morning after Leandro had finally been able to rupture her hymen. Hers were sexual acts in a domestic setting, but they were also moves in a contest over labor conditions and personal autonomy — a fact underscored when Aguilera denounced Leandro to the police for the offense of "deflowering" his "ward" and demanded Sebastiana be returned to his custody.

Called to perform the requisite vaginal exam, Dr. Benjamín de Céspedes described Sebastiana as "a young *negra* who because of her inciting curves must have been sought after with real tenacity by her rapist. . . . [T]he loss of virginity has been consummated without the slightest resistance on the part of a young woman well-built for reproductive ends."[1] The clinical report encased a political claim about which kinds of women should have access to which kinds of state protection. Sebastiana's blackness, her curves, and her sexual willingness were apparently equally visible to Céspedes's trained eye. Of course, the doctor had long experience in such things. Years earlier he had authored a survey of prostitution in his native Cuba and observed that "in the lymphatic organism of Cuban society the suppurating abscess of prostitution is located in the customs of the colored race."[2] In this instance Sebastiana chose not to contradict his views. She was, she insisted, not the victim but the author of her loss of virginity.

That same year nine million banana stems were shipped from Port Limón, loaded onto United Fruit Company (UFCO) steamers within sight of the park where Sebastiana and Leandro took their evening stroll. Rail lines branching west and south from the port city tied together the province of Limón, a vast hinterland where farms large and small were dedicated to growing the green gold. We know much of certain kinds of labor and politics in the banana zone, of plantations and strikes and contracts between San José congressmen and Boston lawyers. But Sebastiana's story suggests new questions: about the work of caring for children and men and how it fit into the export economy, about the role of kinship and social ties as well as cash in structuring labor there, about the household as a site of conflict over resources and authority, about the impact of ideas about race and sexuality on the exercise of power.

Labor and Love in the Export Economy

Working from a dependency framework, intellectuals in the 1970s and 1980s argued that global linkages had determined the course of Central American history, particularly that of the "enclave economies" of the Caribbean lowlands. But as historians have built detailed case studies from a wider variety of primary sources, it has become clear that the impact of global forces was decisively conditioned by regional and local dynamics.[3] There is a common misconception in Costa Rica that banana exports, UFCO power, and Jamaican immigration rose and fell together. Early observers certainly linked the three: company boosters marveled at the power of United Fruit to import black workers to export bananas, while nationalist critics railed against the same. But examining the history of Caribbean Costa Rica with a closer optic and a wider time frame reveals that banana exports and labor migration responded to separate dynamics, neither of which functioned at the will of UFCO officials. In each case, developments in the province of Limón depended on events and processes in a broader region, the Western Caribbean, which encompassed the coastal lowlands from Guatemala to Colombia and the islands of Jamaica and Cuba.

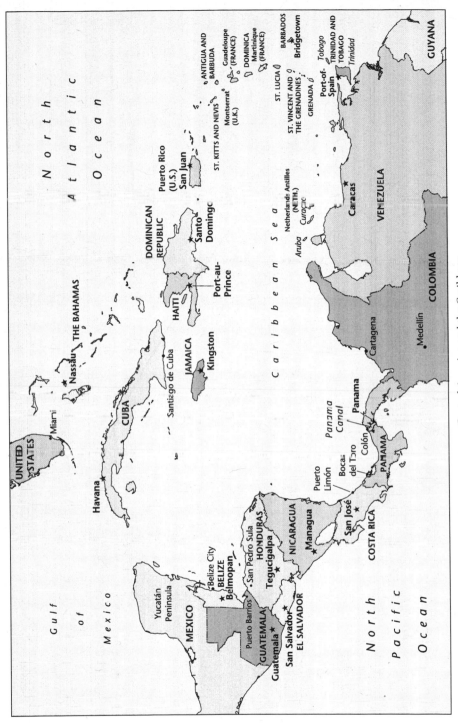

MAP I.I. Central America and the Caribbean

Seafarers had circulated among the islands and rimlands of the Western Caribbean since the 1600s, and travel between Jamaica and Central America intensified in the last quarter of the nineteenth century as infrastructure projects and export agriculture boomed along the coast. Construction of the railroad from highland Costa Rica to Port Limón drew thousands of workers from the British Caribbean in the 1870s; work on the French canal project to the south drew tens of thousands a decade later. Bananas were first planted commercially in Costa Rica by former railroad and canal workers, on lands they claimed for themselves and on plantations owned by railroad concessionaire Minor Cooper Keith. In 1898 Keith merged his Costa Rican holdings with Jamaica-based Boston Fruit to form the United Fruit Company. Keith's company directly managed more than half the banana acreage in Limón before the turn of the century, and the majority of workers on United Fruit Company plantations were West Indians. Other plantations were established by wealthy Costa Ricans and well-placed newcomers from Colombia, Cuba, the British Caribbean, and beyond. Most workers on these noncompany plantations came from highland Costa Rica, with smaller numbers from Nicaragua, Colombia, and the West Indies. During this first banana boom United Fruit's control over those who passed through its employ was limited by the ease of travel, the plentiful employment opportunities across the region, and the lack of legal restrictions on migration. Banana exports from Limón grew continuously from the 1880s through 1907, wavered for several years, and then plunged during World War I. Cultivation practices had exhausted ecosystems and opened the way for plant disease; this, coupled with mounting labor activism, encouraged United Fruit to shift resources to Panama, Guatemala, Honduras, and Colombia.

When strikes in Limón and Sixaola (on the Costa Rica–Panama border) after World War I were met by repression rather than UFCO concessions, young West Indian men left Costa Rica in droves for Cuba's booming sugar industry. In 1920 international banana prices soared, and United Fruit and farmers big and small began planting export fruit again on lands that had been abandoned two decades before. This time the company recruited Costa Rican laborers by the thousands. Company rolls soon shrank, though, as yields again declined. The 1930s were lean years all around. A brief surge in banana planting in the late 1930s tailed off to near-zero banana exports from 1942 to 1958. Yet in those same years United Fruit became once again the largest direct employer in the province, now growing manila hemp and cocoa. On these plantations most workers were recent migrants from highland Costa Rica or from

Nicaragua, alongside some West Indians (by now, second- or third-generation natives of Limón). Within the province homesteads and cocoa smallholds multiplied, but in the broader region wage-earning alternatives were scarce. Workers' lives were no more restricted to Limón than were UFCO investments, and the expansion of United Fruit holdings in Pacific Costa Rica and Panama in these years meant that the company's weight in the laboring lives of people who came through Limón increased, if anything, while bananas disappeared from Limón over the 1930s, 1940s, and 1950s.

Does this chronicle of commodity cycles and the men whose labor fueled them accurately sum up the economic history of Limón? Throughout the decades described above there was a vast amount of work integral to the export economy that was not tallied on company payrolls or shipping manifests. A thorough account of the functioning of the enclave should encompass not only acreage, exports, and infrastructure, but also food grown, bartered, or bought, and then carried, and prepared; water hauled for drinking and washing; trousers patched and dresses starched; and bush tea brewed so agues would pass. The arrangements under which such labor was performed were generally beyond the control—and often beyond the ken—of company managers and plantation owners. As in most places at most times, gender was a crucial component of the organization of production. Here the labor of social reproduction was women's work. One element was generational reproduction: the bearing and rearing of children. But even more basic to the export economy was daily social reproduction: the food, clean clothes, shelter, sex, and companionship that sustained the regional workforce.[4]

Women reached Limón from Kingston and Cartago, St. Lucia and San Juan del Norte. Some came with a male partner by their side, others on their own. (West Indian girls in their early teens were often sent by their mothers to work with an older female relative or friend.) Male migrants outnumbered females by more than two to one in the early decades of plantation expansion, creating a seller's market for female services that gave incoming women abundant alternatives to an exclusive relationship with any given partner. Such was the luck of Jerome Dabney, by his own account, as he yelled at Jane Barnes's boardinghouse door in 1903: "Dam how Beach [Damn whore bitch], I take you from Kingston naked, and I have to give you clothes to cover your ass, and you come in Limón to take man upon my catt [cot]: make your man buy mattress give you."[5] The great majority of women settled in the port city or in the line towns located at railroad junctions. A few chose to follow husbands or lovers into the bush or from camp to camp, cooking, washing, and comforting not for cash but for love, for long-term promises, or for lack of a good way out. Prostitution or "sex work" is an increasingly popular topic of historical investigation, and it is one I explore at length below. But I also describe many other things women and men did that involved both sex and work, like taking a sweetheart, claiming a homestead, or raising a family. Kinship, cash, and noncash exchange each structured a portion of the reproductive labor essential to the export economy.

The Civilizing Mission

Recent work in colonial and postcolonial studies has renewed attention to the moral claims of U.S. and European overseas projects in the late nineteenth and early twentieth century. Contributors do not deny that self-serving profit-taking was fundamental to colonial expansion. However, they do take seriously the ways in which that colonial enterprise affected and was affected by ideologies of racial superiority, gendered virtue, and moral duty.[6] United Fruit publications described the company's tropical endeavor as the American vanguard of the worldwide white man's mission. In Costa Rica, Frederick Upham Adams wrote in 1914,

> [t]he native Indian tribes have absorbed some of the attributes of Caucasian civilization—which is the only way an Indian can acquire the first veneer of civilization. Each succeeding generation of Costa Rican Indians has sloughed off some hereditary tribal trait and substituted for it an energetic habit of the dominant white man. . . . There has been no effective or lasting progress in all of the vast domain from the Rio Grande to Cape Horn which was not the result of Caucasian initiative and eventual supremacy, and the hope of the disturbed sections of Central America lies in an influx of the race which has the intelligence and the courage to fight only for peace.[7]

There is no doubt that the way UFCO managers, investors, and shills understood their place in the tropics was imbued with ideologies of race and gender that justified white northern domination. However, sources generated outside the company's purview give little evidence that UFCO's discursive embrace of the civilizing mission was translated into action. Did United Fruit pursue a project of cultural imperialism in Limón? Did company bosses try to supervise home lives, sexual choices, or moral codes? Workers' personal narratives tell of bananas rejected on flimsy pretense, supervisors lying about the measure of tasks, wounds left to rot by racist bosses. They also tell of instances of open-handed generosity and moments of mutual respect. But in these same frequently critical, occasionally complimentary sources there is no evidence of UFCO agents trying to instill bourgeois values, promote the male-headed nuclear family, or counsel sexual moderation. To judge by the narratives and testimony of those who passed through its employ, the company's energies were directed at impeding unionization (always) and controlling the labor process (sometimes, though hands-off subcontracting and outsourcing were also prominent among UFCO arrangements). Controlling workers' domestic lives was not even on the list. Meanwhile, supervisors sought pleasure and power in ways that were not starkly different from those of the workers they supervised. Company rhetoric about moral improvement remained just that: rhetoric.

In this context it is useful to compare the turn-of-the-century migration of West Indians to Central America—a mix of private recruitment and spontaneous departures—with the migration of East Indians to the British Caribbean organized by the colonial government in the same years. In Trinidad, Guyana, and Jamaica indentured labor schemes were plagued by the costs of repatriating single men who wanted to go home as soon as their contracts were up. While the private contractors who brought West Indians to Central America usually avoided the expense of repatriation by reneging on their promises—assuming they had not gone bankrupt long before—British authorities were in a more delicate position. Both the ideology that justified imperial rule and the practical challenge of maintaining it demanded that commitments to migrants be honored. For the same reason, British officials were more responsive to complaints about the immorality and violence of heavily male plantation labor forces than UFCO officials ever were. With an eye to both stabilizing and moralizing the immigrant workforce, colonial officials mandated the inclusion of ever higher proportions of women in shipments of contracted workers.[8]

As a result, indentured East Indian women labored in sizable numbers on Jamaican banana plantations. The West Indian women who traveled on their own to Central America never did. The United Fruit Company proved perfectly willing to employ women as field workers and dock laborers in Jamaica; that it did not do so in Central America reflected differences in local labor markets and in immigrant women's freedom to maneuver within them, rather than any ideological commitment to a particular vision of femininity on the part of the company.[9] UFCO indifference to workers' domestic morality did not mean that gendered moral claims were unconnected to hierarchies of power in Limón. What it meant was that here laundresses and laborers, preachers and prostitutes themselves instigated the struggles that shaped intimacy and obligation among them.

Transnational Migrants in the Western Caribbean

This study uses microhistorical techniques to create a portrait of migrants' lives not limited to those patterns contemporary observers perceived. Microhistory reduces the scale of observation in order to detect elements obscured in aggregate data. This is hardly revolutionary. A basic dictate in social science is to use the smallest unit of analysis data permits so as to avoid spurious correlations. Claims about ethnic differences in party allegiance, for example, are far more convincing if based on surveys of individual voters than if inferred from state-by-state trends. Similarly, historians may reduce the unit of analysis to the individual life, tracking medieval villagers or nineteenth-century mill girls via nominal record linkage to assess market arrangements, migratory systems, and cultural change. Microhistory does not pursue micro-social explanations—explanations that stress personal skill, virtue, or luck in explaining individual outcomes—nor does it restrict analysis to the actor's point of view. Long-term changes in demography, production, investment, and commerce are often invisible to us even as they shape our lives. Microhistory provides a more accurate picture of large-scale trends and also offers a unique window onto the way in which myriad intimate encounters, patterned in common ways, create collective change.[10]

The impact of this approach is clear in the case of Western Caribbean migration. At the aggregate level, official statistics from the late nineteenth and early twentieth centuries seem to depict successive waves of emigration from Jamaica: to Costa Rica in the 1870s, to Panama in the 1880s, to Costa Rica in the 1890s and 1900s, to Panama during the construction of the U.S. canal, to Cuba after World War I. However, microlevel data—autobiographies and personal accounts preserved in judicial testimony—show a very different pattern. Sebastiana Veragua and her grandmother traveled a well-worn route. Men and women moved back and forth between Kingston, Colón, Bocas del Toro, Port Limón, Santiago de Cuba, and a dozen other ports, working for wages, buying and trading, washing and cooking, planting and reaping. The one-way shifts that appear in aggregate statistics mask a system in which people moved and moved on repeatedly, creating a migratory field that expanded to include new sites of economic dynamism as the decades wore on.

Social networks shape migration. This is a truism among sociologists and anthropologists today, and yet historians have never asked whether migrants' networks affected the enclave economies' labor force formation. In fact, though, personal ties guided migrants' decisions of where and when to travel and often determined how they applied themselves upon arrival. No categorical distinction separated kinship and other ties in this regard. Informal adoption, consensual unions, and same-sex work partnerships all carried obligations both economic and emotional. Frequent moves and multiple encounters created far-flung social networks and reinforced norms of sharing and reciprocity within them. This was equally true of West Indian migrants at the turn of the century and Costa Ricans and other Central Americans a generation later. It was not unusual for a family to include relatives in Kingston, Cuba, Bocas del Toro, Colón, and Limón. A man from Nicaragua might run into a sister in Limón, an uncle on Costa Rica's Pacific coast, and a former lover in Sixaola, and he would certainly find former work companions at all those sites. The paradoxical result of applying a microscopic lens to the history of Limón is to reveal the extent of regional linkages, the interdependence of processes played out in Panama, Jamaica, Cuba, Costa Rica, and Nicaragua.

Sympathetic observers blamed the lack of social bonds among "uprooted" workers for the legendary drinking and violence of the plantation zone. "In his small home community he was influenced by the attitudes of his neighbors. He enjoyed their approval and shunned their disapproval. With these primary relationships gone, many a transplanted worker . . . loses important controls which formerly had guided his daily conduct."[11] But plantation drinking and violence did not reflect a lack of social ties; on the contrary, they reflected the specific character of social ties forged between migrant men. As we shall see, violence between men was highly stylized, almost scripted, as insults and threats culminated in duels of honor with clear standards and known consequences. This was not a reversion to some precultural masculine state of nature. This was a particular local culture, one in which loyalty and reputations were important enough to fight over.

The State in the Enclave

Ironically, the birthplace of United Fruit—in a sense, the original banana republic—has become the only successfully hegemonic state in Central America. Throughout the twentieth century Costa Rica's breadth of political participation and degree of power sharing were greater than those of its isthmian neighbors, and by the 1920s highland intellectuals had laid the groundwork for what would become one of Latin America's most enduring welfare states.[12] Early-twentieth-century critics charged that United Fruit manipulations undercut national sovereignty, suggesting that state power was uniformly diminished by company power. But the state in the enclave was a multiple presence, not a monolith. A thorough account of governance in the zone must consider policemen and judges, appointed bureaucrats and locally elected politicians, and must assess the use of the courts, land titling, patron-client ties, labor laws, and voting. UFCO officials and different state agents worked sometimes in concert, sometimes in conflict, in a series of shifting alliances that benefited different sectors at different times. Within this abiding complexity two clear patterns stand out. First, across the generations women in the port and towns, formally disenfranchised, made active use of state institutions and actors. They used personal contacts and judicial appeals to fight eviction orders, sue foul-mouthed neighbors, intimidate their daughters' deadbeat lovers. Second, at the turn of the century West Indians in Port Limón—men and women alike—made widespread use of local courts and built personal ties to bureaucrats and elected officials. But this informal political access contracted in the late 1930s and 1940s, even as second- and third-generation Afro–Costa Ricans gained formal citizenship and voting rights for the first time.

Thus the present study is an inquiry into the changing contours of gender, kinship, and community among migrants within an enclave and within a state. The employer was uniquely powerful, the state unusually persuasive. And yet neither one seems to have dictated the terms of local debate over sexual virtue, personal deportment, family values, or domestic order. Indeed, as we follow the lives of three generations of men and women in Limón, we will find that targeted official projects and elite moralizing campaigns were rarely central to the processes through which popular behavior and belief were remade.

The Problem of Gender and the State

Gender in academic writing has come to refer to a constellation of related things. What is considered manly or feminine in a given society? What are men and women supposed to do together, and what do they actually do? What are women supposed to do with other women, and men supposed to do with other men? What do they actually do? The questions direct our attention to both public debates and intimate relations, including but not limited to those between sweethearts or spouses. They also imply related questions about sex. How are perceptions of desire or disgust shaped by culture? How are perceptions put into practice? What sanctions await those whose practice runs counter to prescriptions? Men and women, families and sex—what makes them the way they are? Social historians once looked to long-term demographic and economic transitions to explain variations in family patterns, while early feminists examined biology, psychology, and capitalism in seeking to explain women's condition. In recent decades attention has turned to the impact of state policies and to the place of gender reform in class formation. This has shed important light on the role of gender in shaping political projects, and the role of political projects in shaping gender relations.

Yet pursuing these theoretical insights requires facing a methodological dilemma. Most of what we as historians know, we know because someone with access to a filing cabinet or a printing press took an interest. Historians usually study popular practices through documents created and preserved by state institutions, elites, or employers. Moments of attention from above create records; other moments do not.[13] This selection bias creates a methodological challenge. Once one discards the assumption that the practices of intimate life belong to an apolitical *longue durée* to which state action is irrelevant, it becomes very difficult as a practical matter to see when the state did *not* matter. States are in the business of making themselves look important—or, more accurately, those who claim the mantle of state authority are in the business of making their supposed master look powerful, and themselves look efficient. This creates a descriptive bias in official sources, one that can be countered in large part by "reading against the grain." The approach has been helpfully elaborated by scholars of subaltern studies in recent years, but the basic dictum is simple: treat official accounts of social conflict with the same deep skepticism historians have long applied to documents ranging from papal bulls to provincial tax figures. The *selection* bias of written sources, however, is far harder to address. To the extent that our choice of case studies reflects the availability of written sources, we risk creating a literature in which each individual interpretation is exactly right, yet the overall picture is fundamentally flawed.

How can we avoid overstating the frequency or efficacy of top-down interventions in family life? One way is to use alternative sources, such as autobiographies and oral history. Since the respondents were not selected by a particular reformist initiative, these sources offer a more representative picture of the degree to which state acts or elite ideologies affected people's lives or permeated their storytelling. Chapter 4, for instance, compares census data with autobiographical sources in order to describe conjugal patterns among migrants. Another possibility is to track individual lives through nominal record linkage. Although this relies on official sources, by making evident the multiple moments at which individuals bumped up against state institutions, record linkage reveals lives whose trajectories went far beyond particular official obsessions. In Chapter 3 I apply this technique to the lives of women who worked as prostitutes in Limón, demonstrating the limited impact of venereal prophylaxis regulations intended to constrain their movement and employment. Prostitutes were indeed sometimes arrested or remanded for obligatory treatment. They also traveled from province to province, took lovers and discarded them, used the courts to avenge their injured honor, and generally lived their lives in ways which flew in the face of the model reformers sought to impose.

Another technique is to track specific social phenomena over time regardless of official interest, even through years for which sources are scarce. I compare patterns between groups and across generations and ask what best explains them. Sometimes official rhetoric was frankly irrelevant to on-the-ground processes. At other times it was deeply connected to them, either weighing upon them or growing out of them, or both. Exploring the use of the courts in Chapter 5, I find that lawsuits by West Indian women over public insults dropped sharply in the 1920s, in the very years the make-up of the plantation labor force was transformed and West Indian women's services became marginal to the export economy. Their shrinking access to public institutions was compounded at the end of the decade by mounting elite denunciations of black women's deportment and morals. In Chapter 6 I trace patterns in deadly violence against women. At the turn of the century the rate of homicide against women in Limón was by far the highest in the nation. By midcentury it had dropped to a fraction of the previous level. This was not a response to any moralizing effort—there is no evidence that any official ever noted, much less acted on, the problem of deadly violence against women in Limón. Rather, my explanation looks to differences in demography, earning options, and social networks, and how these affected arguments and outcomes between men and women.

Indeed, demography, settlement patterns, and macroeconomic conditions are consistently central to explaining the patterns I find. This does not imply that actors had no choices, or that their choices had no impact. Demography tracks the convergent patterns within a multitude of life trajectories, patterns shaped by perceptions of decency and desire as well as by ovulation and epidemics. As migrants negotiated the geography they encountered, with its particular ecosystems, transit routes, and patterns of settlement and ownership, they shaped the social geography subsequent sojourners would face. What impact state policy had on intimate practice and family values was often indirect or unintended, as public authorities set the terms of institutional access through land titling procedures or civil codes or immigration policy and thus shaped the terrain women and men traversed in their daily lives.[14]

Collective Identities, Race, and Gender

Limón's export booms drew workers from far flung homes, and lines of group identity were reworked on the coast. Even the apparently simple question of geographic origin could occasion multiple responses. A woman might list her place of birth variously as the island of Jamaica, the British empire, and the parish of St. James, each answer implying a different set of allegiances, obligations, and resources. To a census taker she might simply be "una negra," but the connotations of that racial label would have varied significantly over the three generations covered here. This complexity creates a fundamental dilemma for the historian. On the one hand, there were real social divisions between groups of migrants, and we need a vocabulary with which to refer to them. On the other hand, we need to recognize the constructed nature and instability of those same categories.

Certain labels, which united suppositions about racial nature and national character, acquired commonsense authority early on. *Chumeco*, derived from "Jamaican," would become synonymous with *negro* in highland speech, while among West Indians any Central American arrival was a "Spanish man," or later *paña*, from *español*. Within each of these collectives, shades of distinction varied by context and over time. How different were *nicas* and *catrachos*

(Nicaraguans and Hondurans) from *cartagos* or *ticos* (Costa Ricans)? To some observers at some moments these divides seemed as clearly reflected in skin color, and as faithfully expressed in moral character, as the divide between West Indian "blacks" and local "whites."[15] Likewise, it was a commonplace among West Indians in Limón that the man from Trinidad would find nothing to praise in the Jamaican, and that "young ladies of the clearer dye" would look down on their sisters of darker hue. At other times solidarity was the order of the day, as when the local English-language press in the 1930s urged "a greater respect for our women, whether they be nearer white, or ebony black [they are all Negritos]."[16] Across the period studied here, in most contexts the fundamental social divide in Limón was between Spanish-speaking Central Americans (whom I will refer to as Hispanics), and English-speaking Afro-Caribbeans (whom I refer to as West Indians, as they themselves sometimes did). For all their internal divisions, there was a density of ties within each of these groups never matched by links between them.

Recognition of the multivalent nature of collective identity in Limón points to another argument pursued throughout this book, regarding race, gender, and social practice. Race and gender are both culturally constructed hierarchies that justify the unequal distribution of material power with reference to supposed biological difference. Obviously the two are connected, and in the last decade much academic effort has been put into theorizing those connections. At the level of discourse race and gender indeed seem to create meaning in parallel ways. But at the level of practice race and gender are not parallel varieties of similar processes. They are very different kinds of things. The distinctions come to the fore when we consider race and gender with respect to families and networks. In a system predicated on supposed racial difference no white child may have a black mother, yet every male child must have a female mother. The family binds sexes together and keeps races apart.[17] Race can be constructed at a distance; gender is created up close and personal. In Caribbean Costa Rica the negotiations and violence that defined power relations between men and women took place between those who claimed to love each other best, and whose daily lives were most tightly intertwined. In contrast, race was made and remade through national politics, rumors, and workplace encounters. What it meant to be *chumeco* or *paña*, *negro*, *nica*, *tico*, or *indio* was defined by contact and conflict at the fringes of social networks. What it meant to be a man or woman was defined by contact and conflict at their core.

Practices and rhetoric surrounding both race and gender changed over time, but the chronology and causes of change differed markedly. At any given moment there was a wide spread in gender ideals, family values, and women's standing: these varied between individuals and over the course of lifetimes. But the grand contours of that range changed slowly if at all over time. In contrast, both rhetoric and practice surrounding race showed far more abrupt reverses. In general, changes in the language, laws, and customs that defined racial difference were tied to economic shifts, while variation in the system of gender and kinship was tied to demography and social geography. Of course trends in the economy, in demography, and in the contours of settlement were themselves linked, especially here where the population was so very mobile. And economic, demographic, and settlement shifts resulted from social processes shaped in part by ideologies of gender and race. Tracing these multiple connections and mutual influences over time is the task I take up ahead.

Chapter 1 describes the evolution of kinship practice in Jamaica and Costa Rica in the centuries before migration to Limón would begin. In each case, I argue, it was the structure of agricultural production, and the historically specific role of the state in controlling access to land and labor, that shaped domestic life over time and determined the role of legal formalities within vernacular kinship forms. The nineteenth century brought major social transformations: emancipation and the rise of a new peasantry in the British West Indies, the boom of export agriculture in post-independence Central America. Together these processes contributed to the creation of a pan Caribbean labor market after 1850, as direct foreign investment in transportation infrastructure brought together North Atlantic capital and West Indian workers. Chapter 2 traces the lives of women and men who migrated to and through Caribbean Costa Rica in the late nineteenth and early twentieth centuries. The story of Limón in these years is unavoidably a story about other places as well: about Port Antonio and the parish of St. James in Jamaica; about Colón and Panama City and the successive transit routes in between; about Santiago de Cuba and Bocas del Toro and the long hot plains of Central America's Pacific coast. Autobiographies, linked judicial records, and court testimony expose social ties and traveling lives that cut across national boundaries more often than not. Workers were extraordinarily mobile, shifting occupations and crossing borders as a matter of course. Within this overall picture of mobility, economic cycles, local and national politics, and patterned personal ties together shaped migratory trends over time.

During the tumultuous days of banana expansion in Limón—at the turn of the century and in the early 1920s—exhausted young men with cash to spare and an itch for comfort thronged the port *cantinas* and plantation clearings on paydays. Chapter 3 explores the practice of prostitution during the two banana booms. Commercial sex was an enduring feature of the export economy, taking distinct forms in the port, in towns along the rail lines, and on the plantation camps. Like all workers in Limón, prostitutes were on the move. Their travels were facilitated by and in turn reinforced social ties, including kinship ties. Judicial records reveal dense networks of mutual support as well as fierce conflicts between women and within families. While elite observers portrayed prostitutes as hardened females who knew neither honor nor sentiment, prostitutes' testimony describes a social world where both were vitally important. Turn-of-the-century "women of the life" crafted a collective understanding of romantic love in which both suffering sacrifice and flagrant independence were legitimate female roles.

By the late 1920s Limón was both a sending society (for West Indian men) and a receiving society (for Hispanics). Women and children made up an ever-increasing portion of the local populace, and migrants formed couples, households, and extended families in a great variety of ways. Chapter 4 compares kinship patterns between Hispanics and West Indians in Limón on the basis of the 1927 census, noting that contemporary claims about cultural difference are belied by the broad similarity of kinship practice across groups. It then traces the patterns of family and community that guided the work and travels of Hispanic laborers from the 1920s to 1950s, during the years in which cocoa and manila hemp replaced bananas as the precarious mainstays of the export economy. Alternating commitments to *compañeros* (male work companions) and *compañeras* (female consensual partners) syncopated the lives of itinerant wage workers as they moved from the Atlantic to the Pacific, from Panama to Nicaragua and back.

Chapter 5 uses insults suits as a window onto the politics of public space in Port Limón, from the town's origin in the 1880s to the straitened years of the 1930s. During the boom years the heterogeneous port had a boisterous street culture in which personal standing was challenged and defended, at times with profound malice and at times with good-natured abandon. Public battles for prestige brought together men and women, municipal judges and "patio princesses," Colombian madams and visiting congressmen. But with the economic crises and demographic transformations of the 1920s and 1930s, patterns of informal political access changed. Notions of domestic decorum and racialized images of female sexual transgression carried new weight in the public politics of the banana zone, and local West Indian elites fervently pursued public respectability for their community as an antidote to white racism.

Chapter 6 turns to the conflictive male culture of the plantation fields, camp barracks, commissaries, and squatter clearings of rural Limón. It combines workers' autobiographies with a survey of court cases from the 1880s through the 1950s, revealing both remarkable continuities in patterns of conjugal violence over time and marked changes in the frequency of fatal outcomes. Criminal cases describe a world in which a single slight could lead to a machete duel, a social world plainly pathological in the eyes of judicial observers. But autobiographical accounts give a different sense of workers' concern for their personal reputations. In the absence of institutions of enforcement, employees and overseers continually and individually tested the balance of power in the zone. Credit meant local merchants or neighbors willing to take one's good name as collateral. The only safety net in case of accident or illness was the loyalty of friends and companions. These were the structures that encouraged workers' hair-trigger defense of personal respect. At the same time, the habits of confrontational masculinity fostered enduringly high levels of violence against women.

Costa Rica's Caribbean coast was a heterogeneous plantation zone that experienced dramatic economic and demographic reversals over the course of a few generations. For this reason the study of Limón offers multiple possibilities for comparison between groups and over time. Such comparisons highlight the role of demography and social geography in shaping men and women's differential experiences and suggest that the impact of official rhetoric or employer schemes on the making of gender was more circumscribed. At the same time, stories from Limón attest to a different, ongoing link between the personal and the political. Hierarchies of gender pervaded everyday life, not only distinguishing women from men but distinguishing between women and between men. In doing so they helped set the terms of public debate for everyone from aggrieved mothers to striking workers to feuding politicians. For this reason practices surrounding gender, kinship, and sexuality at times became central to class struggle and state formation. But it was not always so, and the legitimacy of these practices as objects of study should not rest on this claim alone. Popular culture and intimate life mattered when they impacted public politics—and when they did not.

ONE

The Evolution of Family Practice in Jamaica and Costa Rica

Distant markets and local initiative have long set goods and people in motion around the western edge of the Caribbean Sea. The migrations that accompanied the booms and busts of export agriculture in Limón in the late nineteenth and early twentieth centuries were episodes in a well-established trend. In coming chapters I seek to compare gender roles and kinship practices in Limón between groups and over time. But what are the baseline cultural patterns against which to measure change? Which are the relevant group boundaries? The answers are not self-evident. The story of each people in the region is a Rashomon tale in which the boundaries of embattled identities are revealed to be themselves the results of previous conflicts and past convergences. Claims about racial essence, national character, and cultural divides came to dominate political rhetoric in the region in the twentieth century. Such arguments depended on a willful forgetting of the stories that went before. Diversity, capitalism, and change did not reach the Caribbean shore on an iron locomotive driven by Yankee impresario Minor C. Keith. By the middle of the nineteenth century no population in the region had been untouched by the world market and European expansion—though the terms of the engagement had varied sharply across localities and over time. No polity was ethnically homogeneous—though some nations were more committed to making that claim than others. Even within a single place, among a self-identified people, patterns of gender and kinship defied simple generalization. No model of domestic authority was unquestioned—though domestic hierarchies received stronger official backing in some places than in others. No gender roles were universal—though some individuals had more culturally sanctioned alternatives than others.

The pages that follow offer a tale of two colonies, the island of Jamaica and the province of Costa Rica. I seek to trace evolving patterns in relationships between men and women and families and states. Official interest in popular kinship was frequently non-existent, occasionally intense. In the final years of the eighteenth century imperial agents made unprecedented efforts to engineer family practice in the colonies, as the British Crown tried to stimulate slave populations' natural increase and the Spanish Crown sought to halt racial mixing by putting the weight of law behind a particular definition of family honor. In both cases, such targeted projects had minimal impact. Instead, the most powerful effects of official policies on kinship practice were indirect. Within each society the evolving articulation of economic elites, state institutions, and labor regimes set the terms of popular access to land, credit, and markets. As the structural conditions men and women negotiated in their daily lives changed over the first half of the nineteenth century, so too did the families they created and the role they allotted the state within their family practice.

The Western Caribbean in the Atlantic System

More than 5,000 years ago footpaths and coastal waterways wound from the heart of modern Mexico to the highlands of modern Colombia. Below Lake Nicaragua, in the narrow southern extreme of Mesoamerica, three mountain chains run from northwest to southeast in what is today Costa Rica. By the years 1000 to 1500 C.E. climate, geography, and long-distance ties had shaped three distinct sociolinguistic regions in the area. The Central Region included the temperate highland basin and the valleys leading south to the Pacific coast; Gran Nicoya encompassed the tropical dry forests and savannas of the Pacific lowlands of modern Nicaragua and northwest Costa Rica; Gran Chiriquí spread over the isthmus of Panama and along the rain forests and mangrove swamps of the Caribbean coast well into what is now Nicaragua. Perhaps 400,000 people lived in these three regions combined.[1] Until the 1500s the rise and fall of expansionist empires elsewhere had important cultural repercussions here, but limited political and demographic impact. With

MAP 1.1. The Western Caribbean

the arrival of military-commercial emissaries from the city-states of Castille and Aragon all this would change.

The indigenous polities of Gran Nicoya were "pacified" and distributed as *encomienda* grants to individual Spaniards in the 1520s and 1530s, those of the Central Region four decades later. This was a land of sparse opportunity from the colonizers' point of view. Descendants of Spanish adventurers who had not ended well eked out an existence in the eastern Central Valley, outside the city of Cartago where colonial officials and wealthy locals clustered. Forced resettlement had combined the tattered remnants of indigenous communities into a handful of *pueblos* in the Central Valley and central Pacific coast. "Free mulattos and *pardos*," descended from African slaves who had managed to secure their own or their children's freedom through purchase or manumission, made themselves indispensable in the colonial militias. Mulatto cowboys ran the Pacific plains cattle ranches of Cartago's wealthy. On the alluvial flood plains of Matina on the Caribbean side, African slaves cultivated the cacao groves of absent masters, and perhaps a few trees of their own as well. Indigenous people from the southern mountains were periodically forced to labor on the Matina plantations of well-connected elites. Cacao was sold illegally to Jamaica-based traders for guns, clothing, and African slaves.[2]

As sugar plantations spread from Barbados to Jamaica, Nevis, and the Leeward Isles, more than 300,000 enslaved Africans were brought to Britain's Caribbean possessions in the second half of the seventeenth century. Among West Africans arriving in Jamaica men outnumbered women by roughly three to two. European planters much preferred to purchase male laborers, while regions within West Africa varied widely in their eagerness to export female slaves. There, enslaved women were crucial to production and reproduction alike. Women performed the bulk of agricultural labor, and female slaves were integrated into their owners' households as additional wives or as wives of their owners' male slaves.[3] Jamaican planters' plans for their human chattel were less complex. The vast majority, men and women alike, were put to work in the cane. If to European observers black women's fieldwork seemed proof of their de-sexed nature, on other points West African and European gender assumptions coincided. Technical or supervisory positions were naturally to be filled by men, domestic labor to be performed by women. In theory, under the plantation system slaves were economic inputs, not economic actors. But Jamaican markets came to depend on the economic initiative of the enslaved, who kept the island supplied with "hogs, poultry, fish, corn, fruits, and other commodities."[4] Kinship ties rather than formal institutions guided production, services, and commerce within the slaves' economy.[5]

The customs that shaped sex and succor among West Indian slaves were those reconstituted by bondsmen and women themselves, within confines laid out by overwork, abuse, and early death. Developing kinship forms were shaped by the specific cultural assumptions brought by enslaved men and women; the greater or lesser heterogeneity of the slave population; the pace of arrival of "Salt-water Negroes"; the strictures of plantation size, work regime, and owner's fortunes; and the distance and degree of contact with other plantations or towns. Given the multiple sources of diversity, the broad similarity of kinship patterns developed among Caribbean slaves is striking. Households with more than one co-residential conjugal couple were rare. Only men of particularly high status had multiple wives, usually in separate households. Women typically entered into co-residential unions after the birth of their first or second child. The small size or sex imbalance of some plantations encouraged a commuting family culture, in which travel between locales maintained contact between husbands and wives, parents and children.[6]

The Caribbean islands had become by the end of the eighteenth century "the most valued possessions in the overseas imperial world, 'lying in the very belly of all commerce,' as Carew Reynell so aptly described Jamaica."[7] The booming trade with the island plantations far outshone the entrepôt trade with the rimlands. Yet European demand for indigo, cacao, turtle-shell, turtle meat, and sarsaparilla continued to bring traders and collectors to the Caribbean lowlands of Central America. Much of this commerce was controlled by the Miskitu, an expansionist indigenous tribe that came to incorporate large numbers of Africans and their descendants: survivors of a legendary shipwreck, escapees from the Honduran mines, refugees from the growing slave economies of the Western Caribbean islands. Miskitu hunted green turtles (*Chelonia mydas*) at their feeding grounds southeast of Cape Gracias a Dios and at their nesting grounds at Turtle Bogue, midway between Matina and Bluefields. Local manipulation of imperial rivalries prevented either Spain or England from gaining control of Mosquitia, whose population had grown to 20,000 by 1759.[8] Two and a half centuries after "conquest," colonial rule in southern Mesoamerica remained limited to the central highlands and Pacific plains, with only a handful of guard posts and two small settlements in the vast Caribbean lowlands. This was in spite of the unprecedented numbers of troops and decrees dispatched into the region in the last decades of the eighteenth century as part of a broad effort by the Bourbon monarchs of Spain to make bureaucracy more responsive, tax collection more efficient, trading monopolies more profitable, and colonial borders more secure.

Race and Honor in Late Colonial Costa Rica

For tightened lines of transatlantic authority to be effective it would be necessary to shore up the internal frontiers of colonial society as well. The Spanish American bureaucracy was designed to rest upon a population neatly split among racial categories, which determined legal obligations and privileges and in theory corresponded to economic position. Geographic, occupational, and administrative divides were meant to maintain Indian tributaries, black slaves, and Spanish nobles as stable and distinct social groups. But by the eighteenth century the rapidly growing numbers of *castas* (people classed by themselves or others as of mixed ancestry) indicated the breakdown of such divides. Booming indigo production around San Salvador drew indigenous workers from their communities of origin. Growing urban economies provided entrepreneurial opportunities for the children and grandchildren of domestic slaves. Intermediate social identities like mestizo and mulatto swelled accordingly, comprising by 1776 the majority within every province of the Kingdom of Guatemala except Guatemala itself.[9] The economic dynamism the Bourbons sought to advance was destroying the social order according to which they meant its fruits to be reaped. Thus the Bourbon state directed its attention to matters of sex and status in the colonies. The Royal Pragmatic of 1778 widened parental control over marriage choice in order to halt the spread of unequal unions that "gravely offend family honour and jeopardize the integrity of the State."[10] Subsequent edicts within the colonies defined precisely which socio-racial groups were subject to consent requirements, thereby delineating those whose couplings were beneath state notice and those who, despite known African ancestry, might have honor to lose.[11]

By 1801 the population of the province of Costa Rica had reached 52,591—which is to say, slightly less than the total number of African slaves imported by Jamaican planters over the previous five years.[12] Contemporaries guessed that 2,500 more *indios* lived beyond the colony's effective borders, in Talamanca, Bocas del Toro, and Guatuso (the densely forested valley south of the Río San Juan). Census-takers tallied 4,942 Spaniards, 8,281 Indians, 30 blacks, 8,925 mulattos and *zambos*, and 30,413 *ladinos* and mestizos.[13] But other documents of the era suggest that in practice racial labels were rarely used to identify social collectives. Rather, the populace was divided into a tiny elite of Spaniards and European immigrants, known as *gente noble* or *gente de bien*, and a heterogeneous but culturally converging mass of *gente del común*—common folk.[14] Over the course of four generations the numbers of people claiming mixed racial heritage, when asked, had mushroomed. Mestizos surged from 4 percent of the population in the 1720 census to 58 percent in 1801, a change in racial identification that must have been the result of both widespread extralegal unions and frequent category shifts. This is evident in marriage records from Cartago, for instance, where church unions between mestizo partners went from 18 percent of all marriages in 1738–47 to 78 percent in 1818–22, without a single marriage between a Spaniard and an Indian being registered in the entire period.[15] The growth of the mestizo category seems to have reflected not a late-blooming sexual intimacy between Spaniards and Indians, but the increasing geographic and social integration of certain mulattos, *pardos*, and *indios* into white society. "Mestizo," a racial category that was officially sanctioned but not claimed in practice by any social collective, was adopted as a euphemistic reclassification—a sort of de facto, plebeian *cédula de gracias al sacar*.[16]

The Royal Pragmatic was meant to prevent just this sort of convergence, to shore up the colonial order by making legal marriage the bulwark against racial straying by men and women of pure or near-pure Spanish descent. In Cuba, where plantation slavery was expanding rapidly in just these years, the Pragmatic was indeed used toward this end.[17] But in late-eighteenth-century Costa Rica the nexus of race and production was quite different. When the Pragmatic was issued in 1778, mulattos, *zambos*, mestizos, and *ladinos* already outnumbered *españoles* by 3.7 to one in the province, and a single generation later the figure was nearly eight to one. Poor whites participated alongside those labeled mulattos and mestizos in the settling of the western Central Valley, and all faced a similar panorama of hard toil and insecure land rights. In Cuba the institution of slavery stood between poor whites and the black majority. In Costa Rica self-purchase and informal manumission had reduced the total of slaves to a hundred at most, and race was ever less salient as an axis of difference among the *gente del común*. Conjugal households, not plantations, structured rural production. In the words of one man facing eviction, "I have a cane field, *trapiche* [cane grinder and boiling house], house, plantains, fruit trees, and cattle . . . all of which I have planted with the sweat of myself and my woman and my children."[18] The male-headed nuclear family the petitioner described was entirely consistent with the kin forms promoted by church and state, and perhaps two-thirds of households were united by the sacrament of marriage.[19]

Peninsular authority in Central America ended with a whimper rather than a shout. Disenchanted with the liberal Cortes governing Spain in the wake of the Napoleonic invasion, and wary of the social unrest accompanying independence movements to the north and south, Guatemalan aristocrats declared the provinces independent in 1821. Absorbed by elite rivalries and struggles for primacy among highland towns, the new national governments of Central America devoted even less attention to the Caribbean lowlands

than late colonial officials had. States pressed territorial claims in treaty negotiations with Britain but in practice conceded a British sphere of influence
from British Honduras to Greytown (San Juan del Norte). The pre-Columbian
Gran Chiriquí had become a land sparsely populated by refugees, entrepreneurs, and survivors. Some, like the Miskitu, had embraced the possibilities
offered by European clients and strategic warfare. Others, like the Bribri of
Talamanca and the *negros de Costa Arriba* in Panama, had fled from violence
and commerce, abandoning coastal resources for upstream isolation. The
African-descended settlers of Matina had worked within the colonial economy, through no choice of their own, and some had prospered. All of these
populations had been shaped by the Atlantic system, by European sparring
and the slave trade. Their existence as collectives was witness to the opportunities for maneuver offered by the fringes of empire.

Nineteenth-Century Transformations: Jamaica after Slavery

After 1789, antislavery activism in England was given a huge boost by events
in French Saint-Domingue, where enslaved African rebels successfully ended
European rule of the most profitable colony in the world. The biological
reproduction of creole slave populations came to seem the fulcrum of the
plantation system's survival, and the black woman as mother became a centerpiece of transatlantic debate. Great Britain outlawed slave traffic by her merchants in 1807. Planters espoused a new paternalism and swore that plantation populations, now free of African troublemakers with their illnesses,
barbarisms, and armed rebellions, would accommodatingly reproduce themselves. They did not. Faced with slave owners' failure to improve plantation
conditions or stimulate slave populations' natural increase, the British Colonial Office pushed the Amelioration Acts through Parliament in the 1820s,
stipulating that "[s]laves should be given religious instruction; marriages and
families should be protected; physical coercion, especially whipping, should
be controlled if not abolished; and manumission should be encouraged."[20]
Planters had long held that abolitionist agitation in Britain and missionary
activity in the Indies would destroy the discipline necessary to maintain the
plantation system, and they were not wrong. Slave rebellions shook Barbados
in 1816, Demerara in 1823, and Jamaica in 1831. The accounts of missionaries
who fled to England in the wake of the rebellions' repression helped turn the
tide of opinion in favor of immediate abolition.

The same moral vision that inspired abolitionists' struggle against slavery dictated particular plans for its replacement. In the eyes of reformers the establishment of male-headed, nuclear, Christian families among former slaves would be both the means of creating a new working class and the ultimate proof of their crusade's success.[21] But the struggle to define the terms of free labor would sculpt Jamaican families along far different lines. Freedmen seem to have been eager to undertake well-paid work, especially when set by the task, but balked at coercive rental agreements and wages arbitrarily set and intermittently paid. Even graver than black men's refusal to commit their labor power to the estates full time was black women's frequent refusal to work there at all. In the separation of women and children from waged labor the postemancipation family looked rather more like the clergy's idealized bourgeois union than it did the planters' idealized dependent proletariat. Yet women's flight from the estates hardly represented a retreat into godly domesticity. For the next 150 years female higglers would be the mainstay of Jamaican public marketing.[22]

It was through the purchase of land that former slaves found the autonomy to manage their households' labor as they saw fit. Sales and registration of holdings under ten acres soared in the years immediately following abolition, with perhaps 20 percent of the former apprentice population residing on such plots a mere seven years after emancipation.[23] Evidence of the kinship forms that sustained and were sustained by rural Jamaicans is found in "family land," a customary institution created in the generations immediately following abolition. In the kinship system defined by church law and common law, property was inherited along lines set by legal marriage, legitimate birth, primogeniture, and male precedence, or it was sold. In contrast, family land was, in the words of a modern informant, "not to be sold, *not* to be sold; *not* selling it. If me even *dead*, it can't sell. Not selling. It's fe the children: all the children." Who counted as "the children" was expansive, for in direct contrast to the British-defined legalities of kinship, family land evolved with bilateral kin reckoning, equivalent male and female access, and entitlement for all recognized (not only legalized) children of corporate members.[24] It is significant that conjugal ties did not establish membership. Life stories of the second generation of Jamaican freewomen describe rural households anchored by mothers and grandmothers in which male mates were valued but not necessarily permanent members. Such unions were not casual—quite the contrary. A co-residential union implied definite obligations, a marriage all the more. Aunty Lou, born 1875, described the proprieties of female labor:

"But you coulden expect him a woman an have him husband, fi go dig [yam] hole! . . . Mi sey dem never work for himself. And him have husband! You hear dere now? Him no have no occasion. Dem woulden allow dem fi go work. Dem go a ground and when dem dig food dem carry it go out a market go sell."[25] Tending and marketing provision crops were appropriate activities for a married woman. Digging yam holes or seeking wage employment were not.

Church formalities were selectively incorporated into local practice. By the second decade of the nineteenth century, baptism had increased dramatically among the enslaved, although marriage had not, even among young Christian couples who together brought their children to be baptized.[26] Marriage grew more common after abolition, though less so than missionaries had hoped. From the start of record keeping in the 1870s through the present day, births out of wedlock have accounted for 60 to 70 percent of live births in Jamaica. While disregarding church doctrine on conjugal unions and sex, Jamaicans embraced other possibilities Christian ritual offered. The 1850s and 1860s saw an outpouring of religious enthusiasm with the creation of Revivalism, myalism, and obeah, all of which combined West African and Christian elements.[27] Christian orthodoxy in style of worship and in family practice was ever more closely tied to class position. Like rising merchants and industrialists in Britain two generations before, members of the emerging Coloured middle class sought to make Christian piety and wealth the twin pillars of their claim to political voice.[28]

Thus Jamaican freedmen and women sought both autonomy and advancement. They purchased land for residence and farming and created customary institutions such as family land, which spread the security landownership offered among as many descendants as possible. Smallholders raised crops and animals for market and soon grew the bulk of "minor staple" exports: coffee, ginger, arrowroot, plantains, and allspice. Wage labor when the terms were right was a desirable complement to independent farming, and in the decades after emancipation it was those regions in which land for purchase and estates for employment existed side by side that saw the largest population growth. Yet over the course of the 1850s and 1860s the conditions faced by freedpeople and their sons and daughters steadily worsened.[29] Jamaican sugar had been in trouble for some time. Cuban plantations combining state-of-the-art technology, fertile soils, and enslaved labor surged after the 1780s, and the expansion of British interests eastward meant West Indian planters now competed against cane growers in India, Mauritius, Singapore, Java, and the Philippines as well. Mismanagement and labor struggles in the 1840s and

1850s accelerated the decline of Jamaican sugar. Planters insisted that only with a labor force available on demand—as freedmen and women refused to be—could production recover. The Jamaican government spent roughly ten times as much on the importation of indentured workers in these two decades as it did on education, achieving a net increase in the workforce of perhaps 10 percent. Given plantations' low productivity, indentured labor could not make Jamaican sugar competitive on the world market, but it did manage to drive wage rates well below subsistence levels. The very survival of the Jamaican working class in an era in which an adult male laborer could barely earn enough to feed himself is testimony to the efficiency with which family networks channeled and husbanded disparate resources.[30]

Meanwhile, British officials were ever more sympathetic to planters' insistence that the people's racial nature required a heavy hand. Vagrancy laws were tightened, access to unoccupied lands restricted, and whipping reinstituted for crimes against property.[31] If in spite of it all some freemen and women managed to put together household economies that combined just enough land, just enough produce, and just enough wages to maintain a measure of rural autonomy, others did not. Former estate artisans swelled the ranks of the Kingston poor. Appalled missionaries watched gangs of boys "swear, swagger, and fight, bluster and blaspheme with a volubility and a recklessness such as is most painful to witness," while "hordes of the lowest prostitutes . . . join [the] banks of [black] soldiers, walk with them, laugh with them, jeer and fight with them . . . following these soldiers in their very walks, their breasts, shoulders, and arms exposed and bare."[32] Little could affront bourgeois observers more than the sight of potential workers unwilling to accept the wages of poverty—unless it was the sight of potential wives selling domestic comfort for cash. This was the milieu that would supply the first West Indian recruits for U.S. contractors seeking a tractable labor force for construction projects on the Central American isthmus.

Costa Rica and Coffee

The southernmost and least populous of the United Provinces of Central America in 1823 would be a generation later by far the most prosperous of the region's independent states. Capital accumulated in short-lived mining and dyewood booms was channeled to a new crop, one for which soil, climate, and world market conditions could not have been more favorable: the mildly addictive stimulant *coffea arabica*. Coffee exports soared from 8,000 *quintales* in 1840 to 100,000 *quintales* in 1848. The typical Costa Rican coffee farm in these years covered less than five *manzanas* (eight and a half acres) of land, densely planted with upward of 1,400 coffee trees. Yet the bulk of exports came from holdings ten times that size.[33] Predictable tensions between small-holder and estate production were evident in plantation owners' complaints about peasants' "'lack of interest' in sustained wage labor."[34] Lacking both inherited institutions of labor coercion and, as yet, the political clout to create them, employers resorted to economic incentives. Average monthly wages rose from 7.5 pesos in 1844 to 15–18 pesos in 1856 and 25–30 pesos by 1870 and still barely mobilized enough workers for harvest. Unable to reduce costs by monopolizing land or labor, local elites dedicated themselves to raising profits by controlling processing and export. The rise of wet-pulp processing in the 1840s consolidated the position of those select few able to build large *beneficios* (processing mills) and link them to both local suppliers and overseas buyers. In the 1820s and 1830s processed beans were sent by oxcart to the Pacific port of Puntarenas and then shipped to Valparaíso, Chile, for re-export to Europe. Direct shipment to London along the same route began in 1840.[35]

By midcentury food crops and pasture had disappeared entirely from the landscape around San José, replaced by the shiny dark green of row upon row of coffee trees. Cane, cattle, and corn were farmed several days' walk to the west now, in the valleys around the thriving towns of Heredia and Alajuela. There peasant settlers grew food for sale back east and tended young coffee shrubs of their own that would soon bear fruit. *Denuncias de tierras baldías* (concessions of government land) in the western valleys tended to be large, many over 2,400 acres in the 1830s, the majority 600 acres or more in the 1840s and 1850s. Large claims were often subdivided and portions resold to migrants and potential laborers, whose purchases were made possible by access to credit, including advances against harvests or labor and short- and long-term cash loans.[36] The risks of borrowing were clear in the rashes of foreclosures that accompanied market downturns in 1848–49, 1856–57, 1874–75, and 1884–85.[37] Yet detailed analysis of lending patterns shows not a sharp division between haves and have-nots but rather multiple ties between have-lots, have-somes, and want-mores. "The vast majority of creditors were not wealthy, did not lend large sums, nor did they have more than two or three debtors. . . . Access to borrowing was socially biased, but it was neither an exclusive privilege of the wealthy nor a means for massive expropriation of the poor."[38] Investment in coffee also took the form of deferred consumption in peasant households, especially on the agricultural frontier. Settlers planted coffee seedlings alongside food crops destined for market and got by on wages, crop and cattle sales, and home-grown produce during the three to five years in which the coffee they cultivated yielded nothing at all.[39] Husbands and sons worked part-time for wages throughout the year. In the harvest months wives and daughters joined them picking coffee on nearby estates. Private land titles were increasingly important for such families, both as surety for loans and as a safeguard on the investment that mature coffee shrubs represented.[40]

In Jamaican family land we saw an institution evolved to transmit property along kinship lines quite foreign to those enshrined in law. Among Costa Rican peasant proprietors we see in contrast a broad adherence to both legal principles and legal mechanisms of property transmittal. The poorest families, urban and rural, passed along what goods they had without recourse to the costly legal inheritance system. But for those who claimed title to real property—the majority of country folk by midcentury—use of *mortuales* (wills) and postmortem inventories was crucial. Spanish jurisprudence held that all legitimate children must receive equal portions of their parents' estate. Nineteenth-century parents followed both the spirit and the letter of equal property division between daughters and sons, often in the form of land, tools, or capital advanced to a child leaving home to form an independent household.[41] Church marriage, household formation, and the start of sexual reproduction increasingly coincided for Costa Rican women. In the Central Valley births out of wedlock dropped rapidly from their late colonial high of around one-third of all births. Where coffee was most established, illegitimacy rates were lowest, holding steady around 10 percent across the second half of the nineteenth century. In contrast, outside of the Central Valley illegitimacy rates were 50 percent or higher, far more typical of Latin America as a whole.[42] Enthusiasm for church marriage was of a piece with the centrality of legitimate inheritance to smallholder life in the coffee regions. In the cities rather different family patterns were emerging, with the proportion of female-headed households (30 to 40 percent) twice as high as in rural villages, and the fraction of female heads who had never married (40 percent) notably higher as well.[43]

While inheritance law as practiced in this period insisted on gender parity, civil and criminal law insisted on male primacy. No one thought male authority could or should be absolute. Husbands were required to administer their wives' property sensibly; to feed, clothe, and house their wives and legitimate children as best they could; and to get their way without using excessive physical force. Male authority was contingent and partial, but when push came to shove husbands and fathers usually found they had the strength of law behind them. And the law, in the form of municipal councils, *alcaldes* (mayors), courts, and justices of the peace, was rapidly following the coffee frontier across the Central Valley. Judicial records confirm the increasing role of legal forums in domestic disputes.[44]

Despite their disparate pasts and divergent futures, by the mid-nineteenth century the fertile inland valleys of Costa Rica and Jamaica had arrived at structures of agricultural production with distinct similarities. The great majority of rural people in each country would at some point in their lifetimes hire themselves out for a daily wage, contract themselves by the task, work a neighbor's land in a noncash exchange, and cultivate provisions and export crops on land they claimed as their own. This was true of both men and women in both countries. For a married woman to work for wages other than at harvest time was an insult to her virtue and her husband's virility in both societies, although straitened Jamaican peasants found themselves forced into such a compromise more often than their Costa Rican counterparts. Overall, Jamaican women enjoyed a far wider range of culturally sanctioned economic roles. The higgler who worked her land, marketed its produce, and administered the profits herself had no equivalent in nineteenth-century Costa Rica. On the other hand, elite women in early republican Costa Rica played a variety of public commercial roles that might have raised eyebrows among the Jamaican plantocracy or Coloured bourgeoisie.[45]

In each country plantation owners complained repeatedly about the shortage of laborers, which they correctly linked to the availability of unoccupied land for squatting or colonizing. Of course the difference between squatting and colonizing is not merely in the eye of the beholder but rather in credit and titling policies, and it is here that the differences between the two agrarian regimes come into focus. Jamaican elites sought to mobilize labor through economic coercion at its most heavy-handed, while the colonial state faltered between conflicting commitments to the protection of new Crown subjects and the stability of the plantation system. In Costa Rica coffee planting was shaped from the start by an open frontier and the absence of institutionalized forms of obligatory labor. Costa Rican elites relied on economic incentives rather than direct control, and the national state they dominated was to find in this arrangement a wellspring of ideological and practical support.

In the eyes of the emergent Liberal elite, national expansion, both economic and territorial, would depend on the properly channeled initiative of peasant producers. "*Poblar es gobernar* [To people is to govern]" ran the slogan of the day.[46] This vision underlay the extension of credit and titles and fostered a climate of official support for the family structures assumed to inhere in settler households.

Rates of marriage and illegitimacy may reflect patterns in relationships between men and women. They may also reflect patterns in relationships between families and the state. Where the structure of public power is such that men and women make active use of the courts, we would expect the legal proprieties of kinship to exert a greater pull on popular practice. Rural society in the nineteenth-century Central Valley of Costa Rica displayed a remarkable degree of overlap between church ideals, state legalities, and popular kinship practice. In Jamaica the opposite was true. As men and women from each of these sites traveled to the Caribbean coast of Costa Rica they would form families in a variety of ways. The spectrum of domestic and conjugal forms that they created would look quite similar across migrant groups, and quite different from the elite ideologies and legal proprieties of kinship in either of the lands from which they came.

TWO

Sojourners and Settlers

Economic Cycles and Traveling

Lives, 1850s–1940s

Two currents of periodic migration have long overlapped on Costa Rica's Caribbean coast. The first, flowing between Jamaica, Panama, the Caribbean lowlands of Central America, and Cuba, carried tens of thousands of West Indians to and through Limón near the turn of the century and carried thousands of young black men away in the 1920s, 1930s, and 1940s. The second, encompassing Nicaragua, Costa Rica, and Panama, carried thousands of Spanish speakers through Limón during the first decades of the century and saw most of them depart during the lean years around World War I. It then poured nearly 10,000 itinerant Hispanic workers into the region in the 1920s alone, and a like number over the course of the following generation. Within each of these spheres of migration, ties of kin and acquaintance routinely crossed national borders. Indeed, national boundaries could be almost irrelevant — or deeply relevant, as when politicians acted to restrict entry or condition employment on the basis of citizenship or race.

Between 1850 and 1910 some 200,000 British West Indians traveled to the Central American rimlands.[1] If we attempt to understand the processes that brought working men and women from Kingston to Limón with reference only to developments within Jamaica and Costa Rica, we are like the fabled blind men attempting to describe an elephant from the feel of trunk and tail alone. The elephant in this case was a regional economy encompassing the

Caribbean rimlands from Belize to Colombia and the Antilles from Cuba in the northwest to Barbados in the southeast. Panama formed a crucial node in this regional economy, its enduring centrality to migrants' lives the inverse of its enduring absence from both Central American and Caribbean historiography. At first laborers' migration was largely orchestrated by prospective employers, who set up recruiting agents in Kingston or Bridgetown (Barbados), provided free passage, and supervised workers' placement on arrival. But as the regional export economy expanded, independent travel became proportionately cheaper and ever more varied. Workers hauled their kit up the gangplanks of inter-island passenger steamers, perched between piles of coconuts on motorboats ferrying up and down the coast, poled in *pangas* (flat-bottomed canoes) through coastal canals, and stowed away on the refrigerated steamers of United Fruit's Great White Fleet.

Banana estates began to expand in Jamaica at the end of the nineteenth century, raising land values and first halting, then reversing the trend of widening ownership. As conditions for small growers worsened, the sons and daughters of the embattled peasantry looked for wage-earning opportunities abroad. These were the men and women who left for Panama and Costa Rica around 1910 and for Cuba after World War I. And when jobs disappeared and state violence worsened in Cuba after 1920 many Jamaicans moved on, taking work where they could find it: harvesting cane in Jamaica, "licking down bush" in Costa Rica, laboring on the Panama Canal. The enterprises that drew West Indian workers in the 1930s reflected a coastal geography reshaped by the railroads, ports, and canals built with their grandfathers' and great-grandfathers' toil. The legal restrictions and local hostility that confronted West Indian workers at these sites reflected notions of national sovereignty reshaped in the same era.

Direct Foreign Investment and the Creation of a Pan-Caribbean Labor Market

With the discovery of gold in Alta California in 1848, tens of thousands of young men from the U.S. eastern seaboard swarmed to the New Granadian province of Panama to cross to the Pacific. The U.S.-owned Panama Railroad Company raced to build a rail line across the isthmus. Kingston artisans headed to Panama to join the bonanza, and railroad labor recruiters soon targeted the Kingston poor. Several thousand Jamaican men made the journey.

Upon the railroad's completion in 1855 laborers were summarily dismissed, and muleteers and brothel owners alike saw earnings slashed as travelers spent hours rather than days on the isthmus. Some Jamaicans headed home. Others squatted in the hills around Colón or in the neighborhoods of Panama City.[2]

Meanwhile, in the decades after emancipation the circulation of traders and collectors between the islands and rimlands of the Western Caribbean had intensified. Some West Indian sojourners settled in established towns like Bluefields and Greytown (San Juan del Norte) in Nicaragua, Salt Creek (Moín) in Costa Rica, and Bocas del Toro (then claimed by both Costa Rica and Colombia). In the 1860s and 1870s their children built *rawa* palm huts at turtle-collecting sites in between: Turtle Bogue and Parismina south of Greytown, Cahuita and Old Harbour on the Talamanca coast. Local tradition in Old Harbour recalls first settlers like William Shepherd of Bocas, Ezekiel Hudson of Nicaragua, and Celvinas Caldwell of San Andrés—descendants of men and women who had left the British Caribbean for Central America a generation or more before.[3] Still, at midcentury the vast majority of the 20,000 inhabitants of Costa Rica's Atlantic slope were indigenous: Guatusos, Viceitas, Cabécares, Bribris.[4] The area around Matina remained tied to the North Atlantic economy. In 1858 E. G. Squier noted "an open anchorage at Salt Creek (Moín) and Matina, with which points a small commerce is kept up, chiefly with Jamaica, in sarsaparilla, turtle-shells, and cocoanut oil."[5]

Overexploitation for markets abroad could hit individual species hard. But overall, locally organized extractive economies had minimal impact on ecosystems. Fifty years after Squier's visit dense vegetation would still cover most of the coastal wetlands of the Western Caribbean. Visitors to Cape Gracias a Dios around 1910 saw "malachite-green palms rustle in a constant soft breeze. Waterbirds haunt the lagoon, there are acres of water hyacinths, and there is a queer secrecy about the forest with its blue veil of haze; quite edible oysters cling to the low-growing mangrove bushes."[6] Quetzal feathers, mahogany logs, and contraband gold were being transported through the bay as they had been since the 1650s. Decaying frame houses stood across the lagoon, relics of an abortive mining-railroad-port-and-tourist-resort scheme organized by U.S. investors years before. Local entrepreneurs ferried passengers up and down the coast in the flat-bottomed steamer the hapless investors had left behind. In contrast, where externally financed infrastructure and export projects were successful they drastically reshaped landscapes as well as livelihoods along the Caribbean littoral.[7]

The continuing growth of coffee production convinced Costa Rican elites that it was time to invest other people's money in that nineteenth-century symbol of national progress par excellence, a railroad. A rail line from the Central Valley to the Caribbean coast would provide coffee growers cheaper access to North Atlantic markets. As a bonus it would open the untapped riches of the eastern hinterlands to the beneficent influence of civilization and capitalism. In a series of mismanaged London bond issues in 1871 the government of General Tomás Guardia managed to acquire £3,400,000 in foreign debt and only £1,300,000 in working capital for the project.[8]

Under the leadership of Henry Meiggs Keith, construction began in 1871— and halted two years later, the company bankrupt and Keith long gone, with fifty-two miles left to complete. Guardia's government struggled to complete the line on its own. Chronically short of currency as well as funds, the state paid workers and suppliers in "railroad greenbacks" (*billetes verdes del ferrocarril*), which could be used to pay taxes or purchase land, or (in theory) be exchanged for silver pesos in San José. Merchants accepted the scrip from workers at a steep discount.[9] Land speculation, government contracts, and trading posts had become the main sources of profits in Limón, and the scrip system made combining all three the most profitable of all. The man who would do so most effectively was Henry Keith's younger brother and commissary manager, Minor Cooper Keith. From 1883 to 1886 Minor Keith renegotiated the debt with bondholders in London on behalf of the Costa Rican government, having first negotiated for himself the concession to build the remaining stretch of line. The result was a somewhat lighter debt burden and the "Soto-Keith" contract, under which Keith's new Costa Rican Railway Company would complete the line in return for property in Port Limón, long-term tax exemptions, exclusive rights to the railroad for ninety-nine years, and 800,000 acres of public land (roughly 7 percent of the nation's territory).[10]

The salience of race to railroad labor recruitment seemed self-evident to Costa Rican leaders. The retroactive whitening of the highland population's forebears—a process that had begun with the adoption of the label "mestizo" by the descendants of mulattos and *pardos* in the eighteenth century— was well advanced. Describing his nation in 1890, *don* Joaquín B. Calvo could write without fear of contradiction, "In Costa Rica, while a primitive people still exists, its numbers are few, and it is completely separate from the civilized race. The latter is white, homogeneous, healthy, and robust. . . . The

Railroad work camp, Limón, ca. 1880. Fotografías 3449-1,
Archivo Nacional de Costa Rica, San José, Costa Rica.

morality of the people and their respect for authority is well known."[11] The
future would be whiter and more respectful still, if legislators had anything
to do with it. An 1862 decree forbade colonization schemes involving "African
or Chinese races."[12] Shortly after work on the railroad began in 1871, General Guardia wrote to remind Henry Meiggs Keith that German, Belgian, and
Swiss immigrants would be particularly congenial.[13] But such eugenic fanta-
sies had little impact on the actual course of labor contracting.

Construction westward from Port Limón began in April 1872 with crews that arrived on their own from Belize and Cartagena, evidence of the strength of Western Caribbean circuits of information and travel. Keith's steamer rounded the region as well, reportedly contracting 600 workers in the Jamaican interior, 400 in Curaçao, 500 in Honduras (including 200 Chinese laborers), and more at ports in between. Many new arrivals stayed in the railroad's employ briefly, if at all. By official estimate 1,000 men, all "Jamaican Negroes," were working on the lowland track when Henry Keith went bankrupt in 1874.[14] In 1872 and 1873 over 1,000 Chinese indentured laborers were brought to Cartago by Keith and his associates. Not only would the indentured Chinese provide a captive workforce for the most difficult stretch of highland rail construction, but their labor contracts could be sold at a profit if cash got tight.[15] The government newspaper assured prospective employers, "We recommend the acquisition of these workers especially for coffee processing, given their recognized ability and dedication in labors of that class, and we congratulate ourselves on the introduction into the country of such useful laborers."[16] An internal company memo reveals the standard of treatment these useful men received: "I'm sending you the four Chinese captured in Pacuare. Please use whip and irons as necessary and put them to work."[17]

If Afro-Antilleans were never the object of nationalist wooing like European workers, neither were they systematically abused like the indentured Chinese. After all, West Indian immigrants were on home ground in Limón as much as highland migrants were: no further from home in travel time, and with a claim to representation by men who mattered. As Crown subjects they repeatedly petitioned British diplomats and navy officers to intervene on their behalf. Typical was the British consul's complaint of harassment against Jamaicans in 1883. Called to account, the Limón police chief swore the opposite was true. Before his tenure, dances had only been permitted on Saturday nights. But Limón's governor, "in view of the great numbers of Negroes who left on every steamer [for Panama], gave me the order to permit them their diversions on any day and whenever they request, and so I have."[18] Time and again West Indians' ease of exit improved the conditions local officials were willing to offer.

When railroad work ground to a halt after 1874 the government was left with hundreds of indentured Chinese workers, some of them now maimed or ill, a rapidly depreciating investment. Sale prices dropped to half their former level and the subsidized importation scheme came under retroactive attack.

Called to justify his actions before congress in 1874, the minister of commerce spouted anti-Chinese credos with the zeal of a new convert.

> The Chinese . . . have vices of rearing which are highly prejudicial to our customs; at the same time they have ills of organization or race that are even more prejudicial to public health. In general they are gamblers and thieves; insubordinate, cruel, and vengeful when they find themselves in the majority and with the upper hand. . . . As to organic defects, experience has shown that the immigrant Chinese race bears within itself a principle or germ of one of the diseases which has caused and continues to cause the greatest harm to humanity and which appears to develop in a mortal fashion in the case of union with our race. For these reasons the Government will permit no further Chinese immigration, and is today attempting to sell off the contracts of those now in the railway's employ.[19]

Accusations of syphilis and sexual vice would remain the mainstay of anti-Chinese racism in Costa Rica for generations to come. All further Chinese immigration was outlawed in 1897, yet surreptitious arrivals continued at night and far from port authorities along both the Atlantic and Pacific coasts. In coming decades Chinese immigrants would spread throughout Costa Rica, relying on kin-based commerce and lending to become the owners of *pulperías* (corner stores), *cantinas* (bars), and *hoteles de chinos* (boardinghouses of ill repute).[20] Even as they prospered economically the Chinese continued to be vilified, by Costa Ricans and West Indians, public health officials and prostitutes alike. In contrast, Jamaicans would enjoy a generally positive official image—as long as they stayed on the coast, and as long as their labor was needed for laying track or planting bananas. Only when a severe economic crisis rocked the highlands and the banana zone simultaneously in the 1930s would racial degeneracy and sexual immorality be imputed to blacks in public debate, in terms remarkably similar to the charges leveled at Chinese laborers sixty years before.

The Settling of Limón

As each stretch of construction brought workers farther west and made transport easier, towns sprang up further inland along the line. When Henry Keith's

Family in southern coastal region, Limón, ca. 1890. Colección fotográfica, 10147, Museo Nacional, San José, Costa Rica.

bankruptcy halted construction in 1874, laid-off Jamaicans were enticed to settle with offers of free government land, a quarter *manzana* lot for any worker willing to establish a farm between Limón and Camp Two.[21] Despite the rhetoric of national incorporation surrounding the railroad project, the Costa Rican state was evidently willing to continue the long-standing pattern of coastal settlement by dark-skinned migrants from nearby lands. Terrain farther from the line was sparsely populated but likewise tied to local, national, and international markets. In 1882 Swedish naturalist Carl Bovallius rode south from Siquirres, finding indigenous Chirripós who "have minor plantings of maize and bananas, but live off the sale of rough hats and mats woven from palm fiber." The rain forests north and east of the rail line drew "Jamaican Negroes, who more and more are moving into this area to collect rubber." Bovallius's German hosts purchased slabs of rubber from them for export.[22]

For the next generation the social geography of Limón would develop along lines already visible in Bovallius's narrative. The mountainous valleys to the south were home to indigenous communities whose precarious autonomy depended on their inaccessibility. The coastal plains were ceded to well-connected outsiders as plantations or remained *terrenos baldíos* (government land) where individual cultivators and collectors used what resources they could with little hope of permanent title. The rail line was bordered by West Indian homesteads: Bovallius described Matina as "two long strings of houses, the majority of them Negro huts made of palm trunks and piles of crates and similar materials."[23] And then there was Port Limón itself, whose population topped 1,000 within a few years of its founding in 1871. By company policy the work camps along the line housed few or no women, and the rural areas of Limón would remain heavily masculine in subsequent decades as well. But from the start the dynamic port service economy gave scope to the initiative of female entrepreneurs. Roughly one-third of the city's residents in the 1880s and 1890s were women.[24]

Like their male counterparts, women came to Limón both directly from the British West Indies and by way of established settlements on the Nicaraguan or Colombian coasts. In 1882, for example, Wilhemina Connell, a widow from San Juan del Norte (Greytown), petitioned the *alcalde* of Limón to evict Jamaican Henry Davis from her Cieneguita River plantation. Connell had purchased the eight and a half acres of bananas and plantains from Henry Brown (also Jamaican) a few months before.[25] Female migrants traveled widely, just as men did, and frequent moves made for frequent reunions. In 1882 Emilia Barton and her fourteen-year-old daughter were invited to the home of Walter and Margaret Grant "in order to celebrate the arrival of myself and my daughter from Colón." They spent the afternoon singing and drinking champagne with old friends.[26] This cheery gathering at a time when railroad construction in Costa Rica was at a standstill reminds us that individual fortunes in Limón did not always track those of Minor C. Keith. The ease, if not comfort, of coastal travel, together with the sequential dynamism of Central American construction projects, meant that people might find ways to do well even where large-scale investment had ground to a halt. As in the case of Henry Brown and Wilhemina Connell, when some were ready to sell and move on, others could buy and reap the fruits of their labor.

The French Canal: Panama, 1882–1888

When one traces individual workers' lives rather than the genealogy of the United Fruit Company, it is the French Panama Canal project and not the

Costa Rican railroad that appears as the crucial antecedent to the expansion of banana planting in Limón in the 1890s. Triumphal accounts of the subsequent U.S. canal effort have shrouded the French project in an aura of failure: fevers rampant, money squandered, lives lost. But between 1881 and 1886 the infusion of $125 million from French citizens' subscriptions created a boom economy the likes of which even Western Caribbeans, long accustomed to the booms and busts of Atlantic export cycles, had rarely seen.[27] Men and women poured into Colón from Jamaica and Barbados, Colombia and Costa Rica, points in between and points far beyond. At its height in 1874 Costa Rica's Atlantic railroad employed 2,500 workers. Ten years later the Compagnie Universelle du Canal Interocéanique de Panama employed seven times that many.

Early recruitment for the French canal centered on Kingston and adjacent St. Andrew parish, where increasing numbers of rural migrants as well as returnees from the Costa Rican railroad swelled the ranks of the urban unemployed. In 1882 the island's governor estimated that 1,000 migrants were leaving each month for Panama, Mexico, and Yucatan, many of them returning and re-migrating repeatedly. In 1883 alone, departures from Jamaica for Panama were estimated at 24,300, and returns at 11,600. Revolving migration was the bane of isthmian contractors but fit workers' ideas about prosperity, pleasure, and obligations. One governor wrote, "It seems now a recognized course for the men after earning a fair amount to return to Jamaica to visit their families and friends and after a short time return to the Isthmus to work again."[28]

By 1884 the Compagnie Universelle had nearly 19,000 employees, including 16,000 black laborers. Black employees were mainly West Indian, and these were mainly Jamaican. The company's direct payroll reached 200,000 francs a day, over $1 million a month.[29] But partisan political conflict escalated in Panama in these years. Colombian troops responded by targeting all blacks as rebel sympathizers, in 1885 slaughtering a group of West Indian workers in their barracks. Hundreds of Jamaicans fled the isthmus.[30] While the governor of Limón in early 1885 had deplored the continuing exodus of workers "due to the variety and abundance of enterprises and the fabulous salaries in Panama," by the following year he could report that "the appalling torrent which threatened to leave the settlements of this territory desolate has ceased a bit" (421 workers had departed, but 658 had arrived). A year later he could celebrate the arrival of 2,083 workers, offset by only 479 departures.[31] The direction of magnetism between Colón and Limón had shifted once more.

As was the case with Henry Keith's Atlantic railroad, poor advance engineering and high-level skimming bankrupted the French canal company long before the project was completed. In December 1888 all work stopped, and some 13,000 West Indian workers were left stranded in Colón with no passage home. Over 7,500 Jamaicans were repatriated with the aid of that island's governor. Thousands more stayed squatting in the hills around Colón. Countless others headed north along the coast.[32] While in mid-1887 railroad labor recruitment had meant expensive promises to Italian artisans, upon the canal's bankruptcy Minor Keith hired workers by the boatload in Colón for merely the cost of transport up the coast. By December 1890 this largely West Indian workforce had completed the final fifty miles of track.

Fat Years in Limón

In the 1880s wealthy Costa Ricans and immigrants established large banana plantations along the Old Line to the north, while government concessions encouraged workers to settle the "miasmic" lowlands along the Main Line just west of Port Limón. But the Main Line's alluvial soils proved perfectly suited for banana cultivation. The Old Line's porous lateritic soils did not. By the 1890s many upper Old Line estates had converted to cattle ranching, while vast banana plantations wholly or partly owned by Minor Keith spread over the Main Line region, displacing smallholders in the process.[33] Meanwhile, along the Talamanca coast, turtle-men who had arrived from Nicaragua and Panama a generation earlier were now joined by former railroad and canal workers who planted coconuts, fruit trees, ground provisions, and cocoa for consumption and sale. Farther south still, at Bocas del Toro, banana planting boomed at the hands of former canal workers, who farmed plots as large as fifty acres in "gangs of four or more negroes," ferrying their produce by canoe to traders' steamers that frequented the bay. In 1895 Bocas del Toro exported more bananas than Port Limón.[34]

In the early 1900s banana planting spread outward from the Main Line along the alluvial soils bordering the Matina, Reventazón, and Banano Rivers. But after 1908 Main Line yields dropped, due to soil depletion and the spread of the fungus *fusarium oxysporum* ("Panama disease"). Keith's United Fruit Company claimed lands farther south along the Estrella River, while wealthy private growers expanded their holdings in the north along the Parismina River—all seeking the high yields that would make growing profitable. From

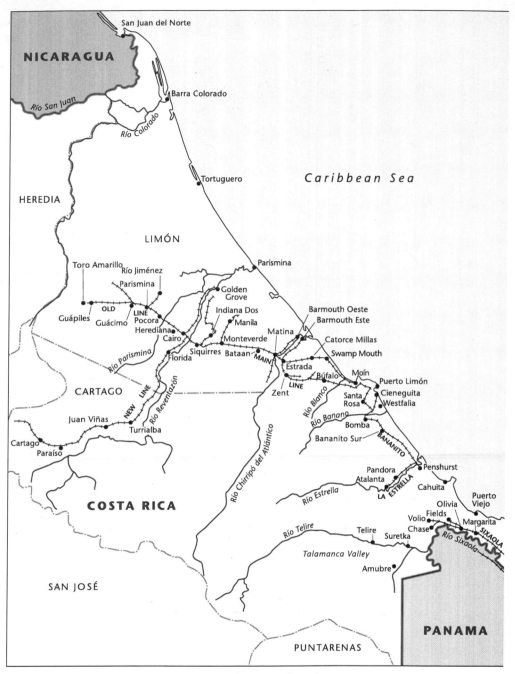

MAP 2.1. The Lines of Limón

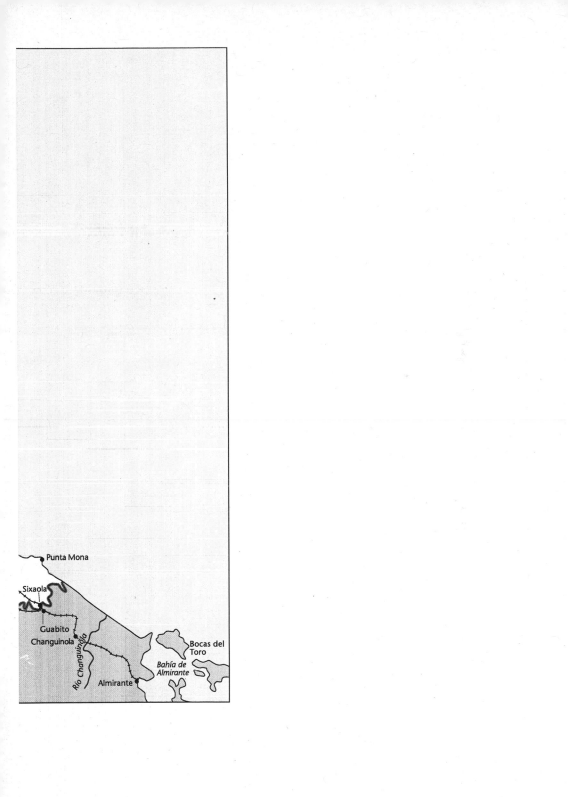

Settlement near Zent, lower Main Line, ca. 1905. Colección fotográfica, 10931, Museo Nacional, San José, Costa Rica.

1908 onward the Chiriquí Land Company, a United Fruit subsidiary, claimed and cleared vast tracts of land northwest from Bocas del Toro in the Sixaola River valley of Talamanca, the heartland of Bribri settlement and the political center of the indigenous tribes of the Atlantic slope. Meanwhile, former plantation workers using mixed cropping patterns and labor-intensive disease controls grew export bananas on abandoned lands in the hollow core of the expanding plantation frontier.[35]

The terms on which former pick-and-shovel men, highland entrepreneurs, and Yankee magnates alike participated in the banana business were set by national legal reforms enacted in the mid-1880s. Championed by a rising cohort of progressive educators and lawyers later known as the Olimpos, the reforms aimed to unleash individual economic initiative, toward the goal of national progress, through the means of export agriculture. The 1884 contract that gave Minor Keith rights to 800,000 acres of public land in return for completion of the rail line was one enactment of this Liberal vision. But other reforms concluded that same year were equally important in shaping land use and ownership in Limón. A decree governing *denuncios de baldíos* (claims of public land) stipulated that debts for public land purchases would be forgiven if claimants planted crops worth twice the land's stated value. Each new municipality was endowed with 8,400 acres of land to rent out or auction off. The Código Fiscal permitted those who held farms under 124 acres to acquire title via a simple declaration before the local judge. And the Civil Code ratified that same year conclusively abolished "common goods," erasing the judicial basis for indigenous groups' communal landholding.[36]

Over the following decades *denuncios de baldíos* would put tens of thousands of acres of land into the hands of wealthy and well-connected claimants from Costa Rica, Colombia, the Spanish Caribbean, and Europe. A British observer in 1894 estimated that three-fourths of exported bananas were grown on large plantations, "two of which produce more than 350,000 stems a year."[37] On the other hand, official policy welcomed small claimants, West Indians in particular. The minister of development reported in 1884 that "[i]n order to attract to the Atlantic coast African immigrants, the only ones who can bear the elevated temperatures of those localities, the government expanded . . . the land concessions made previously with that same goal, removing all restrictions and facilitating the means to acquire property."[38] Those who claimed plots on these terms planted cash and food crops side by side, as highland settlers and Jamaican smallholders had for generations. One set of parcels in Piuta, just outside Port Limón, were planted in the 1890s with cocoa, *ñame* (yams), *tiquisque* (*Xanthosma sagittifolium*), yuca (*Manihot esculenta*), ginger, coffee, *hule* (rubber trees), plantains, coconut palms, *zapotes* (*Pouteria sapota*), mangos, oranges, avocados, breadfruit, and bananas.[39] Such plots produced a quarter of all bananas exported in 1894.

Large holdings dominated banana growing, but hourly wage labor did not. Even on the largest plantations cultivation was organized by complex layers of subcontracting, job work, and payment by the task.[40] As proof of cultivation was required for subsidized title, all would-be estate owners were obliged from the start to enter some sort of agreement with those willing to work the land they claimed. Hiring wage workers was one approach, though it meant that the costs of planting and labor control had to be assumed by the aspiring owner. An alternative requiring less up-front investment and less direct supervision was the "rental" of lands to independent cultivators in exchange for money, a portion of their produce, or eventual ownership of the *cultivos* (established crops). Success with this strategy depended on the claimant's ability to use the local courts to maintain de jure control of the land in question, no simple matter when the cultivator's residence might well predate the claimant's claim, giving the "renter" technical legal precedence in titling.

House near Port Limón, ca. 1900. Fotografías 3185, Archivo Nacional de Costa Rica, San José, Costa Rica; originally published in Próspero Calderón, *Vistas de Costa Rica* (1901).

Effective use of the Limón courts was facilitated by wealth, whiteness, influential relatives and business partners, and command of the Spanish language. The disadvantaged nevertheless managed to obstruct legal proceedings in any number of ways: preventing legal notification by changing their names and signatures at will, selling their rights and crops to hapless third parties and leaving town, seeking out their opponents' enemies for support. Speculators and future *finqueros* (estate owners) combined legal and extralegal forms of coercion in response: forcing cultivators to sign documents in Spanish they did not understand, mounting eviction proceedings against "tenants" with prior claims to ownership, tearing down fences to allow livestock to eat the crops of those who refused to leave.[41] Although squatters or tenants rarely won possession in the face of a concerted assault, at least they might negotiate compensation for the *mejorías* (improvements) they were forced to leave behind.[42] By structuring disputes over land rights as adversarial processes, Costa Rican agrarian law set the stage for small farmers to exploit elite rivalries and patron-client ties through the courts. Conversely, by abolishing communal goods the Civil Code transformed conflicts between indigenous communities and outsiders interested in their land into private disputes. Far from the courts, ill-versed in judicial processes, isolated from the fray of port politics, the indigenous residents of the Talamanca and Estrella Valleys were hard-pressed to mobilize allies on these terms.

Migrants, Gender, Work

Who came to Limón during the early years of banana expansion? People from Antigua, Barbados, Belize, China, Colombia, Cuba, Curaçao, Demerara, Dominica, El Salvador, England, France, Germany, Grenada, Guadeloupe, Guyana, Honduras, Italy, Jamaica, Martinique, Mexico, Montserrat, Nassau, Nevis, Nicaragua, Panama, Providencia, Puerto Rico, Russia, St. Kitts, St. Lucia, St. Thomas, St. Vincent, Spain, Sweden, Syria, Trinidad, Tunisia, the United States, and Venezuela all appear in turn-of-the-century records from Limón. But the great majority of immigrants were Jamaican.[43]

Kingston and the parish of St. James were proportionately overrepresented among Jamaicans in early Limón. In contrast, the central island parishes where peasant freeholds had multiplied in the generations after emancipation —St. Elizabeth, Manchester, Clarendon, St. Ann, and St. Mary—were starkly underrepresented.[44] The pattern bears the imprint of networks established during construction projects in Costa Rica and Panama, when urban artisans were among the first to seek opportunities abroad, and the urban poor were recruiters' first targets. The northwest parishes, in particular St. James with its port of Montego Bay, had been "heavily involved in the emigration to Panama [in the 1880s], both through the numbers who emigrated and through the lucrative trade in foodstuffs which these parishes maintained with the Canal Zone while work was in progress."[45] It seems that St. James's close integration into Central American economic cycles and migratory circuits during the French canal project was reflected in the make-up of the Jamaican populace of Limón two decades later.

In migrants' societies of origin, as in most places and times, the labor that ensured daily social reproduction was usually performed by women rather than men and provided under the structure of kinship obligations rather than market exchange. In Limón this was not the case. Here most men found themselves far from aunts or mothers, sweethearts or wives. Of course in theory

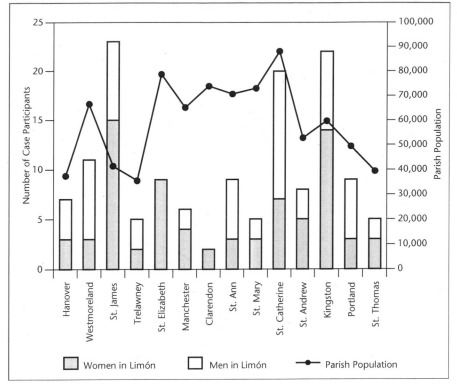

FIGURE 2.1. Comparison of Jamaican-Born Limón Judicial Case Participants'
Declared Place of Origin, 1901–1915, with Jamaican Population by Parish, 1911

Sources: Archivo Nacional de Costa Rica, San José, Costa Rica; G. E. Cumper, "Population
Movements in Jamaica, 1830–1950," *Social and Economic Studies* 5 (1956): 275.
Note: N = 158; median year, 1908.

men could perform maintenance chores for themselves, and sometimes they
did. A knife-and-pistol duel in 1901 began when Jamaican Simon Clark, a
"contractor who weeds banana farms [*contratista en limpia de banano*] . . . went
with my crew [*mis peones*] down to the river to wash our clothes, as we do
every Sunday," and James Taylor, also Jamaican, came by and with "vulgar
words" ordered the men away from their accustomed spot.[46] But every evidence is that men preferred to pay women to do their laundry when they
could afford it—and that they preferred to pay for more intimate comforts
as well, rather than improvise on their own or with each other. Hot meals,
sliced fruit, a close dance, and sex were just some of the goods and services
that female migrants might profitably offer for sale in Limón. In years when
male laborers were earning 1.50 to 2.15 *colones* a day ($.70 to $1.00) and skilled

male artisans five *colones* at most, a washerwoman or cook earned up to two *colones* a day in Port Limón. Women who worked as prostitutes earned a good deal more, between one and five *colones* for a single sexual encounter at the turn of the century.[47]

As line towns replaced construction camps and the regional population grew, local trade expanded. Who sold what, and where they sold it, was patterned by both origin and gender. "Turks," "Syrians," or "Arabs"—most born in "Monte Líbano" (modern Lebanon)—were prominent in the retail trade, particularly in the sale of dry goods and sundries. Chinese men owned a third of commercial establishments in Port Limón and more than a third of liquor licenses throughout the province. Each group formed tight-knit merchant communities in the larger line towns.[48] Meanwhile, the purchase and resale of provisions and the manufacture and sale of savories and sweets was the purview of West Indian women. The word "higgler" was never widely used in Limón, but that was the exact role of women like Sarah Simon, who rode the train back from San José to Zent in 1899 with a market basket filled with eighty eggs and three pounds of coffee, or Ella Kelly, who left her home in Matina center at 4 A.M. as usual one morning in 1906 to "see to her obligation, that of picking up the milk at Mile 23 and carrying it to sell at Zent Junction."[49]

The petty trade in West Indian women's hands was carried out through ongoing ties of kin and acquaintance, borrowing and credit, visits and rumors. In 1898 Jamaican Ada Gale owned a storefront in Cimarrones with a room behind, where she lived with her four teenage sons and daughters and her consensual partner, Daniel Louis of Grenada. Her daughters, Anna James and Ethel Gordon, ages twelve and fourteen, often traveled to Pacuarito or other towns to sell on her behalf. Around the same time, eleven-year-old Bertha Henry, born in Colón, was living with Jamaican Letitia Davis in Matina. Everyone called Letitia Bertha's aunt, although apparently there was no blood tie between them. Gossip had it that Davis had recently left her husband and entered *la vida alegre*, that is, begun selling sex for cash. In any case, she was in the business of lending money and selling goods as well, and when Ada Gale sent the message that she was ready to pay some money she owed, Letitia sent Bertha to stay with Gale's family for a few days and collect the debt.[50]

Informal fostering or child-borrowing was common throughout the West Indies in these and later years, as mothers with conflicting commitments or too many mouths to feed entrusted their children to friends or relatives with more resources or more work for idle hands. Judicial testimony suggests the arrangement was quite common in Limón. Women who worked as traders, shopkeepers, midwives, or confectioners brought girls from Jamaica to help them in their businesses or to look after younger children.[51] Nine-year-old Caroline MacArthur had lived with Francis Prince and her husband in Jamaica for three years, and with her parents' permission the Princes brought her along when they came to Limón in 1898. Francis Prince made candy in her home, and Caroline walked the docks and plaza selling the sweets from a tray.[52]

Fostering occurred among Costa Rican and Nicaraguan migrants as well, though less commonly. Like most kinship forms, child fostering combined hierarchy, labor, and love, in degrees that varied from home to home. At their best those who took in children provided affection and security for the long haul. Black youth Samuel Mude, born in Port Limón and reared in Nicaragua, testified at age fifteen: "I never had a father, my mother died when I was small, *la señora* Emilia Ruíz is the one who has raised me ever since."[53] Foster parents could also be as cruel as the worst natural parents. Everyone in Matina knew that ten-year-old Domingo Álvarez was beaten constantly by his god-mother after his mother's death in 1913. But he only entered the official record when he tried to burn down the home of two West Indian matrons because, the boy told a neighbor, "they called him 'damn' t'ief" [*le decían dean Tiff*]." The court doctor found Domingo malnourished and mentally impaired, and the boy ran away before officials could decide what to do.[54]

Men, women, and children all participated indirectly in the export economy. Some women did so directly as well. Legal constraints on female proprietorship were reduced by the Liberal reforms of 1884, which established women's judicial personhood and legalized divorce. Some women invested in land and managed its cultivation. William Carter sued his wife for separation in 1902, after she began to experience attacks of spirit possession and left to travel the lines as an itinerant preacher. Although he claimed they had no goods in common, she reported that at the time of their marriage she had owned two houses, one in Parismina and one in Dos Novillos, which Carter had sold "to invest the proceeds in work on two farms which together we established."[55]

Amelia Pardo y Figueroa, originally of Colombia, sued her Nicaraguan-born husband, José Andrés Vargas Lobo, for separation in 1898. She asked the judge to order Vargas out of the house on her farm in Moín, as "his actions there bother my workers, who are occupied in the cultivation of my *finca*, and once my husband vacates said house I will be able, acting with the *depositario* [court-appointed interim administrator], to organize the agricultural labors necessary to make the farm produce enough for my subsistence."[56] Among the residents Vargas had been bothering was Lucía Cuen, long a dependent of the Pardo family, "an aged and suffering Costa Rican," in her lawyer's words. In 1901 Amelia Pardo attempted to reclaim the ten-acre parcel that Lucía Cuen had farmed for more than twenty years. When Cuen refused and sought legal counsel from prominent lawyer and politician Lucas Daniel Alvarado, Vargas cut through a fence and let his livestock into her parcel, where they destroyed the "banana, cocoa, fruit trees, and provisions" she cultivated. Amelia Pardo did her best to mobilize personal ties both up and down the social hierarchy in her favor. She wrote to Alvarado—"Esteemed sir," "*don Lucas*"—begging him to disregard his political rivalry with her nephew Rogelio and stop harassing her through the courts. She also wrote to Cuen—"with warm affection from your friend and *comadre*"—imploring her to desist. After two years of legal maneuvering Pardo and Cuen reached an unspecified extrajudicial settlement, and Vargas kept the farm.[57]

Such evidence suggests that among the proper and the prosperous, women might take an active role in supervising agricultural investments, and that on occasion a poor woman alone or with a male partner might work land herself.[58] However, such cases were the exception rather than the rule. No evidence suggests that women were prominent among the squatters and small farmers who cleared land, planted root bits, and harvested bananas on the expanding agricultural frontier. And no women were employed as agricultural laborers on banana plantations here.[59] The same pattern prevailed on the southern coast where bananas were not yet grown. Old-timers in Cahuita remember that when Jamaicans began settling there in the 1890s, the men would travel every day to plots in the "woodlands" or "bush" to the west, clearing forest and planting *ñame*, plantains, yuca, coconuts, and cocoa. The women stayed near their houses along the beach, grating and pressing coconut meat to make oil, boiling cauldrons of yuca to make starch. The products were shipped for sale in Port Limón and beyond.[60]

Geographic and Occupational Mobility

A police inquiry in 1904 provides a telling portrait of the diversity of routes that brought West Indians to Limón. On 24 June local officials began gathering evidence against thirteen *jamaicanos* they were eager to expel. The men were vagrants and thieves (according to authorities and their hand-picked West Indian witnesses), all of whom had "bad reputations [*malos antecedentes*] in Jamaica, Colón, and Bocas del Toro."[61] The personal histories the accused men related in order to refute these charges need not, of course, have been true. Yet if they are not factual the following accounts were those deemed most plausible by the men involved. These must have been the kind of stories you heard from young black men on a street corner or down by the docks, if you happened to ask how they came to Port Limón.

John Ivery Akeman, a twenty-seven-year-old carpenter from Jamaica, had been in Limón for two years, working first on the railroad in Zent and now at odd jobs around the city.

Federico Adolphus, a twenty-one-year-old painter, had left Jamaica to look for work in Bocas del Toro; finding none there, he headed up the coast to Limón. After a week in the port, he went south to Talamanca with a friend named David (whose last name he could not recall) with merchandise to sell. He had only just returned.

William Howard Gale, a twenty-six-year-old carpenter from Jamaica, had been in Limón for a year and a half. He had worked as a foreman in Cedar Creek for a year, spent three months as a stevedore on the docks, and for the past month had worked on the plantation of George Smith.

Walter Christian Williams was a twenty-five-year-old baker from Jamaica who had arrived in Limón in 1896 at the age of seventeen "in the company of many others contracted by Mr. Keith to work in the Company." Williams had worked for United Fruit "at different places along the Line" and now worked in Mrs. Emily Grant's bakery in town.

William Brown Douglas, a twenty-three-year-old tinsmith, had left Jamaica along "with many others contracted by Mr. McDonald to work on the railroad in Ecuador" and eventually made his way to Bocas del Toro. He had come to Limón from Bocas for a brief visit "because all my family and things are here" and a relative in the city was ill. He planned to leave the following week.

Samuel Walker Wilson, twenty-six, a painter, had left Jamaica for Colón "in search of better luck." He had come to Limón from Bocas del Toro fifteen months earlier because he was sick. He was living off money he had brought from Bocas.

Frederick Gordon Merril, twenty-four, had left Jamaica for Limón three years earlier. He found work "in the banana fields, and on the docks, but four days ago I had to stop working because my testicles became inflamed."

Julio Johnson Davis, twenty-three, was a baker from Venezuela who had been in Limón all of ten days. "I came searching for my brother, because he was working here, but as I didn't find him I plan to leave for Bocas del Toro as soon as I can."

David Cole Williams, a thirty-eight-year-old brakeman from Jamaica, had come to Limón three years earlier "when Mr. Keith made the contract to grow bananas." Since arrival he had been working along the line, most recently cutting bananas in Bar Mouth. He had left that job a few days ago due to a pain in his stomach.

James Super Smith, twenty-five, veterinarian, had left Jamaica for Nicaragua along with others contracted by Keith to work on the railroad. Four years ago he had come to Port Limón planning to take a steamer to Jamaica and "hasn't had occasion to leave." He worked caring for the horses of two West Indian gentlemen. When arrested the night before at 6 P.M. Smith had been on his way to the docks to look for work, since "whenever the United has abundant work, they always give me some."

John Fenton Ortiz ("known as John Bull"), a twenty-year-old from Colombia, had left Bocas two years earlier "due to the revolution which broke out there." Since then he had worked on the Limón docks loading and unloading bananas and coal.

Edward Johnson Onfrei, a thirty-year-old brakeman from Colombia, declared, "I left my country after my parents died, and headed to Bocas del Toro first, and then here, in search of better luck." Of his six and a half years in Limón, he had worked two and a half years "with the United Fruit Company and the rest of the time as a brakeman."

"Steven Swat," reputed ringleader of the band of swindlers, described himself as a thirty-eight-year-old blacksmith who had left Jamaica under contract to work for José María Sánchez in Sixaola. Four months ago he had come to Limón "to find something better" and had since worked stringing telegraph line, first in Banano River and now in Zent.

The thirteen men were condemned to three months of municipal labor and then expelled from the country by executive decree.[62]

The stories told by Steven Swat and his crew remind us that not all those labeled *jamaicanos* in Limón were Jamaica-born, and not all Jamaicans came to Limón directly from Jamaica. For West Indian migrants in these years departures were frequent and destinations rarely final. By the 1890s steamers carried several thousand passengers between Limón and Colón each year. Hundreds more traveled on scores of smaller craft.[63] A. Hyatt Verrill rode one such "Panama coaster" around 1910. It was a made-over sloop with a fourth-hand oil-burning motor attached, "[p]lying up and down the Isthmus from Port Limon to Colombia, carrying cargoes of cattle, pigs, coco-nuts, logwood, fruit, lumber, fish. . . . Men, women, and children—black, brown, and yellow; shouting, cursing, chattering, laughing; chaffing in English, French, Chinese, Spanish, and Jamaican patois-cockney, they swarmed on board accompanied by their multitudinous possessions."[64]

News, people, and earnings circulated continuously between Kingston, Colón, Bocas del Toro, and Port Limón. When Florence Thompson was about to board the steamer for Kingston in 1898, her cousin Samuel French and his wife, Dorothy, gave her a packet with money to carry to his mother on the island. In August Florence returned to Limón, preceded by rumors that she had delivered only eight paper shillings to her aunt and kept one pound sterling for herself.[65] Bluefields and San Juan del Norte remained part of the migratory circuits, although no large enterprises drew migrants there in numbers comparable to those of Limón or Colón. Roberto Drescher was born in Bluefields in 1891 of a German father and Trinidadian mother. In 1913 he was working as a scribe in the Limón mayor's office and courting his landlady's daughter—María Cristina Arguedas, a sixteen-year-old from San Juan del Norte—with offers of free English lessons.[66]

Working people were likewise on the move within Limón itself: from job to job, from town to town, from plantation camps to port boardinghouses to shacks in the bush and back again. Thomas Green was shot dead by his lover's former lover on the railroad tracks at San José Creek east of Matina on 29 June 1895. Seven residents of the houses facing the line (all Jamaicans) gave declarations to police. When the judge summoned the witnesses to repeat their testimony eighteen months later, none were still there. One had moved to Mile 12, one to Mile 20, one to Siquirres, one to Matina, and three, separately, to Port Limón.[67] Costa Rican workers in the region were equally mobile. In 1898 an argument among work companions near Jiménez on the Old Line lead to machete blows and the death of Juan Álvarez, a laborer born in Tres Ríos, Cartago. The witnesses, fellow *peones*, hailed from Tres Ríos or San José. When the judge attempted to reinterview them six months after the event all but one had returned to the Central Valley.[68]

Almost invariably observers have exaggerated the prevalence of blacks and banana plantations in Limón and ignored regions, farms, and individuals that did not fit this image. Foreign visitors in the 1920s and 1930s confidently reported that the province was 90 percent black, although in fact Hispanics made up at least 40 percent of the population by then and comprised the great

Loading bananas along the line in Limón, 1909. Fotografías 3245,
Archivo Nacional de Costa Rica, San José, Costa Rica.

majority of plantation workers.[69] A characteristic 1926 account described the
scenery as "forests and banana lands and negroes; negroes individually, in
gangs, in huts on stilts, in villages on stilts,—everywhere. And not one Costa
Rican of any shade or color. All this is the United Fruit Company's land, and
the labor is from Jamaica and other British West Indian islands. . . . The black
belt and the banana belt climb together."[70] This may have been a roughly accurate description of the view from the salon-car window along the lower Main
Line, but it was certainly not an accurate summary of the banana industry as
a whole in that year, nor even two decades earlier.

Periodic wage work had long been a crucial component of smallholder
household economies in the Costa Rican Central Valley. Need for such cash
inputs increased markedly after the collapse of coffee prices in 1897 brought
the more marginal of small properties to the brink of foreclosure. In 1904
United Fruit reported 5,600 workers on its payroll in the Limón division,
4,000 of them Jamaican. But growers other than United Fruit produced 54
percent of bananas exported from Limón in that year.[71] A rough estimate suggests that at least half the company payroll consisted of transport workers
rather than field workers, and that over 2,000 men tended bananas on non-

UFCO farms of varying size.[72] A few hundred of these were own-account farmers, most of them West Indians. But the bulk of bananas were grown on large plantations owned by wealthy Costa Ricans or others and centered around Siquirres, Parismina, and the upper Old Line.[73] In light of regional mortality statistics, and given United Fruit's predominantly West Indian workforce, by 1907 half or more of all non-UFCO banana workers must have been Hispanics.[74]

Construction of the U.S. Canal, 1904–1913

The flight of second-generation West Indians like John Fenton Ortiz ("alias John Bull") north from Colón and Bocas del Toro to avoid the violence that accompanied the secession of Panama from the Republic of Colombia in 1903 was the first in a series of eddies and flows within established migration currents that came with the resumption of canal construction under the control of the United States government. When the governor of Jamaica, wary of another costly repatriation crisis, set prohibitive conditions on recruiters, the U.S. Isthmian Canal Commission (ICC) chose to do all formal contracting in Barbados. From 1905 to 1913 20,000 male Barbadians—40 percent of the island's adult male population—left under contract for work on the canal. By 1913 the ICC and its subcontractors employed over 56,000 men.[75] Meanwhile, an estimated 80,000 to 90,000 Jamaicans traveled to Panama on their own account. Steerage fare from Jamaica to Panama was only $5, two weeks' wages for a laborer on the island, or five days' wages at isthmian rates.[76]

Winifred James observed steerage passengers on a Kingston-bound steamer around 1911. "The travelling kit of the decker is well worth seeing. A canvas stretcher on folding legs, a magnificent white-frilled cushion, a number of bursting brown-paper parcels and a kerosene tin. The kerosene tin down there is called the nigger's steamer trunk. On the journey they all lie about inert, listless and unwashed. But on the day of arrival there is a great awakening. The parcels are undone, clean dresses and marvelous hats appear out of the brown-paper parcels. The ladies comb their wool vigorously, puffing it out in the very latest fashion, with twists and rolls and tortoiseshell combs, and powder their chocolate faces with all the thoroughness of a lady of style."[77] In the eyes of a European contemporary, even a progressive feminist such as James, the sight of poor black women in fancy clothes seemed burlesque at best. But what James captures is a Caribbean world in which sea-faring migration was neither orchestrated from above nor a desperate flight from below,

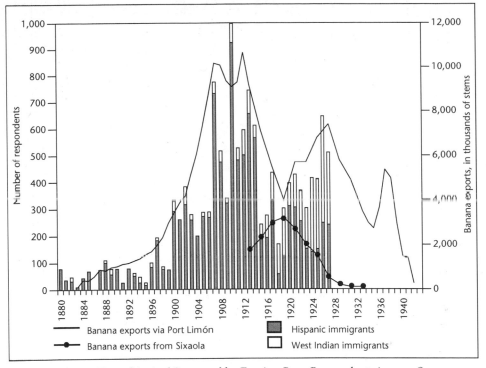

FIGURE 2.2. Year of Arrival Reported by Foreign-Born Respondents in 1927 Census, with Annual Costa Rican Banana Exports, 1880–1942

Sources: Author's analysis of CIHAC 1927 census database; Reinaldo Carcanholo, "Sobre la evolución de las actividades bananeras en Costa Rica," *Anuario de Estudios Centroamericanos* 19 (1978): 145, 167; Clarence F. Jones and Paul C. Morrison, "Evolution of the Banana Industry in Costa Rica," *Economic Geography* 28, no. 1 (1952): 2.

Note: Figures expanded to reflect total population size. N = 1,165.

but rather deeply integrated into working-class lives, its comforts and discomforts predictable, its rituals of status and self-presentation well set.

The established circulation of people, news, and ships meant that Port Limón was in many ways closer to Colón than to either Kingston or Cartago. West Indians from Costa Rica were likely among the first workers to reach Colón—after all, Jamaicans leaving the island had to deposit £1 5s. with local authorities and present two backers to guarantee their return passage, while Jamaicans in Limón faced no such restrictions. By 1913 annual remittances from the Canal Zone to Costa Rica reached $4,852, the bulk of it West Indians' earnings going to their families in Limón.[78]

The years of canal construction were also the height of banana employment in Limón. Established districts were still producing, and huge new areas were being cleared for planting in Sixaola to the south. Government correspondence from 1906 to 1908 mentions for the first time Nicaraguan workers coming to the *zona bananera* in large groups. The increasing arrival of Costa Rican laborers drew notice as well.[79] The immigration of West Indians to Limón reached its height when canal employment was highest, around 1907–13, and began falling at the same time the canal workforce was reduced.[80] While in early years the canal had pulled migrants away from Limón and diverted others who might have arrived, that effect was soon drowned out by a countervailing wave.[81] More people were coming from the islands to the coast than ever before, and some of them, finding work in Panama uncongenial or unavailable, headed north. Such was the tale of Robert Samuel Buchanan Sterling, his son recalled seventy years later. "My father went to Panama in the days of the contract to build the Panama Canal but he could not get work and he would not stay in the country, because the police don't allow you to light on the street in the daytime. So he had to leave that country and come to Costa Rica," where he worked on the railroad in Siquirres and then in the Estrella Valley.[82]

Like Sterling, most West Indian migrants had headed on or headed home by the time canal construction was winding down. Demographers set net emigration from Jamaica to Panama between 1891 and 1911 at 26,000, only a quarter of the number who made the journey from Kingston to Colón.[83] The governor of Jamaica visited Panama in 1911 and reported to his superiors that the ICC planned to discharge some 5,000 Jamaican laborers in the coming year. "The Barbadians, I was informed, have given more satisfaction as labourers than the Jamaicans: the latter, doubtless owing to their being nearer home, more familiar with the opportunities of Central America, and not under Contract having been found more 'independent' and 'captious.'"[84] With the ICC's blessing United Fruit recruited between 5,000 and 6,000 West Indian canal workers in 1912 and 1913 and shipped them to Costa Rica, Bocas del Toro, and Honduras.[85]

The United Fruit Company was recruiting labor at a time when it had a surplus on its own rolls. By 1910 Main Line plantations were in frank decline, and established Old Line farms soon followed. Declining yields, labor activism, and a threatened export tax had all contributed to the UFCO decision to cut Limón operations to a minimum and transfer capital and fixed stock to Bocas del Toro and Honduras. Of the 30,000-plus acres that UFCO owned in

United Fruit Company buildings in Bocas del Toro (point of embarkation for Sixaola division bananas), 1916. "House No. 3—Bocas— 1916," Box 27, Panama, United Fruit Company Collection, Baker Library, Harvard Business School.

Zent, only 1,250 acres remained in cultivation by 1913.[86] Bankruptcies swept local business, and arson became common as merchants attempted to cash in on hefty insurance policies acquired in better days.[87] The collapse of old farming regions meant an intense demand for labor in new regions being cleared and planted. Acreage under cultivation by United Fruit dropped by a third from 1908 to 1910 and then nearly doubled between 1911 and 1913 as over 22,000 acres in Sixaola were brought into production.[88] Yet after 1913 new plantings were not enough to shore up Limón's export totals. In 1915 there were over 3,000 unemployed men in Port Limón alone.[89] Some workers may have chosen not to follow the plantation frontier, for skilled and steady work in settled districts was being replaced by hard and dangerous labor in distant camps with few amenities. But the company's decision to recruit in Panama while unemployed workers thronged the streets of Port Limón suggests a strategic choice to oversupply the new districts with new men and to leave the Limón labor force—with its increasingly sophisticated union organization and negotiating strategies—behind.[90]

Most Nicaraguan and Costa Rican workers had been employed on large private farms on the Old Line and in the Estrella Valley. As the bonanza of the first decade of the century gave way to sharp contraction during World War I, fewer laborers returned to the zone after trips home, and fewer of their neighbors arrived to take their places. The thousands of Costa Rican and Central American *peones* who labored in Limón's first banana export boom left no second-generation Hispanic populace in Limón.[91]

Peons and Pioneers: Limón during the Second Export Boom

As exports plummeted in 1917–18, United Fruit and other local employers cut wages and rolls. In December 1918, 1,200 West Indian workers went on strike in the Bocas del Toro division, where real wages had fallen by half since 1914. Costa Rican police and UFCO agents murdered two workers, assaulted scores more, forced strikers "to work at the point of bayonet and with revolvers," burned their homes, and uprooted their provision gardens. British diplomats helped negotiate an end to the strike, but the 15 percent wage increase brought little relief.[92] In the Limón division in January 1921, the (West Indian) Limón Workers' Federation, recently affiliated with the San José–based Confederación General de Trabajadores (CGT), called a general strike to protest layoffs and demand wage increases. The company refused to negotiate and fanned a border dispute between Costa Rica and Panama. When war broke out the CGT called on Limón strikers to return to work in the name of patriotic unity and the collective action collapsed.[93] Company intransigence, official violence, and unreliable allies were the order of day, and increasing numbers of West Indians sought greener pastures abroad. Cuba's booming sugar industry drew many. Old-timers report that "after World War I 'everyone' was going to Cuba. Houses were sold for a few dollars, and the owner of one even traded it for a grip to hold clothes for the trip."[94] Then, between 1920 and 1921, the U.S. market price of bananas leaped by 50 percent, and United Fruit as well as other growers suddenly found it profitable to cultivate bananas on lands abandoned a decade earlier.[95] Limón's second banana boom was under way. United Fruit recruited Costa Ricans by the thousands for the new planting. A company official reported in 1920 that "at least

90 percent" of new laborers hired that year were Costa Ricans.[96] The human landscape of Limón was being remade.

In 1927, 55 percent of Limón's residents spoke English as their mother tongue; 37 percent spoke Spanish. The majority of the remaining 8 percent were indigenous Talamancans. Three-fifths of the English speakers had been born abroad, 86 percent of them in Jamaica; one-quarter of the Spanish speakers had been born abroad, 72 percent of them in Nicaragua. Limón was notoriously heterogeneous, and yet the census describes a remarkably straightforward architecture of race and ethnicity. Ninety-six percent of blacks spoke English, and 95 percent of English speakers were black; 90 percent of Spanish speakers were white, and 96 percent of whites spoke Spanish. That is, "color or race" as classified by census takers mapped almost perfectly onto linguistic divides, despite each migrant group's demonstrably diverse ancestry. This should not surprise us. Racial categories always depend on cultural cues that guide the perception of bodily difference. When a dead body was discovered along the rail line near Siquirres in 1911 the police report noted: "Due to the dead man's color the witness believes that he belongs to the black race."[97] The witness believed, but he could not be sure. For that he would need to hear the man speak, or know where he lived, or see him among friends. Costa Rican highlanders were inevitably labeled *blanco* by census takers in Limón, as were the majority of immigrants from the northwest province of Guanacaste. Apparently *guanacastecos* looked whiter in Limón than they did back home: census takers in Guanacaste described 67 percent of residents as mestizos in 1927, but less than 6 percent of *guanacasteco* immigrants were labeled mestizo by census takers in Limón that same year. In sum, the census classifications of *negro* and *blanco* for "color or race," and of English and Spanish as "mother tongue," are both nearly coterminous with the groups I have referred to as West Indians and Hispanics.[98]

In Search of the *Hombres Solos*

Writings about Limón have made much of the pattern of *los hombres solos* — the lone men — that shaped the region in its early years. The phrase is both demographically descriptive and emotionally loaded. A memoir written in 1950 by José León Sánchez about his years on the island penitentiary of San Lucas was entitled *La isla de los hombres solos*, and the sense of men suffering together in a place beyond civilized norms pervades the phrase as applied to the banana zone as well. Demographic patterns in Limón have in fact been enduringly different from those in the Central Valley. Since the start of official record keeping Limón has had a heavily male population, a low marriage rate, and a high illegitimacy rate. It has seemed reasonable to attribute these differences to West Indian behavior, as explained by racial nature, cultural heritage, or imperialist exploitation, depending on the observer's inclination.[99] A closer look at the 1927 census data confirms much of the black men as *hombres solos* hypothesis, for men outnumbered women among West Indian immigrants by perhaps three to one during the years prior to 1899, and over the course of their lives West Indian men in Limón would marry in far fewer numbers than either their island counterparts or their Hispanic neighbors. On the other hand, in the 1920s the male to female ratio for Limón's white population (172:100) was markedly *less* balanced than that of the black population (133:100). Over one-third of young Hispanic men in Limón were foreign citizens, and male predominance was greater among Hispanic immigrants (265:100) than among Costa Rican migrants (145:100). Nonetheless, in the 1920s the weight of Costa Rican women within the provincial population was still small.[100]

Unprecedented numbers of West Indian women had arrived at the height of canal-era migration and had stayed to raise families in Limón as the years passed.[101] Meanwhile, the recent exodus of young West Indian men had created a male to female ratio of only 78:100 among English-speaking young adults. Black Limón had become a sending society in the very years that the region drew Hispanic migrants by the thousands. Whether locally born or childhood immigrants, young West Indian men began to leave Limón as they reached the age of employment, heading for Panama, New York City, Jamaica, and, most of all, Cuba.[102] Their female peers stayed. Young women worked alongside mothers, aunts, and foster aunts in the port and line town service economy and likely dedicated ever more time to caring for their kinswomen's young children—children who made up an increasing portion of the local West Indian population.

The outcome of these various trends was a regional population largely composed of middle-aged West Indian men, young Hispanic men, and black boys and girls.[103] In the 1920s young Hispanic men encountered few potential mates of the opposite sex and of their own heritage in Limón; the same was true for young West Indian women in the 1920s and beyond. Yet census data, oral history, and judicial sources all confirm that mixed unions were exceedingly rare in this era. Young black women remained single, or married or lived

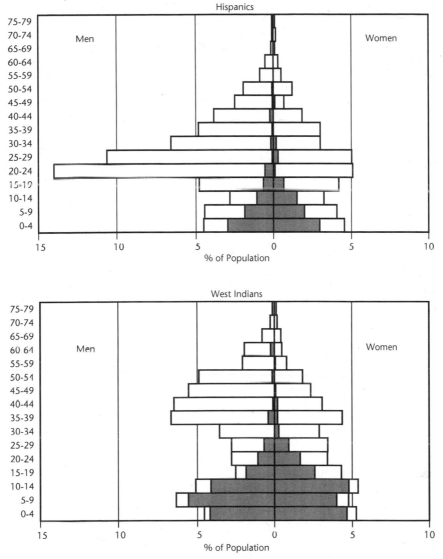

FIGURE 2.3. Age Pyramids of Hispanic and West Indian Populations of Limón, 1927

Source: Author's analysis of CIHAC 1927 census database.

Note: Figures expanded to reflect total population size. Spanish speakers, N = 1,072; English speakers, N = 1,592. Limón-born population shaded.

with older men, or took sweethearts who might soon leave to seek work else-where.[104] Young white men found solace in paid sex or made do without. Carlos Luís Fallas, a banana worker in the Estrella Valley in this era, would later write:

> That's why we kept drinking in desperation, until we fell on our backs like felled trunks. . . .
>
> No one, not even Calero, would have to suffer that night the martyr-dom of erotic dreams, which excite the sleeping flesh of the *peón*. No one would roll trembling, whimpering in the shadows, performing absurd contortions. No one would wake bathed in semen and with a feeling of disgust, of shame, and of rage gnawing on his soul.
>
> The four of us slept, drunk.[105]

West Indians were still coming to Limón in the 1920s, albeit in much smaller numbers than in previous years. Recent arrivals tallied in the 1927 census were evenly split between English speakers (two-thirds of them Jamai-can) and Spanish speakers (three-quarters of them Nicaraguan). More than half of Spanish-speaking newcomers were young men, while less than one-seventh of English-speaking newcomers were.[106] A full decade before United Fruit chose to end banana production and purchasing in the province, West Indian Limón was exporting its young men for work abroad and welcoming (or welcoming back) older men and a few middle-aged women. It was the confluence of cohort life-cycle rhythms and regional economic rhythms that created this pattern, as the life stories of West Indians who reached Limón after World War I show.[107] Most had been born around the turn of the cen-tury; many were raised by their mothers while their fathers worked abroad. Without exception they had begun their travels in their late teens or early twenties and had worked for wages around the Western Caribbean for ten, twenty, or even thirty years before settling on the Talamanca coast.

John Burke was born in St. Andrew parish, Jamaica, in 1901, one of twelve children of a Methodist minister. He left for Cuba at nineteen "because the rest of the boys were doing it—friends. We wanted to know something about the outside. Those days was a big day in Cuba. You get plenty of money. All kind of work. You have men work in the railroads, you work in the farms cut-ting cane, you work in the factories and all different places." Burke left Cuba in 1928 "because they were expecting a big revolution there." He found work on a United Fruit banana plantation in Puerto Cabezas, Nicaragua, as a prun-ing foreman and later worked as a stockman on a plantation in Puerto Valdía, "near to Colombia." His travels took him through Limón several times. Around 1930 he hired on as a foreman, working first in Siquirres, then in Bananito, and then again in Siquirres, where UFCO *abacá* (manila hemp) plantations were centered during World War II. After he "got paid off" in 1946 he farmed along the Old Line. "I had a friend down here in Cahuita and they said if I could get down to Cahuita they'd give me a property to manage, cocoa farm. So we came to Cahuita, 1949."[108]

Ormington Demontford Corbin, born in Barbados in 1903, left school in sixth grade to help his mother farm while his father worked on the Panama Canal. At seventeen a cousin persuaded him to stow away on a boat full of contract workers bound for Cuba, where Corbin's father had found work as a railroad foreman. "When I got [to Cuba] I asked and I asked and I got to find out where he was. We go to there. He said to me, 'Don't I tell your mother not to let you come to Cuba?' I said 'Yes, Dad, but she showed me the letter too late when I had already made up my mind.' . . . I go there in '21, he went home in '22. He wanted me to go but I wouldn't go, I said, 'no, no, let I stay.'"[109] Corbin worked for seven years as a canecutter and then cook in Cuba, then as a trader in Nicaragua, a railway laborer in the Estrella Valley, a stevedore on the canal, a U.S. Army orderly, and a carpenter in Almirante. Like John Burke and others, Corbin traveled with male friends as work companions in his youth. By middle age he had married, and then it was the conjugal partnership, and his wife's needs and resources, that guided his travels. Corbin recalled at length his anxious days in Bocas, working desperately to earn enough money to send for "Miss Ida," whom he had left ill in a boardinghouse in Colón. In 1954 Miss Ida's ailing stepfather asked the couple to return to her native Cahuita and take over his cocoa farm.

The aggregate result of the individual travels and travails that made up the Western Caribbean migratory system in these years was a marked improvement in the collective lot of West Indians in Limón. Even as the number of penniless Hispanics swelled, West Indians came to dominate the ranks of midlevel service employees and small rural proprietors, growing provisions, cocoa, and bananas. Two separate factors drove this upward mobility in the years after World War I. The first was the exodus of the least well-situated young black men. Census data suggests a near absolute rejection of plantation labor by this group in favor of out-migration. In 1927 only 28 percent of West Indian men ages fifteen to twenty-nine were agricultural employees, compared to 80 percent of their Hispanic peers. In fact, according to the census sample projection there were barely 300 young black field workers in the entire province. The second factor was the seniority within the region of West Indian men forty-five and older. With a median year of arrival of 1900, these were men who had worked in Limón during the banana industry's last long decade of prosperity, and they had been well positioned to take advantage of the era of uneven expansion and abandonment after 1909.[110] The stories of West Indians who settled on the southern coast in this era highlight newcomers' access to resources shared and exchanged along a wide variety of social ties. George Humphries's parents were sheltered by his "uncle" when they arrived—whether the title reflected a preexisting blood tie or honorary kinship created through mutual support is unclear in his retelling. Leslie Williams's father was fed by a friend.[111] If in Port Limón and on plantation camps the cash economy included many services more usually assigned to the kinship domain, in the rural hinterlands noncash labor and lending united people not usually thought of as family.

Hispanic Currents during and after the Second Export Boom

And so he rolled up his kit and went to shed fleas somewhere else.
—"Las Penurias del Pobre Mozo" (autobiography of F.J.J.,
born Bocas de Nozara, Guanacaste, 1916)

Just as West Indian workers circulating the Western Caribbean bumped up against fellow workers and former employers, kinfolk and former lovers as they moved from place to place, so too the lives of itinerant Hispanic workers were marked by repeating contacts and enduring ties. The intermittent waves of migration from Nicaragua over the course of the twentieth century are today the focus of much hostility within Costa Rica, expressed in nationalist terms. But the autobiographies of *campesinos* who ended their days in Limón describe not an ongoing Nicaraguan invasion but rather a unified social geography within which people with relatives on both sides of the border moved back and forth over the course of their working lives. Political violence in Nicaragua sent Nicaraguans south to Costa Rica seeking work and respite; political violence in Costa Rica sent Costa Ricans north in search of the same, albeit in smaller numbers.[112] By the time Nicaragua-born M.M. was thirty-four years old he had traveled to the United States, Colombia, the Philippines, Japan, Peru, the Galapagos, New Zealand, Samoa, Spain, and Mexico as a sailor and port worker. Yet his trajectory after arriving in Puntarenas in 1929 could not have been more typical. He worked on the Estrella Valley railroad, labored on the Penshurst Banana Company plantations outside Cahuita, left for Puerto Cortés de Golfito (the Pacific banana zone) in 1938, spent time in Puntarenas, cleared and planted a farm in San Carlos, and ended up farming a parcel he had purchased in Cariari de Guápiles in Limón.[113]

Sizable numbers of Costa Ricans left for Panama in the late 1930s and 1940s for canal or plantation work. A.H.Ch. recalls subcontractors recruiting in Limón around 1940 for work on the United Fruit plantations in Sixaola: "[A]ll the *compañeros* were going to Panama and so I signed up too."[114] A.H.Ch.'s life—as he titled it, "The Life of a *campesino*, who has known the whip of Poverty"—typifies the experience of itinerant Costa Rican wage workers in the decades after World War I. As a landless youth in Heredia in the 1920s he worked picking coffee on wealthy relatives' plantations. Hearing the stories of "men who traveled to the Line of Limón to work with the Banana Company and said one earned well there," a group of boys decided to try their luck in Guápiles in 1935. A.H.Ch. was seventeen. He would work on banana plantations in Matina and Parrita, on a ranch in Guanacaste, digging canals in Quepos, preparing *abacá* fields in Monteverde de Siquirres, running a dredge on the Río Cimarrones near Zent, cleaning overgrown cocoa groves in Sixaola, planting *abacá* in Changuinola, clearing pasture for a dairy ranch in San San, Panama, pouring cement floors for plantation barracks in Bocas del Toro, weeding cocoa in Cahuita, and clearing his own *parcela* from the rain forest near Punta Uva on the Talamanca coast.[115]

Like West Indian workers a generation before, men like A.H.Ch. worked many jobs at many sites, acquiring skills and friends who served them well in times of need. Yet the landscape that drew them was dominated by a single employer to a degree that the Caribbean rimlands that drew West Indians at the turn of the century had never been. At all but two of the stops above, A.H.Ch. was employed by the United Fruit Company, one of its subsidiaries, or one of its subcontractors.[116] Little wonder the company became known in these years as El Pulpo, The Octopus.

Race and Citizenship in the 1930s and 1940s

The collapse of the 1920s banana boom coincided with the worst economic crisis highland Costa Rica had ever seen, as well as with the height of scientific racism's worldwide prestige. The impact of this conjuncture on the politics

West Indian children traveling by burro along rail line, Limón, ca. 1925.
Plate 597, "Children coming in from surrounding country, sometimes as far as
five miles," Box 76, Recreation (Welfare, Schools), United Fruit Company Collection,
Baker Library, Harvard Business School.

of race in Costa Rica was unmistakable.[117] The paragraph that followed tables
on citizens' race in the official report of the 1927 census declared, "As can be
judged by these figures the population of Costa Rica includes a high percentage of [the] white race. . . . With good reason the conditions of social and
political order which have prevailed in our country, and which have endowed
us with those habits of peace and work so traditional among our people, have
been attributed to the racial homogeneity of the Costa Ricans."[118] The preceding statistics would have been far less reassuring had census officials not
excluded all West Indians—many of them second and third generation *limonenses*—from the figures. They were not legally citizens. Nor would they ever
become so if leaders like Census Office director José Guerrero had their way.[119]

The preliminary census report caused a public scandal and political crisis, for it revealed a national population far smaller than expected, more than 19,000 *negros* in Limón, and—worse still—832 *negros* in the Central Valley and 301 already settled on the Pacific coast. All analysis of census data was halted, and the tally sheets disappeared.[120]

Accusations about black workers' biological nature and moral character suddenly assumed a central role in long-standing debates over the banana industry's impact on the national economy. In 1930 José Guerrero published an influential article entitled "What Do We Want Costa Rica to Be—Black or White? The Racial Problem of the Negro and the Current Banana Negotiations." Citing census data on the provincial distribution of black residents, Guerrero denounced the proposed expansion of United Fruit plantations beyond Limón. "The Negro is the shadow of the banana [*El negro es la sombra del banano*]," he wrote. "As a human I have nothing against anyone, whether white, Chinese, or Negro." This was a simply "a biological matter, or more specifically, a eugenic one." Economic nationalism demanded racial separatism. "Those who manage nigger workforces [*negradas*] in foreign lands don't have to worry about the fate of peoples of other races already settled there, for all they care about is extracting wealth which can be turned into cash, but how can we Costa Ricans who live permanently on this soil be indifferent to the Negro invasion of the rest of our nation?"[121]

The depiction of West Indian blacks as an alien element within the national organism, whose earnings were sent abroad and who had no allegiance to the nation, became standard among Costa Rican intellectuals in the 1930s and 1940s.[122] (The same image of the enduring alienness of the banana workforce, stripped of its explicit racism, would shape the concept of enclave economy developed by intellectuals in the 1960s and 1970s.)[123] Anti-black racism pervaded the demands of Hispanic workers and the posturing of Costa Rican planters alike in the 1930s and found direct expression in the 1934 law that forbade the employment of "colored people" on United Fruit's new Pacific coast plantations.[124] Communist Party leader Manuel Mora was the only member of congress to speak out against the racially restrictive article, and both deputies from Limón voted with the two-thirds majority that supported the contract.[125]

Up to the 1920s there had been significant overlap in the migration circuits of West Indian and Hispanic workers who came through Limón, all of whom might cultivate bananas and cocoa in Costa Rica and Panama, tap rubber in eastern Nicaragua, northern Limón, or western Panama, or log wood at any of these sites. Yet by the end of the 1920s, race-based immigration restrictions at Central American ports and informal restrictions on black movement within Costa Rica were truncating West Indian travel in unprecedented ways. "We are fearing that in the near future a very drastic immigration act will be introduced against peoples of Negro decent in this country, which up to now is the only free port for Negroes in these parts," wrote the editors of the Limón *Searchlight* in 1930.[126] Their fears were well founded. After 1936 the trajectories of West Indian and Hispanic migrants diverged sharply, as United Fruit's new Pacific coast plantations became integral to Costa Rican and Nicaraguan itinerant wageworkers' circuits.[127] And in 1942 "the black race" was added for the first time to the long list of peoples ("Chinese, Arabs, Turks, Syrians, Armenians, Gypsies, Coolies, etc.") forbidden entry to Costa Rica.[128]

The politics of race and nation were changing across the region, shaping the prospects of young black men like Martin Luther, born in Matina in 1914. In 1919 his mother left him with her mother in Jamaica while she sought work in Cuba. In 1926 she brought Luther to join her and enrolled him in school. "But I couldn't get along with Spanish children so much. . . . [In Cuba] they have colored Spanish and the white ones, but in those days when them know you can speak English and they know you are from Jamaica, they call you 'jamaiquino' and we used to fight a lot." Luther left school to sell newspapers on the street. By 1932 there was no work in Cuba. Although he had no "Jamaican documents" he finagled free passage on a steamer for returnees. But the situation in Kingston was little better, and Luther found it hard to find work, "for I didn't grow there." He stowed away with a Cuban-born friend, but they were discovered and shipped back from the Canal Zone. On their second attempt they made it to Port Limón.[129]

Presenting his Costa Rican birth certificate on arrival, Luther was given a "free pass" by Costa Rican immigration officials, but his friend was refused entry "because he wasn't born here, it would be $200 against us to admit him here." His friend slipped off the boat regardless, and the next day the two headed west to Puntarenas. "But at that time there was a President name León Cortés, that was in 1937, and he show a law that the colored people should not go on the Pacific side of the country." A United Fruit supervisor "gave me fifty *colones*, telling us to go back. He try to help us but he not able to employ us because it's against the law." In Matina Luther sought out his mother's closest friend from twenty years before, who helped him while he learned to work as a railroad foreman and tried his hand at logging. In 1941 he went under contract to the Canal Zone. "I didn't like the system." Public spaces were segregated by law: silver meant black. "The [water spout] marked gold, if we make a mistake and go drink water there, we may be locked up in jail." In the commissary, "we weren't allowed, we the Costa Rican weren't allowed to purchase in that place. The boss had to go in and purchase our lunch." In 1943 he cut out for Port Limón.[130]

Martin Luther describes nationality, color, and ethnicity as three separate matters. He refers to himself throughout as a "Costa Rican"; he had a friend who was a "Cuban." They were both "colored" rather than "white" but could communicate with both "English" and "Spanish people." The territory he traveled, though, was cordoned off by nation-states that had made whiteness a prerequisite for full citizenship. Luther tells his tale as a picaresque adventure in which his birth certificate and linguistic skills allow him to leap each unjust barrier in turn. But in this his life was exceptional. For thousands of Limón-born West Indians, migration in the 1930s and 1940s was a one-way street that led away from Costa Rica.[131]

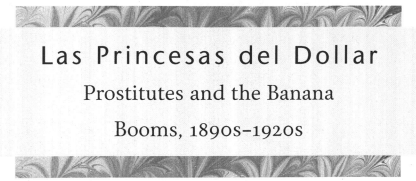

THREE

Las Princesas del Dollar

Prostitutes and the Banana

Booms, 1890s–1920s

In the opening scene of Joaquín Gutiérrez's novel *Puerto Limón*, Paragüitas, a Nicaraguan union organizer, holds forth to a group of striking banana workers about the time he rented a "room with a bath" in a Honduran hotel:

"I crossed the patio and went in. *¡Ay juemialma!* My mouth waters just remembering it. Figure it out: six months chopping down jungle, alone with myself, so horny that at night I had to rub it on my own just to get some sleep. And what do you think? Well *negro*, there she was, a *cholita* with chinky eyes that squinted up with pure pleasure to see me. In the center of the bath was a bench where I sat, and a gutter came down from the roof where they sent down the water. And her standing there with a bar of soap and a brush ready to wash me. 'Is this the bath?' I asked. 'Aha,' she said. 'And you're going to wash me?' 'Aha.' All she would say was 'Aha.' 'So, now I get naked?' She moved her head up and down and I stripped down, ripping off buttons; I sat on the bench, the *chola* opened the hatch and the water poured down. So she started to soap me and rub me all over with the brush, and when she started in on my armpits she worked so hard tickling me that I ended up falling off the bench. When she saw me on the ground she got scared and ran to a corner and froze, gasping, like a trapped deer. Well, let's just say I didn't even stop to get the soap off!"

"Shit!"

"No way, Paragüitas, don't lie."

"Why don't we end this fucking strike and all head for Honduras?"

"And that's what they call a room with a bath?"[1]

Carlos Luís Fallas, one of the founders of the Costa Rican Communist Party, worked in the Estrella Valley in the 1920s, returned to Limón as a labor organizer in the 1930s, and published the autobiographical novel *Mamita Yunai* in 1941. In Fallas's narrative, sex and its absence syncopate the lives of laborers on Camp Andromeda, defining the worth of wages and marking the passage of time:

> "Son of a bitch!" [Calero] shouted. "You assholes. You know who I was dreaming about when you called me? About Mister Clinton's big *negra*! And she'd finally made up her mind to take off her clothes—when you come and wake me up! Bastards!"
>
> And I, swallowing my laughter:
>
> "Payday's coming soon enough, so you can stop masturbating already."
>
> "Pay?" he exclaimed, flashing his eyes and making an indecent gesture. "Look! It's been two paydays already with no whores come out, and I'm not going into Limón to waste the chickenshit I earn!"[2]

Prostitution, Production, and the State

In contrast to fictional and autobiographical accounts, United Fruit Company publications were carefully discreet when discussing the role of sex and companionship in maintaining the plantation labor force. In 1925 the Panama division report noted that "frequently there are small villages adjacent and many of the employees are drawn to the places of amusement there."[3] Outside observers were more explicit. That same year, as labor shortages prompted United Fruit to renew recruitment efforts, the U.S. consul in Limón wrote to his superiors, "Gross sexual immorality among the negroes and the lower class of 'Natives' is the rule, in fact the presence of loose women on the farms is said to tend toward holding laborers on the farms and keeps them more contented."[4] Touring Limón in 1911, Jamaican governor Sydney Olivier noted that "in Jamaica every man of this class has his sweetheart, with whom he has relations which, if civically irregular, are at any rate natural and healthy: in

Costa Rica there is an immense plurality of young men, with the result that the largest building in Siquirres—(the centre of a large banana district)—a pile of four stories,—was pointed out to me as the local brothel—an institution quite unnecessary in Jamaica, and with the further result that great numbers contract disease and on their return to Jamaica disseminate a very active and virulent form of syphilis."[5]

Unlike Lord Olivier, the UFCO Medical Department rarely focused on venereal disease as a plantation health problem, much less on the specific risks of congenital syphilis. The company's approach stands in sharp contrast to prostitution regulation policies adopted by U.S. medical personnel elsewhere around the Caribbean in these same years. Where U.S. troops were the customers, as in Puerto Rico during World War I or along the Panama Canal, mandatory medical exams and forced quarantines of infected women were the norm.[6] But on the United Fruit Company plantations those at risk from venereal disease were, as the U.S. consul noted, "negroes and the lower class of 'Natives'"—not U.S. servicemen who might return home to infect wives and engender defective children.

The United Fruit Company had little interest in the generational reproduction of a plantation labor force. The expected productive life of a prime-soil banana plantation was eight to ten years at the turn of the century and dropped to as little as two to three years by the 1930s as Sigatoka disease spread through the zone.[7] United Fruit and other corporate banana planters practiced what one scholar calls "shifting plantation agriculture," using accumulated soil fertility and hydrological resources as intensely as possible and then moving on when yields fell and when pathogens followed banana plants into disrupted wetland ecosystems.[8] In their dependence on geographic mobility, foreign-owned banana plantations were the exact opposite of foreign-owned mines, although the two are often described together as "enclave" economies. At the El Teniente mine in northern Chile in this era, the Braden Copper Company worked hard to transform male and female migrants into stable, wage-dependent husbands and frugal, feminine, legally married housewives. Properly educated as to "good manners," "controlling your passions," and "women's emotional hygiene," such mothers (the company paper insisted) "initiated and prepared children to arrive, as they are supposed to, at the jobs that workers occupy today and that they will occupy tomorrow."[9] In contrast, United Fruit paid lip service to the need to civilize its workforce but put little effort into paternalist social engineering. A second generation of banana workers tied to their homes and eager to step into their fathers' shoes was the last thing the United Fruit Company needed. Maneuvering through the political fallout of labor dislocations caused by the shifting plantation strategy was delicate enough as it was.

Historian Avi Chomsky has shown that the UFCO Medical Department concentrated resources on combating those health problems most costly for the company's short-term profits. Under this calculus the highest priority was malaria, which filled hospital beds with the critically ill and reduced productivity among the chronically ill. Diseases with higher mortality but lower morbidity—that is, diseases less likely to keep you sick and more likely to kill you off—received less attention.[10] Despite the company's generally laissez-faire attitude to commercial sex and venereal disease, worries that workers' nighttime rambles would frustrate malaria control did draw some official attention to patterns of sex and sociability on the camps. The superintendent of the Medical Department wrote in 1929 that camp populations must be "stabilized and not permitted to fluctuate between sanitary and insanitary districts [referring to mosquito control] without daily supervision. No matter what his civil status, man is a social animal and seeks companionship, irrespective of the distance he must travel. . . . To meet these requirements in malaria-infected districts, wherever possible, segregation in villages or camps is essential and married quarters must be provided."[11]

In practice married quarters were rare. The great majority of camp residents were men living with other men, and this was particularly true during the early years of clearing and planting in any region. In the era of Main Line and Old Line plantation expansion around the turn of the century, the great majority of arriving women settled in Port Limón or in the junction towns along the lines. This gendered division of residence was replicated in Sixaola as UFCO plantations expanded northward from Bocas del Toro. A company report on that district recalled in 1918, "It was the rule in the early days for laborers to keep their women and children in settlements in crowded rooms. . . . The country was overcrowded with negro women, who were constantly travelling back and forth from settlement to farms."[12] The pattern was repeated as Siquirres and the Estrella Valley were replanted in the 1920s. More than three-quarters of Hispanic *peones bananeros* in the 1927 census resided in all-male households.[13] In migrants' home societies the labor of social reproduction was traditionally carried out by women, in the context of kinship relations. As Lord Olivier had accurately observed, this was true for sex as well. But in Limón most migrants paid for their meals, paid for clean clothes, and paid for a room with a bath. And pious pronouncements about married quarters aside, it was widely assumed by workers and employers alike that most migrants would pay for sex.[14]

As various scholars have noted, prostitution is not a "natural" response to a disproportionate number of young men in a society. To privilege commercial sex with women over alternative practices (masturbation, homosexuality, celibacy) is a culturally constructed choice.[15] In the autobiographical novel *La isla de los hombres solos*, written in 1950, José León Sánchez recounted his experiences in the late 1930s and 1940s on the island penitentiary of San Lucas off the coast of Puntarenas. Sánchez described in detail patterns of sexual relationships between male prisoners, which included both established couples with clearly marked masculine and feminine roles and prostitution by cross-dressed adolescent boys in exchange for bread or tobacco. "[A]lthough at first I found it repugnant, later the loving glances, the performances on fire with tenderness when there were spats, the effeminate and provocative walks and the fervent courting of one man by another who wished to conquer him, and the sweet and tender kisses even before the gaze of all the other *compañeros*— all this seemed perfectly normal."[16]

But while individual men in Limón must have made alternate choices, all observers agreed that female prostitution was the preeminent sexual practice of the *zona bananera*. Of course, there were many different arrangements through which women accepted material resources from men in exchange for care and comfort. Variables included services provided, residence arrangements, duration of union, expectations of exclusivity, and obligations incurred toward other kin (including offspring). In common understanding then as now, a prostitute was a woman who offered such services on the most concrete and time-limited terms: sex, for cash, today. As we shall see, prostitutes in Limón did not only or always have sex with their clients, did not only or always receive cash in exchange, and did not only or always earn their livings in this fashion. Yet despite its blurry edges, "prostitute" was a discrete occupational role and social identity in the *zona bananera*. These women were known as *meretrizes, rameras, prostitutas, mujeres de la vida alegre* (women of the happy life), *mujeres de la vida ligera* (women of the light life), *mujeres de mala vida* (bad-living women), and *mujeres públicas* (public women). Their work and their lives are the subject of this chapter.

The Organization of Commercial Sex in Limón

The organization of commercial sex reflected the social geography of the plantation zone. A municipal tax table from 1909 gives a clear picture of the spatial hierarchy of public consumption in Limón. Fees—which reflected profitability—decreased both with distance along the rail lines from the port, and, within each building, with distance from the street. Commercial sex was spread among all the businesses listed—bars, hotels, *cantinas*, billiard halls, and boardinghouses—which in fact often shared the same buildings and formed unified social spaces.[17] Those that had large numbers of resident prostitutes were de facto brothels and were known, though not licensed, as such. During Limón's first boom, port brothels included El Rincón Bellaco (The Rogues' Corner), El Arca de Noé (Noah's Ark), and the long-lived Casa Azúl (Blue House). One spot popular in the 1920s was known as Las Princesas del Dollar (The Princesses of the Dollar), while others were known by their owners' names: "Arabella de Henriquez's place," or "the establishment of Eduviges de Santander."[18] Business owners' profits came from the rental of rooms and the sale of food and liquor to prostitutes and their clients, rather than through direct control over women or their earnings.

The port also had cheap boardinghouses, where cots or rooms were rented monthly, weekly, and nightly, in which some residents were working prostitutes and others might engage in a variety of sex-exchange relations over time. Jamaican laborer James Henriques was arrested in a port boardinghouse late one night in 1899, after a Costa Rican woman raised an uproar when he entered her room. She was Rosa Zelaya Vindas, seventeen years old and a registered prostitute from San José in town for a short visit. By her own account she was "somewhat inebriated" at the time, having gone down for a few drinks in the *cantina* on the first floor. Earlier that evening Henriques had borrowed money from a friend in order to pay Zelaya five *colones* in advance for her services—two days' wages for a port laborer in those years—and he bitterly asked the arresting officer, "[W]ho was going to guarantee the money he had paid?"[19] In the same era a prostitute in San José might earn a single *colón* per encounter, so it is hardly surprising that many prostitutes from highland cities made long visits to Port Limón or traveled to the junction towns or camps on biweekly paydays.[20] In 1911 the governor of Limón complained of "the public women from the interior [e.g., the Central Valley] who come here for their entertainments on paydays, leaving as is natural venereal diseases spread among the workers of the canton, principally in Guácimo and

Jiménez where there are the largest concentrations of them."[21] Other prostitutes resided on the camps continually. This last situation was patently the least desirable, for the same reasons that life on the plantations was difficult for men: climate, inadequate housing, leprosy, malaria, and parasitic infections.

Urban prostitution was integral to male sociability and public consumption. While elite men frequented private clubs, less privileged men filled *cantinas*, *hosterías* (inexpensive eateries), and billiard halls. In San José these men were artisans, petty merchants, and laborers with wages to spend. In Limón they were port and railway workers, minor public employees, and men in from the lines after payday. Sometimes male play crossed ethnic lines. One night in 1892 "Madame Stefanie" was interrupted while drinking with two customers (one Puerto Rican, one Cuban) by four boisterous young men who had just finished dragging the sail of the official port launch down the main street on a lark. Of the drunken foursome one was Costa Rican, one Colombian with a Hispanic surname, one Colombian with an Anglo surname (likely a West Indian from the province of Panama), and one German. Madame Stefanie herself was variously described as Martinican and French; she specified that she was from St. Lucia.[22] More commonly, however, social spaces were informally segregated. A subscription dance sponsored by a Jamaican businesswoman in 1907 was referred to as a "dance for blacks [*baile de negros*]," though in fact several of the participants were Costa Rican men from the Central Valley.[23]

Such social spaces were off-limits to decent women of any class. Put differently, women seen *en parrandas*, that is, drinking and diverting themselves in public, were assumed to be sexually active with multiple men. Police in San José justified an executive order closing all *hosterías* at 11 P.M. on the grounds that allowing them to remain open until 1 or 2 A.M. "lends itself to those who stay up all night (who are almost always the same men) forming scandals of every kind with *mujeres de la vida alegre*, who are the only women who frequent such establishments at those hours."[24] Yet prostitutes' participation in the *cantina* world did not revolve around sex. In 1914 Enriqueta Sánchez Mayorga was in her room in San José with two men, one of them resting on her bed, the other sitting in a chair with her friend María Lidia Álvarez. When two other men arrived, friends of the women but unacquainted with their guests, the early arrivals sent out for drinks for all of them. After a while the six went down to dinner together and then spent the rest of the evening visiting various *cantinas*.[25] Similar patterns held in the public entertainment locales of Port Limón and the line towns. In 1912 Angela Moreira and Emilia Hidalgo Zúñiga, one a resident of San José, the other living in Port Limón, traveled together by train to Guápiles for the night. Much of their evening was spent in the main salon of the local hotel drinking with a table full of planters and public officials, most of whom the women knew well enough to refer to by their first names and nicknames. Hidalgo's explanation that the men came "with the goal of spending a chatty evening [*un rato de tertulia*] with us" may have been a coy reference to intercourse, but it was also descriptively accurate. Laughter and brazen conversation were part of what Hidalgo and her *compañera* brought to the occasion.[26]

Port dance halls brought working-class men together with women no longer concerned about the appearance of propriety, and when men paid to enter they were purchasing a total experience rather than a carnal act: the chance to move to music with a woman held tight, to challenge other men in games of skill, to drink too much and shout too loud. Letters of complaint elicited by the governor of Limón in support of his decision to shut down Colombian widow Eduviges de Santander's *bailes de negocio* (commercial dances) in 1925 describe the many pleasures such enterprises offered. Dances were held, one neighbor reported, every Saturday and Sunday, "as well as the days when the steamers come in; participants pay entrance fees; women of doubtful conduct attend; liquor is sold and they get wild [*se forman grandes desórdenes*]. On Colombian Independence Day they made such a huge ruckus that the Police had to intervene and as a consequence various people of both sexes were arrested."[27] Santander called on friends in high places (a general, a congressman, a former cabinet member) to lobby the minister of government on her behalf, and the governor of Limón found himself repeatedly obliged to justify his actions against her. Neighbors young and old, he wrote, were "forced to see the scenes of orgy in which the *mujeres de mala vida* and the *hombres de pueblo* [humble men] who attend these dances inevitably end up." In a separate letter he derided Santander's business as "scandalous dances of people of the *bronze* (*sic*) [*bailes de escándalo de gentes del* bronce (*sic*)]," which seems to be a double entendre referring both to their skin color and to their intermediate social status: not of the "gold roll," as whites employed on the Panama Canal in these years were classed, nor of the "silver roll," as West Indian blacks were labeled.[28] The bronze-skinned revelers' loud nationalism, drinking, and sexual commerce were of a piece in the governor's complaints, as they likely were in the experience of the revelers themselves.

In contrast, prostitutes' work on banana plantations was limited to copulating sequentially with many men in a short time. In *Mamita Yunai* Fallas describes payday on Camp Andromeda, when "a group of men would line up in front of the door to an improvised shack of leaves and sticks; they entered two by two and soon left out the back." The narrator sees his companion Calero emerging from the hut, fastening his pants.

> "They even built them a shack, see?" he said, pointing to the hut while he spit, wrinkling his face with disgust.
>
> "Are the broads in there?" I asked, remembering the pair of horrors I had seen [arriving by train] that morning.
>
> "Yeah. They look like pigs, rooting around on that pile of dead leaves." And Calero threw himself on the ground, face up, to imitate the position the women were in.[29]

The disgust that the narrator and his coworkers express toward the women they pay for sex in part reflects Fallas's literary strategy, in which everything United Fruit touches becomes diseased and defiled.[30] But it also underlines how different public women's role on the plantations was from the urban *cantina* world of San José or Port Limón. For the line-men of *Mamita Yunai*, whores are a means to orgasm. At the camp it is boasting of sexual conquests, rather than socializing alongside prostitutes, that combines with communal drinking as the basis for men's bonding.

It seems clear that plantation prostitution was physically hazardous and emotionally degrading for the women involved. Yet it could also be profitable. The narrator and his *compañeros* work from 4 A.M. to noon at the most difficult and dangerous of plantation tasks, dynamiting landslides and hacking through rain forests while hip deep in mud. For this a subcontractor pays them 6.50 *colones* per day. When Calero emerges from the prostitutes' improvised hut, he exclaims, "You know how much those filthy sows are charging? Two and a half dollars! . . . Now I've really pissed away the money I'd gotten together!" It had taken Calero a day and a half to earn the sum he paid the nameless prostitute for a few minutes of uncomfortable sex.[31]

Blurred Boundaries and Constrained Choices

Some sexual arrangements fell into a gray area between prostitution and courting. Several *estupro* (deflowering) cases were brought by parents of adolescent girls who had had sex with one or several men and taken money in return. In 1914 Olivia Brown lived in a port boardinghouse doing chores for Mariah Gordon, who had brought the girl to Limón a year earlier with her mother's permission. By her own account, thirteen-year-old Olivia had been having sex with neighbor John Johnson every few days for a month before "Miss Mariah" found out, receiving from him "a quarter coin, or a *colón*" each time. Olivia testified that she had never had sexual contact with any man before Johnson, "and that she entered his room the first time because she didn't know what it was to be with a man and she wanted to know."[32] Mary Graham, a thirteen-year-old who lived with her parents in Germania, Siquirres, in 1913, used to visit a room shared by three young black men on a nearby United Fruit farm. It seems that one—Sammy, a guitar player from St. Kitts—was her steady lover, and that she also had sexual relations several times with his fellow worker Ernest McKay. She did so once in return for a promise not to tell her mother that she was sleeping with Sammy, once after telling Ernest "that if he gave her a *colón* she would give him 'a chance,'" and once in return for a UFCO commissary chip (*vale*) worth one *colón*.[33]

In 1922 a Chinese storekeeper was accused of deflowering a fourteen-year-old Jamaican girl. According to Caroline Davis's testimony, José Wing Chong had offered her some candy in exchange for sex, and she agreed. A fellow Chinese shopkeeper testified that the girl had a "bad reputation" because she sold yams and other things in the streets and "is always entering stores of my countrymen and joking with men." The witness went on to say that he himself had had sex with her two years earlier. When she first proposed that he "make use of her," he had said, "But you're so little," to which she replied "that she had already been with many of her own countrymen, and some of his as well." He and a third man testified that they had paid the girl five *colones* the first time they had sex and two or three *colones* on subsequent occasions.[34] There is no way for us to know what fears or hopes, anger or need pushed Olivia, Mary, and Caroline to have sex with the men they did, and no way for us to assess what satisfactions they may have gained in return. But their experiences of informal, semicommercial sex exchange set into relief some relative advantages of formal prostitution. Working together, as most public women usually did, prostitutes marshaled mutual aid and collective pressures: lending money, fixing prices, and maintaining working relationships with local police, who generally backed them up when conflicts with clients turned ugly.[35] Girls who had sex with men for money on an informal basis faced the same risks public women did—pregnancy, venereal disease, male violence—but they earned less in immediate material terms. And in the cases cited, at least, the long-term benefits were nil, for the men involved insisted their obligation went no further than the sex-for-cash transaction, and in each of these cases judicial authorities agreed.

Nor was there a clear divide between prostitution and coercion. Autobiographical sources suggest that forced sex was not rare in this era, especially for young women in domestic service or living with men who were not blood kin.[36] Several formal accusations of rape were filed each year in Limón in the first decades of the century, most involving prepubescent girls.[37] Yet accounts of coerced sex surfaced even when authorities did not seek them, even when the young women who spoke sought no redress. Apprehended at her mother's behest after she ran away to live with her boyfriend, sixteen-year-old Ana Luísa Vargas declared that she had lost her virginity long before, when her employer, *don* Víctor Araya, pushed her onto a bed and, "gripping me by the wrists," forced himself upon her. He "then told me not to say anything, that he would give me all I needed . . . [and later] gave me this white shawl I am wearing, and money from time to time."[38] Like Ana Luísa, other young women who described coerced sex with men in positions of authority insisted that what was done to them was violent and wrong, yet they clearly expected—correctly—that no legal action would ensue against the men in question.[39] Shared knowledge (or personal experience) of poor women's vulnerability to nonconsensual sex was among the structural conditions within which women in prostitution made their own history: not as they pleased, but with as much mutual support, monetary return, and personal dignity as they could muster.[40]

Prostitution Regulation in Theory and Practice

The theory and practice of prostitution regulation in turn-of-the-century Costa Rica made evident the tensions between the foundational tenets of Liberal ideology: individual and commercial liberty and due process on the one hand, the promotion of public morality and economic progress by a strong and active state on the other. An Hospicio de Sanidad was established in San José in 1875 with the aim of forcibly isolating women infected with venereal disease. A decade later the Hospicio was abolished, and for the next eight years internal debates, jurisdictional conflicts, and budget woes made it impossible for the government to pass any anti-venereal legislation at all. The minister of police wrote in 1890:

Of course the confinement which was imposed in that establishment [the Hospicio] on women affected by venereal disease was an insult to individual liberty, in no way justified by the obligation of the Government to provide whatever public welfare demands, aside from the fact that in any case official intervention is never authorized to avoid evils which prudence and individual efforts are sufficient to combat.

On the other hand the state of public customs and the necessity of fostering in every new nation the development of a vigorous and healthy population, justifies the adoption of any measures which under other circumstances would have to be judged as exaggerated Government solicitousness on behalf of individual well-being, as long as on the other hand such measures do not contradict any of the cardinal principles upon which the nation's organization is based.[41]

The contradictory principles (and twisted syntax) enunciated here were no mere window dressing for a repressive project of state control. For the next four decades, attempts to control commercial sex and the lives of individual prostitutes would be hampered by the use that women and business owners made of judicial appeals procedures and of the division of powers between branches and levels of government.

The Law of Venereal Prophylaxis (Ley de Profilaxis Venérea) of 1894 laid the groundwork for official control of prostitution. All women who "trafficked in their bodies" had to register with hygiene officials. Those who did not do so voluntarily could be compelled to do so by police, after a formal investigation. Registered women were required to undergo periodic vaginal examinations and were forcibly interred for treatment in the Hospital de Profilaxis Venérea when found infected. Public women could be fined or sentenced to the Casa de Reclusión for missing medical exams, for defying the authority of hygiene officials, or for a variety of "scandalous" public behaviors.[42] Police records give evidence of frequent abuses of power by the officials involved.[43] But as a whole the system was never effectively repressive and was often entirely unworkable. Appeals from prostitutes to be removed from the lists for good behavior clogged police courts, and ad hoc social control by police was hampered by registered prostitutes' immunity to prosecution for vagrancy.[44] Only five years after the Ley de Profilaxis Venérea first established prostitution regulation, key articles were revoked pending revision, and they were never replaced. In historian Juan José Marín Hernández's survey of San José police records, 65 percent of prostitutes who served prison terms were jailed for less than five days, and 82 percent of those fined paid less than five *colones*. Punitive action against public women was, as Marín Hernández puts it, "symbolic and instructive."[45]

It is instructive to compare this system to prostitution regulation in Guatemala in the same years. While macroeconomic developments had followed similar outlines in the two nations after independence, labor relations and the role of the state in enforcing them differed sharply. In 1887 Guatemala instituted a system of prostitution control that combined "the state-regulated bordel prostitution . . . current in Europe and the United States" with an expanded role for state coercion.[46] Any woman convicted of "bad conduct" could be legally remanded to a house of prostitution for three years. Individual women and their debts were bought and sold between madams (a practice legal until 1906), and state officials rigorously enforced these contracts.[47] Meanwhile, in Guatemala's banana plantation zone, Guatemalan women accused of "bad conduct" for living with Jamaican men were forced to perform labor service grinding corn for local garrisons, in what began as an extralegal exaction by local military officials and became standard practice in the zone.[48]

The articulation of state authority and commercial sex in Costa Rica was starkly different, both in the highlands and on the coast. In Costa Rica brothels were one among a great variety of sites were prostitutes might legally work. Even when unregistered women were processed for "bad conduct," "defiance of authority," or "immoral acts," the sanction was not mandatory labor in a brothel or garrison but confinement in the Casa de Reclusión. While some women fought confinement with every means they had (stabbing the arresting officer, getting men to declare them honest concubines, tying up police courts with endless appeals), others seem to have accepted it with relative equanimity. To be sure, the conditions of the building and the state of medical knowledge were such that inmates were almost as likely to contract new illnesses as to be cured of the ones they brought in (by the director's own admission, one woman came down with typhoid fever in 1895 due to "the bad state of the latrines").[49] On the other hand, the strictness of discipline within the Casa is a matter of doubt. Complaints about scandalous behavior among inmates abounded, young men came to serenade the inmates during nights on the town, and on at least one occasion a female head nurse was accused of taking an inmate out for drinks in order to "win her favor."[50]

The same factors that made enforcement difficult in the metropolitan area were magnified in Limón: political rivalries between local authorities, police corruption, the population's mobility. Sound and fury in official rhetoric might signify little action on the ground. Prompted by an article in a San José newspaper in July of 1906, the minister of police ordered the governor of Limón to crack down on houses of prostitution illegally operating in the vicinity of schools. Local officials responded with a flurry of well-documented excuses, promises of action, and declarations of resounding success. Seventeen Costa Rican "public women" were sent from Limón to the Casa de Reclusión in San José for vagrancy, and forty-eight foreign-born women were processed for expulsion on the same grounds.[51] Twelve months later identical complaints were lodged against the very establishments so recently declared vanquished.[52]

To some, sexual immorality seemed so inevitable in hot, dark Limón that it was hardly worth prosecuting. As one politician wrote to the minister of government on behalf of beleaguered Colombian madam Eduviges de Santander, "Dear 'Filo' . . . I beg of you, gentleman that you are, that you have pity on that poor widow, in such a hot climate and with an itch to dance, and that you will use, if not your authority, at least your influence, so that they let her dance."[53] Instances of officials willing to turn a blind eye for a price abound. Such unofficial taxes were the cost of doing business in Limón, surfacing in police correspondence only when rival higher-ups needed ammunition for internal power struggles. Typical were the accusations lodged with the minister of government by the minister of public health in 1925 that in Siquirres a certain "Negro healer named Frank Heron" gave out certificates of venereal health to infected prostitutes that the local hygiene police officer and *jefe político* rubber-stamped, "doubtless due to profitable arrangements."[54]

Official statistics tell us little about the number of prostitutes who actually worked in Limón at any given time. Two separate processes influenced prostitute registration here: the waxing and waning of official zeal, and the export booms and busts that shaped employment prospects for sex workers in Limón. The height of official activism was in 1896 and 1897, and in those two years the newly founded Department of Venereal Prophylaxis published extensive statistics on registered prostitutes in each province. In 1896 113 women were registered in Limón: 12.5 per 1,000 inhabitants, as compared to 4.5 per 1,000 in Costa Rica as a whole. Even when measured against the male population the rate of prostitution in Limón was nearly twice the national average, and this in spite of officials' acknowledgment that in "the provinces" (that is, everywhere outside of San José) "even well-known prostitutes are not registered, and those familiar with those places know the totals registered to be ridiculously low."[55] More than two-thirds of the women registered in

Limón in 1896–97 were foreign-born, the great majority from Jamaica, others from elsewhere around the Caribbean.[56] Official prostitutes in Limón were the most mobile in the nation: 14 percent of them formally transferred their residence in 1896 and 1897 (and many more surely did so without notifying officials), as compared to 6 percent of women registered in San José. Prostitutes in Limón were only half as likely as those in San José to be granted exemptions from the registry, probably because given the minimal activism of local prophylaxis officials, women in Limón did not bother to appeal. Over a three-year period hygiene officials averaged only eight medical inspections per woman registered in Limón, compared to thirty-six per woman in San José. In the same period only 3 percent of prostitutes in Limón were sanctioned for noncompliance of any sort, compared to 42 percent of *josefinas*.

In the decades following this burst of activity the number of official prostitutes in Limón rarely totaled even half of the 147 registered in 1896, yet no one seemed to think commercial sex was on the decline. Statistics are scattered and contradictory, and the only constants are complaints from hygiene officials that the majority of sex workers were avoiding the system entirely. In 1910 the circuit doctor for Guápiles complained that medical examinations were useless under current legislation, which had no provision for obligatory confinement or treatment. Certain local women were "true sources of filth and decay." "But the woman isn't a vagrant," the doctor wrote, dripping with sarcasm. "[S]he isn't scandalous because she works by the light of the day, and at night she's as tranquil as moonlight: doesn't drink, doesn't cause scandals."[57] Three years later a different official in the same post concluded, "If the Government doesn't start taking seriously in these distant regions the crucial matter of venereal prophylaxis, I don't know where this *pueblo* is going to end up with so much gonorrhea, chancroids, and syphilis, extremely malign in some cases."[58] These complaints and a flurry of others came from Guápiles, Guácimo, and Jiménez between 1910 and 1914, when plantation expansion in the Old Line region was at its peak and Hispanic workers were arriving in unprecedented numbers. A small but prominent minority of arrivals were female entrepreneurs, or as the governor described them in his annual report, "public women who take the liberty of coming from the interior to entertain themselves on paydays, leaving as is natural venereal diseases rampant among the workers of the canton, principally in Guácimo and Jiménez where the arrival of workers is greatest."[59] It was on the frontier of plantation expansion that care and comfort were most likely to be purchased on a cash-and-carry basis from a small number of women. In contrast, public officials made no mention of payday prostitution in the Main Line and Banano River districts, where plantations were long established and production in decline.

Health officials in Port Limón and Siquirres in these years complained instead about the evils of clandestine prostitution. Some of the women they referred to may indeed have been in the business of commercial sex and managed to avoid registration and its compulsory vaginal exams. But the label "clandestine prostitute" might as easily be applied to any woman whose domestic arrangements did not conform to hygiene officials' own ideals. Thus complaints about clandestine prostitution also reflected officials' racialized perceptions of local kinship patterns. In 1913 the port doctor attributed the spread of venereal disease to the prevalence of clandestine prostitutes who "belong in their majority to the Negro race."[60] In the same year the *jefe político* of Siquirres wrote of that locale's public women: "The *negras* although numerous excuse themselves from registry presenting a fake husband."[61] The official doctor of Siquirres was sincerely confused about which lower-class women were available to whom, if his own drunken behavior is anything to go by. The local police chief wrote to the governor in 1908 that *don* Mauro Aguilar had for the second time "caused a great scandal late at night forcing open the doors of several women who, although it's true they are not married, certainly have steady conjugal arrangements [*sí llevan vida marital arreglada*]." Out of respect for Aguilar's "position and family," police had merely escorted him home, but if it happened a third time the chief would be forced to take action.[62]

By 1921 the prefect of Pococí dismissed the entire question of prostitution as a matter of "a few cases," and the police chief of Port Limón observed that of ninety-six prostitutes registered there at the start of the year, thirty-seven had officially transferred residence elsewhere.[63] Limón offered little market for their services. Banana exports had dropped precipitously during the Great War. Several thousand young West Indian men had abandoned the province for Bocas del Toro or Cuba, and the Costa Rican and Nicaraguan migrants who had kicked up a ruckus on Old Line paydays a decade before were long gone. In 1922 the local hygiene chief wrote in his annual report that "hidden prostitutes abound, but the only women who come in for exams are a handful of women who signed up years ago."[64] This was the profile of port prostitution during the bust.

Even as he wrote, however, the export economy was reviving, as United Fruit and private growers cleared and replanted tens of thousands of acres of abandoned banana farms to cash in on soaring prices. Hispanic workers flooded into the zone. "In two years' time the railroads of Costa Rica transported five thousand itinerant laborers from the west coast to the east coast. It was reported that they resembled military convoys because of the absence of women and children."[65] The market for commercial sex turned bull once more. These were the years in which Eduviges de Santander's *bailes de negocio* gave rowdy voice to Colombian pride in Port Limón, in which "Negro healer" Frank Heron made a business of forging certificates of venereal health in Siquirres, in which line-men like *Mamita Yunai*'s Herminio and Calero spent their days redigging the contours of the Estrella Valley and their nights dreaming of sex. As during the previous heyday of export production, prostitution was once again highly visible, intermittently targeted, and little controlled.[66]

Working Women, Traveling Lives

The legal definition of a clandestine prostitute, a woman who "in addition to being occupied in the various duties appropriate to her sex, also traffics in her body," in fact described the occupational patterns of most women in prostitution most of the time. Women combined sex work not only with unpaid domestic labor (the "various duties appropriate to [their] sex") but also with the paid occupations available to lower-class women, including cigar making, dressmaking, and food preparation. Such work was combined with prostitution sequentially or simultaneously as need and opportunities arose.[67] Prostitutes' geographic mobility rivaled their occupational mobility and was similarly frustrating to officials who tried to regulate them. "Women of the life" followed the cyclical economic rhythms of regional and national economies, their migration made possible by the infrastructure built to facilitate export agriculture: railroads within Costa Rica, steamers around the Caribbean. Just as prostitutes from the Central Valley worked banana plantations on paydays, they might travel to coffee regions for the weeks of the yearly harvest. They also moved between the Central Valley cities of San José, Cartago, Alajuela, and Heredia, relocating for weeks, months, or years. A crackdown on prostitutes in one area might spur an exodus, as when the newspaper *La Prensa Libre* noted in 1914 that activism by hygiene police had sent "flocks of low-flying birds" down the line toward Limón, to the consternation of upstanding citizens of Atlantic slope towns.[68] The governor of Limón noted the same phenomenon the previous year, observing that *mujeres de mala vida* "arrive to take refuge in the various towns of this jurisdiction, coming from the interior where they can't find any means to support themselves, or perhaps fleeing from the persecution of the Venereal Prophylaxis authorities, which I deduce from the reports of the local police chiefs and hygiene officials."[69]

Prostitutes' lives and work routinely spanned regional economies and social worlds usually analyzed in isolation: coffee, bananas, urban artisan production; the Pacific port of Puntarenas, the Atlantic port of Limón. A typically circuitous path was that followed by María Dobles. A registered prostitute, she was living in San José in a rented room with her *querido*, or steady lover, in 1905.[70] The pair moved to Limón in 1906, where she worked briefly in a brothel and he tried his hand at petty theft. Ten months later María was on her own, earning a living as a seamstress and cigar maker in Puntarenas. The following year she was back in San José participating in the *cantina* social world (though one character witness noted that while Dobles had previously been a *mujer pública*, in the last six months she had "moderated her conduct" and was now living with her mother and maintaining relations with a single lover).[71] María Dobles reappeared in the judicial record twenty-four years later when Esteban Martínez sued her for illegally retaining his belongings, which included 1,650 *colones* in IOUs. This was a considerable sum of money: more than a full year's wages for a well-paid skilled artisan. María indignantly responded that Martínez—her legal husband of ten years, although he had neglected to mention the fact—had made this false accusation in an attempt to liquidate their mutual assets before they could be frozen as part of the divorce suit she had brought against him. Martínez worked for the Pacific Railroad, and the couple had built a business lending money to his fellow employees in exchange for promissory notes against their salaries. These IOUs "are the product as much of my labor as his, and therefore belong to both of us. . . . I have many witnesses and many ways of proving how hard I have worked, in many cases contributing more money than that which he contributed through his salary."[72] The judge in the case admitted the legal propriety of her actions and acquitted her of all charges, but only after he had handed the disputed notes over to her former husband. Esteban Martínez and his much-younger female lover may have managed to flee the country with the money, just as María feared.

María Dobles's reference to the profits she invested raises the question of how significant prostitutes' earnings were in the economy as a whole. Many examples exist of older prostitutes who accumulated enough capital to act as money lenders or start their own businesses.[73] Paid sex may have been a significant factor funneling wages from Costa Rica's various export sectors into the national economy. Remember the image of payday provided in *Mamita Yunai*: a long line of banana workers waiting to spend one-seventh of their two-weeks' pay for a few minutes of sex on a dirt floor. Or recall James Henriques, the Jamaican worker who paid two days' wages several hours in advance for the services of a *josefina* prostitute passing through the port. The cash earnings of women in prostitution could be sizable. In 1906 Juliana Rojas Umaña accused Luís Carranza of stealing sixty *colones* from the bundle of bills and gold coins she had given her friend Claudia López Cabrera to hide under her mattress. The sixteen-year-old Carranza was the live-in lover of López Cabrera's younger sister Trinidad, who was twenty-two. All three women were "public women." In pursuing the case Juliana Rojas was obliged to prove that the money had actually been in her possession. Two witnesses, owners of a *cantina* in Limón, testified on her behalf. They explained that during a several-month stay in the port Rojas had periodically given them sums of money for safekeeping, by the end of her stay accumulating a total of 160 *colones*. Judicial officials also investigated Luís Carranza's earning pattern, to prove that the cash and new clothes found in his possession had been come by illicitly. A coworker testified that Luís earned seventy-five *céntimos* a day as an "official apprentice" in a carpentry workshop and added that the youth habitually missed several days of work each week. At that rate it would have taken young Luís ten and a half months to earn *in gross wages* the sum that Juliana had managed to accumulate *in savings* from a few months in prostitution in Limón.[74]

One of the most striking cases of financial success in the commercial sex industry was that of Pacífica Bermúdez and her family. Born in San José in 1860 or 1861, Bermúdez worked in her twenties as a "public woman" in the capital's Central Market. In 1893 she participated along with two men—a lawyer and a merchant—in several *denuncias de tierras* totaling thousands of hectares in Limón. Bermúdez claimed additional lands on behalf of her sons, ages two and nine. The two-year-old child was described as illegitimate but bore the merchant's unusual Christian names, which suggests that a relationship of some intimacy and endurance may have existed between this man and Bermúdez. One of the land claims was lost after a lengthy legal battle with Minor Keith over the latter's "prior claims," but Bermúdez and her friends apparently had enough political pull to prosecute two other claims successfully.[75] By the end of the decade Bermúdez owned rental properties in Port Limón as well as a house and farm in Cartago, although her main business was running an *hostería* in San José. By 1905 she had hired an *apoderado generalísimo* (lawyer with power of attorney) to manage her Limón real estate while she ran her business in San José. Four years later she had relocated to the port, where she opened a popular eatery.[76] It is impossible to know if Pacífica Bermúdez's life was a happy one. Her daughter Antonia frequently brawled with other public women and kept contracting bad debts her mother was forced to cover. But there is no doubt that Pacífica Bermúdez managed to build a significant fortune at a time when high-profile female entrepreneurs were few and far between.[77]

Just as the localized bonanzas of export production inspired Costa Rican prostitutes to move in search of better earnings, by all accounts the massive temporary migrations of young men around the Caribbean in these years created a parallel demand for commercial sex in each spot. Meanwhile, the pull of women toward Panama was ongoing, because even after demobilization reduced the male workforce upon the canal's completion, there was constant demand from sailors passing through. In 1895 Pacífica Bermúdez's daughter Antonia threatened a customer in her San José eatery with a table knife when he mocked her for claiming to have visited Paris. He thought her, as he later testified, "incapable of having traveled." In this he was incorrect. When authorities tried to ratify Antonia's testimony a year later they sought her first in San José and then in Limón, only to be told that she had left the port for Colón. How she spent her time there—and whether she ever made it to Paris—we do not know.[78] Other female sojourners were certainly obliged by circumstance to sell sex in Panama. In 1911 the governor of Colón urged the governor of Jamaica to halt "the emigration from Jamaica to Colón of children who are abandoned here and become criminals and prostitutes." The occasion of his complaint was the pending deportation of "two girls of Jamaican origin [ages thirteen and fifteen] who are at present detained in prison for persistent prostitution on the streets."[79] Neighborhoods like Boca Grande in Colón and New Caledonia in Panama City became identified early on as centers of prostitution by immigrant women.[80] Women born in Panama, Costa Rica, Colombia, St. Lucia, Barbados, Spain, France, and Berlin ("a Hebrew") all appear in Panamanian judicial records, working as prostitutes in the Canal Zone or terminal cities in the first quarter of this century.[81]

Social networks facilitated prostitutes' frequent moves, and the multiple encounters occasioned by their travels in turn reinforced social networks. This pattern was brought to the fore by an investigation into the death of sometimes public woman Eva Barrantes on an isolated banana farm in Limón in 1912. Emilia Hidalgo Zúñiga, a prostitute and resident of Limón, testified that about three years earlier she had met Eva, "who was then going by the name 'Simodocia,'" and who stayed in her house in the port for "quite some time" before leaving for Cartago. Emilia later ran into Eva in San José, and Eva said "that she had been living in the house of Angela Moreira and that presently she was living with Rafael Bonilla" as his lover, on his father's plantation outside of Siquirres. The two women met again, though Emilia could not remember when or where, and Eva told her that she and Rafael had been fighting. A while later Emilia heard rumors in Limón that Eva had killed herself. Angela Moreira (who a few months later would entertain a table of local notables in Guápiles together with Emilia Hidalgo Zúñiga, as mentioned above) testified that a young man she did not know had recently come to her home in San José and, "standing in the door, in front of many people though I don't now remember who, said, 'You know girls, that pug-nosed girl who's a friend of yours died [*Saben muchachas se les murió la ñatita amiga de ustedes*],' referring to Eva Barrantes." Emilia Hidalgo Zúñiga and several other women Eva had lived with at different times in different places happened to be in Angela Moreira's house to hear the announcement.[82]

One historian of Costa Rican labor has pointed out that the Venereal Prophylaxis legislation created a de facto guild of prostitutes, complete with membership registration, exemption of practitioners from vagrancy laws, and incentives to residential segregation.[83] The state hygiene apparatus continually brought public women in contact with one another, in the Casa de Reclusión, the Hospital de Profilaxis Venérea, in municipal doctors' offices for weekly exams. Likewise, the communal sociability of urban prostitution brought women together, whether sharing rooms in brothels, meals in *hosterías*, or a bottle of whiskey in the back of a coach.[84] Indeed, it seems likely that patterns of male sociability resulted in part from women's preference for working in groups or pairs rather than in isolation. Linked judicial records testify to the repeating contacts, widely spread over time and across space, that shaped public women's lives. Dense networks of mutual support connected sisters and brothers, mother and daughters, coworkers and friends.

Women shared housing, money, and information; paid for each other's medical treatment; backed each other up in court. Such habits were remarked by observers at the time. In 1898 a judge in Alajuela refused to prosecute a trespassing case involving two prostitutes, reasoning that given the norms of mutual aid between *mujeres de la vida alegre*, Zoila Sánchez Mayorga might reasonably have assumed that she had Julia Romero's tacit permission to use her room for a tryst with a client—breaking a padlock to do so—while Julia was out of town for the week.[85]

Frequent moves might prevent close acquaintance. In 1914 Pilar Cisneros was sitting on a bench in a Siquirres billiard hall chatting with five women who lived, like her, in the brothel upstairs. Apart from her own sister, she could not give the last name of any one of them.[86] Yet evidence suggests that norms of reciprocity held among fellow *mujeres de la vida* even when their acquaintance was brief. When María Dobles woke up with a toothache for the second day in a row a few weeks after moving to Limón, "all the girls who live in the Casa Cubiller like me treated me to some drinks," and by midmorning she was "so drunk I couldn't walk" (and, one imagines, temporarily cured of her toothache).[87] Women in brothels also helped protect each other against their clients' excesses, on several recorded occasions helping friends take guns away from men they judged too drunk to be trustworthy.[88]

Sometimes mutual support extended to an enduring partnership between women. In 1900 Enriqueta Sánchez Mayorga moved from San José to Alajuela when her friend Miriam Ávila "sent for me," and the two of them split the rent on a small house near the city center. When Enriqueta was remanded by hygiene officials to the Prophylaxis Hospital in San José, Ávila broke her lease in Alajuela and moved to the capital. She left her furniture with their landlord to cover rent in arrears and explained, in his words, "that when she returned to this city maybe she would pay me though it would take a while because what she earned wouldn't be enough to cover the medical treatment of her *compañera* 'Little Bird.'"[89] In other cases, evidence of possessive jealousy suggests intense emotional ties. In 1897, when both were registered as prostitutes in San José, this same Miriam Ávila and a woman named Sara Chávez León moved together to the suburb of Escazú and stopped attending medical exams, for which each was sentenced to forty days in the Casa de Reclusión. Three months later, when Ávila was confined to the Prophylaxis Hospital— where Sara Chávez was already interned—the two created constant scandals by their screaming arguments and fistfights with each other. A fellow patient explained their battles, saying that Ávila "gets very jealous of nurse Custodia

Pérez because she shows preferential behavior toward *la* Chávez," adding that "*la* Pérez, wanting to attract *la* Ávila, would invite her to go out to the street and drink liquor, and she would accept and they'd go out drinking together."[90]

Such cases bring home the irony that by earning a living through sex with men, prostitutes actually managed to live much of their lives surrounded by women. Whether residing in brothels, sharing rented quarters with *compañeras*, or traveling the rails of the plantation zone, prostitutes lived beyond the influence of husbands and fathers. Their relative autonomy is clear on various levels. They controlled their daily comings and goings; they controlled their migratory choices; they controlled their earnings; and often, but not always, they controlled whom they had sex with. None of these choices could be taken for granted by women who lived with their families of origin or with male partners.

Family Ties

Socially engaged thinkers at the turn of the century alternately presented prostitution as crucial to the preservation of the bourgeois family, or the cause of its ruin. The socialist editors of San José's *Hoja Obrera* in 1910 decried prostitution as a menace to working-class families, as wealthy young men (*monos de leva*, the editors called them—monkeys in tuxedos) preyed upon the daughters of the proletariat.[91] Elite reformers in the 1930s and 1940s attributed prostitution to the lack of family control in the lower classes: either the physical absence of one or both parents or the lack of moral guidance on their part.[92] Yet a quite different image of the connection between prostitution and family emerges from linked judicial records. These reveal dozens of examples of families in which sisters, cousins, mothers, and daughters were together involved in commercial sex.[93] Some of these family groups functioned like the support networks described above. These women lived together, at least periodically, worked together, and backed each other up. In 1906 Agustina Cabrera and her daughters Maurilia and Angelina Vásquez Cabrera got into a screaming fight with a woman to whom they owed money in San José. Six years later Maurilia was living in a boardinghouse in Limón, in a room next door to her mother and brother; her sister Angelina and their cousin Claudia López Cabrera also lived in the port and were in daily contact. All of the women had been registered prostitutes at one time or another.[94]

Kinship ties shaped lives even when relatives did not travel or live together.

This is clear, for instance, in the intertwined life stories of the Sánchez Mayorga family. Enriqueta Sánchez Mayorga, who rented a house with Miriam Ávila in 1900 as noted above, was sister to Zoila Sánchez Mayorga, who borrowed Julia Romero's room without her permission in 1898. Originally from San José, Zoila, Enriqueta, their parents, and other siblings had traveled to Limón in 1895. The entire family was arrested and sent back to the capital due to their public "scandals." The father "is usually seen in taverns and other places of drunken corruption, giving a bad example to his daughters, who usually follow him in his drunken sprees." In 1897, just before the trespassing incident in Alajuela, Zoila had jumped bail in Limón while on trial for insulting a local *cantina* owner. In the years following she was rumored to be in Guápiles or Guácimo; she eventually surfaced in Puntarenas in 1901. That same year her sister Enriqueta was among thirty-odd prostitutes rounded up in a burst of hygienic zeal in San José. Nine years later Enriqueta was still registered as a prostitute in San José, though she did not show up for a single medical exam; a note scrawled in the municipal register next to her name reads "Limón."

In 1904 Zoila and Enriqueta's mother, Juana Mayorga, died on a banana plantation near Guápiles, where she had lived "maritally" with a West Indian man for seven years. At the time of Juana's death another daughter, Mariana, had been staying with the couple for two months. A younger son, Bernardo Sánchez Mayorga, had lived with Juana until two years earlier, when "my father Matías brought me to San José because he didn't like me living with said *negro*." Although the siblings seem to have lived apart most of the time, their relationship was widely known. Enriqueta and Mariana were both nicknamed *Pajarita* (Little Bird); an older brother accused of insults in Puntarenas in 1897 was referred to as *Pajarito*; and when the police agent of Guápiles sent a telegram announcing that "the mother of '*las Pajaritas*' has died," he assumed his superiors in Limón would know whom he was talking about. Even when the Sánchez Mayorgas' support came from friends or lovers rather than kin, family members kept in touch. When Miriam Ávila broke her lease to follow her *compañera* Enriqueta to San José, Enriqueta sued their landlord for the illegal retention of her furniture—even though he had already returned it—"because she wanted to screw that bastard so he'd treat her with more respect the next time; this had been her father's advice to her." [95]

Family ties could be coercive, as relatives sought to back up material claims through the use of force or law. Records contain several examples of mothers pushing their teenage daughters to have sex for cash and managing their daughters' clientele. Potenciana Cubillo brought her fourteen-year-old daughter, Manuela, to a remote plantation in Pococí in 1913, where she supervised her sexual relations with at least six men. When the girl resisted her mother's attempts to set her up in an exclusive union with one of them, running off with another instead, Potenciana accused the second man of deflowering her daughter and demanded her immediate and forcible return. Authorities complied. The *curador* (court-appointed guardian of Manuela's judicial interests) remarked that it was evident that no crime had been committed by the young man who had accompanied Manuela in her flight, and that all that could be done "would be for local authorities to sequester this girl and place her in the custody of some relative or of the mother herself, so that she [the mother] can correct her and oblige her to work honorably as long as she is a minor." But Manuela's testimony had made it abundantly clear that her mother was already obliging her to work, and the *curador* made no mention of how he thought Potenciana might be convinced to make honorability—or her daughter's welfare—her guiding principle in the future.[96]

Lowell Gudmundson has written of turn-of-the-century Heredia that "[t]hose most likely to fall out of smallholder society into the ranks of the laboring poor and servant populations were those whose father or mother died very young and indebted, or those whose home and yard needed to be sold to cancel debts and pay probate inventory and burial expenses."[97] Confronted with precisely this situation, Pilar and Isabel Cisneros rejected the onerous intimacy of domestic service and found their way into prostitution in Limón. The sisters were fourteen and eighteen respectively when their mother died in 1904. They and three younger brothers were left homeless in Alajuela, for their father was exiled to the island penitentiary of San Lucas. Their mother had placed the girls as servants before her death, but within months Pilar had run away and Isabel had been dismissed.[98] Six years later the two were in Heredia, accused of having stolen 275 *colones* from a Chinese laundry owner with whom Isabel had arranged for her sister to live. Apparently police officials were sympathetic to Pilar's claim that "they had fled because they didn't want to live with *chinos* ever again," and to Isabel's insistence that Sing Achon's accusation was "vengeful" because "that *chino* is madly in love with Pilar who doesn't love him." In spite of extensive evidence against the women, the case was dropped.[99] Two years later Pilar and Isabel, by now in their late twenties, were living in a brothel in Siquirres. Isabel's "clothing, trunks, baskets, and other belongings" were lost in a fire in her room, apparently started when "a rat, or perhaps the cat I keep which was in the room," knocked over a candle while Isabel was playing a lottery in the billiard hall next door.[100]

Jamaican women working as prostitutes in Limón were likewise bound together by multiple ties. They shared rooms, borrowed clothes and jewelry, and traveled together to the plantations on paydays. In 1906 Martha Darling sued Bell Brown and Jessie Smith for publicly insulting her in the port brothel known as Noah's Ark. Brown had declared "that Martha Darling had stolen clothing in Jamaica and in the market on said island had stolen yams and hidden them up her ass." When Martha replied in kind, Jessie said to Bell, "I'm your cousin and no one can insult you, much less Martha Darling who I've known for a thieving whore since Jamaica."[101] Two years later Martha was visiting Jessie in a different brothel and got into a fight with one Mary Jane Brooks, calling her a "rotten-assed whore who was full of putrefaction [*puta culo podrido que estaba llena de purgación*]." This time Jessie testified in Martha's defense while Sarah Sampson, a witness on Martha's behalf in yet another insults suit earlier that year, supported her opponent Mary Jane instead.[102] As these cases show, feuds were as much a part of social networks as was mutual support. The same documents that record shared housing and shared drinks give evidence of fierce conflicts between women and within families, of personal betrayals and shifting allegiances. All of this differed in degree but not in kind from the social networks of other migrants.

Race and Prostitution in Limón

Circum-Caribbean and Costa Rican circuits of prostitution intersected in Limón. There Costa Rican and West Indian women often lived in the same boardinghouses and brothels and traveled the same rail lines. In a 1914 case Eugenia Méndez reported that Martha Darling had stopped by her room in the Casa Azúl and invited her to the bar for a drink, because "she wanted me to help her celebrate" the five *colones* a drunken client had given her before he passed out on her bed. Eugenia declined but soon after went down to the *cantina* and saw Martha, "who had given me fifteen *céntimos*, and who was drinking together with some *negritas*, one by the last name of Green and the other called Fanny McGregor."[103] The solidarity implied by the sharing of windfall profits is set against the social distance implicit in the phrase "some *negritas*." Overall, there is no evidence of a density of social contacts across groups anything like that which existed within each.

Both in the port and on the camps, male sociability was informally segregated.[104] Likewise, prostitutes and clients tended to belong to the same ethnic groups, though cross-group commercial sex seems to have been more common than cross-group consensual union or marriage. An elderly Afro-Limonese man interviewed in 1980 described West Indian men lining up to visit— "quick, quick"—the four or five black women who lived on the upper floor of the Casa Azúl (they were known as "Blue Belles," he joked).[105] Philippe Bourgois reports ethnic specialization by the women (all Hispanic) who work today in brothels on the United Fruit plantation in Bocas del Toro. Hispanic and Guaymí men refuse to have sex with women who have black customers, a stance "legitimized with the pseudo-scientific explanation that the abnormal size of the penis of blacks 'stretches' the woman."[106] Similar prejudices may have played a role in keeping Jamaican women out of Costa Rican prostitutes' circuits in the Central Valley.[107]

The complexities of racial identification and personal identity are illustrated by the life story of Raquel Montezuma, the foster daughter of sometimes prostitute, sometimes procurer, sometimes moneylender Raquel Barrantes. Raquel Montezuma was born in San José in 1891 to a Jamaican mother and a Barbadian father. As she lay dying, the mother commended Raquel to the care of Barrantes, the child's godmother. Raquel was two months old at the time. A year and a half later the girl's father, Albert Louis, found work in Nueve Millas and removed her from Barrantes's home. Raquel Barrantes cried inconsolably for days and begged police to return the "kidnapped" baby to her. When arrested, Louis insisted that Barrantes had cared for the child at his behest, and that he had never ceded his role or rights as father. Barrantes's own witnesses admitted that everyone knew the girl as Louis's daughter, one adding, "[A]ll [I] can say is the child loves that Negro a lot." The charges against Louis were dropped, but the toddler remained in Raquel Barrantes's care.[108] In subsequent years neighbors would describe the girl variously as "a little girl called Raquel who is as black as a Jamaican . . . whom Sra. Barrantes treats as if she were her daughter," "the *negrita* of Sra. Raquel Barrantes," and "a *negra* who lives with her [Barrantes]." Race may have been a factor in one woman's identification of the fifteen-year-old as "a maid of [Raquel Barrantes] who is also called Raquel." Clearly, though, the emotional ties between the two Raquels were close and enduring. In separate cases seven years apart, Raquel Montezuma specified with respect to Barrantes that "I call [her] Mamá because she raised me." Barrantes referred to Montezuma as "my little girl" when she was young and as "my adoptive daughter" in later years.[109]

Eventually Raquel Montezuma moved to Limón, where she worked in various brothels along the Old Line. Her clients included both West Indian and Hispanic men. It may be that her skin color made the *zona bananera* either more congenial or more profitable for her than the Central Valley. In her late teens in 1907, she married Luís Pérez, a Costa Rican policeman with whom she had maintained a sexual relationship for some time. Pérez beat her frequently, and on multiple occasions she left him and tried to regain her economic independence by working as a prostitute. They were reunited once by the Siquirres police chief, Pérez promising not to mistreat her in the future, but soon they separated again. In 1912 Pérez shot and killed Raquel, insisting that her "infidelity" had forced him to it.[110]

Los Preferidos: Romance and Tragedy

Prostitutes' cash earnings and female social networks enabled them to live beyond the confines of intimate male authority. But many chose not to. Judicial records contain multiple references to public women's *queridos* or *preferidos*. In some cases the *preferido* was a wealthy man who maintained the woman economically in exchange for an exclusive sexual relationship. In other cases the man in question was essentially a pimp (a role usually labeled *chulo*, *alcahuete*, or *rufián*) who lived off of the profits the woman earned from sexual commerce. In general, however, a *querido* was simply the consensual male partner of a woman who earned her living by having sex with other men. As with the consensual partnerships of women not in prostitution, any number of arrangements might govern the sharing of income, expenses, and housing between the two, and these might vary over time. In some cases the union was thought by one or both partners to be incompatible with commercial sex as a livelihood, and in other cases it was not.

Defending the man accused of killing prostitute Bernarda Rivera Arias in 1912, a Limón attorney declared it self-evident that for a "public woman . . . affection does not exist because vice, or better said its indulgence, has killed in her all honorable sentiments."[111] But on the contrary, there is evidence of a great deal of sentiment, and sentimentality, in prostitutes' social world. Men fell deeply in love with *mujeres de la vida*, though testimony of their feelings generally reached the documentary record only after their "amorous, delirious passion" (in the more generous words of the same attorney) inspired them to assault the object of their affections. And women in prostitution, in spite of their familiarity with male violence and sexual coercion, sustained a deeply romantic vision of what love between men and women could be. In the case above, Bernarda Rivera and Daniel Ramos had lived together "as if married" for several periods, splitting up in response to his discomfort over her continued contact with former customers. Without her testimony it is impossible to know what she thought the terms of their partnership were, or what she actually did with the other men. All we have is a faded postcard with a drawing of a red rose, inscribed on the back:

> Sr. *don* Daniel Ramos.
> My sweet love: The aroma of these roses makes me feel the love I only think of you and long to see you and with these roses and you alone can I live. This card I send you as proof of the love I profess for you
> yours until the tomb
> BR [112]

Some prostitutes' steady lovers were sanguine about their partners' sexual encounters. María Dobles and Guillermo Castro, for instance, had a long-running relationship. They lived together in San José for almost two years, separated briefly, and within months were together again, living in a brothel in Limón. When María and Antonia Alfaro went off to bathe at the beach north of town with several men, allegedly as part of a plot to steal a purse of money from one of them, Guillermo stopped by Ester Fonseca's room at a neighboring brothel. Ester teased, "Oh, now you're back here missing me because your lover just walked past with another man, cheating on you," to which Guillermo replied, in his own account, "She can't cheat on me because she's a prostitute, and wherever she finds a hog she's got to kill it." Ester recalled his words a bit differently: "No woman cheats on me—I don't care if she goes with him because we're taking a fat pig to slaughter at the beach and if he's got a thousand dollars on him they'll end up in my pocket, so he can do whatever he wants with her." Apparently such straightforward cynicism was neither expected nor admired in a *preferido*, for Ester and her roommate, Salvadora Núñez, together replied, "That's no way to treat a woman you love." [113]

In 1912 Eva Barrantes wrote to a childhood friend from the isolated banana plantation in Siquirres where a wealthy young man had installed her: "Well Chabela I'm living with Felo again and I'm very happy Felito is treating me very well I don't plan to separate myself from him again until I die belonging to him. . . . I want you to come visit for a few days, Felo has said you

Eva Barrantes, [1890?]–1912. This photograph was presented to police by
Eva's childhood friend Isabel Segura, whose insistent inquiries pushed officials to
investigate Eva's death. Limón Juzgado del Crimen, 520, Seric Jurídica,
Archivo Nacional de Costa Rica, San José, Costa Rica.

should come stay, he sends greetings, we have a phonograph and every night we play it come on Chabela ask your mom for permission and let me know." Eva died not long after writing this, and when rumors of her death reached Chabela in San José she began pushing authorities to investigate. When finally interviewed, Rafael Bonilla—the "Felo" named above—denied any intimate involvement, calling Eva "my cook" and claiming that she "died on my father's plantation" while he himself was back in San José. He claimed that "she always talked about wanting to poison herself because she said she was bored with life and her family disdained and abhorred her." But if anyone's disdain drove Eva to suicide it was Bonilla's own. Emilia Hidalgo Zúñiga recalled, "She said she'd had an argument with Bonilla, that she was very much in love with him and if he didn't feel the same she was going to kill herself." Eva Barrantes spoke of suicide as if reaching for the chance to be, for one final moment at least, the heroine of her own life story.[114]

If these stories are melodramatic, it is because the men and women who enacted them scripted their lives around a belief in tragic and transcendent love. But the fact that romantic passion was invoked by men and women alike does not mean that theirs was an egalitarian vision. Cases abound of men killing their female lovers out of jealous or unrequited love; in not one recorded instance in this period did a woman kill a man in Limón for any reason. Eva Barrantes may have valued love over life, but Raquel Montezuma and other women like her chose sexual autonomy instead, and some of them died for it.[115]

Defending Honor, Demanding Respect

Of course, most interpersonal conflict in the banana zone culminated not in bloodshed but in raised voices and nasty words. Like other people, prostitutes fought with neighbors, coworkers, and kin over money, love, and respect. Conflicts over bad debts or stolen affections were expressed through insults to a person's honor. But honor was not only a medium for expressing material conflicts. It was also a possession worth fighting for in itself. According to the classic tenets of Mediterranean honor, the prostitute is the very embodiment of shame and transgression. In matters of honor public women should have had nothing left to lose, yet they acted as if quite the opposite were true. In verbal battles on the streets or in brothel hallways, prostitutes attacked others' honor and vigorously defended their own. Their opponents might be male lovers, *cantina* owners, or fellow women of the life. They framed their insults in the same terms as everyone else, that is, in accusations of sexual impropriety. And like everyone else, they eagerly turned to the judicial system to back up their claims, suing for *injurias* or insults to their reputation, and thus using the local judge's office as a theater of retribution when they had been bested in a verbal battle for public prestige.[116]

Self-righteous and willfully vulgar at once, angry women taunted others with accusations of transgressive sex. When Vicenta Salazar tried to collect the three *colones* owed her by Agustina Cabrera and her daughters Maurilia and Angelina Vásquez Cabrera, Maurilia called her "a big-mouthed thieving whore [*una puta ladrona bagrón*]" and swore "that her sister Angelina was better than Vicenta Salazar because no one had ever seen her with *chinos*," while Angelina called Vicenta a *mamona* and *culiola* (a woman who engages in oral and anal sex) and repeated "that even *chinos* had had anal sex with her [*que hasta los chinos la habían culiado*]."[117] Similarly, when Ramona Morales tried to collect money Juana Sánchez owed her for meals she had prepared in the Limón brothel where both lived, Juana yelled "that all the money Ramona Morales had came from sleeping with *chinos*," that she herself "wasn't as low as Ramona Morales who rolled around with *chinos*; that she preferred to sleep with four *negros* before doing so with one *chino*."[118]

Thus female honor was defined and defended in terms of sexual propriety even among women who were categorized by elite observers as possessing neither honor nor propriety. The same women also enacted the rituals of masculine valor: threatening violence, fighting with knives, brawling in public. Sometimes confrontation was directed at agents of state control, as when Felicitas Montealegre slashed the face of the policeman taking her to the Hospicio de Sanidad, declaring that "if she had a revolver she would have killed him because it was an oath she had sworn that if he took her to the Hospice she had to take him down [*agarrarse con él*]."[119] More often, though, challenges were aimed at other women, as when Antonia Bermúdez Solano called to Manuela Urbina in a dispute over a *querido*: "Come suck my cunt, you *negros'* used-up whore [*Vení chúpame el mico, pellón de los negros*]"; "You're not even a maid to my ass [*No sos ni criada de mi culo*]"; "If you're a woman, let's go to the Sabana park where we can go at it [*Si sos mujer, vení vamos a la Sabana para que nos demos las manos*]."[120]

Judicial authorities, generally eager to fine public women for public brawling, agreed with participants that a woman faced with such a challenge had the right—even duty—to defend herself with her fists. María Luísa González

"Los bajos" de la Cuesta de Moras, San José, 1920, site of the Vásquez Cabrera sisters'
shouting match with Vicenta Salazar. Colección Fotográfica, E 60-99-79,
Museo Nacional, San José, Costa Rica.

was charged with attacking Maurilia Vásquez after having been taunted, "Female pig, shameless one, come out here in the street and let's go to the Sabana
so I can prove you're not woman enough for me [*Chancha, sinvergüenza, salte
a la calle y vente por la Sabana para probarte que no sos mujer que me aguantes
a mí*]." The police court ruled that González had been "impelled by an irresistible force, since under the circumstances she was left with no other means

of making her rights respected," and absolved her.[121] Macho boasting among Jamaican prostitutes in Limón was similar. Martha Darling threatened a former friend in a port brothel: "Damned whore, I plan to go to San Lucas because I'm going to buy a switchblade to kill you and stick it in you up to the handle."[122]

One San José evening in 1895 Fernanda Jiménez and her *compañera* Petra Chéves faced off against Antonia Bermúdez and her *compañera* Juana Pereira. Fernanda challenged Antonia "to come on out, if she was woman enough [*que si era tan mujer que se saliera*]." She then stabbed Antonia in the face and chest and told arresting officers "that it was a shame she hadn't killed that slobbering pug-nose." Although some witnesses said Antonia had started things by hitting Fernanda with a switch, Juana Pereira insisted her friend had carried no switch, "but only a novel, 'La Dama de las Camelias,' with a lead-colored cover; and with this book she defended herself against her aggressor, hitting her on the head with the book."[123]

Juana's claim invites us to rethink the question of romance. The heroine of Alexandre Dumas's wildly popular 1848 novel is a courtesan who falls in love with a young man of privilege. In order to protect Armand's reputation and save his sister's betrothal, Marguerite breaks off their affair on a false pretense and ends up penniless, ill, and alone. Finally learning the truth, Armand returns to Paris to swear his undying love, and Marguerite dies in his arms. The narrator concludes, "From this tale, I do not draw the conclusion that all women of Marguerite's sort are capable of behaving as she did. Far from it. But I have learned that one such woman, once in her life, experienced deep love, that she suffered for it and that she died of it."[124] For Dumas the possibilities of redemptive love were not open to prostitutes as a class—"Far from it." Yet in the tropes of literary romanticism women in prostitution could find validation of their sentiment and suffering, indeed, could refigure their trials as the prelude to transcendence rather than the proof of degradation. To take solace in such stories did not consign the reader to a life of silent sacrifice. As Antonia Bermúdez and Juana Pereira knew, high culture had multiple uses. You could read *La Dama de las Camelias* for romantic affirmation, you could smack a rival upside the head with the book in a brawl, you could even flaunt your literary leanings when you stood before the judge.

In his annual report in 1890 the governor of San José lamented that "public women, forgetting the need for social respect and forgetting their own despised position, live today more than ever given over to the most scandalous prostitution."[125] He was partly right. Public women did act without regard to their supposedly dishonored position. Through their scandals—verbal and physical battles with each other and with others in public spaces—they aggressively asserted their personal standing in both the masculine and feminine idioms of honor. It is unlikely that they "forgot" the social stigma their livelihood entailed. Rather, they chose actively to ignore it.

Prostitution was one among many arrangements under which women offered services of social reproduction to men in the banana zone. It could be combined with other strategies simultaneously or over time. The complexity of such lives was reflected in the frustration of public health officials at the behavior of "clandestine prostitutes" and their "fake husbands," or the confusion of census takers faced with women who lived in consensual unions, declared their occupation as prostitute, and—most shockingly—declared themselves heads of their households and their male lovers as junior partners.[126] That such arrangements were not always harmonious is obvious in the shouting matches between *compañeras* over infidelity, in the cases of women killed by *queridos*, and in the court battles between girls and their parents over who would set the conditions for their sexual activity. In novels of the banana zone line-men dream of the day they will have enough money to buy a sharp suit and return home to impress the girls or to pay back the mortgage on their parents' farm. Like them, prostitutes accepted hazardous working conditions, risked life-threatening disease, and migrated frequently to take advantage of ever-shifting labor demand. They did so in a seller's market that put accumulation within reach for some, and amid social networks that meant that even when penniless they were not homeless.

Commercial sex in Costa Rica presents a sharp contrast to state-regulated brothel prostitution or prohibitionist systems elsewhere. Prostitutes here were legally free to structure their own work process. As long as they registered with police and showed up for periodic exams (and in Limón the majority never did even that and went largely unsanctioned), they could choose the site and set the terms under which they labored. They could rent a bed in a boardinghouse, take a room in a brothel, borrow a shack near a banana camp, or travel the rails. Nevertheless prostitution was not simply another service sector job in the export economy. In the particular dangers it entailed—venereal disease and the violence of jealous men—sex work looked far more like other kinds of sex than like other kinds of work. The densely woven bonds and the well-worn migratory circuits that united women in prostitution confirm their status as a distinct social group in turn-of-the-century Costa Rica. Yet if their daily lives set them apart, their common sense and their stated values were of a piece with local culture. Women in prostitution invested their world with meaning borrowed widely, figuring themselves sometimes as virtuous victims, sometimes as romantic heroines, sometimes as righteous avengers. They were not ignorant of what observers—from local bureaucrats to French novelists—had to say about prostitution and its practitioners. But just as their daily lives were not limited to having sex with men, the webs of meaning through which they experienced those lives were not limited to other people's ideas about paid sex.

FOUR

Compañeros
Communities and Kinship,
1920S–1950S

A group of ten people carefully selected to typify the origin, gender, age, and occupational structure of Limón in 1927 would have looked something like this: There would be a man from Jamaica who had arrived around 1900 and now in his mid-forties worked as a mechanic with the Northern Railway. There would be another Jamaican man who had arrived around 1912 and now in his late thirties worked as a laborer on a cocoa plantation. There would be a Jamaican woman in her mid-thirties with a teenage daughter and young son, both children born in Port Limón. There would be a woman from San José and a man from Cartago, both in their late twenties and both recently arrived. She would be unmarried but perhaps pregnant, he a *peón bananero*. There would be a newcomer from Nicaragua as well, a *jornalero* of around thirty clearing forest for bananas. There would be a native Bribri speaker, a woman, perhaps, living in the upper Talamanca Valley and raising pigs to sell in Sixaola. The last spot would fall to someone who did not fit into either of the two predominant socio-racial categories of Limón (English-speaking blacks and Spanish-speaking whites): a light-skinned mulatto pharmacist from Jamaica, say, or a Chinese man working in an older relative's store.[1]

The communities these people came from had varied repertoires of family forms, and within each sending society the relationship of church and state legalities to the popular practice of kinship was different (the contrast between the Costa Rican Central Valley and Jamaica was particularly strong).

Yet within Limón the conjugal patterns and domestic forms of different migrant groups overlapped broadly. In the first section of this chapter I use the 1927 census to argue that West Indian households were not markedly matrifocal in Limón, nor were Hispanic households particularly patriarchal. To understand kinship practices among migrants of different origins over the course of their lives, we need to explore not just household structures but also patterns in personal ties and how they varied across time and space. So I turn to autobiographical sources to trace the entwined domestic and productive lives of Hispanic migrants from the 1920s to 1950s. The trajectory of male laborers' lives was an ongoing counterpoint between months or years spent *trabajando en fincas* (working for wages on plantations) and those spent *haciendo finca* (making a farm of one's own). This rhythm was echoed by the counterpoint between stretches spent with a *compañero* (steady and exclusive male work companion) as domestic partner and stretches spent with a *compañera* (female lover) in the same role.

Family Life in the 1927 Census

In both absolute and relative terms black women had more children than white women in late 1920s Limón. Rural black women's childbearing patterns were wholly responsible for the difference, for in Port Limón and its surroundings the child-woman ratio was virtually identical for blacks and whites. Even for rural women, the distance that separated West Indian and Hispanic fertility in Limón was considerably less than the difference between each group and its sending society. Both white and black women in Limón were far less likely than their sisters back home to bear children and see them survive their early years.[2] Nevertheless, by 1927 children under the age of ten made up one-fifth of the province's populace. What kinship practices shaped reproduction? What practices guided the care of children once born?

Census takers had at their disposal a vast array of terms intended to describe the relationship of each individual to the household head and to clarify whether each person's presence in the home was based on kinship, friendship, or cash. Yet just five labels—*jefe* (head), *hijo* (son or daughter), *alojado* (lodger or consensual partner), *huésped* (guest), and *esposo* (husband or wife) —accounted for 90 percent of all those tallied, in that order of descending frequency. Comparing children's ages, patronyms, and parents' civil status on the first two sheets of the manuscript census reveals that those labeled *hijo* stand in a number of very different positions with regard to their household heads. Most important, the term is used for both male household heads' children and their female partners' children from prior unions, even though official terminology included several terms intended to specify variants on that status, including *pupilo* (foster child), *hijo adoptivo* (adopted child), and *hijastro* (stepchild). Only in one case is the label *hijo natural* (child of unwed parents) used, although that would have been the correct label for at least fourteen of these youths according to the official kinship system of the time.

Census takers' de facto application of *hijo* implies the recognition of a social reality quite apart from the legalities of domestic authority. The social identity of the young people involved was tied more closely to their (ongoing) relationship with their mother than to their (potentially temporary) relationship with their mother's lover, the nominal household head. The same principle is illustrated by labels assigned the family headed by Eva Mata, an English-speaking black seamstress of forty-five. Eva lived with her mother, a sixty-five-year-old widow who had been in Costa Rica for fifty-four years. The next person listed in the household is Luiza v. de Caward ("the widow Mrs. Luiza Caward"), whose relation to the household head is given as *hija* although she is forty-eight years old and clearly must be Eva's older sister rather than her daughter. Implicitly, *hija* describes her status as a daughter in her mother's home. The next four household members listed are the Caward children, ages sixteen to twenty-two. Two of the young men worked as shop attendants, another was employed at the UFCO commissary, and their older sister was a seamstress in a dress shop. Each was labeled *hijo* or *hija*, although in fact they were the nieces and nephews of the household head.[3]

All of this suggests that the label *hijo*, although located in the "relationship to head of household" column, in fact signifies a particular social identity—that of a child or dependent adult living with one of his or her natural parents—rather than a relationship to the man or woman paying the rent.[4] Although one would have no way of knowing it from the "relationship with household head" listings on these census sheets, most homes had been shaped by serial unions and early death. Of forty-three children under age fifteen listed, only seventeen were living with two married parents in a household that did not include either parent's prior offspring. I do not claim the population tallied on these two sheets is a microcosm of the province. Quite the contrary—these two pages correspond to Port Limón's downtown business district. Fully 84 percent of the 200 residents listed are white. More than one-fifth of the adults had a secondary or professional education, compared with an average of 3 percent for the province as a whole. Probably nowhere in Limón were census takers confronted with a population so thoroughly exposed to the elite Hispanic culture whose kinship taxonomy official categories were intended to mimic. And even here the fit between available labels and social practice was poor.

Before we can compare conjugal patterns on the basis of census data, we need to consider the categories census takers had at their disposal, and how they chose to use them. Questions of conjugal status and household arrangements carried a great deal of moral weight for census makers and respondents alike, and conflict over who should be labeled what is visible on the manuscript returns.[5] In 1927 the categories provided by census designers included no label for consensual unions, either as a civil status or as a household role. But most census interviewers followed the practice of labeling female consensual partners as *alojada* S.S.L. in the "kinship or relationship to head of household" column and So[SSL] in the "civil status" column. Literally translated as "unmarried woman without legal ties," *soltera sin ligamen* (S.S.L.) was used to designate women living in free unions that ranged from enduring and exclusive partnerships like those that British jurisprudence classed as common-law marriages to arrangements far more limited in duration and obligations. No equivalent code was assigned to these women's male partners. But in fact 13 percent of Hispanic and 17 percent of West Indian men in the census sample were living with consensual female partners.[6]

The superscript SSL was a clever innovation on the part of census interviewers. In essence it created a supplemental category for women, that of current domestic status. The suffix allowed interviewers to recognize the distinction between a woman's legal status and her present conjugal state and to note down independent values for each. Indeed, in addition to So[SSL], the original manuscript sheets include women labeled V[SSL] and C[SSL], that is, widows or wives living with men other than those to whom they were wed. Yet this on-the-ground adaptation of imposed categories to local practices was erased in subsequent reporting. In the official summary prepared for publication the manuscript distinction between So and So[SSL] was dropped, and only the categories of *soltera* (single), *casada* (married), *viuda* (widow), *separada* (separated), *divorciada* (divorced), and *desconocida* (unknown) listed. This is despite the fact that for Limón at least, the number of women designated So[SSL] was on par with the number of those married, was three times the number of widows, and was ten times the number of those either separated or divorced.

Family in Brooklyn de Siquirres, ca. 1923. Colección fotográfica, 1120, Museo Nacional, San José, Costa Rica.

The patriarchal legal model of kinship, in which a young woman was presumed to pass directly from her parents' to her husband's authority, described the experience of less than one-third of the province's adult women. This was true for West Indian and Hispanic women alike. What differences existed were of degree. Young West Indian women were nearly twice as likely as their Hispanic peers to live with a parent, and as they aged they were half-again as likely as Hispanic women to head their own household without a resident partner. Across all age groups, Hispanic women were one-quarter more likely to live in consensual unions than were West Indians. Judging by the census returns neither group's households were either consistently "matrifocal" or "consanguineal" (centered around a woman and her blood kin) or consistently "conjugal" or "affinal" (centered around a conjugal couple).[7] Forty-one percent of West Indian households with children under the age of ten were headed by a man and his wife, 24 percent by a consensual couple, and 22 percent by a woman alone. Thirty-four percent of Hispanic households with children under ten were headed by a man and his wife, 27 percent by a consensual couple, and 19 percent by a woman alone.[8]

Less than one-tenth of men fifteen to twenty-nine in Limón were married, and less than one-third of men thirty to forty-four. The rates were identical for West Indians and Hispanics and were markedly lower than marriage rates for their peers elsewhere in Costa Rica or in Jamaica.[9] But while 61 percent of Hispanic men forty-five and over in Limón had married, only 36 percent of West Indian men had done so. These aging Caribbean immigrants, whose median year of birth was 1876 and median year of arrival was 1905, had the smallest average household size and the largest fraction of single-person households (39 percent) of any cohort in Limón. They were disproportionately rural, disproportionately likely to own land, and disproportionately self-employed— backwoods patriarchs ruling over no one but themselves.

One-person households were extraordinarily common among two groups in 1927 Limón: these aging Jamaican immigrants and Hispanic men a full generation younger, the current mainstay of the plantation labor force and at the opposite pole of prosperity and economic autonomy. More than a third of Hispanic men aged fifteen to twenty-nine lived in one-man households, yet their *average* household size was highest of any group other than indigenous Talamancans.[10] This reflects a few cases within the sample, anomalous at first glance, in which large groups of men living in plantation barracks were listed as "guests" or "lodgers" within a single family. In most other cases such men (and their *compañeras,* in the rare instances in which they had them) were listed as separate households within a single dwelling. The anomaly is a telling one. In a handful of other cases men living in similar circumstances were enumerated with unique family numbers, but as lodgers rather than household heads—a direct contradiction of enumerators' instructions. This suggests a chronic uncertainty that goes to the core of the notion of *hombres solos.* Distant from families of origin, rarely tied into families of choice, these men lived a togetherness equally intense. They were *compañeros,* at times in groups, at times in pairs. Indeed, among young Hispanic workers in the 1920s and beyond, the role of preferred *compañero* was so distinct in its social, economic, and emotional obligations that it should probably be considered a kinship role, the most important one in many men's lives for years at a time.

By the time of the 1950 census, decades of out-migration by young black men together with low rates of childbirth and survival among black women had reduced the total black population of Limón by 25 percent. Meanwhile, the steady accretion of itinerant workers from highland Costa Rica, Guanacaste, and Nicaragua, and increasing rates of childbirth and survival among Hispanic women in Limón, had more than doubled the province's white population in the course of a single generation. By 1950 barely one-third of the province's 41,360 residents were "Negro," while 63 percent were "white or mestizo." Only among the elderly were West Indians still a majority. So the story of rural workers in Limón during and after the second banana boom is largely the story of young Hispanics, men and women.

The search for decent work at a decent wage carried itinerant workingmen from San José, Cartago, Nicaragua, and Guanacaste to the Caribbean lowlands, the Pacific coast, the rain forests of Western Panama, and back again. A single life might encompass each of the export crops whose cycles of expansion and collapse punctuated the economic history of the region in the first half of the twentieth century. Around 1930 E.S.C.'s family moved to Pejivalle de Turrialba, where his father worked hauling bananas on a large plantation. From there they moved to Florencia de Turrialba, where E.S.C. worked in the cane fields. Heading out in his late teens "to adventure," E.S.C. found work in Matina pruning cocoa. Later he and his father cleared a plot in the rain forest west of Guápiles, but his father drank up all the money they earned. E.S.C. moved on, first to Port Limón to work on the docks, then to San Alberto to tap rubber, from there to Manila to clean *abacá* fields, and finally to the UFCO plantations at Golfito. By the time Standard Fruit was replanting bananas in the Atlantic lowlands around 1960, E.S.C. and his wife had cleared and claimed a farm of their own in Cariari de Guápiles, where they grew food to eat and bananas to feed the pigs. E.S.C. sold his banana stock to the company for seed, and with the money he received bought mules for hauling his produce to market.[11]

Itinerant laborers' lives were shaped by repeating contacts and enduring ties. Friends and family from back home and those acquired along the way were their steadiest resource, the only real security they could claim. *Compañeros* and kinfolk provided job references, shared skills, and lent money, houses, and land for planting. When M.G.L. needed to outfit his quarters for a new woman around 1954, he borrowed 300 *colones* from a *compañero* whom

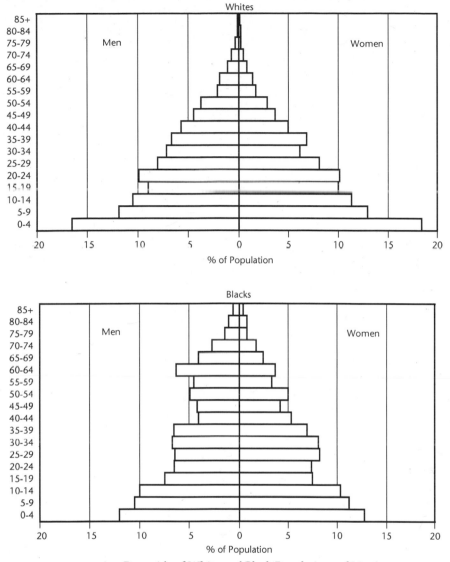

FIGURE 4.1. Age Pyramids of White and Black Populations of Limón, 1950

Source: Costa Rica, Dirección General de Estadística y Censos, *Censo de Población de Costa Rica, 22 de mayo de 1950* (San José, 1953), 181.

he had worked with ten years earlier in Parrita and had just run into on UFCO Finca 18 in Puerto Cortés.[12] And when M.F.A.'s infant son and four-year-old daughter died in a measles epidemic in Limón around 1960, "I was real poor then but thanks to my friends nothing was lacking at the wake because all my friends helped me almost every one who could brought a box full of things for the wakes even the coffins were given as a gift." With his *compañera* and surviving children M.F.A. then left for Nueve Millas in search of work. "[M]y older kids were crying to their stepmother for food and we didn't know what to do but thanks to God a friend sold me something to eat [on credit] while we got ourselves settled."[13]

These were not occasional episodes. This was the daily texture of the lives of migrant workers. When Nicaraguan-born M.G.L. arrived in the banana plantations at Puerto Cortés around 1943 a woman recognized him. She turned out to be an old friend of his mother's; her first husband had been his father's cousin. Eventually M.G.L. landed in Port Limón, where he stayed with his father's sister. She got him work with a friend's husband in Hone Creek, where he met up with a "friend and *paisano*" whom he had known on Finca 14 in Parrita a decade earlier. A few weeks later a new *compañera* convinced M.G.L. to go to Manila, where her sister lived. When they arrived the sister had gone, but M.G.L. found a group of old friends, "*nicas* and *ticos*," who convinced the foreman to give him work in the *abacá* fields even though the company was no longer hiring. Arriving in Puerto Cortés a few years later, M.G.L. found one of the men who had helped him in Manila now working as a foreman. He was hired on the spot. When a stranger on the streets of Puerto Cortés asked him to become baptismal godfather to his infant child M.G.L. agreed immediately, borrowing money from a local tailor in order to pay the priest—and rightly so, for the norms of diffuse reciprocity among *peones* in the plantation zones had served him well throughout his life. Of course, M.G.L. did not become the *compadre* of a stranger in need because he calculated the cost of his action against the probability of positive return. He did it because loyalty to friends, solidarity against enemies, and giving when asked made up the moral code of men like him, of men like the man he wanted to be.

In early 1935 a group of young men left San Rafael de Heredia together to look for work in Guápiles. "Shortly before there had been a strike," A.H.Ch. recalled, "and so you couldn't work directly with the company only through intermediaries." After "digging ditches felling trees and planting banana bits" on various plantations, A.H.Ch. left for Parrita with a contractor in 1936. By then only two of his *compañeros* from San Rafael were still with him. Within weeks one had headed home and the other had shot a policeman and fled to Nicaragua. "Upon finding [himself] alone without *compañeros*," A.H.Ch. abandoned the camp and headed with some friends to the *fiestas* (yearly fair) at Liberia, where they ended up broke and had to work to earn money to leave town. His companions—now transformed from mere friends to work partners—"knew the work of blasting with *chicharra* [a kind of dynamite]." So they headed to the UFCO Quepos division and hired on together, all claiming to be experienced blasters. Fifteen years and many travels later, A.H.Ch. was building barracks for United Fruit in Panama. A Nicaraguan *compañero* suggested they get their severance pay and head to Costa Rica, where they together accepted a contract to weed and prune a cocoa farm in Cahuita; when they finished, together with some Hondurans they knew from Panama they contracted to clear a farm in Punta Uva. A.H.Ch.'s coworkers moved on, but this time he stayed, working for a West Indian *patrón* and clearing a farm for himself in the bush.

Prime wage-earning destinations shifted rapidly within lower Central America in this era, as international politics created swings in demand (as for *abacá* and rubber during World War II) and as the United Fruit Company and individual entrepreneurs exhausted natural resources at one site and moved on to the next. Far-flung networks of once and future coworkers were in part the result of these employer strategies, but they were also the best defense workers could build against dependence on a company wage. A man who had been A.H.Ch.'s *compañero de trabajo* in Parrita in 1937 happened to pass through Punta Uva in the 1950s. "[W]hen he came to work on the coast here I took him to see the possible sites so he could make his farm, and here he is with his family getting old . . . and there's another neighbor named Francisco A., who was living with us while he made his *finquita*." A few years later A.H.Ch.'s *comadre*, the wife of a former *compañero* whose daughter was A.H.Ch.'s goddaughter, wrote him from Liberia asking if work was good where he was. He urged the family to come and helped them clear a farm. "[S]oon the oldest girl, who was already a *señorita*, was my wife, and she was one of the little girls I'd cared for in Panama, by now we have five children four boys and a girl." When A.H.Ch found himself outside the clinic in Puerto Viejo around 1960, his gravely ill daughter in his arms and his pockets empty, "God is never lacking, a friend happened by and he lent me for the trip to Limón."[14]

As A.H.Ch.'s experiences in Guápiles, Cahuita, and Punta Uva suggest, work partnerships among traveling men were encouraged by the small-scale sub-contracting that characterized UFCO banana cultivation in Limón, especially after the 1934 strike, and by the even smaller-scale contracting by private land-holders (many of them West Indian) that characterized cocoa growing and woodcutting in Limón after the banana industry's collapse. On UFCO banana farms in the 1920s and 1930s harvesting was done by three-man teams made up of a *cortador*, who cut the banana stem from the plant; a *conchero*, who received the stem onto his back and hauled it to a nearby hut; and a *mulero*, who ferried the stems by mule to the nearest tram line. The pay, calculated by the piece, was split among the three.[15] Harvesting on United Fruit *abacá* plantations was organized as two-man tasks, J.V.O.G. recalled: "I got to the Finca San Miguel . . . and the next day real early I headed with my mule to the *abacales*, with my *compañero* because that work was done in pairs, and [paid] by the ton."[16] Logging contracts went to pairs too, as the work was done with a *serruchón*, or two-man saw.[17] Those who worked the jungles needed partners as well. L.O.M. almost died of a snake bite while tapping rubber inland from Barra del Colorado during World War II because, he explained, "I was going about without a *compañero*."[18]

All coworkers were *compañeros*, but for a man to refer to *mi compañero* meant something rather different. It implied exclusivity, ongoing mutual obli-gations, and a commitment to travel together until circumstances intervened. M.G.L. left one *finca* after only six weeks' work "because Antonio R. came from Parrita and pulled me along so as to travel accompanied [*me sonsaco con el fin de irse acompañado*]." In Puntarenas M.G.L. ran into his father, whom he had not seen in decades; his father urged him to stay, but M.G.L. replied, "For now I can't because I'm traveling with a companion [*voy acompañado*] and I don't want to make the *compañero* I've come with travel on alone." When Antonio R. remained with his mother in Parrita, M.G.L. paired up again. Soon his new companion, Silvano, asked M.G.L. to accompany him to Puerto Cor-tés to track down a former *compañero* who had betrayed Silvano by stealing 3,000 *colones* he had promised to take to Silvano's mother in Nicaragua.[19] Silvano—"my new *compañero* who was 28, light-skinned, with a gaze down-wards like this and a frank expression, a native of Bagaces"—accompanied M.G.L. up and down the Pacific coast for three years until they were sepa-rated by fighting during the 1948 civil war. Many consensual unions endured less. M.G.L. wrote of a female lover who tricked him into taking her on, "The

Hunting companions, Guadalupe (San José province), 1913.
"Patricio Mora junto con otro cazador, Guadalupe, 1913," Colección fotográfica,
E 60-99-60, Museo Nacional, San José, Costa Rica.

damn woman only accompanied me for three months because she wouldn't obey me, one day when the boat was leaving I took her to the dock I bought her a ticket I gave her 100 *colones* and said I hope things go well for you."[20]

Gender, Conjugal Practice, and Working Lives

Once here he tried many times to economize, in order to buy himself a blue cashmere suit with crossed lapels and three buttons and show up as a surprise at his rancho. *His mother would fall down from happiness and he would give her a pile of bills so that she could buy another cow, pay the mortgage and leave poverty behind forever. But the salaries were not in dollars but in* fichas *[company scrip] that slid away like salt and water in the Company commissaries. And the years passed. One day when it was pouring rain his little brother showed up at the camp. "What are you thinking, you great idiot?" Filiberto apologized and told him that the cow had died and they'd had to rent the field. So they drank a bottle of rum together and began working together for the Company.*
— JOAQUÍN GUTIÉRREZ, *Puerto Limón*, 1950

Migrants' choices about when and where to travel and about which jobs to accept on what terms were shaped on the one hand by their access to resources, which was structured by kinship as well as by class, and on the other hand by their goals for consumption or investment, which were molded by ideas of proper male and female behavior. Shared kinship forms and common gender ideals shaped the lives of Hispanic men and women in consistent, and consistently divergent, ways. Men's and women's experiences of labor and migration differed drastically because of it.

According to many men who came to Limón in this era, it was the need for extra money to support a new wife or *compañera* that forced them to seek work at the highest wage wherever that might be. After three weeks of courting in 1938, M.G.L. got permission from María U.'s stepfather to visit their home as her formal *novio*, or fiancé. A week later he told her he was leaving to seek temporary work elsewhere: "Since Dec. 22 I haven't earned a cent, it's true that I've been working for my brother harvesting his grain, but not for money. . . . She told me don't go there's lots of work here I Answered yes that's true but here they pay cheap and in San Antonio one can earn in a day what one earns here in a week and this is no time for playing it slow."[21]

At twenty-one Chonsito M.J. fell in love and asked his father's permission to leave his hometown, where men earned only two *colones* per *tarea*, or task, a day's work weeding a quarter hectare.

Rural family, Costa Rica, ca. 1910. Colección fotográfica, F. 60-99-47,
Museo Nacional, San José, Costa Rica.

> Yes he said; To Río Jiménez I went.
> Working among Men; I earned five and six *colones*
> At those jobs. Soon I earned the money and married
> In the month of September the year 1935
> My dad was so poor he didn't help me with one cent.

Neither Chonsito's family nor his wife's could offer the young couple a home of their own.

> I started thinking, where can I look
> And now with a wife; Where am I going to put her[22]

A local man loaned the couple a house, but Chonsito decided he could not support his wife except by returning to Río Jiménez, where United Fruit was engaged in a short-lived bout of banana replanting.

Conjugal obligations guided the working lives of West Indian men in similar ways. S.T. was born in Clarendon, Jamaica, in 1901 and came to Limón as a child with his widowed mother. He worked as part of a three-man cutting crew in the Estrella Valley from 1918 to 1922 while maintaining a visiting union with a woman back in town. "I had a *compañera*, she was living with me. I had her here in Limón, and while I was there working, sometimes every month, sometimes every three months, I would come to Limón. When I didn't come that month, she would come to me. Sometimes stay with me for a few weeks, like that." After his sweetheart died S.T. spent two years as an ironworker on the docks of Port Limón earning $1.10 to $1.35 a day. But when he entered another steady union, he had to leave town again. "By then I had another woman, had to live. Staying right here in Cieneguita. I had to prepare the room, maintain the woman, right? It [dock work] was too cheap. So I went back to La Estrella."[23]

While male memoirists emphasized the lengths to which they went to support wives, *compañeras*, and children, female memoirists described a world in which male support was far from reliable. Both men and women agreed that men should provide for their families and that women should be respectful and faithful in return. It was in their perceptions of how well this conjugal pact was fulfilled that they differed. For male migrant workers drinking, brawling, and sexual conquests were the natural expressions of manhood. As one aging line-man summed up his seventy-page autobiography: "I ended up having various women, I have sixteen sons and daughters scattered around, I was about to marry six times and I always 'got in' ahead of time."[24] "I was a great carouser I smoked and drank a lot of liquor," explained another proudly.[25] In practice these mainstays of male sociability were hard to reconcile with the breadwinner role working men also claimed. I.P.R. returned to Limón in 1932 after five years in Bocas del Toro, accompanied by a Panamanian woman and their three children. "[W]hen I got here bad luck three men drunk on their passion for liquor were going to kill me I hurt them bad I ended up in jail I lost my woman and children." He boasted in his memoir, "I'm 82 if I die my sons and daughters can be proud That their father died still fighting in this life like a hard-living man I was jailed once because a man has to defend honor life and capital I was defending my life."[26] But one can imagine that for I.P.R.'s *compañera* his brawling was anything but a source of pride. It cost the family its income and left her alone in a foreign land with three small children to feed, and she moved on to make her way as best she could.

Most of the women born before 1930 who submitted autobiographies from the province of Limón were forced to seek wage work as young teens, left to fend for themselves by their fathers' abandonment and their mothers' early deaths.[27] Only one woman—J.M.L., born in Nicaragua in 1876—lived in her parents' home until marriage. "I had good luck in marriage because he was very good and he loved me very much," she wrote.[28] Her experience of marital stability seems to have been exceptional. The life stories of women born in the highlands who came to Limón in the 1930s, 1940s, and 1950s are uncannily similar. Most worked as domestics or in the fields during their early adolescence and bore their first child in their late teens. Sometimes marriage or co-residence preceded their first pregnancy, but often it did not. Those who lived with male partners while their children were young did not work outside the home at the time. But for most of the women, these marriages or first consensual unions ended within a few years due to their partner's drinking, infidelity, physical abuse, or abandonment.[29] With small children and no reliable husband or *compañero* by their side, women struggled to mind their children and earn money to feed them at the same time.

One alternative for women no longer willing to tolerate their current partner was to find a new one. Around 1944 O.C.C. was living in Port Limón with her two youngest daughters (her eldest daughter had been taken from her by her first husband in San José; her second eldest daughter was in the care of a female relative in the port). A man recruited her for farm work in the Estrella Valley, saying that his wife would watch the girls. "I get there and what wife he didn't have one and perfectly cool he says you're alone and with kids I want to take care of you and this was the only way I could get you here and me what could I do I was dead broke; as if I were some dog; what could I do I stayed."[30] When she could bear the man's drinking, jealousy, and threats no longer, O.C.C. accepted the suit of a male neighbor. "As soon as he took me [to his claim] I started to raise my animals we were doing very well and another child arrived this one a boy and everything was going well," until her new partner took up with another woman. "[H]e'd go out Saturday nights to *parrandear* [carouse] and by then I was *pan dulce* [pregnant] again and with all and that he left me ditched and abandoned off there in the wilds."[31] That new men bring old problems is the moral of many women's tales. When E.G. de L.'s husband tried to win her back a decade after infecting her with syphilis and abandoning her with two toddlers and no home, she told him "that I'd set myself the goal of not giving my daughter a stepfather and I had turned down good men for fear they'd turn out the same, the last thing I'd do was go with him."[32]

A woman might try homesteading on her own. After O.C.C.'s *compañero* left her, *pan dulce*, she supported her four young children by farming his claim. "I planted corn and beans, I had one hectare of bananas which I would cut and sell to the Compañía Bananera, but living was cheap then I had a little bit of everything but thanks to God we weren't in need."[33] When J.S.A. was nine, in 1951, her parents separated and her mother moved the children from Port Limón to a *finquita* ten miles out of town. "I went to work with my brothers clearing, planting, I helped my brothers saw wood to make the house . . . we had hens pigs cows not many but at least we had enough for us we always had milk and eggs and we ate chicken every week we always went to fish and we also got shrimp because there was lots there we also went hunting and we were always lucky because we always brought back either a *tepezcuintle* or a *guatuza* well any old animal we brought my mama would cook it up." The family was resource rich but cash poor. "[O]nce we even ate a *león* and it tasted good to us of course we didn't have anything to prepare it with because that was for sure anything we had to buy we never could, halfway through the week we were already running out of things some times we would run out of coffee and my mama got horrible headaches and sometimes we had to go to a neighbor to borrow some even just a little other times mama would go to a patch of coffee we had planted to pick the green berries that was all there was."[34]

For women without access to land, or with children too young to farm and hunt, the precarious independence of homesteading was not an option. Selling services to itinerant male workers or working for wages as a domestic or in the fields were the alternatives. Most women would do all of these at one time or another.[35] After her husband left her, E.G. de L. lived with the *jefe político* of Guápiles and his wife for three years, cooking in exchange for her children's room and board. In 1936 she was recruited "to go provide food for *peones*" on the new UFCO plantations in Parrita. There her children contracted malaria, and her son died. She returned to Siquirres "and put my girl in school and kept working washing and grinding for other people so I could at least give my girl her Primary." Once her daughter had completed grade school and town residence was no longer crucial, E.G. de L. became a laborer on the UFCO cocoa plantation Indiana Dos.[36]

In the Central Valley women had rarely labored on plantations except at harvest, when most picked coffee, either for relatives or for wages, or for relatives for wages.[37] But plantation labor by women and children became more common as hard times hit in the 1920s and 1930s.[38] In eastern Cartago and

Coffee harvest, San José province, ca. 1920. Fotografías 5282,
Archivo Nacional de Costa Rica, San José, Costa Rica.

Turrialba in the 1930s and 1940s it was common for whole families to labor on haciendas that nominally employed only the fathers as *peones*. L.R.A., whose father was "a dark-skinned man" from Turrialba and whose mother was "a mostly Indian woman from Lari," was born in Villa Colón, San José, in 1921. In 1930 the local sugar mill shut down, and her parents sold their goats and hens, left their house to her uncle, and moved to an hacienda in Tucurrique (east of Cartago). There her father weeded and handled oxen, her mother prepared meals for *peones*, and L.R.A. swept coffee berries in the *beneficio* yard. They were not paid separately for their labor, and the structure of authority that guided their work mimicked that of family labor on peasant smallholds.[39]

Without the mediating figure of the male household head and *peón*, rural wage work for women was far less acceptable. When L.R.A.'s father died, her mother refused to stay on the hacienda. L.R.A. "had to work in Juan Viñas dressed as a boy to find work because they didn't give work to women and I cut my hair and wore a straw hat suspenders shirt and pants."[40] As she reached adolescence the arrangement became uncomfortable for L.R.A. because local girls, thinking she was a man, began to flirt with her. But she wrapped a cloth belt around her developing chest and continued, until her mother decided the family should return to Villa Colón. By then L.R.A. had no female clothing that fit. "I have to work to buy clothes but my features are rough and hard and my habits those of a man heck what can I do, well, work at whatever I can and I get work on the *finca* of *don* Salvador A. there you see me planting

Rural family, Villa Colón (San José province), ca. 1920. Fotografías 2186, Archivo Nacional de Costa Rica, San José, Costa Rica; originally published in *Album Gómez Miralles* (San José, 1922).

beans planting peanuts driving oxen yoking up a pair or more and haul up the ox-cart that's easy for me and my mama doesn't say go there or do that my mama doesn't say anything about nothing to me and I have enough clothes now but my life was made for work and this is what I do."[41]

Within a few years, though, L.R.A. wrote, "I'm starting to understand more and I think more and I go to work and I don't like the jokes of the men who are my *compañeros* because they call me *marimacha* [tomboy or dyke] and so I'm going to look for work elsewhere this very day and I go to my paternal grandfather's house." On her grandfather's farm L.R.A. did equally heavy labor, cutting cane, running the cane grinder and boiling house, driving oxen. But apparently, once structured by kinship ties her agricultural labor did not require a gender compromise. When L.R.A. herded oxen on horseback, "my godmother would dress me in a skirt with flounces a blouse and a hat with ribbons she would say I looked very good but not only that she would send me to water the oxen at the river that ran the machine and the boys who saw me flirted with me with words of love."[42]

Neither West Indian nor Hispanic women had worked on the banana plantations of Limón, either at the turn of the century or during the 1920s replanting. It was the cocoa boom of the 1940s and 1950s that brought women into plantation fieldwork in Limón for the first time. Tending the groves and harvesting and packing the one-foot cocoa pods was considered less physically taxing than the harvest and transport of four-foot, seventy-pound banana stems. (Bananas' weight did not prevent women from routinely carrying the stems, balanced on their heads, on Jamaican plantations and docks in this era.)[43] As on Turrialba sugar and coffee haciendas, whole families, including children, worked on cocoa plantations. But here individual women were also employed directly by United Fruit, both in the fields and at the central processing plant in Zent.[44] In 1948, when A.C.C. was twelve, her family relocated from Cartago to Siquirres. Her father soon moved on. The three younger children and their mother weeded, pruned, and harvested cocoa on the UFCO plantations at "los Indianos," while an older sister found work "in the Zone" as a domestic in the home of a high-level employee. In 1960 A.C.C.'s mother retired after twelve years of fieldwork on UFCO plantations.[45] West Indian women tended cocoa on plantations in these years as well. Dalia, born in Limón in 1945, lived comfortably while her father worked as a foreman at the UFCO *abacá* processing plant in the late 1940s and early 1950s. But when he left her mother for another woman and moved to Panama around 1958, the family was left with no income. Dalia and her older brother were sent to their maternal grandmother in Port Limón, while her mother took the younger children to a *finca* where they worked cutting and cleaning cocoa. In 1960 the cocoa groves were "burned" by heavy rains and Dalia's mother returned to Port Limón, working as a hotel maid by day and ironing for customers by night.[46]

The Homestead Alternative

The Hispanic workers who came to the region from the 1920s onward sought the security of smallholding as eagerly as West Indian workers had a generation earlier. Aging former *peones* recounted their travails as they moved back and forth between plantation labor and own-account clearing and farming. As

J.V.O.G., born in Nicaragua in 1927, wrote, "I know many *paisanos* [country-men] who if they had the smallest patch of land would never work for the *bananeras* [banana companies], I spent thirty years with the *bananeras*; what did I achieve I just got more stupid and I damaged my spine, there's no cure for that, the only medicine is rest and us poor folks can't buy that, if we buy it we go hungry."[47] E.S.C. concluded, "Earning wages you always die with nothing."[48]

Like West Indian workers before them, Hispanic laborers found family life and plantation labor incompatible in the long haul. A.M.R. wrote of becoming a father in the 1940s: "After our child was born I tried to seem happy, but the truth is I was sad, thinking about how I was going to manage to raise a family drifting about the banana zone. So I contracted myself to work in Almirante Panama, thinking to improve my situation. . . . There in Almirante our sixth kid was born I didn't know what to do with so many children and drift-ing from one *finca* of the *Bananera* to another, because I didn't want them to grow up *zoneros* [plantation zone laborers] like me."[49] "With much sacrifice" A.M.R. purchased a little farm in Gandoca, Sixaola, and was able to raise his children with the stability he sought. At the age of sixty-one, L. Campesino could brag of his son, "Of course the boy hasn't had to go out to earn his living because we have our *vida propia* [own life, that is, own farm] built over the course of a struggle that was hard but faced with valor and care, many times deprived of things we needed to live but always with conviction."[50] As among West Indians a generation earlier, it was support and sharing among com-munity and kin that made small proprietorship possible at all. When R.J.G. headed northwest from La Pascua de Guápiles to homestead with his uncles around 1940, they built a ranch together and rotated cooking chores while each staked his own claim. Three days a week R.J.G. worked for his uncle; the other three days his uncle "lent" his son to R.J.G. to help him on his own parcel and compensate his labor.[51] When a friend lent M.F.A. "a little piece to plant" in 1950, he sold his house, built a shack, and successfully planted corn, yuca, and papayas and raised hens and pigs to sell in Port Limón.[52]

While maintenance and comfort on plantation camps could be had on a cash-and-carry basis, a pioneer in the bush needed either a *compañero* or a *compañera* for company, for care when ill, for support against rival claim-ants, for hot meals. A.H.Ch. recalled that it was a *cholita* (young indigenous woman) he was living with who encouraged him to clear a plot near Punta Uva. Even after she had moved on with her parents he continued to work the land, spending more and more time on his claim and less and less time working for his *patrón*. When he moved to his claim definitively it was with a male companion. "In '57 I went to live on the *finquita* because I had enough to eat there, bananas, plantain, rice, beans, cane, corn, I had chickens and pigs and a few dogs and a shotgun which we got lots of use out of and I had a *compañero* who was Salvadoran and whose name was Jaime S."[53]

The goal of possessing one's own farm was in practice inseparable from the goal of finding a domestic partner whose fidelity and frugality would see one through good years and bad, and as working men aged they were more likely to seek these qualities in a wife or *compañera*, who could bear them children to carry on the farm. Chonsito M.J. described the rural laborer's dream as he remembered living it:

> And so I continued working, I made a straw hut
> That's how my God wanted it: to be able to dwell on
>   my own property
> My wife and I very happy
> These were our assets:
> A dog with a litter, a colt, some hogs
> A number 28 rifle, me planting agriculture
> My wife pregnant[54]

A decade and a half later, after Chonsito had built up three separate smallholds through his waged and own-account labor and his wife's and children's hard work—and lost each one due to work accidents, bad business deals, and animal diseases—his wife left him. Despite her betrayal, wrote Chonsito, he let her keep his livestock, hens, and crops, and with a friend's help he cleared yet another farm. But his "twisted luck" continued.

> How terrible my life, so difficult, and dull.
> I'd get back tired from working and then have to cook.
> I thought, I have to find another woman
> Indeed I found her
> What happened to me? She turned out half crazy.
> We couldn't get on. She didn't last me long.[55]

For women, like the wife of many years and the lover of short duration who left Chonsito for reasons he could only chalk up to twisted luck, homesteading brought heightened risks as well as shared dreams. Some *campesinas* ended their lives happily ensconced on a viable smallhold with a loyal and reliable companion. Around 1935, after an unhappy first marriage, H.C.A. met "a Gentleman named Julian M. who accepted me as *compañera* and we went to the Old Line where I lived with him almost 34 years until he rested in peace."[56] Around 1948, after an unhappy first marriage, E.G. de L. married "a *nica* who was poor but humble and hard-working." He was a field boss on a cattle ranch in Pocora on the Old Line, "and I helped him in what I could." Bit by bit they purchased livestock of their own "and now we have quite a bit of cattle and we're little old folks way out in this wilderness serving the Lord in his works and humanity as well."[57] But H.C.A. and E.G. de L. were exceptional. For most Hispanic women in midcentury Limón, rural home-steading was marked by isolation from kin and community and heightened dependence on male partners. For some, perhaps for many, grinding poverty and bitter submission were the result.[58]

West Indian pioneers in the first two decades of the twentieth century had formed rural communities amid abandoned Main Line or Río Banano plan-tations or along the southern coast. Their villages were nucleated and their farms, located on land rented from the United Fruit Company or on *terrenos baldíos*, were not too far away. The West Indian women who lived in Cahuita and Puerto Viejo around midcentury were not cut off from their kin—on the contrary, they were often locals born and bred. Their husbands were more often the outsiders, who gained access to local resources through their wives' families.[59] After decades of wage work in Cuba, Jamaica, and Panama, Martin Luther fell in love with Miss Esther in Port Limón in 1943. "She invited me down" to Cahuita where "her people" were, and her stepfather gave him work.[60] When Ormington Demontford Corbin and Miss Ida Corbin moved to Cahuita from the Canal Zone in 1954, they were returning to the village where Miss Ida had been born, and where her sister Miss Maud Kelly and other family members still lived, to cultivate her stepfather's cocoa farm.[61]

When homesteading alongside male partners proved unprofitable for Daisy Lewis, she had family and support networks of her own and could try a new approach.

[W]hen I was young, several times I got together with a man and I helped him out on the farm. One after the other got tired of me and left me with nothing. I loved farming, and I always helped them, but the farm was always the man's property. In those days men thought marriage was too hard and so on. You would help them and then two days later, they see another woman they like and all of a sudden they are bored with you and they leave you behind. Until I said to myself: I better work for my own self because it's not worth it to struggle all the time and lose all you've worked for.

As soon as I start to work for myself, some twenty years back [ca. 1955], I see the difference. I planted coconut, I built this house, then I get a chance to buy myself a cocoa farm.[62]

Hispanic pioneers in the 1930s and later staked claims mostly to the north in Pococí or Siquirres, regions with the necessary mix of abandoned or uncut land for clearing, on the one hand, and still-functioning plantations for earning cash, on the other. The ongoing struggle to obtain formal title to the plots they appropriated for themselves or purchased from their fellows (plots almost invariably located on land already titled to United Fruit or absentee owners) often meant multiple relocations. There was a premium on continuously residing on the homestead, both in order to maintain de facto possession against rivals and to reinforce de jure claims pursued through the state. The *ranchitos* of Hispanic pioneers, huts hastily built from palm trunks, palm leaves, and untrimmed lumber, were the basis of a dispersed settlement pattern that would prove enduringly characteristic of Spanish-speaking northern and western Limón.[63] Like their menfolk, the women who lived in the *ranchitos* were far from home. Unlike the menfolk, whose periodic plantation labor maintained their ties to the paired task work and communal drinking that cemented male migrants' social networks, women on rural homesteads were often quite alone.

United Fruit gave A.C.C.'s *compañero* his severance pay in the early 1950s, most likely when the *abacá* plantations shut down in 1952. She begged him to buy a house, thinking of their four small children and fearing that otherwise he would fritter the money away on drink. Instead he purchased a claim in Santa María de Río Jiménez, barely accessible by road, whose *rancho* had no windows, no doors, and no water nearby. "[W]hen our money ran out I went through many calamities because sometimes there wasn't food for us much less milk for my children a lady sometimes would give me a bottle of milk which I would mix with water so that there would be enough for the littlest ones and for the others I would find lemon grass and give it to them in tea, I had a squash plant from which I would make hash and on that we survived while my *compañero* had no work, since we were newly arrived and we didn't have friends and we couldn't plant anything because the *finca* was more jungle than fields."[64]

A.C.C. suggested her *compañero* go to her uncle in Pocora and ask him to advance them some food from his *pulpería* (corner store) in exchange for odd jobs. But her access to her own kin was mediated by her husband, for she stayed on the *finca* with her children. "[H]e left on a Saturday, there I was with just a little bit of coffee and some salt, but Saturday passed and he didn't arrive, the desperation was worse when Sunday passed and he didn't come either, well to make a long story short he didn't come back until Monday night, that day since he still wasn't back I had a laying hen which had been a present and I killed it to make some broth for the children I thought if he doesn't come today I'm going to beg some money or pawn my watch and leave." As on this occasion, her *compañero* often brought only the remnants of Saturday's pay when he staggered home on Sunday night. A.C.C. cobbled together what resources she could: her own labor and that of her children, borrowing and credit. "When the harvest came I went with him to harvest corn and left the babies with my little boy, who was the biggest one, so we got some pennies together and could pay for what we'd borrowed on credit and pay some debts and buy some food to sustain us."[65]

In 1960, at the age of twenty-four, A.C.C. gave birth to her sixth child. By then the family was living on a different parcel, slightly less isolated, so that although her husband continued his weekly binges she was economically less dependent. Buying a few coconuts on credit she began making *cajetas* (candies) for her children to sell, and through the slow accretion of profits she was able to start a business selling meals on credit to *peones* at nearby *fincas*. However, the same social contacts that brought her economic independence were fodder for her husband's jealousy. "There were paydays when my husband was waiting for me maybe drunk and beat me, because he said that I was off whoring when I'd been off with my kids collecting what I was owed for meals. . . . So there were days we waited until he came home to go out and sleep in the *monte* [wilds] and days when we slept under the floor of the house."[66]

A woman caring for her children, her man, and his property on an isolated rural homestead and a woman working as a prostitute in a port brothel in a sense represent opposite poles on the spectrum of female strategies. A prostitute provided services to many men and managed the income she received in return herself. A settler's wife put all her eggs in one basket and prayed for the best. The prostitute might count on cash earnings and the ongoing support of steady *compañeras*, but her occupation guaranteed chronic venereal infection and placed her at risk of the potentially violent jealousy of many men.

The wife could hope for security for her children and the respect and care of a grateful family as she aged, but she could also fear the poverty and blows that might be her lot if the man she was with turned out badly. For both, their status within a given conjugal unit cannot be evaluated without reference to the world outside the door—the location of their home and workplace within the social geography of Limón, the nature of their daily contacts with kin and companions, the sorts of resources that their particular community was willing to offer a woman in need.

Life stories from Limón confirm the overlap in domestic and conjugal patterns across ethnic groups that we found in census data from 1927. Both marriage and consensual unions were part of most people's lives at one point or another, as were households both with and without resident adult men. To understand this pattern, we moved back and forth between numbers and stories, using narrative sources to hone our knowledge of the vernacular forms obliquely reflected in official data, and using a collective portrait drawn from census returns to contextualize the lives we read. Ultimately, patterns in household composition and conjugal status offered only weak clues to broader family practice, for the lived experience of domestic arrangements depended as much on the integration of the household into a web of social relationships beyond its bounds as it did on the internal structure of the household itself.

Domestic patterns in Limón present many of the characteristics that in other societies have been taken as evidence of the disintegration of the family, including conjugal instability, high rates of illegitimacy, low rates of marriage, and large numbers of children raised in homes that do not include their fathers. Households consisting of a conjugal couple and their children were exceedingly rare among both Hispanics and West Indians in Limón in 1927, and autobiographical and judicial evidence suggests that this was a long-standing and enduring fact of social organization there. Furthermore, the domestic units that looked most like the discrete nuclear family—the isolated rural homesteads of the 1940s and 1950s—provided little security for many women and children, by their own account. And yet, if the nuclear family was not a haven in a heartless world, family in a broader sense surely was. Life stories from Limón show family less as a structured series of relationships branching out from a biological core—whether a sexually reproducing couple or a mother-child dyad—and more as a matter of intense bonds forged from more diffuse social ties. Community was always on the verge of coalescing into kinship: when coworkers partnered up as *compañeros*, when neighbors fell in love, when someone took a child in need into their home.

Indeed, it is in the widespread practice of informal fostering that the continuity between community and kinship is most evident. West Indian V.P. was born in Port Limón in 1922; her mother died when she was ten months old. "[T]hanks to the fraternal spirit you could feel in that *pueblo* . . . I was not abandoned. There was a house whose owner was Chinese and all the women of the neighborhood would gather every day to make their purchases and tell each other the news of the day." There Miss Matilda learned of the orphaned infant, took her in, and raised her as her own.[67] As with so many kinship practices, child-borrowing was common across all ethnic groups in Limón. In 1899 black youth Samuel Mude told interviewers, in Spanish, "I never had a father, my mother died when I was small, *la señora* Emilia Ruíz is the one who has raised me ever since."[68] In the same years, brothel owner and moneylender Raquel Barrantes was raising Raquel Montezuma as her daughter in San José. Even when ideologies of racial difference were unchallenged common sense, people could disregard supposed barriers of language or blood and turn a child of another origin into one of their own. On the other hand, personal loss could heighten perceptions of difference instead, as when ten-year-old Domingo Álvarez, orphaned by his mother and abused by his godmother, set fire to the home of the West Indian matrons who called him a "damn' t'ief" in a language whose insults were all he knew. As they built such ties or deepened such divides, sojourners and natives alike shaped the contours of family and the boundaries of community in the Western Caribbean.

FIVE

Facety Women

Rudeness and Respectability,

1890s–1930s

For a few heady years at the turn of the nineteenth century Port Limón was a boomtown beyond compare. The city's population increased tenfold in the early decades of banana expansion, reaching over 7,000 in 1913.[1] The streets, wrote the chief of police in 1912, looked as if "the majority of the nations of the globe—Costa Ricans, Europeans, North and South Americans, Antilleans, Africans, and Asians—all have arranged to meet here."[2] This chapter is about the politics of public space in Port Limón: about how individual and collective status was asserted, challenged, and defended; about the contradictory roles state institutions and actors played in that process; and about the campaign for decency and decorum promoted by local West Indian leaders in response to mounting racism in the 1930s. I begin with two anecdotes. In 1899 Louise Gordon sued Jane Parker for insults before the *alcalde* of Limón, claiming that the previous morning while she was chatting with Annie Cummings at her stall in the market, Parker had called out "that I was a whore, a filthy pig . . . I asked, who are you talking to? and she repeated herself, saying it was me she was insulting, since I was talking about her."[3] On a nearby street in 1902, according to a telegram sent by the governor to his superiors in San José, "[d]ue to personal disputes motivated by despicable articles published in one of the so-called 'newspapers' of the capital, *don* Eduardo Beeche gave *don* Lucas Alvarado several blows with his cane: there were no serious consequences."[4] Beeche and Alvarado were both wealthy and influential citizens, active in electoral politics—indeed, Alvarado was a former *alcalde* himself. Their conflict seems far removed from that of two Jamaican marketwomen; certainly Beeche and Alvarado would have insisted it was. In fact, however, there were both parallels and direct connections between battles for status in these two social worlds.

The scholarly literatures on honor and shame in Latin America and on reputation and respectability in the Caribbean both address connections between individual status, intimate relations, and social structure, yet they are rarely read in tandem. Perhaps this is because supposed differences in kinship forms and associated values have been central to scholars' division of the world into cultural regions. Machismo, patriarchy, and honor have been "gatekeeper" concepts for the study of Latin America, shaping observers' interests and guiding perceptions of where the region's true boundaries lie.[5] In the past decade historians have borrowed from anthropological work on honor in the Mediterranean to depathologize Latin American masculinities and explore the opportunities for maneuvering that the honor/shame system provided. Closely attuned to links between the personal and the political, such scholarship has explored the interaction of gender ideologies, family structures, and church and state.[6] Historians of colonial Latin America have argued that the maintenance of family honor, and thus social standing, relied on the control of female sexuality. Men's honor was enhanced by the conquest of other men's women; conversely, it was made vulnerable by the sexual activity of their own wives, daughters, and female kin. The honor/shame complex reinforced social hierarchy because both wealth and political power were necessary to enact the gendered ideals of female seclusion and male sexual access to multiple women and dominion over multiple men. In turn, claims by members of the elite to embody a privileged morality served to legitimize their exercise of material power.

Quite different notions of kinship and values have been central to scholarship on the Caribbean. In the crudest version, family values in each region were the problem, but in opposite ways. Latin American families had too much hierarchy and too much male power; Caribbean families did not have enough of either. Social scientific interest in the Caribbean originated with the Moyne Commission, appointed in 1938 to investigate the social and political crises rocking Britain's Caribbean colonies. The investigators claimed that moral failings among the lower classes were central to the region's ills. Unrestrained sexuality and male irresponsibility created impoverished households in which women dominated, children multiplied, and men were marginal at best. Ethnographic research, even when sympathetic, seemed to confirm the essentials of this portrait, and debates in the next decades centered on the origins and functioning of Caribbean kinship systems. Were the West Indies a plural society in which different socio-racial groups had different value systems? Or did the Afro-Caribbean masses aspire to a more "normal" family life, which economic disenfranchisement prevented them from achieving?[7]

Peter Wilson's 1973 account of social relations in Providencia seemed to synthesize these divergent views. In his account men seek reputation among their male peers, gaining prestige from sexual success with multiple women, defiance of public authority, and verbal dexterity. Women, in contrast, seek respectability through organized religion and aspire to a moral code borrowed from the British bourgeoisie, which legitimates social hierarchy.[8] Subsequent scholars questioned the rigid gender division of Wilson's model while at the same time confirming many of its specific elements. Rather than pit "liming" men against churchgoing women, recent work asks how presentations of self and sexuality fit into conflictual class relations.[9] Literary critic Carolyn Cooper has traced ongoing skirmishes between elite "Culture" and popular "slackness" in Jamaica. Her description of the opposition between civilized decorum and rude self-assertion echoes many of the elements of Wilson's concepts of respectability and reputation, but she sees these as class-based strategies that cut across gender.[10] Together, these two literatures have much to offer our analysis of sex and standing in Port Limón. Gendered notions of sexual honor were central to conflicts over individual status and were also invoked to naturalize social hierarchies. Selective rudeness and public rowdiness could both build individual reputations and challenge the social order. On all these points Hispanic and West Indian migrants show considerable cultural overlap.

Insults Suits in Turn-of-the-Century Limón

Lawsuits over *injurias*, or insults, filed in Limón during the first banana boom offer an intriguing set of paradoxes. Insults suits were quite common in Limón, far more so than in the rest of the country. Seventeen times as many insults cases were filed per capita in Limón than in San José in these years.[11] According to the Penal Code of 1880 *injurias* consisted of expressions or actions intended to bring "dishonor, discredit, or scorn" that harmed the recipient's "reputation, credit, and interests."[12] Yet the women who sued for in-

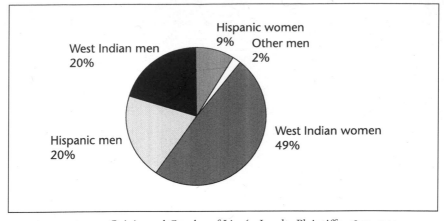

FIGURE 5.1. Origin and Gender of Limón Insults Plaintiffs, 1897–1910
Source: Archivo Nacional de Costa Rica, San José, Costa Rica.
Note: N = 224.

sults—washerwomen, bar owners, prostitutes—were precisely those women with the least honor to lose in the eyes of elites and officials. In contrast, the men who filed such cases were frequently themselves elites and officials: plantation owners, contractors, police commanders. While the gender ratio and social standing of insults suits participants varied markedly across ethnic groups, the specific content of the insults did not. Women were accused of sexual impropriety—often in lavish detail—and men were accused of theft or dishonorable business dealings.

The breadth of participation in insults suits was remarkable. Spanish store owners and St. Lucian laundresses, Colombian madams and Tunisian traders, fruit magnate Cecil V. Lindo and the men who hauled his bananas on the docks—all appear among the ranks of those who filed suit for *injurias* in turn-of-the-century Limón. Just over half of parties to insults cases were women. Patterns in national origin differed sharply by gender. Four-fifths of female plaintiffs were West Indian, while only half of male plaintiffs were.[13] Costa Rican men were twice as likely to sue as to be sued. West Indian men were half again as likely to be sued (almost always by West Indian women) as to sue. Eighty-five percent of cases involved parties from the same region of origin. West Indian women, West Indian men, Hispanic women, and Hispanic men were each twice as likely to sue someone of their own origin and gender as anyone else. This matches a basic pattern of status similarity between participants. Insults cases involved two stages of confrontation: the original act of insult and the subsequent decision to sue. For a case to result, at the first stage one party had to find the other neither too inferior to bother with nor too powerful to risk offending, and at the second stage the other party had to make the same evaluation. Insults cases embodied "the logic of challenge and riposte, in which a challenge both validates an individual's honor by recognizing him as worth challenging, and serves as a 'provocation to reply.'"[14] Not infrequently the case itself served as an additional provocation to reply, inspiring the filing of a countersuit.

Patterns in the relationships between parties and in the inflammatory words themselves have much to tell us about the bases of male and female honor in Limón. Classic analyses of honor in the Mediterranean described men's control over female dependents' sexual behavior as the centerpiece of the honor/shame system and argued that male hypersensitivity to affront evolved to both defend and display this patriarchal power.[15] Thus men compete with each other by challenging the honor of female kin — as in this letter, the object of an insults suit in 1908:

> Dear Mr. Lloyd, I understand that you called Mrs. Powell a "common woman." I would like to know your meaning. Suppose I tell you that there are many around here more common than she, would you doubt me? Do you know a man anywhere around here who is cloaking up a sister, and trying to pass her off as a young lady? Suppose I were to tell you that that very sister has had a child in Jamaica, would you doubt me? Remember my friend, news never hide. So don't look at motes and try to hide beams.
>
> You will not call the name of the mischief maker in that he told on Mrs. Powell, now Sir allow me to tell you that I am going to compell you to call it.
>
> In haste, W. M. Powell[16]

Yet as a motive in insults actions, male defense of the reputations of mothers, sisters, wives, or lovers is most notable by its absence.[17] The social geography of turn-of-the-century Limón, in particular the gendered division of labor that concentrated men on the plantations and women in the port, worked against the establishment of rigid domestic units. Even if the men of Limón had wished to be patriarchs, few had patriarchal households over which to rule. Mr. Powell's insinuations about Mr. Lloyd's sister aside, male vigilance over female kin could hardly be the central axis of honor in the port.[18]

Sexual impropriety was indeed the substance of almost all actionable insults against women. But female sexual honor was not a symbol in status struggles between men. Rather women's sexual choices were seen as instrumental to their own social and economic status, to their standing vis à vis other women as well as men. This is clear in the insults suits filed days apart by Martha Brown and Isabel Jamieson in 1907. Brown had called the younger woman over to her doorway, saying, "I'll tell you not to keep company with my son any more," or, in another witness's version, "You evil woman, you took all my son's money last pay day." Jamieson answered, "Oh, I take [or fuck: the meaning is ambiguous in the interpreter's Spanish] anything I want if there's money behind it," to which Brown replied, "If you want to be a whore I'll go to the Governor and have him ship you out as a prostitute." Jamieson turned her back, saying, "Don't you break my ass this morning."[19] In this case the imputations against Jamieson's sexual honor stemmed logically from the substance of the conflict. But in fact sexual dishonor was the idiom through which women's status was challenged and defended no matter who the women were or what the conflict was. Thus Matilda Thompson sued Edith MacLean for saying "that she was a 'whore,' that she was always getting money from a man to sleep with him, that when that man goes to her house, she shuts herself up with him and three others and they keep cohabiting until midnight." Queried about the case, the local justice of the peace reported that the two women were constantly in disputes due to a land title conflict.[20]

In this boomtown full of striving entrepreneurs, business disputes were most often the occasion of actionable insults between men. In 1902 Frederick Davis sued Jerome Bright for saying "You were a thief in Jamaica, a thief in Colón, and a thief here." The occasion, according to Davis's witness, was that Bright had tried to collect "the rest of the pay owed him for a job that they had done together in Banano River, to which Davis replied that he didn't owe anything, as the remaining money the company commissary had deducted for goods Bright had bought on credit; and Bright said this was a lie, and Davis a lying thief." In Bright's version, Davis responded to his request for the money owed by saying "that he didn't have the means to pay me now, and anyhow that Negroes as stupid as I should work for free." When Bright answered in kind, Davis "called me a son of a bitch and threatened to take me up before the authorities," which indeed he did.[21]

A similar dispute occurred between two Cuban contractors in 1906. When Manuel Ulyett went to collect the 100 *colones* that Miguel Xirinach owed him for carpentry work, Xirinach said "that he owed me nothing because I had taken some of the lumber for myself, that I had no right to complain about

Main street of Port Limón, ca. 1920. Fotografías 2148, Archivo Nacional de Costa Rica, San José, Costa Rica; originally published in *Album Gómez Miralles* (San José, 1922).

the cow I said I had given him, and that any way he had lost money on the business of building the hospital in Guápiles; to which I answered that if he had lost money on that contract it was because he'd been planning to steal a profit of four to eight thousand *colones,*" upon which "he threw himself at me, and attacked me, calling me a *bandido* [crook], *sinvergüenza* [shameless one], and thief."[22] Monetary disputes likewise underlay the insults exchanged by Florence Thompson and her cousin, who accused her of stealing the pound sterling he had given her to take to his mother in Jamaica; or those between Sarah Simon and David Newcome over her brand-new market basket, filled with eighty eggs and three pounds of coffee, which she claimed he had taken off the train at Zent Junction while her attention was elsewhere.[23]

In such cases the specific insults that served as the basis for the lawsuit might be almost incidental and the accusation itself a strategic maneuver— sometimes an openly expedient one. Jamaican plumber William Williams had been fighting for weeks with "the *chino* Joseph Lyng" over whether the pipes he installed in Lyng's store had been ten-cent tubes or fifteen-cent tubes. After Lyng again refused to pay and publicly called Williams a thieving son of a bitch, Williams replied "that he could insult him all he wanted, since he knew where and how to get his money," that is, as damages through an insults suit.[24]

In many cases though, the public affront itself became more significant than the ephemeral conflict that had sparked it. Ethel Forbes sued Harold Franklin in 1902 after he called her "in English, 'Jamaica Bitch' which is to say in Spanish *jamaicana puta perra puta*." Franklin's prepaid laundry had not yet been ironed when he came to pick it up.[25] Disputes over a few cents' change at the pharmacy or the butcher's shop led to court cases in which the parties invested many times that amount.[26]

One could lodge an oral accusation for free at the *alcalde*'s office, but to pursue a case further involved increasing outlays. The next stage was to bring witnesses to the *alcaldía* to testify on one's behalf. The summoning party was by custom obliged to reimburse the witness for a full day's lost wages, from 1.50 to 4 *colones* in these years. (Testifying included long hours waiting for the relevant case to be called.) Then, before the *alcalde* would officially charge the accused, the plaintiff had to present a *fiador*, a local resident of known means who guaranteed payment of court costs if the plaintiff defaulted. Over three-fifths of parties to insults cases sought legal representation, which ranged from purchasing a single-page writ of complaint that the clients themselves presented at the *alcaldía*, to specifying a lawyer's office for the receipt of notifications of decisions (and presumably getting legal advice on those decisions), to officially registering an *apoderado* (attorney empowered to act on one's behalf).

Lawyers took on cases under a variety of arrangements, including quid pro quos and patron-client ties. Such ties are exemplified by a case involving Juan José León, prominent leader of the local Chinese community. León sued two young Jamaican women in 1909 for calling him (in his lawyer's account) a "thief, *bandido*, *sinvergüenza* and other words so against morality that I omit to mention them, although I am forced to add that they also said that his mother was a Chinese whore." One of the accused women, Emma Charles, explained that the conflict had begun on the day when presidential candidate *don* Ricardo Jiménez came to visit Limón. "[T]he *chino* saw that I was wearing a *civilista* badge [that of the party opposing Jiménez] and began to insult me, saying that I was a vagabond, *bandida*, and that only *sinvergüenzas* and thieves and drunkards wore *civilista* badges, because the *civilistas* were idiot sons of bitches." She avoided León's store for a while but then returned one day to buy meat. "At the moment that one of the *chinos* was cutting the meat, as they were speaking in their language I laughed, and so the *chino* who apparently is the owner of the establishment asked me if I liked to have sex with *chinos*, to which I replied that only a woman who was totally shameless could sleep with a *chino*, as it's well known that *chinos* are really filthy."[27] Incensed, León sued, hiring a prominent lawyer tied to Jiménez's Partido Republicano. The *civilista* electoral effort was heavily backed by Minor Keith, and former *alcalde* Lucas Alvarado was local counsel for United Fruit. Alvarado joined the case on the women's behalf, and the suit was soon dismissed. As in this case, the majority of insults suits never made it past the initial writ of complaint and perhaps a few witnesses' declarations. Less than one in seven actually reached judgment, and in at least half of these the defendant was absolved. All told, less than 5 percent of accusations ended in conviction.[28]

Boardinghouses and *Cantinas*

A few insults cases began in junction towns along the lines, but the vast majority came from Port Limón itself. The bulk of accusations stemmed from conflicts between neighbors, in which monetary disputes, malicious gossip, and moral judgments were inextricably mixed. When Elena Cervantes demanded that police sergeant Rogelio Fonseca pay the seven *colones* he owed for rent on the sublet room she shared with Rogelio's woman, he answered, according to one neighbor, "that no, that he wasn't *pendejo* [idiot] enough to pay for her whoring," to which Elena replied, according to another neighbor, "that he was a filthy *sinvergüenza* who was used to freeloading off his woman and not paying for his lodging." A third neighbor observed the fight through the partially open door and a fourth through the room's back window, all wary lest Rogelio draw the service revolver he wore.[29]

Such cases highlight the relationship between the built environment, social networks, and popular culture in Limón. Working folk in the port lived either on the outskirts, in wooden shacks built on the public domain or on rented plots, or in the center of town, in boardinghouses and multifamily dwellings. Known as *casas de vecindad* or, more crudely, *chinchorros*, these were two-story buildings with lines of eight to ten rooms opening onto a corridor on the first floor, a balcony on the second.[30] In the rear patio was a standing water pipe, and sometimes a separate kitchen to reduce the risk of fires. Landlords often built one-room shacks of corrugated zinc or scrap wood beyond the back patios and rented these as well. Governor Daniel Víquez saw the urban geography as a menace to authority. "The centers of the city blocks form a second population . . . and it is precisely there that the greatest danger [of arson, in this case] exists. There live those who are lost to fortune or looking to economize; the front sides of the blocks are inhabited by the well-off, or occupied by storefronts. These dens of crime and misery are in darkness because the electric plant is not able to provide for all who request electricity. . . . Each block has so many hidden alleys that the police cannot effectively watch them, and each of those is an escape route which mocks the policeman's good-faith attempt to exercise his duty."[31] Official doctor Benjamín de Céspedes described similarly decrepit conditions and placed the blame with landlords who refused to make urgent repairs "to improve their foul slum barracks which earn them as much as 2 percent per month from the resident niggers."[32]

The patios of the *casas de vecindad* and the shared water pipes of the back lot shanties were the locus of most women's daily activities, in particular the cooking and washing they did for themselves, for kin, or for customers. Many insults cases had their origins in words shouted "from the *altos* [second floor]," from doorway to doorway, or through the partitions between rooms (a row of planks that often stopped several feet from the ceiling). Even more than the public market, it was the *casas de vecindad* that facilitated the informal economy of working women. They were the centers not just of laundry and food preparation but of money lending, small-scale retailing, and services like dressmaking and hairdressing. Whatever residents' wishes, there could be little distinction here between public and private domains. Such a division had no spatial basis in a world in which only five flimsy boards separated your bed from your neighbors', in which you literally washed your dirty linen in public, and in which your financial borrowing power depended on your neighbors' opinion of the man you had been keeping company with. In the *casas de vecindad* social networks, political connections, intimate liaisons, and economic well-being were all connected, and judgments about all of these came together in personal reputations.

It was not uncommon for a dozen neighbors to testify to a particular verbal battle they had all witnessed, giving versions that differed dramatically depending on whose side they chose to take. In a 1908 case, Roberta Thompson said she and her husband had been sitting peacefully in front of their door when Edith Carter called out, "Why is this bitch laughing at me, why don't you go to Jamaica and whore with the man you left behind there?" One witness claimed Roberta had replied "that [Edith] was a damned nothing, 'patio princess.'" Others, testifying on Carter's behalf in her countersuit, remembered a more colorful response: "that [Edith] was a whore all her life, that she had given birth in a chamber pot; that she smelled worse than chicken shit;

Woman in back patio, Port Limón, ca. 1930. Colección fotográfica, 9354, Museo Nacional, San José, Costa Rica.

that she was a shaved-head, no more than a vulgar woman of her class; and that if she didn't like it she could take it to the judge."[33] Similarly intimate public conflicts occurred among Costa Rican and Central American boarding-house tenants. The argument between Vicenta Hernández, a Costa Rican, and Isabel Montoya, a Nicaraguan eighteen-year-old, began in the public market with hurled accusations of malicious gossip involving several other women as well and carried over into a string of insults in their shared patio (including the classic repartee, "She said 'tu madre' to which I replied 'la tuya'"). The fight culminated with Vicenta declaring in front of Isabel's consensual male partner "that I [Isabel] am a whore, so low that I whore with *chinos*."[34]

Although most insults cases involved participants from the same region of origin there were exceptions, shaped by the social geography of the port. West Indians and Hispanics formed distinct communities here, yet residential and commercial spaces were never segregated. Any boardinghouse or back lot included residents from Jamaica and Costa Rica, Barbados and Nicaragua, Colombia and China.[35] In the tight quarters of boardinghouse life the attempt to keep someone in her place might be enacted literally. One morning in 1900

Amelia Esquivel, consensual partner of Isidor Stein, nailed a canvas sheet across the corridor behind their *cantina* to prevent Maud MacPherson from walking by. Esquivel declared "that filthy whores like [MacPherson] could not pass here," but MacPherson paraded back and forth, milk jug in one arm and baby in the other, daring Esquivel to stop her and taunting "that if she was dirty it was from caring for her one husband and her child" (implying that Esquivel was morally dirty for living with Stein). "One Colombian woman there was urging Amelia to hit [Maud], but Amelia instead brought out her chamber pot as a sign of disrespect and put it in front of Maud saying that she should talk to the chamber pot, that she [Amelia] didn't want more trouble." Meanwhile, Stein came out of the store and began insulting MacPherson, at which point MacPherson's mother joined the fray, demanding to know why he was calling her daughter a whore. Esquivel spoke little English and MacPherson no Spanish: bystanders had to translate for each throughout (although Esquivel's attorney, Lucas Alvarado, wrote that MacPherson "knows how to swear well enough in Spanish, and besides which *señor* Alcalde, anyone who hears 'God Dam Son of a Bitch' [in English in original] knows he's been called *hijo de una perra*, even schoolchildren know that").[36]

Amelia Esquivel belonged to a category clearly overrepresented among insults plaintiffs: women who ran *cantinas* owned by their male consensual partners.[37] The line between *cantinas* and brothels was blurry, as was the line between a materially advantageous consensual union and commercial sex. Such female entrepreneurs were sometimes former prostitutes themselves and were always suspected of being so. Their honor was precarious, and perhaps hard-won, and they defended it with a vengeance. Ramona Méndez sued Fidel Gómez in 1907 because when she refused to serve him twenty *céntimos* of cane liquor on credit, he yelled "very loudly that I couldn't cure a burn I have on my hand, because I had been the concubine of *chinos* and was syphilitic." The offense occurred while she was tending the *cantina* owned by Ramón Sárraga—with whom, she emphasized, "I have lived honorably and maritally for more than three years."[38] Arabella Levi sued Isaac Fraser for insults in 1899 (both were Jamaican). She had served Fraser a drink "in my *cantina* establishment. . . . He brought the glass to his nose and then said that those of us working there were 'dirty' and that I in addition was 'a daughter of a whore,' 'damned,' 'a prostituted *mulata*.'" Fraser's lawyer countered by promising to prove that "Arabella Levi is an unmarried woman and she has lived for more than four years with [*cantina* owner] José Fontaine," who had abandoned his wife and children in Jamaica because of her. Levi quickly settled out of court.[39]

Accusations of prostitution undercut the rising status of women who had worked their way up in the liquor-and-entertainment sector and prompted vigorous responses. But insults suits were also brought continuously by working prostitutes like Martha Darling of Limón or the Cabrera sisters of San José.[40] How can we understand the apparent contradiction of prostitutes filing lawsuits to restore honor they claimed was injured when other prostitutes accused them of being prostitutes? The answer illuminates the dynamics of insults accusations as a whole.

Courts and the Vindication of Honor

The heated exchanges reported in insults cases were a street theater of personal standing, fueled by righteous indignation and animated by an aesthetic of verbal artistry. Insults suits were brought by those who felt they had been bested in public battles for prestige. A suit was a way to trump one's opponent, to continue the same argument by other means. In filing suit the plaintiff proved she had money or connections enough to carry a case through the criminal system—or at least bluffed that she was willing to do so. One could place an accusation for free or spend a few *colones* for a single lawyer's writ, but as we have seen, the costs for both parties grew heavier as the case moved on. To file for insults suggested one was willing and able to raise the ante. Indeed, bragging about one's ability to afford to carry cases through the courts became part of the standard repartee of public insults. Roberta Thompson ("patio princess," above) apparently kept former judge Enrique Jiménez Dávila on retainer for just such occasions. According to one neighbor, Thompson "makes a habit of insulting her neighbors, bragging that she has money, and has already paid a lawyer for the year to carry her defense."[41] The act of mobilizing witnesses further flexed the muscle of both parties' social support, and "putting witnesses"—asking onlookers to testify on one's behalf in a future court case—became a ritual part of verbal duels. In a typical reference from 1898, Hermione Edwards and Leonore Green were chatting "about the bad state of business" when Letitia Phillips interjected, "What are you going on about, don't you remember the time [when things were so bad that] you stole yams from that coolie and hid them under your bed?" Green counseled Edwards "that she should not get angry, but just go to the authorities, and so she did, she put witnesses and didn't answer Phillips back."[42]

To sue for insults occasioned a second performance, as participants and witnesses came forth to repeat lines from the first engagement. But valences attached to dialogue were different in the new forum—indeed, in many ways they were reversed. In the eyes of the law, clever insults counted against the speaker, and sexual boasting lowered her standing. Thus in 1901 Barbadian carpenter Alexander Barnes sued Mistress French, who he said had "accused his wife of having illicit relations with one 'Barefoot,' a neighbor of French's."[43] His wife, who identified herself pointedly as Cassandra Maxwell *de* Barnes, included a copy of their marriage certificate as part of her formal complaint. Her writ of accusation noted that "the act which was imputed to me consists of a grave insult, as I am a married woman and this could bring about the dissolution of my tranquil home and bring down the wrath of my husband." Yet the alleged insults took on a rather different tone in her own witnesses' testimony. Apparently Cassandra Barnes had gone to another woman's room to buy some vegetables. Mistress French, who happened to be there, picked up a yam and boasted, "My man John Belfore can get any married woman he wants with that yam of his." In a petition written by Lucas Alvarado, Mistress French claimed she never meant to offend. "I have a very high regard for Mrs. Barnes, and if I said anything, which I don't remember, it certainly wasn't referring to the plaintiff, as the testimony so far makes clear."[44] Yet the vulgarity of the jest may well have been intended as an affront to *la señora de* Barnes and her cultured pretensions.

Parallels for such competitive wordplay can be found in "slanging matches" in Providencia, "cussing out" in Barbuda, "tracings" in Jamaica, or "the dozens" in the United States.[45] But in Port Limón this was not an exclusively Afro-Caribbean practice. The heterogeneous city blocks facilitated casual contact between migrants of every origin, and when conflicts arose standing was challenged and defended in much the same terms whether within or across group lines. One of the few ethnic differences in actionable insults were West Indian women's creative bodily references ("You stole a watch in Jamaica and hid it up your ass"; "You stole tripe in the market in Jamaica and hid it in your brassier"; "A piece of your ass fell off in Jamaica and your mother had to tie it up with rags").[46] But in general even the content of insults was similar across groups. Not only did Nicaraguans, Costa Ricans, and Jamaicans all use "whoring with *chinos*" as emblematic of the worst female degradation, but among all groups insults having to do with Chinese men were most commonly uttered by debtors confronted with their inability to pay.[47]

What are we to make of the similarity of insults among migrants of every origin in Limón, and, more generally, the similar strategies through which they sought to affirm their public standing? Contemporary observers from both sides insisted that West Indians and Costa Ricans were culturally different, and that that difference had much to do with gender roles, domestic arrangements, and sexual morality. As we shall see, such claims became the centerpiece of anti-black racism in Costa Rica in the straitened years of the 1930s. But the contemporary conviction of difference, and its political salience, has masked the common elements in the two regions' heritage, commonalities accentuated by migrants' self-selection. The uncertain prospects of the banana zone did not draw all potential workers evenly. It took a certain degree of facetyness or brazenness simply to arrive, whether from Kingston, Colón, or Cartago.[48] In addition, the built environment of the city favored certain developments for migrants of all origins. The *casas de vecindad* strengthened female social networks and the informal economy associated with them and thrust intimate relationships into the public domain.

The very notion of regional cultural difference is predicated on an idea of cultures as bounded and consensual systems that is itself increasingly questioned. As ethnographers and historians attend more carefully to conflict and power, culture begins to look less like a matter of shared norms and occasional deviance and more like an ongoing dispute over meaning: a "language of argument," as David Sabean has termed it.[49] The metaphor illuminates the cases at hand. Think back, for instance, to the insults suits between Maud Mac-Pherson and Amelia Esquivel. The former spoke only English, the latter only Spanish, yet clearly the two shared a language of argument. Underlying the insults and their aftermath was a series of common understandings—indeed, the insults could not have been insulting if this were not the case.[50] Esquivel tried to assert class privilege by barring MacPherson from the corridor behind her store and calling her a dirty tramp. MacPherson replied that she *was* dirty, but not from whoring: she was dirty from caring for her husband and legitimate child. She challenged Esquivel's claim to superiority by implying that Esquivel's economic status came from her advantageous but immoral liaison with the store's owner and insisted that her own domestic strategy—church-sanctioned marriage and hard work—entitled her to a higher standing. The women relied on bystanders to translate the words of this exchange, but the content of the insults made perfect sense to each. Both assumed that access to public space was symbolic of social privilege, that sexual practice and personal status were linked, that the ways women negotiated this link were subject to moral judgment, and that resultant claims to decency and precedence could be made either on the streets or in the courts—either by brandishing a chamber pot or by buying a lawyer's time.

In one sense, even the judicially sanctioned version of female honor was not so distant from the versions espoused by MacPherson and Esquivel, or by Martha Darling and friends. Honor for women meant sexual propriety. It was simply the definition of sexual propriety that varied. In the letter of the law, sexual propriety meant fidelity to a lawfully wedded husband; on the streets of Limón, it meant not sleeping with *chinos* for cash (or not cohabiting with three men at once in the kitchen, or not having sex in the *bananales*). West Indian and Latin American popular cultures drew on European traditions as developed in colonial caste societies, in which elite male privilege included sexual freedom and poor women's plight included sexual vulnerability. Thus when working-class women laid claim to personal status in public verbal duels, they did so by asserting their sexual self-determination. They claimed virtue not as virgins, but as willful actors who enforced their own moral discriminations. In contrast, for upper-class women merely to appear in court might compromise their reputations. As one lawyer explained regarding a wealthy Costa Rican, inadvertent witness to a conflict outside her door, "As the *señora* Ana *de* González is of good character [*buenas costumbres*] and does not frequent public offices, I beg you to go and receive her declaration in her own home."[51]

In this context it is worth remembering that while Costa Rican women made up only a small fraction of insults plaintiffs in Limón, insults cases were eagerly filed by certain women in San José and other Central Valley cities —in particular by registered prostitutes. Like peddlers and market women in Limón, like men everywhere, such "public women" claimed the right to occupy public space. They did so loudly and aggressively, in battles against each other as well as against the policemen and hygiene officers who tried to regulate their lives. An argument between two San José madams in 1892, for example, over whose establishment a traveling player piano should play at next, led to a brawl involving a dozen public women, several knife wounds, and multiple arrests.[52] Strident self-assertion was not unique to women in prostitution. A raucous attitude of entitlement was the modal form of public deportment for a significant number of poor urban women.[53] Again, these parallels belie the fixity of regional cultural difference, calling our attention instead to the role of social structure in shaping personal demeanor.

Class and the Claim to Public Space

At the beginning of this chapter I noted the apparent paradox that insults cases were filed by the lowest of women and the highest of men. What these groups had in common was their use of public space for personal conflicts. For both groups, the streets served as settings for individual conflicts within the group, while at the same time the very claim to a street presence was a collective act with political implications. U.S. traveler Harry Franck captured this dynamic in his description of the battle for public space in Kingston in the 1910s (in his view, the forces of good were losing).

> The white residents of Kingston seem to live in fear of the black multi-tude that makes up the great bulk of the population. When hoodlums and rowdies jostle them in the street, they shift aside with a slinking air; even when the black hooligans cling to the outside of street-cars pouring out obscene language, the white men do not shield their wives and daughters beside them by so much as raising their voices in protest. When cursing, filthy market women pile their baskets and unwashed produce in upon them and crowd their own women out of their places, they bear it all with humble resignation, as if they were the last survivors of the civilized race wholly disheartened by an invasion of barbarian tribes.[54]

Market women, with their oversized baskets, were required by custom to sit in the rear seats of Jamaican buses. Those who considered themselves their social betters would sit far to the front—unless the bus was so crowded there was nowhere else to sit. Jamaican poet Louise Bennet captured the daily strug-gle for public space and personal respect in her rendering of a comment over-heard on a Kingston bus in the 1930s:

> Pread out yuhself de Liza,
> one Dress-oman dah look like seh
> She see di li space side-a we
> And wan foce harself een deh.[55]

In Bennet's account, market women physically spread themselves out so as to leave no room for the middle-class interloper (derided as a "one-dress woman") to squeeze into their domain at the back of the bus.

One component of West Indian women's assertive occupation of public space was the aggressive display of sexuality that so troubled Harry Franck in the "loose-mannered females" of Kingston. But all was not slackness on the streets of Limón.[56] The popular occupation of public space incorporated cultural forms borrowed from disparate sources, including many that were more often associated with middle-class respectability than with lower-class reputation. Travelers often commented on West Indian women's fondness for haberdashery. George Putnam described women on the 6 A.M. local train to Zent Junction, returning to the lines after visits to Port Limón and its stores. "One buxom coloured lassie was envied much in the eyes of her sisters, thanks to a vivid hat of rainbow hues and broad scope which she bore proudly on her head, while in her hand she carried the discarded creation of the last season."[57] Such descriptions aim for parody as Euro-American authors try to laugh off the travesty of poor Jamaicans dressed as proper ladies. But the women themselves were the original parodists. They appropriated symbols of bourgeois respectability in a manner that was not only potentially subversive but—more important—stylish. Wallace Thompson's first impression upon docking in Limón was of "[a] large, very dusky lady, gaudy in green satin, and smoking of the immortal 'whopping big cheroot,' . . . selling native candies."[58] This peddler not only mixed female and male symbols of bourgeois privilege (the dress, the cigar) but did so within an aesthetic of sensual pleasure that was anything but respectable (the color and texture of the satin, the indulgence of the tobacco).

Limón's docks were more often the province of male workers and masculine display, as West Indian longshoremen "sang the bananas into the holds."

> On the opposite end of the ship was a rival concert, but at times some singer with a powerful voice would sound a strain which would ring clear above the hum and racket of the conveyor machinery and the shunting of trains, and the workers from end to end of ship and dock would join in. On the night which I am attempting to describe, a huge Jamaican negro took artistic advantage of a slight lull in the noise. He was black as night, with huge shoulders and massive torso. For hours he had been handling seventy-pound bunches of bananas as if they were bouquets. In a splendidly modulated baritone voice he suddenly began the second verse of "Nearer, My God, to Thee."[59]

The longshoremen's nightly performance was a vocal "spreading out" paralleling Bennet's market women's physical one. It was of a piece with their claims to public space at other moments, as Putnam described in 1912: "Just before daylight the next morning we heard those workers going home, when the ship was loaded and underway. A more varied or unearthly conglomeration of sound than that produced by a pack of paid-off Jamaicans, with the work day behind them, it is impossible to imagine."[60] The dockside hymns were the object of paternalist approval by northern observers, while the rowdy retreat met racist disdain, but there is no reason to think workers themselves drew any such distinction. For these young men, who had traveled far to earn decent wages for back-breaking work, both the songs and the streets were occasions for individual virtuosity, manly competition, and boisterous communal pride.

Status and Public Display among Limón's Elite

The public displays organized by high-status men were less tuneful, but often just as loud. In discussing local elites I refer not to those UFCO officials who would move on once their tour of duty was over, but to the handful of wealthy and well-connected residents who had made fortunes in the region and sought to make more. They included both Costa Ricans and immigrants from Colombia, Cuba, North America, and Europe, many of whom married into prestigious highland families. Their wealth and political activism went hand in hand, since the national and municipal governments controlled almost all local resources not already in the hands of United Fruit, particularly land concessions and municipal contracts. Court documents and internal government correspondence record intra-elite battles as boisterous, public, and vindictive as those of any *casa de vecindad*. Elites' economic and kin-based alliances were institutionalized in party structures, and because their rituals of public assertion involved *fiestas cívicas* and electoral tallies in addition to "cussing out" and ritual shaming, the political nature of their conflicts has been comparatively easier to see. But like the popular struggles embodied in insults cases, elite conflicts were expressed in the idiom of gendered honor, were fought out in public with words and occasionally with blows, and were fueled by the links between social connections, personal prestige, and economic leverage.

Limón's elite rivalries were unusually rowdy even by the standards of the day. In the words of one exasperated governor, "If anywhere in this country there's a big ants' nest, it's here."[61] Conflict was endemic between the centrally appointed governors and the locally elected *regidores* (municipal councillors), whose cycles of collusion and obstinacy with regard to United Fruit rarely seemed to coincide. In general the local elites who controlled the municipality identified their interests with those of the company, while the central government periodically adopted a more contrary stance.[62] Tensions within the regional political economy were fought out in battles over office space and social clubs, in the quest to secure a prime appointment for the protégé who "is like a son to me," in the cultivation of networks of clients whose legal petitions (say, appealing eviction orders) could make life hell for a rival businessman.[63]

Thus in 1906 Governor Ricardo Mora complained to his superiors in San José regarding his difficulties with the *regidores municipales*. Not only had they approved a street construction swindle that was going to cost the government 35,000 *colones* for the extension of a single avenue (not coincidentally, the avenue led to the newly completed home of *regidor don* Carlos Saborío), but together with the official port doctor they insulted Mora loudly in the streets within his hearing. The origin of the most recent conflict was the governor's opposition to the *regidores'* attempt to impeach municipal treasurer Eduardo Beeche (of the 1902 caning) for embezzlement. "So far things have gone no farther, but it's clear that if they continue in this manner and repeat the affronts that they have been committing against my authority and my person, I will have to demand my respect as an authority and suffer personally the consequences which would follow, because if it comes to that I won't be lacking that which it is necessary I not lack."[64] Mora threatened to take the law into his own hands—which, he implied, he would certainly have the balls to do—in order to make himself "respect[ed] as an authority." Male honor was figured as a necessary component of legal authority even as the vindication of that honor was predicated on disregard for the rule of law.

The men involved in these quarrels were no second-tier provincial burghers. Their families were at the core of Costa Rica's commercial and agricultural elite.[65] Yet like those of other port residents, elite power struggles depended on the public demonstration of individual daring and social support. And just as boardinghouse dwellers pulled elite actors into their interpersonal conflicts when they denounced neighbors before the *alcalde* or hired lawyers to press their claims, elite conflicts also had need of working-class actors. Recall the case of Chinese storekeeper Juan José León, who sued two Jamaican teens for calling him a son of a Chinese whore. That quarrel began when the girls came into the store wearing the red ribbons and badges of the Partido Civil, while León had his store decorated with blue banners in support of the Partido Republicano. León was a naturalized Costa Rican citizen and thus eligible to vote, but the teens were foreign women and therefore doubly disenfranchised. Clearly that did not prevent them from taking part in the public display and personal affronts that were an essential part of party politics.

Of course, such parallels and ties should not blind us to the fact that the resources elites fought over, that is, access to the state and its spoils, were immensely more valuable than those up for grabs in any boardinghouse battle. This is symbolized by the contrast between William Williams's fifteen-cent pipes, or Sarah Simon's market basket full of coffee and eggs, and the 4,000–8,000 *colones* that Miguel Xirinach had allegedly planned to skim off the hospital construction contract (an accusation that may well have been accurate, if Governor Mora's figures on street construction are anything to go by).

It was urban artisans and entrepreneurs a few steps below the status of *regidores* like Saborío and Alvarado who were the most enthusiastic male insults plaintiffs. Insults suits between men pitted upstart successes against uppity strivers—men who, in the dynamic port economy, might tomorrow find their positions reversed. Only rarely did insults cases pit two workingmen against each other. Dock hands, construction workers, and day laborers show up in the judicial record not in insults suits but in assaults, brawls, and homicides. Not infrequently the verbal conflicts that led to such outcomes were identical to those that led women, and wealthier men, to file suit for *injurias*. But when the conflict was between two young, able-bodied, working-class men, they did not take it to the judge: they took it outside. A machete fight between a Jamaican and a Martinican worker on the Cuba Creek plantation in Zent began one night with a series of boasts. A fellow worker who was trying to sleep at the time recounted, "Hansen was saying that he knew Spanish, and Jullistein French, this they were saying in English. They were arguing for a while, about who spoke which language better, then Jullistein said 'I'll teach you French'; then I heard the noise of two machetes and sounds of blows." Jullistein died from the wound he received—to Hansen's horror, by all accounts, as the two men had been close friends.[66]

The "culture of male bonding and rivalry that blends play, risk, and a ratification of masculine courage amidst life's adversities" has been a crucial component of accounts of both "machismo" in Latin America and "reputation" in the Caribbean.[67] While scholars of Latin America have usually taken this as evidence of the downward spread of elite Iberian values, whose effect was to increase the legitimacy of social hierarchy, scholars of the Caribbean have seen in confrontational working-class masculinity a reaction against the elite imposition of British respectability—and the last, best defense against internalized colonial dependency.[68] The similarities between West Indian and

Latin American male street culture in Limón should make us question these divergent accounts of causality and impact. Competitive claims to honor among men both echoed traditions of dominance and sometimes subverted them in the process. (What this meant for private lives and public struggles in Limón is the subject of the following chapter.)

Compared to the physical confrontations of working-class men, there seemed something vaguely sissy about saving it for the judge. A defensive note sounds in Lucas Alvarado's insistence, in an insults suit against fellow lawyer Salomón Zacarías Aguilera, that "although as a man I could demand satisfaction directly, I want it to be the tribunals of justice which impose on this criminal the sentence mandated by law." [69] A case from 1900 underlines the assumption that manly honor should rest on physical defense. Alfred Dibbs explained to the court that his *querida* (female lover) had reprimanded James Murdock for almost hitting her son with a bag of potatoes he was lifting from the train, to which Murdock had replied that

> if she didn't get out of the way, he'd throw it on top of her instead; to which she answered that that couldn't be, because she had a man (meaning me) [said Dibbs] who would answer for her, but Murdock said he didn't care because I don't have the hands to hit him. . . . When I met him in the market the next day, I asked him why he was calling me "*mocho*" [literally, a bull without horns] when I wasn't bothering him, to which he answered that yes, he could call me that since I couldn't hit him; I replied that it was true that I couldn't hit him, as I have only one arm, but that he must stop bothering my woman.[70]

Creative Scripts

Thus there were multiple models for how to claim public space, for when to defend honor with words, when with fists, when with a legal writ. The invocation of different models was patterned by gender and class, but individuals were not wholly constrained by those patterns. Rather than thinking of class-specific, culture-specific, or gender-specific "norms," it may help to think of these models as familiar scripts available for performance. The meaning of the scripts varied with the context in which they were performed, and neither actors nor audience had the ultimate power to affix meaning. Illustrative of the "serious play" of cultural reference and riposte were the threats and insults exchanged between neighbors Frederick Davis and Wilhemina Prince in 1906.[71] According to Davis's witnesses, after a particularly vivid string of insults Prince declared, "Mary Jane Davis, if you think you are man enough for me I'll wait for you tomorrow along the rail line."[72] Apparently she did just that. A neighbor described how Prince stood outside Davis's doorstep at dawn "dressed in her husband's clothing, wearing his [Masonic] lodge regalia," calling, "Davis, I'm your man this morning." Knife in one hand and machete in another, she blocked Davis's passage as he tried to ride his horse along the tracks, and again on the street past the nearby church. According to Davis, "In that spot she again insulted me, saying that she would not denounce me as a damned son of a bitch before the courts, because she could settle things by herself [by fighting] and pay a fine, since her husband earned sufficient money."

Prince first assaulted Davis with the verbal aggression that was one resource within the public personae of West Indian women and then implied that femininity was weakness by calling him "Mary Jane" and announcing that she was "his man." If we analyze this as a simultaneous invocation and inversion of gender hierarchy, however, we get the gist but ruin the joke. Prince's performance must have been fierce, and fiercely funny. Her early-morning drag routine referenced multiple strategies of male status: physical violence, lodge membership, the ability to pay for the pleasure of breaking the law. In her version of events, Prince acknowledged all of this—the insults, the threats, the knife—and threw in a dash of feminine piety and domesticity as well: "I answered, 'Davis, watch what you say, your words are abusive but I will leave it in the hands of God, and the tears of your mother, your wife, and myself shall be your punishment.' He responded, 'You are no more than a filthy woman and if you keep answering back I'll smack you across the mouth until you pee,' to which I was obliged to answer, 'Very well we will settle this between ourselves tomorrow at four in the morning if you are man enough to meet me out at the rail line; I'd come after you now but I'm ironing.'"[73] Prince's detailed narration was excellent theater but lousy legal defense, and she ended up paying Davis forty-two *colones* in an out-of-court settlement.

Self-sacrifice and religious devotion were central to images of motherhood in the British Caribbean as well as Latin America, both at the turn of the century and beyond. If in theory swearing, brawling, and sexual looseness were the antithesis of this ideal, in practice poor women put the pieces of their lives together as best they could. In her autobiography O.C.C. recounts the following tale—"but this is not a joke, it's true"—from her Central Valley childhood in the 1920s.

Once an old man died who was really poor. His wife and daughter, and the daughter had two kids, [were left living] in the hut which didn't have any partitions, all together, that is, the bed the table the cooking fire practically all together.

They had a few hens a dog a pig, the widow was making some biscuits and cooking them on the *comal* [iron griddle], and the hut was all open so of course the dog the pig and the hens kept coming in. The daughter was cooking and the old lady trying to make biscuits and she was praying the Hail Mary by herself when a group of us arrived and hid while we listened: here's what she was saying.

"God hail thee Mary damn pig get out of here and full of grace fuckin' dog got in here too, the Lord is with you hell girl chase those chickens they're gonna leave me without batter, blessed art thou among all women damn these sonofabitch brats, shut up you noisy bastards—"

and so she went on praying the Hail Mary.[74]

The story of the widow's prayer, surely too good to be true, encapsulates the truth of O.C.C.'s own life as she tells it. O.C.C. had twelve children by five different men—who wooed her, in one case wed her, sometimes beat her, and often drank. Some of them left her, and others she left after one threat too many. Her fate was to suffer, but Jesus and Mary never abandoned her, and religious visions always came to guide her in her hours of need. Like the widow in the story, she knew that when life deals you blows it is best to pray, and if you live in a hut without walls, the pigs and the children get underfoot. To survive you have to be ready, like Wilhemina Prince, to give as good as you get.

The People and the State

The fundamental dynamic between state and people in these particular cases was not one of hegemonic project and popular resistance. This contrasts sharply with other scholars' recent findings. Numerous monographs have convincingly demonstrated that the extension of state authority in turn-of-the-century Latin America often came through the enforcement of gendered morality and domestic order.[75] Indeed, the Liberal state in Costa Rica was deeply concerned with the "demoralization" of the lower classes, and the rhetoric of social hygiene would eventually be called on to buttress discriminatory policies in Limón, as we shall see. But in the early decades of the century,

with the exception of the occasional half-hearted attempt to register prostitutes, neither the local nor the national government showed much interest
in moralizing Limón. From the point of view of local government, sin was
simply too profitable: liquor license sales were the single largest source of
municipal funds during the years in question, and much of the port economy
depended on the provision of entertainment and comfort to visitors passing
through.[76] And while the national government was certainly concerned with
forging a virtuous and healthy population, Limón's manifold marginality—
its blackness, its domination by a foreign company, its transient population—
militated against an activist approach by the state.

State agents did not become involved in the personal disputes recorded in
insults accusations as part of a program of social control. They became involved because participants demanded it. After all, relationships with bosses
or officials were not the only unequal power relationships in most people's
lives, and they certainly were not always the ones that grated the worst. The
cases we have seen document struggles between neighbors and business associates, lovers and kin. The government did not break down doors to get into
these people's private lives. Rather, these were people who dropped everything to run for the nearest policeman, or dressed up in their Sunday best to go
down to the *alcalde*'s office and lodge a complaint. The judicial apparatus and
local elites may have been oppressors, at times in very concrete ways, yet they
could also be manipulated to serve individual ends. This is the dynamic captured by Walter Gavitt Ferguson in the calypso at the beginning of this book.
The soldiers who threaten to deport the singer have been summoned by a certain woman, whose earlier threats and insults were not enough to bend the
calypsonian to her will. In the insults cases that clogged the *alcalde*'s calendar,
legal notions of honor were pulled into the service of battles for public standing in which sex was invested with myriad and contradictory meanings. State
agents appear anything but hegemonic as they earnestly transcribed Cassandra Barnes's claim that her honor was gravely injured by Mistress French's
bragging about her lover's yam.[77]

But it is also evident that the police apparatus was systematically corrupt
and abusive in Limón. Accusations of police harassment against West Indians surfaced periodically from the period of railroad construction onward
(indeed, they continue to the present).[78] In Carlos Luís Fallas's autobiographical novel *Mamita Yunai*, police agents begin fining *peones linieros* as soon as
workers have their pay in their pockets.[79] The local West Indian press published a series of complaints in 1935 about the arbitrary fines issued by a judge

in Matina, where "even commissary chips are accepted in payment." "He is said to be unnecessarily inquiring into the home disputes of the settlers in the vicinity, even when these take place without the attendant scandal, and when the people explain their unpleasantnesses, he imposes fines for which he does not give receipts."[80]

The people who used the judicial system in Limón did not feel the need to theorize the state as either a mechanism of class oppression or an accessible structure providing needed services. They knew from experience that states worked both ways at once. The dual functioning of the police apparatus is evident in published government statistics on *injurias* and *escándalo*. Both charges reflected the same kinds of boisterous verbal battles—indeed, not a few insults plaintiffs mentioned that the incidents they described had already been charged and fined as "scandal" by local police agents.[81] But at the aggregate level the trends for the two categories of misdemeanor were quite different, and this was true for both Limón and San José. In each province annual scandal prosecutions tended to echo total *delincuencia* (police cases filed per year). That is, they reflected overall police activism, official interest in popular moralization, or the desire to increase income from fines (surely these factors were not unrelated). Insults cases show an entirely separate pattern. From 1907 (the first year for which published statistics are available) to 1913, there was an average of 142 insults cases per year in Limón, in contrast to 58 per year in San José, at a time when the population of Limón was one-seventh that of the San José. From 1914 to 1926, insults prosecutions in Limón averaged only 31 per year, while those in San José remained near their former level at 53 per year.[82]

Why did insults accusations drop so steeply in Limón? The continuity in scandal prosecutions suggests that state activism, reporting trends, or abrupt changes in public deportment were not the cause. Rather, the reason must be sought in the demographic reversals the province experienced after World War I, and their social and political consequences. As we saw in Chapter 2, the years after the first banana boom brought both hardship and opportunity to West Indians in Limón. The poor and mobile simply left. The few young West Indian men remaining in Limón at the time of the 1927 census were disproportionately urban, prosperous, well educated, and likely to live in a parent's home.[83] These men would form the core of Limón's black bourgeoisie in coming decades, benefiting as United Fruit and its subsidiary Northern Railway sought to cut costs by promoting West Indians to replace midlevel North American employees, at half the salary.[84] Meanwhile, West Indians a generation older than these upright young men were following a rural road to a different prosperity. Growing bananas, cocoa, coconuts, and ground provisions, these aging squatters and smallholders cleaved to village life inland from the port or along the southern coast.

As young men left, as older men passed away, and as babies were born and raised, women formed an ever-greater portion of the local West Indian population. Yet the cash service economy in which West Indian women had worked and which had served them so well was in decline. By the 1920s and 1930s the mass of migrant workers eager to purchase their daily needs were young Hispanics laboring on plantations around Siquirres, Guápiles, and La Estrella, far distant from the port. The women who provided for them, as meal-sellers, laundresses, *compañeras*, or wives, were Costa Ricans arriving from the highlands and beyond. The economic fortunes of West Indian men young and old were rising, and one imagines that women within their households also benefited. But sources of independent income for black women were shrinking. The urban female population whose facety street culture had fueled hundreds of insults suits was increasingly marginal to the regional economy, and increasingly under attack.

Race and the Emerging Politics of Respectability in Limón

Many of those attacks came from within the West Indian community. The critics were the self-styled "select crowd of intellectuals of Limon," or the "decent ones," as opposed to the "inferior class" or "lower orders." These professionals, business owners, privileged UFCO employees, and planters were all too aware of their tenuous position as "law-abiding sojourners" in an ever more hostile land.[85] The political equation of exports, labor, and race changed radically in Costa Rica in the 1920s and 1930s. With economic opportunity scarce in the highlands, Limón's marginality came to seem less an excuse for inaction than a call to arms. More Costa Ricans were in the region demanding state intervention, and they were heard by an increasingly interventionist state. "National" planters' and "national" workers' groups each urged the government to pressure United Fruit on their behalf, and each used the rhetoric of race and hygiene to bolster their claims.[86] By 1927 the Economic Society of Friends of the Nation, a group that combined highland intellectuals and large private planters frustrated by United Fruit's purchasing monopoly, could refer almost in passing to the new conventional wisdom: "Let us not neglect to

West Indian church congregation, Limón, ca. 1924. Plate 604,
"Going home from church," Box 76, Recreation (Welfare, Schools),
United Fruit Company Collection, Baker Library, Harvard Business School.

mention at least the matters relative to the purely racial question of that immigration the Company principally stimulates: black immigration, which, as
is known, has a higher predisposition to diseases like tuberculosis, leprosy,
syphilis, and madness."[87]

With the economic crisis of the 1930s, and in the context of the upward
mobility of some sectors of the West Indian populace, certain Costa Rican
workers began to define their material interests in racial terms. One petition against West Indian employment that was circulated in 1933 had been
signed by 543 people by the time it was sent to Congress. The authors spoke
of sexual honor as the index of racial virtue and domestic order as proof of
national entitlement. "It is not possible to get along with [the blacks], because their bad morals don't permit it: for them the family does not exist,
nor does female honor, and for this reason they live in an overcrowding and
promiscuity that is dangerous for our homes, founded in accordance with the
precepts of religion and the good morals of the Costa Ricans."[88] Anti-black

feeling was the lowest common denominator of elite and worker opposition to United Fruit Company policies. When the UFCO contract was renegotiated in 1934, in the wake of a failed strike headed by Hispanic workers, the government's only nod to workers' demands was the companion law prohibiting employment of "colored" labor on the Pacific coast plantations.[89] Race-based immigration restrictions were progressively tightened, and government pressure was brought to bear on United Fruit to increase the percentage of Costa Ricans in midlevel positions. As Hispanics entered these jobs they claimed a position equal to white North Americans in the semiformal racial hierarchy of the zone. Meanwhile, light-skinned West Indian elites found themselves less white and more black than ever before.[90]

In these same years racial segregation was introduced in sites of entertainment and sociability such as swimming pools and cinemas. Skin color became the measure of health and worth in a way it had never been before. An article in the *Atlantic Voice* in 1935 noted that "the city fathers . . . have just got alive to the necessity of segregating the 'sheep from the goats' in that it is just realized that our coloured citizens will not be permitted to frequent the City Bath in association with the tourists from both the Exterior and the Interior; therefore the Piuta Bath is also to be fixed so that they, as well as the women of dubious characters, may have their baths there instead of at that in the City."[91] Reader response in the following edition underlined the weight of the insult. "We all know what is meant by the use of the term 'dubious character,' hence, regardless of their moral or social standing, our coloured ladies and gentlemen are all regarded as vagabonds."[92]

The pages of the *Searchlight* and the *Atlantic Voice* pay witness to the fervent promotion of respectability as an antidote to the racist policies justified by the discourse of social hygiene. Community leaders did their best to eradicate Pocomia, revivalism, and other worship forms with African associations.[93] Their reasoning was explicit in the diatribe against "Nine Night Practices" (traditional wakes) published in the *Searchlight* in 1929. "If the lower class of coloured people would just begin to get away from their lower natures and think, they would see that this scandal is not indulged in by any other race. . . . So we write this with the hope that the better informed coloured people will discountenance this practice and advice their less informed friends how hideous this thing appears in the sight of other peoples."[94] The goal was respect for the colored race, the means were education and decorum, and the implicit gaze was white. Yet the external racism that provoked leaders to demonize the lower classes' "lower nature" also prompted a new formulation of race-based solidarity. The *Searchlight* called in 1930 for donations to establish a reform school for West Indian boys and girls, reminding readers that "every waif on the street that incriminates himself by indecent conduct" reflects badly on "Negro blood." "It is a fact that some men do not like to consider themselves coloured, but the fact remains that they are, and it is no fault of their own, but this should not prevent him from endeavoring by any means possible to uplift those below him so as to help them to be above reproach."[95]

In the context of local West Indian leaders' promotion of the politics of respectability, the aggressive public presence that had long been one component of Afro-Caribbean womanhood in Limón came under attack. The editors of the *Searchlight* wrote in 1930:

> From Pacuarito a correspondent writes calling the attention of the police to a band of loose, common young girls who patrol the railway lines from Siquirres to that place throwing out the vilest expressions in the presence of the police as well as the respectable women of the vicinity and continually fighting amongst themselves; the Police does not understand the Filthy language that emanates from these lawless groups of peddlers and hawkers, and so they spit out these vile utterances to jeer the folks that they know abhor them.
>
> These things in human form should not be let loose by the Hygiene officers to inoculate the youngsters of the villages along the lines, a Police man should be engaged who knows English and be able to prosecute these hawks.[96]

Rejecting a racial ideology that compared "our Coloured ladies and gentlemen" to prostitutes, the editors adopted a rhetoric of class that drew the same comparison.

Similar complaints denounced "the daily and nightly assembly of children of tender years, especially boys, at our street corners, the railway station, when the trains are departing and arriving, and other open spaces, playing, quarreling, fighting, and using the most filthy language, that shocks one's sense of decency."[97] The correspondents seemed to suggest that such "things in human form" were a recent plague, and surely it is true that the economic straits of the mid-1930s multiplied the number of young people living off the informal economy of the streets: peddling, shoe-shining, handling luggage with or without its owners' permission. But it was the concerted effort to stigmatize such behavior rather than the behavior itself that was truly new. Like the "scandalous" prostitutes of San José a generation earlier, these young *afrolimonenses* rejected the decorum dictated by a social hierarchy that refused to make room for them. They claimed public space with the same concerted rudeness that had long been the province of market women and lawless urchins, gray-haired matrons and civic leaders alike in Port Limón.[98]

Street comportment and sexual morality were repeatedly linked. For several months in 1931, the *Searchlight*'s weekly column "Philomela's Serious Talk with Girls" instructed readers in the necessary elements of female public decorum.

> For the little time that I have been up here in San José, I have noticed that there exists here a higher social environment than in Limón. The coloured girls feel themselves more important, thus they live up to a higher life. They adopt the social life around them, they are more colour conscious, more intelligent, more refined than their sister in Limón. A girl that is reared in San Jose, moves in a higher social circle than one who is reared in Limón, irrespective of her colour. And why? Because she embraces every opportunity that affords her, she lives the descent life that is around her, her deportment in the streets will have to be in conformity with the customs of San Jose, and more over, she doesn't want her white sisters to say, "Que negrita mas ordinaria."[99]
>
> But our sister in Limón is something of the Pharisee type, she sings and makes a devil of a noise in church. She and her companions walk the streets in groups, and never a one to tell the other her actions are rotter. Little and big, young and old carry on their illicit love affairs without tact and without reasons, such a love affair that seldom leads to the STATE OF MATRIMONY, but very often leads to shame and disgrace [100]

Consistently, the remedy the *Searchlight* and *Atlantic Voice* promoted for female slackness was female education. In 1930 the *Searchlight* lauded the formation of the Young Women Standard Club, whose "aims and objects" were "to promote a higher standard of Social life among the Young Women of Limon . . . through exchanges of opinions in progressive ideas with a view of subduing the darker passions." The editors called for community support so "that the Club may be a means of reclaiming those who might have erred, and strengthening the determination of the steadfast, so as to better fit them for the higher calling of companionship and comradeship for which they are intended."[101] The Young Women formed both a basketball team and lecture society, and on the second anniversary of the club's founding the *Searchlight*'s correspondent enthused, "I have begged the privilege to sing their praise publicly, so that those people scattered over Costa Rica may feel that Limon has intelligent Negro girls."[102]

An article entitled "Immorality among Our Girls" insisted that the parents of wayward young women had only themselves to blame. "I remember having heard [one father] and some of his friends stating that it is folly to educate girl children. The money he had to waste on them would serve him better to give him a drink of rum." Nothing could be more misguided, the article claimed. Irresponsible sexuality had both economic and social roots and could be remedied through education. "Can we not realize the social outlook of our young women? Well no less than one hundred are in 'Embarrassed conditions' which is the more serious in consequence of the 'Conceptions.' We see them running Pell Mell into the Jaws of danger due possibly to our Financial Crisis but due primarily to lack of training."[103] The editors insisted the following week, "The world knows full well what happens to girls who are permitted to run like wild animals on the streets night and day, and the sooner parents are admonished to try to put an end to these careers by education . . . the better for us all." The authors again denounced "the stupidity of some parents in thinking it is a waste of money to educate their girls so as to create *self respect* in their ideas of life."[104]

When West Indian leaders insisted that education and deportment rather than color or origin were the measure of human worth, they were playing to their community's strengths—and choosing a standard by which "Our Girls" especially could shine. West Indians, both young and old, were better educated than their Hispanic peers in Limón. Within each group older women had less formal education than men of their own age. Yet across the board, among Hispanics and West Indians alike, girls and young women were better educated than boys and young men. They were more likely to be enrolled in school, were more likely to be literate, and reported higher levels of educational attainment. Only 73 percent of young white men in Limón (ages fifteen to twenty-nine) could read and write in 1927, compared to 83 percent of young white women and 86 percent of young black men. The highest literacy of any cohort in the province was that of young black women, 98 percent of whom could read, and 90 percent of whom could both read and write.[105]

The denunciations of female sexual looseness and male rowdiness that characterized elite rhetoric in 1930s Limón bring us full circle, back to the origins of the literature on family in the Caribbean that began this chapter. The crisis in commodity prices that raised tensions in Limón in these years was regional in scope. Unemployment soared in the British Caribbean and was made worse by the simultaneous decline in migration opportunities and the drying up of remittances from abroad. The years 1935 and 1936 saw strikes and rioting in Trinidad, St. Lucia, St. Kitts, and British Guiana, and 1938 witnessed the worst labor violence in Jamaica in sixty years. The report of the Moyne Commission, appointed in the aftermath to examine the causes of the British colonies' plight, launched half a century of scholarship on family and values in the Caribbean. The root causes of West Indian social ills were economic, insisted commission members. "[P]overty, uncertainty and casualisation" had begotten "improvidence, theft . . . , promiscuity, inefficiency." The tragic "lack of family life" was no more than could be expected of "a people whose immature minds too often are ruled by their adult bodies."[106]

As we have seen, similar diagnoses were tendered by West Indian leaders in Limón in the same years. The images of the dominant black woman and the shiftless black man, so central to European and North American scholarship on the Caribbean from the 1930s on, were not simply mirages of a racist colonial gaze. These images were *pathologized* by West Indian elites, who attempted to negotiate a particular moment in the history of Atlantic racism by insisting that lower-class practices were the result of social sickness rather than "Negro nature." For the community leaders writing in Port Limón such internal criticism was not racist but rather the best available defense against racism, fully compatible with support for Marcus Garvey, denunciations of local "Jim Crowism," and boycotts of Italian businesses in the wake of Mussolini's invasion of Ethiopia. The politics of respectability was also a politics of "self respect."

West Indian elites' heartfelt embrace of the doctrine of education and civility, coupled with the ongoing exodus of those men and women least committed to social mobility within Costa Rica, would profoundly affect the ideological tenor of the West Indian community that remained in Limón. Public memory and written histories would enshrine the white dresses and lodge meetings, the quadrille dances and Universal Negro Improvement Association chapters, and erase the stories of facety public women like Martha Darling or shoeshine boys whose language could make a sailor blush.[107] Meanwhile, Costa Rican political rhetoric has carried on the tradition established by nineteenth-century Liberal historians who tied national identity to a particular domestic order.[108] *Tica* female modesty and *tico* male restraint have been counterposed to the supposed domestic disorder of Jamaican and Nicaraguan migrants. This has given anti-immigrant sentiment the seal of moral complacency and provided a comfortable explanation for the enduring poverty of regions with large immigrant populations, especially Limón and Guanacaste. It has also put the weight of national pride behind a particular and restrictive definition of female decorum.

I do not mean to claim greater authenticity for slackness than for civility. When Maud MacPherson bragged to Amelia Esquivel that she was legally married and was dirty from caring for her husband and legitimate child—in contrast to Esquivel, who was dirty from loose living—she was asserting her personal virtue through one of the multiple codes available to working-class women. She was no more a dupe of bourgeois femininity than Eduardo Beeche was exposing his internalization of working-class masculinity when he smacked Lucas Alvarado with his cane. Cassandra Maxwell *de* Barnes, clutching her marriage certificate, and Mistress French, waving her impressive yam, each claimed respect through established rituals that tied sex to standing. A generation later the young women who played basketball to subdue their darker passions, and the lawless peddlers and hawkers who jeered respectable women they knew abhorred them, did likewise.

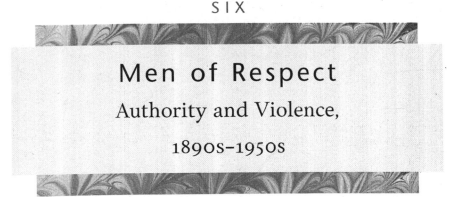

Men of Respect
Authority and Violence,
1890s–1950s

A.H.Ch. left San Rafael de Heredia to seek work in Limón in 1935, when he was seventeen years old. Four decades later he would recall:

> I met a worker there, called Manuel M., a man who when he wasn't liquored up was a good friend, but when he drank a few *cachirucasos* as he called them, the devil got into him and he got like a beast who only wanted to see blood, I saw him on a *finca* called El Bosque whack the head off one man with a single *machetazo* [machete blow], and when he got drunk he would come to the barracks saying boys tonight no one sleeps here and we'd all have to find somewhere else to spend the night; one payday he got drunk and that one day he cut seven people and when the police came from Matina together with some from Limón he left running, but shooting off bullets at the guards, until he fell into a ditch with water and they grabbed him and tied him up and carried him off to [Port] Limón.[1]

Payday on Camp Andromeda in the 1920s was little different, according to Carlos Luís Fallas's *Mamita Yunai*. "Hey, you, think you're rawhide? Here's the tallow that'll soften you up!" When drunken taunts gave way to fists, police intervened, blackjacks in hand. The men "curl[ed] like worms at each blow."

"Wha' dogs dem assholes is!" exclaimed old Jerez, who had come out to watch the scene, referring to the police.

"Yeah," I said. "And those two, their pay won't even cover the fine. The *agente* will stick them for at least a hundred pesos each."[2]

Challenges, machete duels, police abuse, bloodshed, violent and premature death—these are the sinews of the stories that Costa Ricans tell today about the *zona bananera*. "They'd cut your throat for a buck in those camps," I was once told, by a friend of a nephew of an old *zonero*. "The whole night you had to lie on your side, narrow as you could, so that if someone stuck a knife through the gaps in the boards on either side of your cot they couldn't get you in the ribs."

In the pages that follow I argue that threats and accusations of violence were an integral part of claims to authority in Limón on every level, from public politics to plantation production to domestic life. Violence between line-men was the stuff of legend; violence between those who gave orders and those who received them was endemic in the early export economy. Accusations of violence were central to ideas about racial and national character that were forged and remolded along banana walks and in backland villages.[3] But the unmarked victims of the Caribbean coast were women, Hispanic and West Indian alike, who were murdered in unequaled numbers by lovers and former lovers during the very years in which they could claim the greatest economic autonomy, at the height of the first banana boom.

Stories to Frighten Children: The Making of Race in Limón

State racism in the 1930s was a sharp departure from the glowing image of West Indian workers put forth by officials during the first banana boom. In 1891 Governor Balvanero Vargas boasted that the public order was never disturbed in his territory because the "foreign element . . . in the majority here" was "blindly respectful of the law and the authorities."[4] Two decades later Governor Gerardo Lara praised "the Jamaican masses [of Limón], whose race is distinguished by its good customs and hard-working habits, and especially by its natural spirit of subordination and respect for authority."[5] The praise was disingenuous, however. The governors were defending themselves (and the plantation system) against accusations that the immigrant workforce threatened the public order.[6]

Even as officials lauded West Indian subordination as a racial character-istic, individual West Indians defied authorities in the name of racial pride. When the police commander attempted to handcuff Alexander Moodie in the Limón jail in 1897, "he refused, saying that a white man could never dominate a Jamaican Negro." Handcuffed by force, Moodie refused to walk. "I ordered him to go along with the policeman," reported the commander. " 'Like this I'm not going,' he answered. I told him not to resist because it'd go worse on him and we'd have to take him in some other fashion; he answered: That I [the commander] could go ahead and do as I liked, because I was no more than a son of a bitch, *sinvergüenza*, idiot, filthy pig, that what I was trying to do was to harass honorable Jamaicans, and that my day would come."[7] Moodie's combination of individual pathology (he had pummeled a fellow worker to death on Zent plantation) and racially coded defiance of authority was per-fectly calibrated to elicit the most racist version of the judicial doctrine of social hygiene in response. In his sentencing recommendation the *agente fiscal* (state's attorney) wrote, "The fierce rage of the assassin reveals an inhuman cruelty, the savage ferocity of the African. In cases like the present in spite of our lovely modern theories about the inviolability of human life, one feels a great lack, one longs for the death penalty, because such human beasts must be eliminated."[8] When black men rejected public authority in terms of racial allegiance, Costa Rican officials were quick to follow suit: to discover that African savagery justified an expanded role for violence in the exercise of state power.

If there was a gulf between Costa Rican officials' public rhetoric and their private concerns about the character of West Indian workers, the same could not be said of their views of Nicaraguan migrants. Internal correspondence and published statements alike concurred that these were *pendencieros* and *bochincheros*—disruptive, violent troublemakers. The number of Nicaraguan workers in a given locale figured prominently in police requests for extra man-power and expanded budgets in the years between 1906 and 1909, and when civil war across the border reduced arrivals in 1910, the circuit doctor for Siquirres wrote archly in his annual report that "the reduction of criminal acts over the past six months is a clear fact; due undoubtedly to the absence from this coast of certain members of a certain nationality I'll refrain from mentioning."[9] When a knife to the chest ended a gambling dispute on a camp near Guápiles in 1902, the *agente fiscal* crowed that at least "Manuel Ramírez (*nicaragüense*) [who] committed the crime of homicide against the person of Carlos Torres (*costarricense*)" had not managed "to escape the arm of justice as

Workers loading *abacá* onto tram cars, Monte Verde plantation, Siquirres, 1945.
"Field loading of tram cars, Mt Verde 1945," Box 61, Abaca Album 1, United Fruit
Company Collection, Baker Library, Harvard Business School.

so often do those men who under the sole name of *huleros nicaragüenses* [Nica-
raguan rubber-tappers] commit every class of iniquity within our borders."[10]

The violent character of Nicaraguan men was not just a convenient official
slander, though it served state interests well. It was an article of faith among
peones and planters, critics and champions alike, at the turn of the century
and in subsequent generations. An elderly West Indian informant told anthro-
pologist Philippe Bourgois, "The Nicas are a barbarous people, you understand. They chop up one another for joke, man. Right beside me in Talamanca
[in 1921] over a gambling table a Nicaraguan man get his machete and him
go wham whaps, and you see the man's body just do that way and drop. Him
dead."[11] Those who felt more kinship with Hispanic Nicaraguans agreed with
the substance of the account. E.N.B., a self-described *negro crusado* (mixed-
heritage black), was born in Bluefields in 1923 and recruited for work on the
rubber camps in his teens. "When I got there I felt humiliated because there
were approximately two thousand whites and the only Negro among all those
chontaleños was me and since people said they were evil, that in a blink of an
eye they'd chop off your head, I was terrified; it's true that those rubber-men
and rice-men never let loose their knives and revolvers and switchblades, but

for me things changed; from the littlest to the biggest they liked me and they gave me the nickname *Motito* [little foundling]."[12]

A similar character was attributed to *guanacastecos* (men from the northwest Costa Rican province of Guanacaste), for in ethnic stereotypes the border between Nicaragua and Guanacaste was permeable, as it was in migrants' lives. M.G.L., born in Rivas, Nicaragua, met up with a man from Alajuela while looking for work near Siquirres in 1949. When asked, M.G.L. said he was from Puntarenas (the Costa Rican Pacific port where his father and stepbrothers lived). "He told me I'll travel with you, because we all know that *puntarenenses* are true Costa Ricans and where I've been there were only *nicas* and *guanacastecos* and I don't partner up with those folks; I told him don't be afraid of them, those men are like fire if you touch them you get burned, if we don't touch them they'll do nothing to us."[13] At a Saturday night dance at the commissary in La Estrella in 1913, Honduran Salvador Pastora began taunting guitar player Miguel Osés and pulled a knife when Osés answered his insults in kind. Osés's *compañeros* recalled, "We warned Osés to defend himself and he said, 'Don't worry, I'm *guanacasteco*,' to which Pastora replied putting his knife up to the other's chest 'You'd get the best of a *tico* but not an *hondureño*.'"[14] As his words suggest, Honduran migrants were similarly renowned for defending personal and national honor with fists and blades. A.H.Ch. described the United Fruit *abacá* plantation in Sixaola during World War II: "Even though people were afraid of the island [penitentiary] of Coiba, they killed each other like savage animals, there was a feud back then between the *nicas* and the *catrachos* [Hondurans], so on paydays when they came up against each other in the *cantinas* or the dances, the fight would start and someone would end up dead."[15]

Unlike any other ethnic group in Limón, the indigenous inhabitants of Talamanca seem to have been systematically targeted for violence: by state agents, company officials, and private adventurers alike. But the role of violence in the incorporation of Talamanca into the national polity and export economy has been obscured by the rhetoric of protective paternalism that accompanied it. Governor Balvanero Vargas wrote in 1890, "I believe it will take a long time to change the way of life of the *naturales* of Talamanca, since of course that cannot be achieved by the use of force. The schools which the Government has established seem to me the most powerful lever we have to achieve that end."[16] In practice, though, the civilizing project was predicated on the use of force—as Vargas himself revealed on the following page. "If among civilized peoples there's a real desire among both individuals and the collective for

Indigenous women and children, Talamanca, ca. 1900.
Colección fotográfica, 10250, Museo Nacional, San José, Costa Rica.

children to attend educational establishments, unfortunately in Talamanca quite the opposite occurs. Parents don't follow any orders to make their children present themselves in school, on the contrary they advise them and hide them so they won't be found. So it was that due to this difficulty, the political authorities have used the only expeditious means that was left to them, that is, taking the little *indiecitos* by force; several of those who today can be seen docile and obedient in the school, were chased down with lassos and even with dogs, as might be done with the insane [*a semejanza de los irracionales*]."[17] As in the case of Alexander Moodie above, racial savagery might demand violence in defense of civilization. Bribris' resistance to imposed institutions shaped state agents' perception of their racial nature: "With respect to the character of the *naturales* I must say that they are lazy, ungrateful, and indolent," wrote Vargas. At the same time, it was the perception of their racial and cultural difference—their *semejanza a los irracionales*, their similarity to the inhuman or the insane—that served to justify the violence through which civilization was imposed.[18]

Across Limón, perceptions of difference changed and hardened with the demographic and economic shifts of the 1920s and 1930s. An elderly West Indian woman described for Trevor Purcell her recollection of the itinerant Hispanic workers who seemed to flood Limón. "Dey looks to me like dey were barbarians, like dey would kill an' eat people. . . . Dese people were illiterate an' ignorant an' we was always afraid of dem. If you going along de street an' you see dem, you walk on de other side. Dey always carry dere cutlass wid dem."[19] As hard years came in the 1930s, as accusations of black degeneracy filled the speeches of congressional deputies and the pages of highland newspapers, as West Indian leaders preached racial uplift by vilifying poverty, ignorance, and dirt, the stories that people in Limón told about each other got uglier and uglier. Paul Rodman, whose father grew bananas on land rented from the United Fruit Company in Sixaola, lived on Finca Margarita as a child in the 1930s. Forty years later he recalled, "Our parents put the fear into us to keep us from going in to the *paña* [Hispanic] sectors on paydays which is when the *paña* drank, because those *pañaman* would machete dogs, cats, hens, or any damn thing that moved. That was true. But I don't remember that they ever hurt any children, though we sure were terrified I can tell you."[20]

In the same era *los negros de Limón* joined "El Coco" and other bogeymen used to scare highland children into good behavior. Bloodcurdling accounts of "Cocomia" worship by West Indians in Limón appeared in San José newspapers in September 1936, describing "diabolical" rites and hinting at human sacrifice. The sect had been banned in Cuba, authors claimed, after ritual murders of kidnapped children came to light.[21] Pocomia had indeed swelled in popularity in Limón in the 1930s, although the article's accuracy ended there. A variety of Jamaican revivalism, Pocomia drew on Christian and Afro-Jamaican traditions alike. Worshipers sought spirit possession and spoke in tongues.[22] The large, loud congregations drew the wrath of West Indian leaders bent on communal respectability, and they called on Costa Rican authorities to intervene. A prominent preacher and several followers were deported to Jamaica, and many more were detained or harassed.[23] Three decades later E.Z.S. arrived in Port Limón, fleeing with her five youngest children from a miserable marriage in Turrialba. The first night she and her children huddled sobbing on the floor of her brother's house, because "it was so hot and they were afraid of the Negroes."

I also had a horror of them. I was remembering what my "tatica" as we called my grandfather had told me when I was a child [ca. 1940] he told me that in Limón there was a Negro religion called KOKOMIA and that they ate people especially children, they lived in the caves of Portete in Limón. That one day a little white boy was going "llevo llevo" [offering to carry luggage] and he said to a Negro woman who was getting down from the train that he would carry her bag the Negro woman said yes, he took it to the caves and she made him go in and once he was deep in the cave the boy saw with horror that they had a boy of his age, hanging with his head downward and a bowl collecting the blood which their Chief was drinking; their Chief was dressed like the devil with horns and a tail (how awful) and all of this was recounted later by the young boy who managed to escape running from the cave while a legion of Negroes chased after him.[24]

Terrified by her grandfather's tale, E.Z.S. refused to step outside her brother's door. The blood libel that a combination of national politics and West Indian class cleavages had pushed into the headlines in the 1930s was guiding Hispanic migrants' perception of the worst possibilities of black nature a generation later.

Violence, Labor Relations, and Public Authority in Early Limón

Novels and memoirs claim that insults, threats, and blows were an integral part of work relations in the early-twentieth-century banana zone. Scores of judicial cases confirm it. The reckoning of money owed for work completed was often the proximate cause of conflict. In January 1899 Rosendo Sánchez complained about ten pesos missing from payment due him and his crew, deducted for provisions they had not purchased. Plantation overseer Francisco Obando confronted Sánchez as he left with his men empty-handed. A witness heard Obando tell an assistant, "Take charge of the plantation because I'm going to kill that prick." He fired four bullets at Sánchez, fled, and was never captured.[25] Sometimes bosses killed; sometimes they were killed themselves. Ramón Quesada refused to come to terms with Hilario Ramírez over money the latter claimed was missing from his two-weeks' pay for work on Quesada's farm. "Despite the fact that I explained to him that the accounting was quite correct he said to me in a rude manner that we'd settle that later in a different way," Quesada recalled. Hours later Ramírez stepped from a thicket,

Workers and boss on hand trolley, Río Bananito, ca. 1900. Fotografías 3195,
Archivo Nacional de Costa Rica, San José, Costa Rica; originally published in
Próspero Calderón, *Vistas de Costa Rica* (1901)

shot Quesada with his shotgun, and disappeared. Quesada died from fever
and infection several days later.[26]

U.S. citizen Charles Thurgood was a *segundo mandador* for United Fruit, an
overseer on the Estrella Valley railroad extension in 1915. When Thurgood
got into a fistfight with a Spanish worker, Jamaican mechanic James Haverhill stepped in to break it up. In doing so Haverhill claimed a tutelary role
that Thurgood was not willing to let stand. As he passed Haverhill's work site
the next day, Thurgood ordered Haverhill to come forward. When Haverhill
ignored him, Thurgood called him a son-of-a-bitch and slapped him across
the face; in response, Haverhill punched Thurgood once in the ribs. Thurgood
died the next day. Company higher-ups threw their support behind Haverhill,
and the local judge ruled that the Jamaican had acted in legitimate self-defense

given the magnitude of the provocation.[27] No boss could believe himself beyond reach. German-born Juan Stolzmann was hacked to death in his bed in
1904, on the United Fruit plantation in Siquirres where he was head overseer. Investigators never discovered why Stolzmann was killed, or if they did,
they never put it in writing. Several Jamaican workers were questioned under
suspicion but no arrest was ever made.[28]

The picture that emerges is of labor relations pervasively exploitative and
violent. Yet the threats and bloodshed reflected neither a coercive project
from above nor a revolutionary wave from below. Bosses did not employ violence instrumentally, to oblige men to labor against their will: workingmen
were too mobile and, in this early period, too much in demand for the plantation system to rest on coercion. Nor did workers employ violence instrumentally, in the hope that shooting their boss would get them the pay they were
owed. Rather, bloodshed between bosses and workers was part of a spectrum
of masculine confrontation through which power relations were tested, ad-
justed, and confirmed. The ad hoc structure of labor contracting and the lack
of effective institutions on which either workers or employers could depend
to do the dirty work of enforcement meant that there were no established
answers to the question of how far workers could be pushed or what sort of
justice they could demand. With the class structure barely institutionalized,
bosses and workers alike continually tested as individuals (or as they would
have said, *como hombres*) the power differential that divided them.

Public officials staked their claims to authority through the selfsame repertoire of manly challenge.[29] In a letter to his superiors in 1907, the Matina police
agent warned that the Estrada police agent had insulted him behind his back
for all to hear, "so if we ever come to argue face to face I will be forced to wring
his neck, which would be a real scandal seeing as I am myself an authority." [30]
Two years later different men assigned to the same posts ended up in a public
duel. Estrada police chief Miguel Arias reported that when he issued instructions to Matina policeman Vicente Solís, Solís "replied that I [Arias] couldn't
order him around, because he reported to the Matina police chief. So I told
him *que no se comprometiera* [not to place himself in a compromising situation; not to make confrontation inevitable] . . . in response he took two steps
back and shot me three times with his revolver, the last thing I could have
expected." But in fact the conflict had followed a perfectly predictable path,
from insults and challenges repeated secondhand, to direct confrontation, to
bloodshed. Arias said Solís "bore me ill will due to political differences," and
that a week before, in a bar in Estrada, Solís had told others "that I was not

a man and that I should face up to him with revolver in hand and he didn't mind killing anyone."[31]

Given the violence endemic to workplace hierarchy and public authority in early Limón, collective labor actions themselves were remarkably peaceful. Governor Ricardo Mora described one strike in 1905: "The Negroes so far have made no hostile gestures, they simply have agreed amongst themselves to return to their homes and refuse to work until their salary is raised."[32] As plantation abandonment devastated Main Line communities after 1908, waves of labor unrest swept central Limón. A unionization campaign by the Society of Artisans and Laborers in 1910 led to widespread dismissals, a general strike in response, and company recruitment of 700 strikebreakers from St. Kitts who soon joined the strike themselves. Workers attacked the UFCO commissary with stones and sticks; Costa Rican police and troops fired into the crowd, killing one of their own and injuring a striker.[33] The British consul's mediation brought the strike to a close, though sporadic work actions continued over the next two years.[34] By comparison, strikes in Bocas del Toro were markedly more violent, with multiple deaths at the hands of police on almost every occasion.[35]

Several thousand banana workers went on strike in Limón in 1934, with organizational assistance from Carlos Luís Fallas, Manuel Mora, Jaime Cerdas, and other members of Costa Rica's Communist Party. The great majority of strikers were recent arrivals from San José, Cartago, Guanacaste, and Nicaragua. Few West Indians joined them. Not only had the absolute number of West Indian plantation laborers fallen drastically by this time, but the median age of those black men still laboring as *peones bananeros* was well over forty, while most of their Hispanic counterparts were in their mid-to-late twenties.[36] In the strike's first month violence was largely limited to machete attacks on bananas set out by the line for transport. Strikers reached an agreement with the Costa Rican government and private planters in August 1934, which United Fruit promptly disregarded. The strike resumed, this time met by mass arrests. Scores of Nicaraguans were deported.[37]

Nevertheless, compared to contemporary movements elsewhere in Central America, the *huelga de brazos caídos* (literally, strike with arms held downward) in Costa Rica's *zona bananera* was remarkably free of violence on both sides. Historian Victor Hugo Acuña Ortega attributes this to "the guidance of the Communist Party, the clear-thinking and discipline of the strikers, and a certain prudence exercised by President Ricardo Jiménez."[38] It can also be seen as part of an established pattern in central Limón, where strikes had ranged from orderly to tumultuous but rarely brought fatalities. The same ethics that shaped deadly violence on the plantations—confrontational masculinity and the demand for just recompense—undergirded labor movements in Limón. Yet structured collective actions were among the more peaceful labor negotiations in the zone. It was when the terms of employment were up for debate between two men, one of them claiming formal authority, one claiming back wages or respect due, that things turned ugly. When they did, those who could claim to be defending property and hierarchy usually got the benefit of the doubt from judicial officials. But the involvement of public authorities in the endemic violence of early Limón went further. Sometimes officials turned a blind eye to abuses, sometimes they committed abuses themselves, and sometimes they abused each other. Rather than onlookers to the ongoing struggle to define authority and demand respect through challenges and *machetazos*, lawmen in early Limón were part of the fray.

Violence in Women's Lives

The violence that went into the making of race and class in Limón has lived on in heroic tales, festering resentments, and lingering suspicions. When we traced the lives of women in prostitution we encountered another variety of deadly violence in the banana zone: working women killed by their lovers or former lovers. Yet there is no "Ballad of Raquel Montezuma" sung today, no facety heroine to take her place beside outlaw Joe Gordon in Limón's pantheon of sacrificed rebels.[39] How common was violence against women in Limón? Did its frequency change over time, or vary between groups? Official records of most kinds of violence are plagued by multiple biases that make answering such questions nearly impossible. Relatively few reported cases of assault involved female victims, and even fewer involved injuries to women by male partners.[40] Yet descriptions of *mala vida* (ongoing violence from husbands or lovers) come up frequently in other contexts. Arrests for assault between men were plentiful, but their incidence seems to have reflected police revenue-gathering as much anything else.[41] Homicide investigations, in contrast, are relatively free of reporting biases. Public officials were quite diligent about initiating investigations into death by violence. Rumors in Talamanca in 1897 that Jhon Garty had died of a shotgun blast rather than a snake bite led to the exhumation of his decayed body months after the fact. Queries from an old friend into the circumstances of sometimes-prostitute Eva Barrantes's death on an isolated plantation launched a homicide investigation as well.[42] Authorities were far less diligent about seeing cases through to a legally proper conclusion. It was not uncommon for investigations to stall in the Limón courts a decade or more, and then be filed away with the legend *extinguido responsabilidad penal* (statute of limitations expired).

Because violent deaths were appalling and rare they occasioned judicial inquiry whether the parties were women or men, *indio* or black or white, and this makes them a good source for comparing patterns in violence across groups and over time. But their very extremity makes them a dubious basis for analyzing gender relations in general. Conjugal negotiations recorded by homicide cases are by definition atypical, for they ended in murder when most did not. Close attention to participants' own evaluations may suggest how recorded dynamics fit into broader expectations. How did men who killed women justify their actions, and what did others make of their explanations? Which words or deeds did neighbors find remarkable between a man and a woman, and which seemed commonplace? In general, in discussing turn-of-the-century homicide cases I limit myself to analyzing the internal dynamics and relative incidence of deadly violence. In examining violence at midcentury, though, I present autobiographical sources alongside judicial testimony in order to ask how conjugal politics as depicted in murder cases compared to conjugal politics more broadly. The narrators are self-selected storytellers, but there is no prima facie reason to think these men and women were more or less violent or more or less victimized than the population as a whole. The stories they chose to tell have a great deal to say about men's and women's divergent perceptions of loyalty, authority, and the uses of violence in private life.

The basic picture is clear. When women were scarcest in Limón, during the years of mass migration and economic expansion that accompanied the first banana boom, they were most likely to be the targets of deadly violence. Only one homicide victim in ten was a woman in San José at the turn of the century or in Limón itself two generations later. But in turn-of-the-century Limón nearly one-fourth of murdered corpses bore a woman's face. Most had been killed by former lovers, a few by current ones. The frequency of uxoricide in Limón was not the ultimate expression of women's daily subjugation to male authority. Quite the contrary—the women of early Limón were unusually outspoken, well connected, and well paid.[43] Those among them who had grown up in patriarchal households had left them far behind. They made the most of extensive opportunities for independent earning. They were integrated into supportive networks of neighbors, *compañeras*, and kin. In spite of this—or because of it—men who claimed to love them killed them in unparalleled numbers. Men's rate of death by homicide in early Limón—36 per 100,000 men—was elevated but not anomalous: slightly higher than that of Puntarenas, slightly lower than that of Guanacaste. Women's rate of death by homicide in Limón—20 per 100,000 women—was truly extraordinary by both national and international standards.[44]

Patterns in Deadly Violence in Turn-of-the-Century Limón

During the years of the first banana boom West Indian men were less likely to be accused of homicide than their predominance within the population would suggest, and Nicaraguan and Costa Rican men more so. West Indian women were less likely to be homicide victims than their weight within the population would suggest, and other women slightly more so.[45] West Indians made up two-thirds of the male population but only one-quarter of male homicide victims. This is largely because they were less likely than Hispanics to kill each other. In fifteen cases a West Indian man stood accused of killing another West Indian; in thirteen cases West Indian men were accused of killing North American, European, Chinese, or Costa Rican men in a robbery or dispute.[46] In contrast, when Hispanics stood accused of killing other men the victims were almost invariably other Hispanics, killed in the course of duels, feuds, and labor disputes (thirty-one cases).[47] While the incidence of different types of deadly violence varied between groups, the dynamics that led to such violence did not. West Indian men were not quick to kill each other, but when they did so the preceding crescendo of public accusations, injured honor, and fatal challenge was the same as it was in the knife duels between Central American *peones*.[48]

Migrants from the anglophone Caribbean brought with them a cultural repertoire of confrontational manly display both similar to and different from that of Hispanic migrants. Richard D. E. Burton has synthesized ethnographers' descriptions of the social world of rum shop, street corner, and beach, where liming men seem "perpetually poised on the brink of explosion as ego grates against ego and the potlatch of boast and counterboast, insult and retort, mounts to a threshold beyond which violence must surely erupt."[49] While it sometimes does erupt, most often it does not. The dynamic is echoed by Carlos Luís Fallas's account of black *peones* playing dominoes on Camp Andromeda:

> And each time a marker slammed down, an exclamation of joy, surprise, or anger:
> *Jesus Christ!!*
> *Son of a bitch!!*
> And they argued yelling horribly and gesticulating like devils; anyone would have thought that they were about to kill each other. A moment later you would hear their thunderous laughter two miles away.[50]

It is the awareness of self-parody, the possibility of falling back into laughter, that one finds more often in descriptions of conflict between West Indian men in Limón and almost never in accounts of conflict between Hispanics. Confrontations between Hispanic laborers crossed the point of no return earlier and more often. This is captured in the term *comprometerse*. The verb could mean either to commit oneself, to place oneself in jeopardy, or to compromise one's reputation, and as used between men on the brink of violence it meant all these things at once. When Matina policeman Vicente Solís told Estrada police chief Miguel Arias not to order him around, Arias responded "que no se comprometiera," warning Solís not to challenge his authority in such a way as to make escalation unavoidable. But Solís was already committed, and compromised: his response to Arias's reassertion of authority was to fire three bullets into Arias's chest.[51]

Among West Indians and Hispanics alike, jealousy over a particular woman was rarely a motive for deadly violence between men (it was mentioned in only eight of seventy-eight cases). In no cases were injuries to a woman's virtue or her family's honor claimed as provocation, and in only one case did a male kinsman—a grandson—intervene to protect a woman from attack.[52] In the deadly dramas of male standing captured by homicide cases, honor and revenge had little to do with sexual rights in particular women. The mirror image of this was that deadly violence against women was rarely a response to betrayal with a particular male rival, real or imagined. It was rather the last resort of a man whose woman left him against his will.

The accused parties in cases with female victims were all men: two-fifths of them Jamaicans, one-fifth Costa Ricans, one-fifth other Latin Americans. Each one of them had been the lover or husband of the woman killed.[53] In fifteen of the cases the victim had ended the relationship against the man's wishes. In another four she was attempting or threatening to do so. The accused invariably admitted the killing, often in tones of righteous indignation. "Do you know why you are here?" the judge routinely asked the accused when calling him to view the cadaver or make his first sworn declaration. "Because I shot a woman called Annie Elizabeth Carlisle, but she's the one to blame because she provoked me to do it," declared Jamaican Gerald Adams. He had killed his former lover in front of their two children, aged four and six, when she came to him to plead for money to feed them.[54] "Yes, I know her: this is the corpse of Jacinta Anguillén and she herself is to blame for what happened to her," said Colombian José de la Cruz after stabbing his former lover three times in the belly.[55]

In one-third of the cases witnesses recalled ongoing, low-level violence against the woman within the relationship. But in only one case did a woman die from yet another beating that simply went too far.[56] Usually the man's turn to deadly violence was a calculated break from what had gone before, a decision to act on threats that the woman had so far ignored. "I loved that woman so much that so as not to see her in the arms of another I would kill her as many times as she came back to life if such a thing were possible," sobbed twenty-two-year-old Rafael Puertas over the body of María Josefa Mora.[57] "I told her that was fine; that she would never live with another man, nor I with another woman, that I would show her that I would never belong to another woman," recalled thirty-one-year-old Isaac Moore, explaining why he had been obliged to shoot sixteen-year-old Albertina Charles as well as her mother, who had counseled her to leave him.[58]

In seven cases the spurned lover killed himself immediately afterward, and again these cases were split between West Indians and Hispanics. Joseph Andrews and Emma Lightly had lived in a consensual union in Port Limón for more than a year by August 1906 and planned to marry the next month. Both were Jamaican, both around forty years old. They had gone so far as to print up invitations, but Emma warned Joseph that if he did not stop his weekend binges the church wedding was off. Joseph threatened to kill her and himself as well, and bought a revolver, which Emma managed to hide while he was drinking. He demanded it back the next morning, and she returned it. "'Come sit here next to me,' he told me, but I said I was going to mass, so he lifted the gun and shot me twice and then himself." Joseph died instantly, but Emma survived, with a scar on her face and a bullet between her third and fourth vertebrae that left her paralyzed for life.[59]

Church-going Emma Lightly was at the opposite end of the spectrum of working-class respectability from nineteen-year-old prostitute María Pérez, who lived in a back room behind a port *cantina* with her seventeen-year-old *querido* Humberto Ríos in 1911. When Humberto slapped María in the face and drunkenly tried to cut her throat with a knife, slicing his finger instead, María was so incensed she called the girls from neighboring rooms to see the blood in her washbasin. A few hours later María heard her *compañera* Delfina arguing with a drunken North American client, trying to get him to hand over his gun "before an all-too-easy misfortune occurred." "You distract him," María told Delfina, and as Delfina caressed the American, María slipped the revolver from him. She ran through the *cantina* showing it off and entered her room laughing and calling "Take it, take it" as she held the gun out to Humberto. "'Ol rait' para vos [All right for you]," he said as he took the gun and shot her, first in the chest and again in the back as she turned to run, igniting her dress. He then placed the gun against his right temple and fired, while María clung to her *compañeras* outside. "Delfina, Delfina," Delfina remembered her crying. "Ay, Hortensia, I'm on fire," Hortensia recalled.[60]

The Judicial Politics of Jealousy

New or suspected male lovers were assaulted alongside women in only two cases. In another three cases accused men described a betrayal with a particular man, or their former lovers' taunting references to a particular replacement, as a motive for the killing. James King sought his former lover Vivian Black out at the home of her best friend, Etta Harris. He found her cooking. "I said 'for three weeks now you haven't cooked for me, and now that you're cooking I'm going to bring you something to cook for me'; she answered 'I don't cook for you, just for another man I have who can break your ass'; this exact comment exasperated me and without time to think I raised my revolver and shot her two or three times."[61] In their first statements accused men most often blamed meddling females (like Albertina Charles's mother or Vivian Black's friend Etta Harris) for their conjugal troubles, rather than any male rival. In some instances the accused denied outright that his woman had left him for another man. Policeman Andrés Rodríguez sought out his former *compañera* at the house where her father had lodged her after she left him. Rodríguez hoped to win her back.

[B]ut she, far from accepting my entreaties or even giving me the slightest hope, told me that she could not do as I asked, for even though she was free to live with whomever she pleased, it was not in her interest to go on as my lover and *furthermore my very presence annoyed her*; this expression produced such an effect on my emotional state that I don't know when or why, I took out my gun and fired. . . . I was out of my mind when I committed this deed, and I am sure that if anyone had been there to criticize me or make me think I would have stopped, for as is clear I had no motives beforehand; in fact, if I had had any object with me, like a switch, and hadn't been in my police uniform [with gun holster], maybe when she began to express her disdain I could have punished her with it and not waited for the fatal phrase which led me to the outcome I regret. . . .

It's true that some people have tried to make me jealous over *la señora* Victoria, with gossip typical of human lowness, telling me that she accepted courtship from others; but they could never give a specific name and I didn't believe them due to my conviction in her honor, in which I believed and believe.[62]

Rodríguez had declined legal representation when he wrote this declaration, which may explain the candor with which he pinpointed what was at stake: not sexual honor, whether hers or his, but authority, his over her. In contrast, the foremost obligation of defense attorneys in cases where women were killed was to mold the accused's initial explanation—"If I can't have her no one will," or variations on this theme—into a narrative more compatible with the statutory definition of justifiable homicide: "She betrayed me with another and I couldn't help myself." Article 10 of Chapter 2 of the 1880 Penal Code declared exempt of criminal responsibility

9th He who acts while overwhelmed by an irresistible force or impelled by an unconquerable fear. . . .

14th The husband who in the act of discovering his wife *infraganti* in the crime of adultery, kills, injures, or mistreats her and her accomplice; as long as the bad conduct of her husband in the fulfillment of his matrimonial obligations has not made her error excusable.[63]

The following chapter specified extenuating circumstances if an act was committed

6th in direct vindication [*en vindicación próxima*] of a grave offense to the author, spouse, etc.

7th while acting under very powerful stimuli.[64]

From these legal precepts, and from fragments of testimony that they embroidered, or fabricated themselves, defense attorneys wove tales in which the irresistible force of jealousy drove innocent and upright men to commit tragic yet unavoidable acts.[65]

Lawyer José Arístides Méndez was hired to defend José de la Cruz in 1900 after de la Cruz threw Jacinta Anguillén from the porch of her Port Limón home and stabbed her to death on the ground. Jamaican fisherman Alpheus Scott, who ate his meals in Jacinta's home, told police, "I understand that [de la Cruz] lived with Jacinta Anguillén a while ago, but that she had separated from him to live with another who I believe is named Antonio," and added, "I know that for days now that José has been coming to bother and threaten Jacinta, telling her that if she wouldn't live with him again he was going to kill her, but she didn't want to have any more to do with him."[66] José de la Cruz told a convoluted story involving Jacinta's mother and accusations of theft but made it quite plain that Jacinta had been "living with" a certain Antonio, although residing in her own home, for some time. Simply ignoring this, lawyer Méndez claimed that de la Cruz had "discovered" Antonio "in the home where [de la Cruz] kept *la* Anguillén . . . seducing her [*conqui standola*]." The lawyer's story of clandestine betrayal and anguished discovery directly contradicted all testimony so far, including the defendant's. However, as a scenario of judicially excusable homicide it was, if not perfect, at least closer than de la Cruz's. Méndez's story nodded to the 14th clause, above, for it had de la Cruz acting at the moment he discovered his woman's betrayal. Yet, as she clearly had not been *in flagrante* at the time, Méndez based his defense not on the act of adultery but rather on the claim that jealousy—in such circumstances—constituted an irresistible force as defined by the 9th clause.

The lawyer called Alpheus Scott to testify "that when Jacinta Anguillén accepted Antonio Zamorano's romantic promises . . . in the presence of de la Cruz, de la Cruz became completely beside himself, he turned pale, trembling, overwhelmed to the extreme that he could not articulate a single word and full of jealousy—for he understood that an irresistible force had taken over his actions—he proceeded to commit the crime with which he is charged." Scott's response translated the lawyer's speech back into a vernacular understanding of why men did things, which diverged crucially from the legal definition of when they were justified in doing so. He agreed in part with the statement, Scott said, "for the defendant likely did act due to jealousy, and to the anger which he [Scott] could see on his face, for de la Cruz showed in that way that he did not accept *la* Anguillén's indifference and that he still loved her a lot."

Defense attorneys repeatedly put forward the amplified, composite notion of "the irresistible force of jealousy" precisely because it could incorporate the local knowledge reported by defendants and witnesses alike: that lethal jealousy was about possessive anger and spurned love, not the shock of injured honor. Judges, however, cleaved to the narrow definition of *in flagrante* adultery by a legal wife, as set out by law. When Daniel Ramos shot his *querida* Bernarda Rivera in a port brothel, the Sala de Casación confirmed the rulings of the judge and the appeals court on this point. It was clear, the magistrates wrote, that Ramos had killed Rivera out of jealousy (*por celos*) upon finding her on another man's lap. "[B]ut this is not the case of a vehement excitation like that which a husband suffers if he discovers his wife committing the crime of adultery. In that case the husband is not responsible if he kills her in the act, because she with her infidelity dishonors their home, deeply wounds her husband's heart, and gravely offends his dignity." A husband's betrayal cannot be compared with "the case of a public woman killed by one of her lovers who finds her with another, because the consequences in the two cases are not comparable." [67] In order to exalt the sexual contract between man and wife and protect the dignity conferred by legal marriage, jurists consistently refused to condone deadly violence against unmarried women.

Threat and Action

What role did threats of violence play in intimate relationships? This question became central to deliberations in the trial of Jorge Porras. Jorge shot his former lover, public woman Maurilia Vásquez Cabrera, after she not only refused his pleas to renew their relationship but taunted him, flourishing a handkerchief that she said "smells like Guevarita" (her current lover, the son of a local politician). As the investigation unfolded, Maurilia's mother, sister, brother, and cousin each came forward with a story of Jorge's repeated threats in the days before. The *agente fiscal* and the judge took the threats as evidence of premeditation, which the judge treated as an aggravating circumstance in sentencing. In a personal appeal before the court Jorge insisted that he had acted spontaneously in reaction to Maurilia's insults. Her sister and mother must be lying, he argued, for if he had really said what they reported, "they should have denounced me to some authority beforehand, knowing I was preparing such a crime."[68]

Rejecting this logic, the magistrates of the appeals court ruled that the testimony regarding prior threats was credible. Nevertheless, those threats could not be considered evidence of premeditation "because it turns out that what the accused was trying to do was to renew his relationship with the victim, going so far as to use threats as a means to achieve that, for which reason if he had achieved what he wanted, the tragic end which occurred would have been avoided."[69] The logic is similar to that which Andrés Rodríguez followed when arguing in his own defense that if only he had had a switch in hand with which to punish Victoria Barquero when she began insulting him, he could have forced her to stop and the tragic conclusion—his killing her—could have been avoided. This line of argument did not make deadly violence against defiant women excusable: Jorge Porras was sentenced to nine years on San Lucas, Andrés Rodríguez to ten. But it did imply that threats and low-level violence were legitimate means men might use to reassert their authority, maintain their dignity, or get what they wanted.

And when women remained defiant, or worse still, laughed, a few men—the ones who ended up on trial for homicide—made good on their threats. The multiple cases in which women were killed with a pistol they had previously taken away from their killer to prevent just such an occurrence suggests that they knew the risk they faced was a real one.[70] After all, they saw around them a world in which conjugal conflict could and did end in deadly violence. Maurilia Vásquez Cabrera was in the room next door when her beloved *compañera* Bernarda Rivera was shot and killed by Daniel Ramos in 1912. One month and four days later Maurilia herself was shot to death a few blocks away by her own former lover Jorge Porras.[71] Hiding your lover's gun might help temporarily, at least until he could pressure or sweet-talk you into giving it back. A nearby policeman might help this time, though maybe not the next.[72] Doing as you were told might help too—staying with him, not talking back, not going back to your mother, not finding a new man. There is no way to measure how many women took the path of obedience or opted for the "sinuous strategies" of the structurally weak.[73] Judicial cases in general, and homicide cases in particular, index conflict, not compliance.

Here, I believe, lies the explanation of the elevated frequency of deadly violence against women in early Limón. Historian Barbara Fields has written,

"The rule of any group, the power of any state, rests on force in the final analysis. Anyone who gives the least thought to the matter reaches that conclusion, and thinkers as different in other respects as Weber, Marx, Machiavelli and Madison would have no trouble agreeing on that. Rule always rests on force in the last analysis. But a ruling group or a state that must rely on force in the first analysis as well is one living in a state of siege, rebellion, war or revolution."[74] In early Limón, where a woman on her own could earn a decent living and where new suitors were standing in line, individual men's authority within intimate relationships depended on force in something closer to the first analysis. If Jorge Porras could have won Maurilia Vásquez back through threats and pleas, he would have. But she had a new lover and a tight family circle who backed her up, and she was in a strong enough position to laugh at what he offered. Victoria Barquero thought Andrés Rodriguez an inadequate partner who did not provide for her as he should. Her father agreed, and an older female acquaintance provided her a place to stay. If Rodríguez had had a switch, he said—if he had had another means of pressure short of deadly violence—he would surely have used it, and she might have complied. Instead she was, as she told Rodríguez, *free to live with whomever she pleased.* Rather than accept the affront of female autonomy, Rodriguez, like a score of his peers from Jamaica, Costa Rica, Colombia, and beyond, preferred to kill the woman he said he loved.

Deadly Violence in Midcentury Limón

The years after United Fruit stopped exporting Gros Michel bananas from Limón were marked by a series of short-lived booms that drew itinerant laborers to the rubber camps, *abacá* fields, and cacao groves of Limón. Many moved on when markets worsened and payrolls were cut. Others stayed to claim a piece of land, building a *rancho* of palm leaves, then a wooden shack if they could, a *compañero* or a *compañera* by their side, and perhaps children as the years wore on. By midcentury the sex ratio in Limón was far closer to the national average, although still top-heavy with aging men. The Hispanic population of Limón had more than doubled over the course of the previous generation, while the total West Indian population had fallen by one-quarter. By 1950 there were nearly twice as many "whites or mestizos" as blacks in the province.[75] Per capita homicides in Limón continued to be higher than the national average, although the rate had declined over the intervening years.[76]

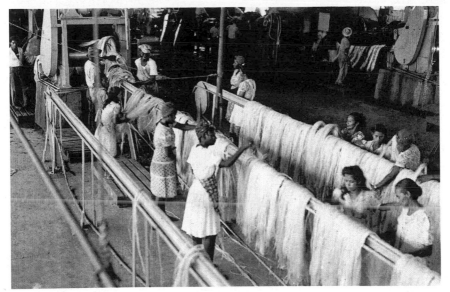

Women hanking and grading *abacá* fiber in United Fruit Company plant at Monte Verde, 1945. "Stripped fiber transferred from delivery end of decortixator machines to hanking and grading rope conveyors," Box 61, Abaca Album 1, United Fruit Company Collection, Baker Library, Harvard Business School.

Both this and the ethnic breakdown of homicide cases fit with the general hypothesis that an outsize number of young men in a community makes deadly violence most likely.[77] The black sex ratio was more balanced, and blacks—women and men alike—were at slightly lower risk of deadly violence. The white sex ratio was less balanced, and whites—women and men alike—were at slightly greater risk of deadly violence.[78] Most strikingly, by midcentury women's proportional risk of homicide was far smaller than it had been two generations earlier. At the turn of the century male victims had outnumbered female by nearly four to one; at midcentury male victims outnumbered female by more than nine to one.[79]

By the 1940s and 1950s deadly violence across class lines had nearly disappeared.[80] In early Limón masculine confrontation often pitted contractor against *peón* or foreman against laborer. By midcentury, labor relations were no less exploitative but were far more stable. Bosses no longer had to prove themselves with their fists. When laborers placed their honor on the line and defended it with a bullet or a blade, the victims were workingmen just like themselves. Robbery, land title feuds, and sexual rivalry each accounted for a handful of cases, but by far the most common pattern was the familiar spiraling path of insult, blows, and deadly retaliation.[81] Mario Madrigal, originally of Panama, and Encarnación Rivera, born in Chontales, Nicaragua, were drinking together in the Hone Creek commissary in 1937. Madrigal asked Rivera to stand him a drink, and when Rivera refused, Madrigal called him *pendejo* and *maricón* (asshole and faggot). When Rivera still ignored him, Madrigal took out his machete and swung at him. Rivera pulled his knife and cut Madrigal on the arm; Madrigal died three weeks later when the wound turned septic.[82]

In 1948 Elí Pérez, of Alajuela, and his neighbor Ramón Ortega, of Nicaragua, were drinking together in the commissary at Bananito. Pérez was looking for a fight, witnesses later reported, but Ortega kept trying to defuse the situation, even handing his machete over to Pérez to prove he wanted no quarrel. But after they walked back to the camp Pérez planted himself in front of the room where Ortega and his wife lived, calling "come out, *maricón*, you're no more than a son of a bitch." As the judge later summed up, "[T]hey began, as drunks do, to taunt and challenge each other as men [*a cuestionar y desafiarse, como hombres*]." When Pérez stepped up to the door, Ortega shot him in the chest.[83] On 24 December 1957, Rafaela Sánchez recalled, Miguel Vega barged into a gathering at her home, "carrying a machete, saying that he was a man and that he'd go at it with machetes with anyone who dared." Vega and Rafaela's husband, Juan Hernández, were both wounded in the ensuing brawl. Five months later Vega came upon Juan Hernández and his two daughters crossing a cocoa grove. The men quarreled, and Vega shot Hernández in the back.[84] West Indian men, as before, were less likely than Hispanics to kill or be killed in the course of a machete duel or brawl.[85] In several cases West Indian men were charged with killing Hispanic men who had first taunted, then assaulted them. Generally the courts judged the accused to have acted in self-defense. In part due to this pattern, the conviction rate for West Indian accused men (46 percent) was notably lower than that for Hispanic accused men (78 percent). Judicial rulings seem to have served as a counterweight to local black-baiting.

Turn-of-the-century homicide cases portrayed a world in which lines of state authority were barely formalized, frequently challenged, and not always enforceable. By midcentury this was no longer the case. No longer did *agentes de policía* fight duels over jurisdictional disputes. Political violence in early Limón had looked something like jousting between peers. Political violence at midcentury looked quite different. One of the few cases that can be classed as such was a suit brought by the families of six prisoners jailed in Port Limón during the 1948 civil war as *vanguardistas* or *calderonistas*—supporters of Dr.

Rafael Angel Calderón Guardia and his allies from the Partido Vanguardia Popular, the Costa Rican Communist Party. On 19 December 1948, eight months after the armed conflict ended with their party's defeat, the prisoners were placed aboard a special train bound for San José. At a spot near Siquirres known as *el Codo del Diablo*, the six men were taken from the train and executed by machine gun while handcuffed.[86]

Evolving Perceptions of Male Right and Female Betrayal

The paradox of midcentury homicide cases is that while the proportion of female victims was markedly reduced from that of the earlier period, if anything the claims to male authority evinced by case testimony are more absolute, and the means by which accused men seem to have thought themselves entitled to discipline their women more violent. Midcentury cases are evenly split between those in which a man killed his former lover for not wanting to return to him and those in which a man killed his *compañera* for answering back. Federico Obando and Marta Araya had lived together in Puerto Viejo for three years before he beat her to death on the way back from a dance. Federico claimed to have been too drunk to remember anything, but he also testified that as they walked home that night "she smelled of liquor and since I had absolutely forbidden her to drink, this bothered me and that was why I got angry and hit her."[87] Later he learned that it had been his own father who had served her wine at the dance. "Let me clarify that Marta is to blame for all of this, for if she had been more frank and had told me that Papa was the one who gave her the wine to drink, nothing would have happened, but when she refused to tell me I became suspicious and proceeded to do what I did." According to Marta, interviewed shortly before her death, his last words to her were "Today is the day I kill you, whoring slut, you think you can play with me?"[88]

In turn-of-the-century cases, killers' first statements rarely mentioned sexual betrayal, although it was basic to judicial wrangling over culpability. But in later decades female betrayal, its prevention, and its revenge became central to the stories men told about gender and justice.[89] This was true of men who killed, as recorded by homicide testimony, and it was true of men who did not, as recorded by scores of manuscript autobiographies. "Autobiografías campesinas" written in the 1970s about events in the 1920s, 1930s, 1940s, and 1950s evince a fundamental divergence in male and female perception. Male authors insisted that women betrayed them with other men: out of "fragility," lack of appropriate male discipline, or greed. Women insisted that they stood by their men as long as they could and left only after their partners' drinking, cruelty, or inability to provide for their children left them no other choice. Sometimes women moved into a new partnership immediately. Just as often they made their way alone or with the help of friends or kin.

Men's autobiographies suggest that although the violence with which Federico attacked Marta was extreme, it stood at one end of a spectrum of justifiable male responses to perceived female betrayal. This comes forth clearly in the life story of M.F.A., born in Escazú (San José) in 1919. M.F.A. recounts a series of betrayals to which he responded according to two sometimes contradictory principles: the need to defend his dignity as a man and the will to show mercy toward those under his authority, especially children. Around 1947 M.F.A. was living with a *compañera* in Guácimo. "We soon separated but I still loved her and one day she tried to make fun of me at a dance at the Jiménez dancehall, so I got so angry for the way she was laughing at me that I tried to go after her with a machete to teach her that *con los hombres no se juega*—you don't play with men."[90] Several years later another *compañera* betrayed M.F.A. with his male work companion, who was living with the couple on an isolated homestead. His *compañero* accepted the blame and told M.F.A. to send him away instead of the woman. M.F.A. agreed: "I'm going to pardon her this once. Because after all poor little child [referring to the woman's toddler daughter by a previous partner]. She's not to blame for what us old folks do. And so it was, from then onwards the woman behaved herself."[91] They were together for eight years until another *compañero* "betrayed me with my *compañera*" and told him about it. This time when she begged for forgiveness he refused. "I gave her some money and she left."[92]

Eventually M.F.A. married a woman who bore him four children and then left home with another man. When M.F.A. tried through the local *agente de policía* to oblige her to "come see her children," she responded "that it was up to me to find where to stick myself and my children [*que viera a ver donde me metía con mis hijos*]." This public insult was too much. M.F.A. left his children at his in-laws' house, saying "Emilse laughed at me but it's going to go badly for her, because when I got married I told her that she should never try to play me for a fool because it would go badly for her."[93] He found Emilse in a field watching her new man work and hid himself along the path. As they passed, embracing, he fired a single bullet that wounded them both. M.F.A. spent three months in jail pending sentencing. Finally he was called before the judge. "He said to me, what was Emilse M. to you, I said she was my wife where were you married In the church at Siquirres and how long have you been married I answered seven years and eight months. I see. I am going to send for your marriage certificate and if this is true you'll be a free man tomorrow."[94]

M.F.A. recounts the judge's words as ringing vindication of the righteousness of his act. But violent revenge was not the only respectable response to finding your woman with another man. J.V.O.G.'s wife's long trips to Matina made him suspect infidelity, so he strapped on his machete, fed their children dinner, and went out to look for her. His worst suspicions were confirmed when he saw her walking home in the embrace of another man. But at that moment, thinking of his mother and of the children he would leave orphaned, he decided to forbear action. He moved out of the house the next morning. In the following days J.V.O.G. concluded that his drinking had been partly to blame, as well as the fact that he had let his wife travel to Zent alone to collect money farm workers owed them for meals. "Some woman will read this and say that wasn't why it happened, but the truth is that even if the woman is proper, even if she is honorable, she should avoid or at least not get thrown together too much with *los hombres solos*."[95]

Women's moral fragility could place their men in situations where deadly violence was the obligatory response. "That woman is going to compromise you [*Esa mujer te va a comprometer*]," one *compañero* warned another.[96] A judicious man should avoid trouble by restraining his wife's movements, as J.V.O.G. concluded, or by appropriate physical discipline. J.V.O.G. wrote of another *compañera*, "The fragile woman I had brought here with me some time ago, I'd had to beat so she would leave me [after she spent the night in town with another man]. I didn't hit her for what she did I did it because otherwise they wouldn't have left."[97] Hitting a woman was neither always right nor always wrong. When M.G.L. saw a man beating a woman on the streets of Puerto Cortés around 1950 he intervened. "[I]t made me angry and I said don't be a faggot hit a man instead."[98] Earlier in his autobiography M.G.L. described stepping in to stop a man from beating his wife on a farm in Nicaragua around 1940. The man begged M.G.L. not to tell the overseer. "He told me it was because he had found her on D.T.'s lap and I said you're in the right but if I didn't stop you you were going to hit me too, the boss won't find out from me but I warn you if you want to beat her do it far away because the Boss doesn't want women here because of such scandals."[99]

To judge by court testimony and women's and men's autobiographies, sometimes men who claimed to have incontrovertible evidence of their woman's infidelity were deluding themselves, sometimes they were attempting to delude others, and sometimes they were quite correct. Surely some women took lovers behind their man's back. But the consistent discrepancies between men's and women's accounts of conjugal practice suggest fundamentally divergent perceptions of just when a relationship ended: when the woman announced she was leaving or when the man accepted it. "I came here to make a *finca* for myself with a *compañera* I lived marital with her 11 years she betrayed me with a *peón*," wrote I.P.R.; he said later, of the same event, "She turned whore [*Se iso pta*]."[100] O.C.C. wrote, "My current husband almost killed me from jealousy and not [that I had done anything] because I was always faithful when I was governed by a husband [*sugeta al marido*], when I was alone I let myself loose but that doesn't weigh on me because the two *rebuscas* [children from unintended pregnancies] I got myself in Limón are very good children to me."[101] No woman described herself as having been unfaithful to a husband or partner, although many described having left a man against his will and found another. From the scores of tales of female betrayal and mockery, written by men, and the dozens of tales of men whose jealousy and improvidence forced their families to leave, written by women, the inescapable conclusion is that all are describing a single pattern from opposite points of view.

Confrontational Masculinity and Class Consciousness

An acute awareness of just where they stood in the structure of power and plenty drives the tales that aging *zoneros* chose to tell about themselves. In several narratives a childhood anecdote crystallizes both the author's dawning sense of self and his recognition of the poverty and powerlessness that had already shaped him. At age twelve A.H.Ch. worked long hours hauling coffee on his father's uncle's farm. "I asked him uncle why don't you buy a pair of oxen and he answered no boy don't you know that as long as we have poor people we have no need of oxen?"[102] When M.G.L. was five his mother was a servant on a plantation in Rivas, and he watched the planting and harvest of broad beans called *chonetes*. "I didn't have a *chonete* nor did I know that you could buy with money." So when he found a ten-dollar and a five-dollar coin in his older sister's room he ran to plant them. "When Virginia that was my sister's name couldn't find the coins she asked me and I said yes, that I had planted them. Where? she said. I took her to the spot where in addition to watering them I had put a stake. She dug down took out the coins and said this is metal it doesn't grow you get it working and when you work we'll live better because we're very poor."[103]

Among poor rural men the transition from childhood to manhood was marked by the entry into full wage-earner status. Author after author described the day he first proved himself worthy of a *jornal completo*, a full day's wage, or as F.R.S. put it, "the wage of a man now up to his work [*el jornal de un hombre lla en todo oficio*]."[104] At the age of fifteen R.J.G. sought a new *patrón*, no longer wishing to work on the Turrialba plantation where his father collected a partial wage for the work his son did by his side. In his first week he surprised all by earning the "complete salary." "You have walked with [kept up with] the *peones* and I can't rob you," said his employer *don* Rosendo—words R.J.G. swore he would never forget.[105] Plantation labor was often organized in such a way that such comparisons were unavoidable. The task was defined as a set length of rows to be cleared, weeded, or pruned, and laborers worked their way across the field in parallel. Laggards were all too obvious, as when wasps attacked young Chonsito M.J. on his first morning of work in the cocoa fields of Limón among *hombres muy campeones*—"men who were real champs." "There I was crying and the *chaperos* [weeders] were coming back, I had 100 meters to go to get to where they were working their way back from." After long days of the same humiliation Chonsito's pride was unmatched on "the day that I could stay even with the *peones*."[106]

The work challenges fostered by this arrangement surely benefited employers, but they were also part of a confrontational male culture that could drive collective action and demands for the bosses' respect. Itinerant workers in Limón knew hard labor as both the confirmation of a man's worth and the index of his oppression. "[T]he worker who never gets paid for the sweat with which he irrigates the ground every day, with skill and heart," wrote J.V.O.G.—"Those are really the men of valor [*Esos sí son hombres de valía*]."[107] "I'm a hard-working man," J.A.B.B. bragged to his interviewer. "I'm a rough-hewn man, understand me. . . . Now I have six animals I've bought with my sweat. I don't owe my presence here to any bank, what I have is mine."[108] C.Q.D.H.D. described working for a North American company as an *hulero* during World War II, tapping rubber for sale to the U.S. Army. "The work was rough and risky, we used to say it was work for '*machos y muy machos*.'"[109] The subversive humor comes from a pun on two meanings of the word "macho" in Costa Rica. The bosses might be *machos* because they were blond and light-

The "riveting gang" from United Fruit's Pacific coast port, Golfito, 1941.
"Golfito Pier: The riveting gang. 2/18/41," Box 19, Golfito, United Fruit Company
Collection, Baker Library, Harvard Business School.

skinned, with all the privilege their origin implied, but the workers were *muy
machos* because they were true males—and did the work to prove it.[110]

Of the rural highlands during the first half of the twentieth century Lowell
Gudmundson has written, "Paternalism, patriarchy, and familial honor, tied
to an inherently ambiguous class structure, made it extremely difficult for
those less favored by coffee culture to articulate an ideology of class antago-
nism and exploitation of their own."[111] This was not the problem in Limón.
Here notions of male honor were perfectly consistent with class consciousness, its articulation, and its sometimes violent expression. Among West Indians in turn-of-the-century Limón, reference to the rights of "honorable Jamaicans" could justify violence against white authority or explain the formation
of labor unions to defend the dignity of working men.[112] In the same years a
young Jamaican named Marcus Garvey was employed on the lines as a time-
keeper for the Northern Railway. In later years Garvey made manly racial
pride the basis of his Universal Negro Improvement Association's international appeal. A membership card issued in Bocas del Toro in the 1920s declared the organization to be "striving for the FREEDOM, MANHOOD, and

NATIONALISM of the Negro."[113] In Jamaica in the early 1930s three Central American returnees each began preaching the cult of Ras Tafari among men of the urban poor, including thousands of laborers recently arrived from Cuba. Rejection of public authority, identification with Africa, and the affirmation of male supremacy would become the entwined tenets of Rasta pride.[114]

Combative rituals of male work and leisure undergirded fierce solidarity among Hispanic *peones bananeros*. Itinerant laborers' shared identity provided the basis for mobilization in the 1934 strike, and their habits of mutual support sustained them through the unpredictable and localized cycles of export prosperity that followed. When José Figueres pulled together disgruntled employers and a handful of highland farmers to overthrow the Calderón-Communist coalition in 1948, the ragtag national army did little to defend the regime. But Carlos Luís Fallas recruited a *columna liniera* (line-men's battalion) on the banana plantations of the Pacific coast. In four days' fighting more than half the *columna* was killed or wounded. Only 40 of the 140 *linieros* had carried weapons, Fallas told reporters at the time. The others had marched into battle "prepared to fight with the rifle of any *compañero* who fell, or to arm themselves by seizing the enemy's guns."[115] Three weeks later coalition leaders capitulated to Figueres on the condition that he uphold the Garantías Sociales, the pro-labor legislation so recently won.[116]

An accurate and expansive perception of social injustice drove migrant workers' definition of masculine valor. But their vision of the exigencies of manhood was costly. Male solidarity was of a piece with machete duels that cut lives short, with drinking binges that left families penniless and babies without food. The same men who were fiercely faithful *compañeros* to their male companions could be cruelly irresponsible *compañeros* to their wives and lovers. The particular understanding of masculine pride that line-men brought to Limón, and goaded each other to prove again and again once there, drove a wedge between laboring men and the women who could have been their best allies in their struggle to grab something lasting from a world that had given them too little: to stake a claim, build a farm, and educate their children; to die knowing they had been someone.

Conclusion

What you see depends on where you stand. Seen from San José, West Indian arrivals to Costa Rican shores seemed creatures of the United Fruit Company, imported Jamaicans employed at the will of the bosses. But seen from the British West Indies, Costa Rica was simply one destination among many in an era in which every household seemed to have someone "gone to foreign." From the point of view of government negotiators, dealing with foreign monopoly capital was drastically different from dealing with other owners or employers. But from the point of view of those who worked in or around the export economy this was not necessarily the case. While critics and boosters alike have emphasized the coordinated functioning of United Fruit's vast empire in green and gold, for those whose labor sustained it the internal divisions within that empire were deeply significant.

Some years back I telephoned an elderly Afro–Costa Rican and asked to interview him about the importance of family ties among migrants to the banana zone. His voice became icy. "Apparently you have been misinformed. Many people see a black man and assume bananas are all he knows. I never worked in the banana zone: I worked for the Northern Railway, twenty-seven years. I won't be able to help you." His reaction pounded home a distinction I had somehow never grasped. *La zona bananera* was not synonymous with the export economy. It referred specifically to the banana *plantations*: a world of sweating gangs of single men, overcrowded barracks, and aggressive UFCO overseers. Since the 1920s, and all the more so since banana exports resumed in 1960, the *zona bananera* has been the province of Nicaraguan and Costa Rican newcomers, the least educated and least advantaged of Limón's labor force.[1] In contrast, railroad employees had steady work, stable pay, homes in town, and a chance at promotion. By associating my would-be informant with the banana zone I had badly mistaken his class position and perhaps questioned his moral standing. I had also echoed the racist stereotypes that have helped highland Costa Ricans misread the socioeconomic structure of Limón for the past three generations.

The Northern Railway was until 1972 a wholly owned subsidiary of United Fruit. This did not mean that tending a locomotive was the same thing as hauling bananas. As we have seen, Limón's agroexport economy included dock work, railroad employment, independent cultivation, fieldwork on established plantations, and felling forests on the agricultural frontier. The experience of each of these occupations differed, not because certain workers misunderstood their class position, but because the structural conditions that shaped employment in each of these arenas were objectively distinct. Furthermore, the organization of production varied markedly for each of the crops exported from Limón: Gros Michel bananas, cocoa, manila hemp, and, after 1960, Cavendish bananas. Across the seven decades we have surveyed, many of the men who cultivated export crops were not employed by United Fruit, and many of the men employed by United Fruit were not banana workers. During the first banana boom, from the 1880s through World War I, non-UFCO plantations produced from one half to three-fifths of bananas exported from Limón. The great majority of workers on United Fruit's farms, railroads, and docks were West Indians, while Hispanic migrants predominated on non-UFCO farms. Some of their wages circled back to Boston through purchases at company commissaries. But everywhere except the most remote and recently established plantations, export workers were surrounded by independent entrepreneurs—mostly women—selling cures for what ailed them, be it homesickness or hunger, fleas, grime, or desire.

The second banana boom began in 1920 and peaked in less than a decade. United Fruit's own plantations provided three-fifths of exports during the first few years but less than a quarter by 1929.[2] About three-fourths of banana plantation workers were Hispanic newcomers, as young West Indian men left Limón for greener pastures elsewhere, Cuba in particular. One-fifth of West Indian men worked on or around the railroads and docks, a like number labored on cocoa plantations, one-sixth were banana laborers, and one-ninth were own-account farmers. Women arriving from the Central Valley and points north provided meals and comfort for the new plantation workforce, while multigenerational families took up ever more of West Indian women's time. The 1930s hit hard across the board. Banana plantations shut down and cocoa prices dipped so low that United Fruit left ripe pods to rot in the fields. Many Hispanic workers followed United Fruit to new banana plantations on the Pacific coast and in Panama. West Indian families, prohibited by law from doing the same, got by on food they could grow, remittances from abroad, and urban improvisation. In 1940 United Fruit revived plantation production in Limón, growing first manila hemp under contract to the U.S. Army and then cocoa as prices soared after World War II. Women and children joined the export economy as field workers for the first time on United Fruit cocoa farms. West Indian smallholders along the southern coast prospered as multiple exporters competed to buy their beans. Meanwhile, increasing numbers of Hispanic migrants, once and future plantation workers, cleared homesteads to the north and west of the reborn plantation zone.

The Transnational Enterprise

Scholars have long emphasized the mobility of capital in the early-twentieth-century Caribbean: the fruit companies' voracious appetite for new lands, the rails pried up and reinstalled elsewhere in a matter of months. But the mobility of capital was matched by the extraordinary mobility of workers within the same system, an aspect of the story invisible in macrolevel statistics but unmistakable in microlevel sources. In the Western Caribbean, infrastructure built to facilitate agricultural exports linked population centers as well. Fruit company steamers circulated between Kingston, Port Antonio, Colón, Bocas del Toro, Limón, and Santiago de Cuba. Workers purchased passage for a few days' wages or chose among countless smaller craft making the same rounds. Within Costa Rica railroads filled the same role, connecting the highland cities of San José, Cartago, Heredia, and Alajuela to Port Limón on the Caribbean and Puntarenas on the Pacific. Sooner or later, most of the men we have met in these pages worked for United Fruit or one of its subsidiaries. It might have been in Cuba, Guatemala, Costa Rica, Panama, or Colombia; behind a desk, on the docks, along the rails, or in the fields; handling sugarcane, cocoa, *abacá*, or bananas. The time they spent in UFCO employ was almost invariably sandwiched between stretches spent with other employers or farming claims of their own. The women we have met were slightly less mobile.

Most worked in four or five places in one or two countries over the course of their lives, their labor structured by a great variety of kin forms as well as by cash and noncash exchange.

The variety of routes that brought men and women from St. James, San José, and Masaya to Limón, Bocas del Toro, and Puerto Barrios, the diversity of employment within the export economy, and the frequency with which workers moved from one role to the next all make the migrant workforce of the Caribbean rim look less like a sui generis outcome of UFCO actions and more like migrants elsewhere at other times. Indeed, they look much like today's immigrants, whose transnational lives are sometimes hailed as a sea-change in human belonging.[3] In the Western Caribbean, as elsewhere in the Americas during the heyday of mass migration (around 1870 to 1930), the ease of travel and strength of social networks became mutually reinforcing.[4] As migrants circulated among centers of economic dynamism they encountered the same faces again and again, and the ties they formed sped the flow of information and lowered the cost of moves. Far-flung networks of kin and acquaintance were the collective outcome of countless individual decisions about whom to love, whom to leave, whom to help, and where to go next. As such, they bore the mark of overarching constraints as well as personal initiative, for those decisions were shaped by patterns of transportation, land access, and employment, by macroeconomic and regional political structures beyond any individual's personal control.

Dense webs of horizontal ties guided men through the formal economy of agriculture and transport and women through the informal economy of services and petty commerce. The dispersed resources embodied in the linemen's code of loyalty helped workers reconcile the rhythms of regional economic cycles and individual life cycles. Men traveled far to earn the highest possible wages when young. As they aged, male laborers faced an increasing risk of illness and work accidents and found it harder to relocate in response to regional economic shifts. Men's social networks, centered around docks, rails, and plantation fields, offered a hedge against the worst outcomes and a leg up toward the best. Women's laboring life cycles were different, as was their link to the export economy. Women traveled to boom sites as service sector entrepreneurs, not wage laborers, and though some kinds of service work (such as prostitution) were largely the province of young women, other kinds were equally or more profitable for older women (renting rooms, selling meals, nursing and midwifery). Like men, women faced illness and accidents.

But the most common calamities for women were unintended childbearing and unreliable men, and these risks were highest for women in youth and early middle age. Where women lived amid neighbors and kin—especially in the port and coastal villages—their social ties served as a hedge against conjugal misfortune as well.

In describing the trends shaping our world today we tend to equate corporations with global forces, laborers with local action. But UFCo investors and supervisors acted in concrete locations, though their decisions could affect distant locales. The same was true of working men like Ormington Demontford Corbin, whose decisions in the 1920s and 1930s about where to invest his labor affected his mother in Barbados, his father in Cuba, his brother in Costa Rica, his wife in Panama, and potential employers at each of those sites. The same was true of J.V.O.G., who moved from Nicaragua to Limón to Puntarenas to San Juan del Sur (Nicaragua) to Puntarenas to San Pedro Sula (Honduras) to Puerto Barrios (Guatemala) to Chichicastenango (Guatemala) to Guanacaste to Puntarenas to Quepos to Bataan to Zent—and was never far from home.[5] Through their travels and ties, Ormington Corbin, J.V.O.G., and Minor Cooper Keith each participated in the creation of transnational social fields. This did not erase the power differential between them, which was a matter of political access and economic scale rather than geographic scope.

Direct Foreign Investment and Moral Reform

At the start of the twentieth century United Fruit Company publications waxed eloquent about the moral burdens facing "Caucasian civilization" and its avatar, the Yankee banana man. Yet when we explored prostitution during the banana booms, conjugal practice among itinerant workers, female vulgarity in Port Limón, and male sociability on plantation camps, we found no evidence that United Fruit put into practice the civilizing mission it preached. Did the company attempt to shape manly men and womanly women in a particular mold? Did it seek to instill bourgeois values and recast domestic order? Did a project of moral reform permeate the company's labor policies and thus mold daily struggles in the export economy? Across the three generations whose lives we have traced, the answer to each of these questions was no. Company policies tolerated or encouraged prostitution. Supervisors showed no interest in their workers' female partners' personal virtue or maternal skill. Line-men's extravagant displays of sexual jealousy, drunken boasting, and bloody revenge were the antithesis of bourgeois self-control. At the turn of the century the bosses joined the fray; at midcentury they turned their backs.

This stands in sharp contrast to other cases where North American investors abroad actively pursued moral reform through comprehensive policies that promoted particular gendered virtues. Thomas Klubock has shown that steady manly labor and docile female homemaking were core goals of the Braden Copper Company's management strategy at the El Teniente mine in Chile from the 1920s onward.[6] Interventionist paternalism was not exclusive to foreign employers: Ann Farnsworth-Alvear has described Antioqueño industrialists' zealous supervision of the chastity and deportment of female textile workers.[7] Steve Striffler has shown that United Fruit itself pursued an interventionist welfare capitalism on its Ecuadorian plantations in the 1950s that was far removed from what we have seen in Limón.[8] On the other hand, Catherine LeGrand suggests that in Santa Marta, Colombia, in the 1920s and 1930s, United Fruit's weight as purchaser and employer was not accompanied by attempts (much less successful attempts) to mold local communities or culture.[9] The plantations' short time horizon under a particular cultivation strategy, the mobility of the workforce, and the political moment in the United States and abroad together seem to account for the difference.[10]

The lack of commitment to a civilizing mission on the part of those who ran Limón's early banana industry was not an unadulterated plus. If United Fruit's agents on the ground had in fact championed domesticity and moral betterment, workers might have been able to force the company to improve housing, health care, and pensions. At Hacienda Tenguel in Ecuador, paternalist UFCO welfare programs brought concrete benefits, from fresh meat at cost to subsidized soccer teams. At the Braden Copper Company's El Teniente mine, wives made good use of the company's commitment to domestic harmony, acquiring institutional allies in their struggles with wayward, spendthrift, or abusive husbands. In Limón, for better and for worse, this was not an option.

Campaigns to reform the personal habits and domestic order of working-class *limonenses* would come eventually, but from black preachers and Costa Rican educators rather than UFCO doctors or plantation managers.[11] As we have seen, the crisis years of the 1930s witnessed fervent calls for community uplift by church and civic leaders. The late 1930s and 1940s also saw increasing attention from government agencies as the institutions and ideology of the welfare state, under construction in the urban Central Valley for a generation, began to make themselves felt in outlying areas of the country.[12] Through it all United Fruit remained fundamentally uninterested. Confirmation on this point comes from the files of the Northern Railway Company, seized by the state after the railroad was nationalized in 1976 and only now available to researchers at the Costa Rican National Archives. The vast collection of correspondence, minutiae, and internal reports from the 1940s, 1950s, and 1960s more than confirms United Fruit's reputation for political interference and union-busting.[13] But the same files offer no evidence of UFCO interest in workers' values, sexual mores, or domestic lives.

In terms of direct U.S. investment in Latin America, Limón was the belly of the beast: birthplace of United Fruit, company town extraordinaire, a place where the only roads were UFCO railroads and even a body's final trip from church to burying ground was made in the Northern funeral car. But United Fruit's economic weight and political machinations were not matched by control of the representational sphere, of popular culture or intimate life.[14] Here managers' schemes never targeted the domestic arrangements of working-class reproduction. Indeed, through most of the period studied, nobody paid much attention to what went on between men and women other than men and women themselves, neighbors and coworkers, enemies and friends. They were the ones who found sexual virtue and family values important enough to argue over.

Gender, Power, and Politics

Women and men together and apart do many kinds of things, from growing bananas to making love to trying to get the people in charge to show a little respect. How they do so is shaped by assumptions about male and female nature, inherited patterns in the division of labor, demography and geography, and international politics. All of these tend to evolve together over time. Yet the gendered balance of power—the distribution of costs, benefits, risks, and opportunities between men and women—can differ starkly across the multiple realms that make up a single life or a social system. Gender relations do not form a single continuum from equity to abjection, and this is as true when we compare individuals as when we compare societies. Local structures of residence and work shaped women's life chances, in part by determining their access to social networks. The experience of nominally similar kinship forms could differ drastically because of this. Men were not necessarily bad for women, but isolation often was. In the port city, line towns, and nucleated villages women benefited from supportive neighbors and kin, independent earning opportunities, and working relationships with agents of the state. On plantation camps women found many customers for female services, but public space there was male space alone, and migrants of every origin agreed the camps were no place for decent women or growing families. On isolated homesteads women had limited mobility, especially while their children were young. They had fewer ways to earn income, and fewer means of exit when relationships turned bad. It was Hispanic *compañeras* at midcentury who most often found themselves accepting the heightened risks homesteading brought women. Meanwhile, their West Indian peers lived amid cousins and grandparents in old Main Line towns or southern coast villages, vulnerable to commodity cycles but sheltered from conjugal calamity.

Men's lot was no more uniform. Men of all groups seem to have been generally convinced they deserved to dominate, but the extent to which they did so varied widely among men, and for any one man in different realms of his life. Autobiographical sources highlight the painful contradiction between working men's conviction that they should be in charge and a world in which they rarely were. There were grave costs to a system that taught men to take female defiance as a challenge to the core of their self-respect. Certainly some men managed to turn away from that challenge, to heed another of the available scripts of male virtue: to think of the children who would be left orphaned, or the grandmothers who would be left crying, and choose the heavy pain of endurance over the catharsis of action. But we cannot doubt the sincerity of the anguish felt by those who did otherwise. The real tragedy of conjugal violence in Limón was not that evil men did evil things to women, but that good men, trying to do what they were convinced was moral and necessary, could commit heinous acts as well.[15]

According to legal doctrine a chaste daughter or faithful wife of unsullied reputation was the most protected of women, sheltered and supported by her father or husband from day to day and due the full protection of the state if insulted, seduced, or assaulted. Yet what is remarkable in the record of judicial action in Limón is how many women who were anything but honorable in the eyes of the law got the courts to work for them. We saw this in the lawsuits brought by women in prostitution over money owed or damages done, and again in the myriad insults suits brought by working women of every sort in Limón.[16] Of course they did not always prevail, especially when their opponents were wealthier or better connected than they. Even if they ultimately lost, though, judicial action might work to their advantage as a delaying tactic or means of pressure. As seen through the statutes that covered family, marriage, and honor, the law appears as one element among many—economic and political structures, religious doctrine, kinship custom—that subordinated women to men. But in practice judicial action more often worked to counterweight in part the unequal distribution of power between the sexes than to exacerbate it. Women's legal personhood and formal access to the courts, their informal access to lawyers, and the adversarial process together allowed women to use the courts to exact partial compliance from men, even when they themselves complied only partially with what the law demanded.

Many recent studies of gender and politics spotlight cases in which popular practices and ideas were remade through conflictive cross-class negotiations over virtue, citizenship, and entitlement. Other studies emphasize the way conceptual vocabularies reliant on distinction between male and female (sometimes called gendered discourses) permeate public rhetoric, and in doing so set the boundaries of the politically possible. We have seen examples of each of these phenomena in the history of Limón. Yet with a research design open to tracking periods of elite disinterest, to noting the frequent irrelevance of official rhetoric to popular habit, we have also glimpsed the contours of a different dynamic. Tracking changes and continuities in everyday life, we found that most (though not all) were unconnected to attempts by rulers to intervene, educate, moralize, or reform. The structure of markets, population, and settlement were consistently important in shaping the divergent contours of male and female lives. The impact of top-down projects was far more circumscribed.

Modern states issue harangues and decrees at a dizzying rate. Do they sway hearts and minds at the same clip? In attempting to compel change, do state projects at least dictate the arenas of resistance? The Costa Rican state sought order, progress, and eugenic vigor as fervently as any in Latin America in these years. Yet in Limón men drank, brawled, and partnered up; women cursed, brawled, and gave birth out of wedlock; and public officials alternated between inaction, abuse, and indulgence. The state did devote much bombast and some resources to controlling the travels and sexual health of women in prostitution. But juxtaposing governmental publications to the reconstructed life histories of prostitutes themselves revealed how profoundly ineffective such attempts were. Meanwhile, mothers and others pulled policemen and judges into their own struggles, creating a system of ad hoc intervention quite separate from official policy. By the 1950s, as the institutions of the welfare state were extended to Limón, local families witnessed more sustained state action. Schoolteachers, social workers, and police officers coordinated their response to perceived problems like juvenile delinquency. But even then most interventions were initiated by parents, uneasy collaborators or eager instigators of the moral reform of the youth of Limón.[17]

William Roseberry called our attention to "the problematic relationship between the talking state and the distracted audience." Even this image gives the state greater coherence and a more central position than it seems to have had in early Limón.[18] There the state hardly looked like an orator onstage. It looked more like two men in frock coats jostling on a soapbox at one end of a crowded marketplace. The frock-coats performed enough routinized functions within the market that no one questioned their right to be present. They sold licenses, exacted bribes, settled personal disputes for a fee. Periodically they called orders to a policeman wandering among the stalls, and sometimes the policeman got carried away with his nightstick. Beyond that, what the frock-coats said to each other or shouted to the crowd was none too relevant to the selling, swapping, cursing, and wooing going on all about them. By the 1930s and 1940s the men on the soapbox (now dressed in double-breasted suits) were leading the crowd around them in chants, and some onlookers were making an active effort to elbow others out of the way and claim the platform for their own. The state mattered more, and elite projects made themselves felt in popular practice, especially when the pressures brought to bear coincided with shifts in the economic and demographic terrain.[19] But even then, much remained beyond the ken of those who struggled for the soapbox.

Gender and Local Culture

Communities among migrants were neither bounded nor grounded. Instead they were diffuse and mobile, stretching across national boundaries with bonds intact even when attenuated by years apart. Such communities were both crucially supportive and endemically conflictive, crisscrossed by hierarchy and inequality and scores that needed settling. I suggested above that one might think of the local cultures that imbued social action with meaning as congeries of available scripts. That the lines were formulaic did not prevent improvisation in the act of performance. Affronted elites, dueling policemen, and wronged washerwomen drew on a common repertoire in claiming their due. Within that repertoire there were sharp divides between roles for women and roles for men, roles for the respectable and roles for the rebels. But there was also the possibility of intentional misreading, parody, and play.

This may explain why cultural heritage has proved to be an inadequate explanation for just about any aspect of gender roles or family life among the immigrants we have observed. If asked, people would have insisted on the weight of their traditions. That conviction is relevant but not necessarily accurate. Did inherited beliefs and values in fact set strong boundaries on family formation or personal aspirations? By the late nineteenth century, Jamaican peasants and Central Valley *campesinos* had developed sharply contrasting patterns of kinship practice. Among the latter, childbearing followed church marriage and preceded legalized inheritance. Among the former, it rarely did either. But among Jamaican and Costa Rican migrants alike in Limón, serial consensual union was by far the most common conjugal form. Such relationships were complemented by work and travel partnerships among men that could surpass conjugal pairings in their intensity and endurance. The spectrum of claims put forth about sexual proprieties and improprieties was also quite similar among Hispanics and West Indians in Limón. At the turn of the century, Hispanic women's use of the courts was more circumscribed by social class than West Indian women's—poor women sued; rich *señoras* did not. But migrants of every origin used the legal system in like ways (though with differing frequency) when honor was injured or obligations unmet.

These examples show the malleability of culture in the rapid convergence of West Indian and Hispanic practices in Limón. Cultural heritage also proved a poor explanation for some divergences between them. In Limón as elsewhere, the West Indian descendants of freedmen and freedwomen insisted plantation residence was incompatible with proper family life.[20] Is this the reason why West Indian workers exited the plantation labor force in the 1920s, while Costa Rican migrants eagerly joined it? Evidence suggests not. In 1927 English-speaking *peones bananeros* were four times *more* likely than their Spanish-speaking counterparts to be married, and many times more likely to live with female partners and children.[21] Regional migration flows and life cycle patterns had molded communal tendencies into the exact opposite of what attention to cultural heritage would have predicted. A particular vision of family propriety could hardly be the cause of a labor pattern that directly contravened it.

Where have inherited habits seemed relevant to the social patterns we have found? Across the years West Indian men were less likely than Hispanic men to kill each other in duels and drunken brawls, which I attributed to a cultural repertory of masculinity in which nonviolent exits—laughter, self-parody—were easier to reach for. I also argued that the heightened deadly violence against women in turn-of-the-century Limón reflected the rigidity of men's notions of honor and entitlement, which did not change as fast as the economic and demographic circumstances that empowered women there. On the other hand, the same cases showed the flexibility of women's assumptions as they made ample use of the new possibilities the export economy provided, claiming the right to manage their money, travel where they pleased, and choose whom to love.

In the public writings of the men whose political and economic endeavors most prominently marked the history of Limón, one can find evidence of a civilizing corporate mission, of state concern over licentiousness and blackness, of contested projects of moral reform. But in court cases and autobiographies—that is, in documents generated at the initiative of common folk—the traces of such concerns are overshadowed by the wealth of evidence of autonomous cultural production by working-class actors, production never innocent of power relations, but neither dictated by the powerful nor merely in dialogue with them. Throughout this book, the staple concerns of much "history after the linguistic turn" have been at the forefront of my inquiry. We have explored understandings of race and gender, vice and virtue, sex and self. But the very fluidity and creativity that has made these things so interesting to study has generally kept them from functioning as causal forces. They have been crucial for comprehending what life was like but have rarely explained what happened next.

Limón, Costa Rica, was the birthplace of what would become the Americas' most notorious transnational corporation. Nowhere was United Fruit's direct involvement in banana growing greater at the turn of the century. But worker mobility and the plantations' short time horizon limited employer control and discouraged social engineering. Men and women and parents and children often disagreed over intimate obligations, sexual proprieties, and gendered rights. The small weight of elite ideals and ideologies in their struggles is striking, given the wealth of case studies that have demonstrated that elsewhere it was otherwise. Here the divergent patterns of men's and women's lives were forged in the daily give-and-take through which migrants reworked the cultural scripts they brought to the coast, trying to keep their feet in a new and shifting setting. Gender was manufactured locally, from imported parts.

Appendix

◆

TABLE A.1. Sex and Age Distribution of Spanish-Speaking
Citizens-by-Birth and Spanish-Speaking Immigrants in Limón, 1927

Age	Spanish-Speaking Citizens-by-Birth			Spanish-Speaking Immigrants		
	Men	Women	Ratio	Men	Women	Ratio
0–14	1,185	1,183	100:100	236	246	96:100
15–29	2,303	1,345	171:100	1,224	372	329:100
30–44	1,099	766	143:100	719	169	425:100
45–59	477	207 ⎫		169	83 ⎫	
60–74	64	44 ⎬ 216:100		30	20 ⎬ 185:100	
75–89		⎭		10	10 ⎭	
Total	5,128	3,545	145:100	2,388	900	265:100

Source: Author's analysis of CIHAC 1927 census database.
Note: Figures expanded to reflect total population size. N = 1,069.

TABLE A.2. Childbearing by Black and White Women in Limón, 1927 and 1950

	Children 0–4 Years	Women 15–44 Years	Children per 1,000 Women
1927			
All Costa Rica	73,686	107,181	687.5
All Jamaica (1921)	111,653	212,954	524.3
Urban blacks in Limón[a]	916	2,268	403.9
Urban whites in Limón[a]	593	1,478	401.2
Rural blacks in Limón[a]	761	1,454	523.4
Rural whites in Limón[a]	436	1,043	418.0
1950			
All Costa Rica	132,635	179,412	739.2
All Jamaica (1943)	156,365	303,682	514.9
Blacks in Limón	1,698	2,889	587.7
Whites in Limón	4,511	5,559	811.5
Urban Limón	1,641	2,794	587.3
Rural Limón	4,835	6,011	804.3

Sources: Author's analysis of CIHAC 1927 census database; Costa Rica, Dirección General de Estadística y Censos, *Censo de Población de Costa Rica, 22 de mayo de 1950* (San José, 1953), 64, 181; *Census of Jamaica, 25th of April, 1921* (Kingston, 1922), 24–25; *Census of Jamaica, 4th of January, 1943* (Kingston, 1944), table 8.
[a] Figures expanded to reflect total population size. N = 926.

TABLE A.3. Civil Status of Spanish-Speaking and
English-Speaking Adults in Limón, by Age Group, 1927

	Age	Single (%)	Ever Married[a] (%)	SSL[b] (%)	Total
Men					
Spanish speakers	15–29	3,122 (91)	249 (7)	63 (2)	3,434
	30–44	1,288 (70)	499 (27)	47 (3)	1,834
	45 and over	272 (39)	431 (61)	(0)	703
English speakers	15–29	1,216 (92)	95 (7)	10 (1)	1,321
	30–44	2,017 (71)	812 (29)	16 (1)	2,845
	45 and over	1,675 (63)	961 (36)	10 (0)	2,646
Women					
Spanish speakers	15–29	802 (48)	361 (21)	525 (31)	1,688
	30–44	241 (25)	426 (45)	287 (30)	954
	45 and over	124 (34)	191 (52)	50 (14)	365
English speakers	15–29	1,081 (56)	319 (17)	521 (27)	1,921
	30–44	523 (29)	850 (47)	420 (23)	1,793
	45 and over	280 (26)	664 (61)	146 (13)	1,090

Source: Author's analysis of CIHAC 1927 census database.
Note: Figures expanded to reflect total population size. N = 1,848.
[a] Combines married, divorced, separated, and widowed.
[b] Soltera sin ligamen (consensual union).

TABLE A.4. Origins of Parties in All Preserved Limón Insults Cases, 1897–1910

Stated Origin	Female Plaintiffs	Male Plaintiffs	Female Defendants	Male Defendants
West Indian				
(Anglo)[a]	11	7	12	17
Barbados	2	2	3	4
Colombia (Anglo)[a]	1		1	
Guadeloupe	1			
Jamaica	85	32	64	52
Martinique	1			
Montserrat	1			1
Nicaragua (Anglo)[a]			1	
Panama (Anglo)[a]	2			
Providencia	1			
St. Lucia		2	1	1
St. Thomas	1			1
St. Vincent				1
Trinidad	1	1		
Latin American				
Colombia (Hispanic)[a]	4	6	5	6
Costa Rica	3	11	4	5
Cuba	1	6		4
(Hispanic)[a]	7	20	6	7
Mexico		1		
Nicaragua (Hispanic)[a]	4	1	1	1
Panama (Hispanic)[a]	2		1	
Puerto Rico				1
Venezuela				1
Other				
China		1		2
France		1		1
Italy		1	1	3
Spain		1		3
Tunisia		1		
U.S.A.		1		1
(Not specified)	1		2	2
Total	129	95	102	114

Source: Archivo Nacional de Costa Rica, San José, Costa Rica.

Note: Total cases, N = 202; median year, 1901.

[a] Where origin was not given, or for nations from which both West Indians and Hispanics emigrated to Limón, parties are classified as (Anglo) or (Hispanic) on the basis of surname and language of testimony.

| Province | Median Year of Preserved Cases | Total Victins in Preserved Cases | | Women as % of Victims | Average Annual Homicides per 100,000, 1907–25 | Estimated Male Homicide Victimization Rate[a] | Estimated Female Homicide Victimization Rate[a] |
		Men	Women				
Alajuela	1907	154	9	5.5	14.2	26.8	1.6
Cartago	1911	83	6	6.7	5.1	9.5	0.7
Guanacaste	1910	169	16	8.6	20.2	36.9	3.5
Heredia	1902	88	2	2.2	6.5	12.7	0.3
Limón	1912	99	28	22.0	30.5	35.7	20.2
Puntarenas	1909	96	14	12.7	20.1	31.9	5.7
San José	1906	243	28	10.3	7.6	14.3	1.5

Sources: Archivo Nacional de Costa Rica, San José, Costa Rica; Costa Rica, Dirección General de Estadística y Censos, *Anuario estadístico* (1907–26).

Note: The gender breakdown of homicide victims was calculated on the basis of homicide inquiries in the ANCR card catalog, for there are no published data on this question. In cases where the sex of named parties was ambiguous, the case itself was consulted. Figures here do not include attempted homicide (*homicidio frustrado* or *tentativa de homicidio*) or vehicular manslaughter (train or tram accidents). The card catalog lists the cases' date of conclusion. In general, in San José the duration of each case was little more than a year. In Limón, however, the concluding date might be as much as ten years after the death that originated the case. Average annual homicide rates are calculated from the *Anuarios estadísticos*, which, beginning in 1907, listed the number of homicide investigations concluded each year by province. Because case preservation varied between provinces, the published totals are more reliable than ANCR holdings for comparing the incidence of homicide across provinces. There is no reason, though, to think that the vagaries of case preservation systematically affected the sex ratio of the victims within the set of cases preserved from each province. Because the above rate estimates are based on the frequency of concluded homicide investigations, it is likely that they overstate the frequency of actual homicides by about 15 percent. (In 86 percent of the preserved investigations from Limón a homicide had in fact occurred. The other cases stemmed from accidental firearms discharge or baseless rumors.) Following published population statistics, average annual homicides per capita in Limón would have been 38.23 per 100,000 from 1907 to 1925. However, official figures underestimated the provincial population over this period. See Lara Putnam, "Public Women and One-Pant Men: Labor Migration and the Politics of Gender in Caribbean Costa Rica, 1870–1960" (Ph.D. diss., University of Michigan, 2000). My calculations here assume an average population of 28,000 over these thirty years rather than the 22,342 resulting from *Anuario estadístico* figures. Sex-specific victimization rates take into account the sex ratio of adults in each province at the time: roughly 200:100 in Limón, 122:100 in Puntarenas, 91:100 in San José, and near parity elsewhere. See Jeffrey Casey Gaspar, *Limón, 1880–1940: Un estudio de la industria bananera en Costa Rica* (San José: Editorial Costa Rica, 1979), 229–31.

[a]Per 100,000.

TABLE A.6. Origins of Parties in All Preserved Limón Homicide Investigations with Only Male Victims, 1894–1922

Stated Origin	Male Victims	Female Accused	Male Accused
West Indian			
(Anglo)[a]	10		4
"Antillano"			1
Belize			1
Demerara			1
Jamaica	12	1	28
Martinique	1		
Providencia			2
Trinidad			1
Latin American			
Colombia	3		2
Costa Rica	15	2	21
El Salvador			1
(Hispanic)[a]	22	1	7
Honduras	1		
"Indio"	3		5
Nicaragua	7		10
Panama	1		
Puerto Rico	1		
Other			
China	1		
England	1		
France	1		
Germany	2		2
Italy			1
Palestine	1		
Spain	2		2
U.S.A.	4		1
Total	88	4	90

Source: Archivo Nacional de Costa Rica, San José, Costa Rica.

Note: Total cases, N = 84; median year, 1904.

[a] Where origin was not given, or for nations from which both West Indians and Hispanics emigrated to Limón, parties are classified as (Anglo) or (Hispanic) on the basis of surname and language of testimony.

TABLE A.7. Origins of Parties in All Preserved Limón
Homicide Investigations with Female Victims, 1900–1916

Stated Origin	Female Victims	Male Victims	Male Accused
West Indian			
(Anglo)[a]	5		1
Jamaica	5		11
Martinique	1		
Latin American			
Colombia	1		3
Costa Rica	8		7
Cuba			1
(Hispanic)[a]	3		
Honduras			1
"Indio"	3	2	1
Nicaragua			1
Other			
East Indian	2		1
U.S.A.			1
Total	28	2	28

Source: Archivo Nacional de Costa Rica, San José, Costa Rica.

Note: Total cases, N = 27; median year, 1911. There were no females accused in these investigations

[a] Where origin was not given, or for nations from which both West Indians and Hispanics emigrated to Limón, parties are classified as (Anglo) or (Hispanic) on the basis of surname and language of testimony.

TABLE A.8. Origins of Parties in Sample of Limón
Homicide Investigations Involving Only Men, 1925–1959

Ethnicity	Nationality	Victims (Male)	Accused (Male)
Hispanic	Costa Rica	15	14
	Honduras		2
	Nicaragua	8	5
	Panama	1	
	(Not specified)	11	6
West Indian	Barbados		1
	Costa Rica		6
	Cuba		1
	Jamaica	4	4
	Nicaragua		4
	Panama		1
	(Not specified)	5	2
Total		44	46

Source: Archivo Judicial de la Corte Suprema de Justicia, San Pablo de Heredia, Costa Rica.
Note: Total cases, N = 37; median year, 1949. Ethnicity classified on the basis of surname or language of testimony.

TABLE A.9. Origins of Parties in All Preserved Limón Homicide
Investigations with Female Victims and Male Accused Parties, 1937–1959

Ethnicity	Nationality	Female Victims	Male Victims	Male Accused
Hispanic	Costa Rica	4		3
	Honduras			1
	Nicaragua	1		4
	(Not specified)	5	1	
West Indian	Costa Rica	1		1
	Jamaica			2
	Nicaragua	1		1
	(Not specified)	1	1	1
Indigenous	Costa Rica	1	2	2
Total		14	4	15

Source: Archivo Judicial de la Corte Suprema de Justicia, San Pablo de Heredia, Costa Rica.
Note: Total cases, N = 14; median year, 1953. Ethnicity classified on the basis of surname, language of testimony, or, in the case of indigenous Costa Ricans, the label "indio" for race.

Ethnicity	Nationality	Female Victims	Male Victims	Infant Victims	Female Accused	Male Accused
Hispanic	Costa Rica			2	3	
	Nicaragua					1
	(Not specified)	1	1			
West Indian	Costa Rica		1	1	3	
	Jamaica		1		1	
Indigenous	Costa Rica				1	
Total		1	3	3	8	1

Source: Archivo Judicial de la Corte Suprema de Justicia, San Pablo de Heredia, Costa Rica.
Note: Total cases, N = 7. Ethnicity classified on the basis of surname, language of testimony, or, in the case of indigenous Costa Ricans, the label "indio" for race.

Notes

Abbreviations

AC	Escuela de Planificación Social, "Autobiografías Campesinas," 30 vols., Biblioteca Central, Universidad Nacional Autónoma, Heredia, Costa Rica (mimeographed)
AJ	Archivo Judicial de la Corte Suprema de Justicia, San Pablo de Heredia, Costa Rica
ANCR	Archivo Nacional de Costa Rica, San José, Costa Rica
LAU	Limón Alcaldía Única, Serie Jurídica, Archivo Nacional de Costa Rica, San José, Costa Rica
LJCivil	Limón Juzgado Civil, Serie Jurídica, Archivo Nacional de Costa Rica, San José, Costa Rica
LJCrimen	Limón Juzgado del Crimen, Serie Jurídica, Archivo Nacional de Costa Rica, San José, Costa Rica
LJCyC	Limón Juzgado Civil y del Crimen, Serie Jurídica, Archivo Nacional de Costa Rica, San José, Costa Rica
LJPenal	Juzgado Penal de Limón, Serie Jurídica, Archivo Nacional de Costa Rica, San José, Costa Rica
MGP	Costa Rica, Ministerio de Gobernación y Policía, *Memoria*
SJA1	San José Alcaldía Primera, Serie Jurídica, Archivo Nacional de Costa Rica, San José, Costa Rica
SJA2	San José Alcaldía Segunda, Serie Jurídica, Archivo Nacional de Costa Rica, San José, Costa Rica
SJA3	San José Alcaldía Tercera, Serie Jurídica, Archivo Nacional de Costa Rica, San José, Costa Rica
SJJCrimen	San José Juzgado del Crimen, Serie Jurídica, Archivo Nacional de Costa Rica, San José, Costa Rica
SJJ1Civil	San José Juzgado Primero Civil, Serie Jurídica, Archivo Nacional de Costa Rica, San José, Costa Rica

SJJ1Crimen	San José Juzgado Primero del Crimen, Serie Jurídica, Archivo Nacional de Costa Rica, San José, Costa Rica
SJJ2Civil	San José Juzgado Segundo Civil, Serie Jurídica, Archivo Nacional de Costa Rica, San José, Costa Rica
SJJ2Crimen	San José Juzgado Segundo del Crimen, Serie Jurídica, Archivo Nacional de Costa Rica, San José, Costa Rica
TPP	Transcripciones de entrevistas de Paula Palmer, Fondo Grabaciones, Archivo Nacional de Costa Rica, San José, Costa Rica

Introduction

1. LJCrimen 72 (estupro, 1906). Throughout this book I have changed the names of all parties traced through court cases, such as Sebastiana Veragua and Leandro Chacón, but not those of public officials or well-known figures, such as Salomón Zacarías Aguilera or Benjamín de Céspedes. All translations are my own.

2. Benjamín de Céspedes, *La prostitución en la ciudad de la Habana* (Havana, 1888), 171. On Céspedes's past see "Informe que rindiera la Comitiva de Oficiales de Sanidad del Sur, que visitara Puerto Limón en 1906," in *Crónicas y relatos para la historia de Puerto Limón*, comp. Fernando González Vásquez and Elías Zeledón Cartín (San José: Ministerio de Cultura, Juventud, y Deportes, Centro de Investigación y Conservación del Patrimonio Cultural, 1999), 278.

3. See Catherine LeGrand, "Colombian Transformations: Peasants and Wage Laborers in the Santa Marta Banana Zone," *Journal of Peasant Studies* 2, no. 4 (1984): 178-200, and "Living in Macondo: Economy and Culture in a United Fruit Banana Enclave in Colombia," in *Close Encounters of Empire: Writing the Cultural History of U.S.-Latin American Relations*, ed. Gilbert Joseph, Catherine C. LeGrand, and Ricardo Salvatore (Durham: Duke University Press, 1998), 348-52; Paul Dosal, *Doing Business with the Dictators: A Political History of United Fruit in Guatemala, 1899-1944* (Wilmington, Del.: Scholarly Resources, 1993); Aviva Chomsky, *West Indian Workers and the United Fruit Company in Costa Rica, 1870-1940* (Baton Rouge: Louisiana State University Press, 1996); and Dario Euraque, *Reinterpreting the Banana Republic: Region and State in Honduras, 1870-1972* (Chapel Hill: University of North Carolina Press, 1996).

4. George Chauncey Jr., "The Locus of Reproduction: Women's Labour in the Zambian Copperbelt, 1927-1953," *Journal of South African Studies* 7, no. 2 (1981): 135-64.

5. LAU 492 (injurias, 1903). These insults were reported verbatim in Jamaican Creole in the lawsuit Barnes filed in response.

6. See Amy Kaplan and Donald E. Pease, eds., *Cultures of United States Imperialism* (Durham: Duke University Press, 1993); Frederick Cooper and Ann Laura Stoler, eds., *Tensions of Empire: Colonial Cultures in a Bourgeois World* (Berkeley: University of California Press, 1997); and Joseph, LeGrand, and Salvatore, *Close Encounters of Empire*.

7. Frederick Upham Adams, *Conquest of the Tropics* (New York: Doubleday, 1914), 164–65.

8. George W. Roberts, *The Population of Jamaica* (Cambridge: Cambridge University Press, 1957), 116–32; Verene Shepherd, "Gender, Migration and Settlement: The Indentureship and Post-Indentureship Experience of Indian Females in Jamaica, 1845–1943," in *Engendering History: Caribbean Women in Historical Perspective*, ed. Verene Shepherd, Bridget Brereton, and Barbara Bailey (Kingston: Ian Randle, 1995), 236–42.

9. See Lara Putnam, "Migración y género en la organización de la producción: Una comparación de la industria bananera en Costa Rica y Jamaica (1880–1935)" (paper presented at the 4th Simposio Panamericano de Historia of the Instituto Panamericano de Geografía e Historia, San José, Costa Rica, 10–13 Aug. 1999).

10. See Giovanni Levi, "On Microhistory," in *New Perspectives on Historical Writing*, ed. Peter Burke (University Park: Pennsylvania State University Press, 1992), 97.

11. Charles Kepner, *Social Aspects of the Banana Industry* (New York: Columbia University Press, 1936), 162.

12. Steven Palmer, "Adiós 'laissez-faire': La política social en Costa Rica, 1880–1940," *Revista de Historia de América* 124 (1999): 99–117; Héctor Pérez Brignoli, *Breve historia contemporánea de Costa Rica* (Mexico City: Fondo de Cultura Económica, 1997).

13. Van Young describes historians' sources as "the detritus of private lives and civil society bumping up against the state." Eric Van Young, "The New Cultural History Comes to Old Mexico," *Hispanic American Historical Review* 79, no. 2 (1999): 245.

14. I borrow the metaphor of "shaping the terrain" from Barbara Jeanne Fields, "Slavery, Race, and Ideology in the United States of America," *New Left Review* 181 (1990): 113.

15. Lara Putnam, "Ideología racial, práctica social y estado liberal en Costa Rica," *Revista de Historia* (San José, Costa Rica) 39 (1999): 156.

16. *Atlantic Voice*, 6 Apr. 1935, 7; *Searchlight*, 26 Dec. 1931, 1; *Searchlight*, 13 June 1931, 3. Brackets in original.

17. People classed as of different racial groups do come together and have babies, of course, more often in some systems than others. Since the fiction of race depends on a belief in stable biological categories, both ideological and practical work is required to keep cross-group unions from undermining the system. See Frederick Cooper and Ann Stoler, "Between Metropole and Colony: Rethinking a Research Agenda," in Cooper and Stoler, *Tensions of Empire*, 24–27.

Chapter One

1. Robert M. Carmack, "Perspectivas sobre la historia antigua de Centroamérica," in *Historia antigua*, ed. Robert M. Carmack, vol. 1 of *Historia general de Centroamérica*, coordinated by Edelberto Torres Rivas (Madrid: Sociedad Estatal Quinto Centenario

and FLACSO, 1993), 297–301; Wendy Kramer, W. George Lovell, and Christopher H. Lutz, "La conquista española de Centroamérica," in *El régimen colonial*, ed. Julio Pinto Soria, vol. 2 of *Historia general de Centroamérica*, 78–81.

2. Lowell Gudmundson, *Estratificación socio-racial y económica de Costa Rica, 1700–1850* (San José: Editorial Universidad Estatal a Distancia, 1978), 19–74; Elizabeth Fonseca Corrales, "Economía y sociedad en Centroamérica (1540–1680)," in Pinto Soria, *Régimen colonial*, 137–40, 146–48.

3. David Eltis, *The Rise of African Slavery in the Americas* (Cambridge: Cambridge University Press, 2000), 48, 98–112, 251; Paul Lovejoy, *Transformations in Slavery* (Cambridge: Cambridge University Press, 1983).

4. Edward Long, *The History of Jamaica*, vol. 2 (London, 1774), 410–11, as cited in Sidney Mintz, "The Origins of the Jamaican Market System," in *Caribbean Transformations*, 2d ed. (New York: Columbia University Press, 1989), 200. See also Richard S. Dunn, "Sugar Production and Slave Women in Jamaica," in *Cultivation and Culture: Labor and the Shaping of Slave Life in the Americas*, ed. Ira Berlin and Philip D. Morgan (Charlottesville: University Press of Virginia, 1993), 49–72.

5. Ira Berlin and Philip D. Morgan, "Introduction: Labor and the Shaping of Slave Life in the Americas," in Berlin and Morgan, *Cultivation and Culture*, 36.

6. B. W. Higman, *Slave Population and Economy in Jamaica, 1807–1834* (Cambridge: Cambridge University Press, 1976); Michael Craton, "Changing Patterns of Slave Families in the British West Indies," in *Caribbean Slave Society and Economy*, ed. Hilary Beckles and Verene Shepherd (New York: W. W. Norton, 1991), 228–49; Christine Barrow, *Family in the Caribbean: Themes and Perspectives* (Kingston: Ian Randle, 1996), 241–340.

7. Franklin Knight, *The Caribbean: The Genesis of a Fragmented Nationalism*, 2d ed. (New York: Oxford University Press, 1990), 40.

8. Mary W. Helms, "Miskito Slaving and Culture Contact: Ethnicity and Opportunity in an Expanding Population," *Journal of Anthropological Research* 39 (1983): 179–97; Juan Carlos Solórzano Fonseca, "Los años finales de la dominación española (1750–1821)," in *De la ilustración al liberalismo*, ed. Héctor Pérez Brignoli, vol. 3 of *Historia general de Centroamérica*, 60–63.

9. Gustavo Palma Murga, "Economía y sociedad en Centroamérica (1680–1750)," in Pinto Soria, *Régimen colonial*, 219–74; Solórzano Fonseca, "Los años finales," 17–59, esp. 25–27. I have borrowed the phrase "internal frontiers" from Ann Stoler, "Sexual Affronts and Racial Frontiers: European Identities and the Cultural Politics of Exclusion in Colonial Southeast Asia," *Comparative Studies in Society and History* 34, no. 5 (1992): 514–51.

10. Verena Martínez-Alier, *Marriage, Class, and Colour in Nineteenth-Century Cuba: A Study of Racial Attitudes and Sexual Values in a Slave Society*, 2d ed. (Ann Arbor: University of Michigan Press, 1989), 11, citing Richard Konetzke, ed., *Colección de documentos para la historia de la formación social de Hispanoamérica, 1493–1810*, vol. 3, book 1 (Madrid: Consejo Superior de Investigaciones Científicas, 1962), 406–13.

11. Eduardo Fournier, "Aproximación a un estudio histórico del matrimonio en

Costa Rica (siglos XVIII y XIX)," *Revista Senderos* (San José, Costa Rica) 35 (1989): 5–26; Patricia Seed, *To Love, Honor, and Obey in Colonial Mexico: Conflicts over Marriage Choice, 1574–1820* (Stanford: Stanford University Press, 1988), chap. 13.

12. Average annual slave imports between 1792 and 1807 were 10,700. Mervyn C. Alleyne, *Roots of Jamaican Culture* (London: Pluto Press, 1988), 40.

13. Edwin González Salas, *Evolución histórica de la población de Costa Rica (1840–1940)* (San José: Editorial Universidad Estatal a Distancia, 1995), 12–14. *Zambo* referred to persons of mixed indigenous and African ancestry, *ladino* to persons of indigenous ancestry who had adopted Spanish language and dress and belonged to no *pueblo de indios*.

14. Lara Putnam, "La construcción social de las categorías raciales: El caso de la Costa Rica colonial" (paper presented at the Reunión Internacional: Ruta del Esclavo en Hispanoamérica, San José, Costa Rica, 23–26 Feb. 1999).

15. Claudia Quirós Vargas and Margarita Bolaños Arquín, "El mestizaje en el siglo XVII: Consideraciones para comprender la génesis del campesinado criollo del Valle Central," in *Costa Rica colonial*, ed. Luis Fernando Sibaja (San José: Ediciones Guayacán, 1989), 61–78; María de los Angeles Acuña León and Doriam Chavarría López, "Endogamia y exogamia en la sociedad colonial cartaginesa (1738–1821)," *Revista de Historia* (San José, Costa Rica) 23 (1991): 118–26.

16. See genealogies in Tatiana Lobo Wiehoff and Mauricio Meléndez Obando, *Negros y blancos todo mezclado* (San José: Editorial de la Universidad de Costa Rica, 1997). The formal *gracias al sacar* was a royal pardon, available to petitioners with sufficient cash and connections, which exempted the grantee from legal restrictions to which he or she was subject due to illegitimate birth or "impure" blood.

17. See Martínez-Alier, *Marriage, Class, and Colour*.

18. ANCR, Complemento Colonial 3922 (1691), as cited in Elizabeth Fonseca Corrales, *Costa Rica colonial: La tierra y el hombre*, 3d ed. (San José: EDUCA, 1986), 297.

19. Héctor Pérez Brignoli, "Deux siècles d'illégitimité au Costa Rica, 1770–1974," in *Marriage and Remarriage in Populations of the Past*, ed. J. Dupaquier, E. Hélin, P. Laslett, M. Livi-Bacci, and S. Sogner (London: Academic Press/Harcourt Brace Jovanovich, 1981), 482.

20. Thomas C. Holt, *The Problem of Freedom: Race, Labor, and Politics in Jamaica and Britain, 1832–1938* (Baltimore: Johns Hopkins University Press, 1992), 18.

21. Diane J. Austin-Broos, "Redefining the Moral Order: Interpretations of Christianity in Postemancipation Jamaica," in *The Meaning of Freedom: Economics, Politics, and Culture after Slavery*, ed. Frank McGlynn and Seymour Drescher (Pittsburgh: University of Pittsburgh Press, 1992), 221–43.

22. Douglas Hall, "The Flight from the Estates Reconsidered: The British West Indies, 1838–1842," in *Caribbean Freedom: Economy and Society from Emancipation to the Present*, ed. Hilary Beckles and Verene Shepherd (Princeton: Markus Wiener, 1996), 55–63; Holt, *Problem of Freedom*, chap. 5; Swithin Wilmot, "'Females of Abandoned Character'? Women and Protest in Jamaica, 1838–65," in *Engendering History: Caribbean*

Women in Historical Perspective, ed. Verene Shepherd, Bridget Brereton, and Barbara Bailey (Kingston: Ian Randle, 1995), 280.

23. Holt, *Problem of Freedom*, 144–46.

24. Resident of Martha Brae quoted by Jean Besson, "Family Land as Model for Martha Brae's New History: Culture Building in an Afro-Caribbean Village," in *Afro-Caribbean Villages in Historical Perspective* (Kingston: African-Caribbean Institute of Jamaica, 1987), 118, as cited in Richard D. E. Burton, *Afro-Creole: Power, Opposition, and Play in the Caribbean* (Ithaca: Cornell University Press, 1997), 94. See Jean Besson, "Freedom and Community: The British West Indies," in McGlynn and Drescher, *Meaning of Freedom*, 198–204; Janet Henshall Momsen, "Gender Ideology and Land," in *Caribbean Portraits: Essays on Gender Ideologies and Identities*, ed. Christine Barrow (Kingston: Ian Randle, 1998), 115–32.

25. Erna Brodber, "Afro-Jamaican Women at the Turn of the Century," *Social and Economic Studies* 35 (1986): 38. Translation: "But you couldn't expect a women who had a husband to go dig a yam hole. She would never do that work herself, if she had a husband. She would have no occasion to. Her husband wouldn't allow her to do that work. Instead she would go to her piece of land and when her husband dug up the root crop she would carry it to the market and sell it." Interviews were conducted in 1973–75.

26. Betty Wood and Roy Clayton, "Jamaica's Struggle for a Self-Perpetuating Slave Population: Demographic, Social, and Religious Changes on Golden Grove Plantation, 1812–1832," *Journal of Caribbean Studies* 6, no. 3 (1988), 298–305.

27. George W. Roberts, *The Population of Jamaica* (Cambridge: Cambridge University Press, 1957), 288; Diane J. Austin-Broos, *Jamaica Genesis: Religion and the Politics of Moral Orders* (Kingston: Ian Randle, 1997), chaps. 2 and 3.

28. Raymond T. Smith, *Kinship and Class in the West Indies: A Genealogical Study of Jamaica and Guyana* (Cambridge: Cambridge University Press, 1988), 101–9; Holt, *Problem of Freedom*, 30. In Jamaica "Coloured" or "Brown" referred to light-skinned elites of partial African ancestry.

29. Holt, *Problem of Freedom*, 146–66.

30. Ibid., 127, 199–202; Douglas G. Hall, *Free Jamaica, 1838–1865: An Economic History* (New Haven: Yale University Press, 1959), 157–81.

31. Holt, *Problem of Freedom*, 278–89.

32. *Report on the Moral Conditions of the City of Kingston*, 1865, as cited in Don Robotham, "'The Notorious Riot': The Socio-economic and Political Bases of Paul Bogle's Revolt," Working Paper no. 28 (Mona, Jamaica: Institute of Social and Economic Research, University of the West Indies, 1981), 71, 77. See also Burton, *Afro-Creole*, 96.

33. Héctor Lindo Fuentes, "Economía y sociedad (1810–1870)," in Pérez Brignoli, *De la ilustración al liberalismo*, 156–200; Víctor Hugo Acuña Ortega and Iván Molina Jiménez, *Historia económica y social de Costa Rica (1750–1950)* (San José: Editorial Porvenir, 1991), 85.

34. Lowell Gudmundson, *Costa Rica before Coffee: Society and Economy on the Eve of the Export Boom* (Baton Rouge: Louisiana State University Press, 1986), 76.

35. Iván Molina Jiménez, *Costa Rica (1800–1850): El legado colonial y la génesis del capitalismo* (San José: Editorial de la Universidad de Costa Rica, 1991), 255–56; Jorge León Sáenz, *Evolución del comercio exterior y del transporte marítimo de Costa Rica, 1821–1900* (San José: Editorial de la Universidad de Costa Rica, 1997), 87, 99–100.

36. Mario Samper Kutschbach, *Generations of Settlers: Rural Households and Markets on the Costa Rican Frontier, 1850–1935* (Boulder, Colo.: Westview Press, 1990), 65–75. See also Carolyn Hall, *El café y el desarrollo histórico-geográfico de Costa Rica* (San José: Editorial Costa Rica, 1991).

37. Acuña Ortega and Molina Jiménez, *Historia económica y social*, 81–83.

38. Samper Kutschbach, *Generations of Settlers*, 99.

39. Mario Samper Kutschbach, "Café, trabajo y sociedad en Centroamérica, 1870–1930: Una historia común y divergente," in *Las repúblicas agroexportadoras*, ed. Víctor Hugo Acuña Ortega, vol. 4 of *Historia general de Centroamérica*, 73–78; Lindo Fuentes, "Economía y sociedad," 174–75. Coffee seedlings themselves were not expensive: *beneficiadores* distributed them free or nearly so to potential growers.

40. Samper Kutschbach, *Generations of Settlers*, 81. In contrast, communal lands proved quite workable for the first generation of coffee cultivators in El Salvador. See Aldo Lauria-Santiago, *An Agrarian Republic: Commercial Agriculture and the Politics of Peasant Communities in El Salvador, 1823–1914* (Pittsburgh: University of Pittsburgh Press, 1999), chap. 6.

41. Eugenia Rodríguez Sáenz, "Padres e hijos: Familia y mercado matrimonial en el Valle Central de Costa Rica (1821–1850)," in *Heroes al gusto y libros de moda: Sociedad y cambio cultural en Costa Rica (1750–1900)*, ed. Iván Molina Jiménez and Steven Palmer (San José: Editorial Porvenir/Plumsock Mesoamerican Studies, 1992), 46; Lowell Gudmundson, "Peasant, Farmer, Proletarian: Class Formation in a Smallholder Coffee Economy, 1850–1950," in *Coffee, Society, and Power in Latin America*, ed. William Roseberry, Lowell Gudmundson, and Mario Samper Kutschbach (Johns Hopkins University Press, 1995), 140–41.

42. Gudmundson, *Costa Rica before Coffee*, chap. 3; Pérez Brignoli, "Deux siècles," 483–87.

43. Gudmundson, *Costa Rica before Coffee*, 97–102.

44. Eugenia Rodríguez Sáenz, "Civilizando la vida doméstica en el Valle Central de Costa Rica (1750–1850)," in *Entre silencios y voces: Género e historia en América Central*, ed. Eugenia Rodríguez Sáenz (San José: Editorial Porvenir/Centro Nacional para el Desarrollo de la Mujer y la Familia, 1998), 43–46.

45. See, for instance, Gudmundson, *Costa Rica before Coffee*, 70, 99.

46. Throughout nineteenth-century Latin America, self-identified *liberales* (political and economic elites, often allied in a formal Partido Liberal) sought to centralize state power, reduce church influence, and promote export-led growth. See Lowell

Gudmundson and Héctor Lindo-Fuentes, *Central America, 1821–1871: Liberalism before Liberal Reform* (Tuscaloosa: University of Alabama Press, 1995); Ronny J. Viales Hurtado, "Los liberales y la colonización de las áreas de frontera no cafetaleras: El caso de la región Atlántica (Caribe) costarricense entre 1870 y 1930" (Ph.D. diss., Universitat Autónoma de Barcelona, 2000).

Chapter Two

1. Accurate statistics on this movement are impossible to calculate, for the degree of return migration and secondary migrations is almost unknown. Approximately 50,000 West Indians worked on the French canal, 80,000 Jamaicans and 60,000 Barbadians on the U.S. canal, and 20,000 Jamaicans in the banana zone of Limón. Bonham C. Richardson, "Caribbean Migrations, 1838–1985," in *The Modern Caribbean*, ed. Franklin W. Knight and Colin A. Palmer (Chapel Hill: University of North Carolina Press, 1989), 210.

2. Aims C. McGuinness, "In the Path of Empire: Popular Politics and U.S. Imperialism in Panama, 1848–1860" (Ph.D. diss., University of Michigan, 2000); Elizabeth MacLean Petras, *Jamaican Labor Migration: White Capital and Black Labor, 1850–1930* (Boulder, Colo.: Westview Press, 1988), 60–81. Eisner sets total Jamaican migration at 1,500 to 2,000, while Jaén Suárez places the total of immigrant workers at around 7,000. Gisela Eisner, *Jamaica, 1830–1930: A Study in Economic Growth* (Manchester: The University Press, 1961), 147; Omar Jaén Suárez, *La población del istmo de Panamá del siglo XVI al siglo XX* (Panama City: n.p., 1979), 451.

3. Harry G. Lefever, *Turtle Bogue: Afro-Caribbean Life and Culture in a Costa Rican Village* (Cranbury, N.J.: Associated University Presses, 1992), 58–60; Paula Palmer, *"Wa'apin man": La historia de la costa talamanqueña de Costa Rica, según sus protagonistas*, trans. Quince Duncan and Paula Palmer, 2d ed. (San José: Editorial de la Universidad de Costa Rica, 1994), 39–40; Charles W. Koch, "Ethnicity and Livelihoods: A Social Geography of Costa Rica's Atlantic Zone" (Ph.D. diss., University of Kansas, 1975), 58–59.

4. Juan Carlos Solórzano Fonseca, "Los indígenas en las áreas fronterizas de Costa Rica durante el siglo XIX," *Avances de Investigación*, no. 78 (San José: Centro de Investigaciones Históricas de América Central, Universidad de Costa Rica, 2000).

5. E. G. Squier, *The States of Central America* (New York: Harper and Brothers, 1858), 460.

6. L. E. Elliott, *Central America: New Paths in Ancient Lands* (New York: Dodd, Mead, 1925), 214. Elliott visited the spot "with a party searching for new, cheap and extensive banana lands."

7. I have borrowed the phrase "landscapes and livelihoods" from John Soluri's eco-social history of Honduras's northern coast, "Landscape and Livelihood: An Agro-

ecological History of Export Banana-Growing in Honduras, 1870–1975" (Ph.D. diss., University of Michigan, 1998).

8. Jeffrey Casey Gaspar, "El Ferrocarril al Atlántico en Costa Rica, 1871–1874," *Anuario de Estudios Centroamericanos* 2 (1976): 292–93; Steven Palmer, "A Liberal Discipline: Inventing Nations in Guatemala and Costa Rica, 1870–1900" (Ph.D. diss., Columbia University, 1990), chap. 5; Watt Stewart, *Keith y Costa Rica* (San José: Editorial Costa Rica, 1991), chap. 1.

9. Carmen Murillo Chaverri, *Identidades de hierro y humo: La construcción del Ferrocarril al Atlántico, 1870–1890* (San José: Editorial Porvenir, 1995), 31.

10. Rodrigo Quesada Monge, *Recuerdos del imperio: Los ingleses en América Central (1821–1915)* (Heredia, Costa Rica: Editorial de la Universidad Nacional, 1998), 317–42; Stewart, *Keith y Costa Rica*, 66–70.

11. Joaquín B. Calvo, *The Republic of Costa Rica* (Chicago: Rand McNally, 1890), 51–52.

12. Decreto no. 24 del 3 de noviembre de 1862, in Costa Rica, *Colección de leyes y decretos* (San José: Imprenta La Paz, 1872), 159.

13. ANCR, Fomento 4515 (5 Oct. 1871), as cited in Murillo Chaverri, *Identidades*, 73.

14. Murillo Chaverri, *Identidades*, chaps. 3 and 4; Carlos Meléndez Chaverri, "Aspectos sobre la inmigración jamaicana," in Carlos Meléndez Chaverri and Quince Duncan, *El negro en Costa Rica*, 8th ed. (San José: Editorial Costa Rica, 1981), 74.

15. Moisés León Azofeifa, "Chinese Immigrants on the Atlantic Coast of Costa Rica: The Economic Adaptation of an Asian Minority in a Pluralistic Society" (Ph.D. diss., Tulane University, 1988), 65–78. From the 1870s onward Chinese migrants also arrived independently (and thus illegally) from established Chinese communities in Cuba, Panama, Mexico, Jamaica, and California.

16. *El Ferrocarril*, 12 Oct. 1872, as cited in Casey Gaspar, "Ferrocarril al Atlántico," 319.

17. ANCR, Hacienda y Fomento 1600 (Copiador del ingeniero, 23 Apr. 1874), as cited in Casey Gaspar, "Ferrocarril al Atlántico," 326.

18. ANCR, Policía 5204 (20–22 Nov. 1883), as cited in Murillo Chaverri, *Identidades*, 116.

19. *Gaceta Oficial*, 19 June 1875, as cited in Meléndez Chaverri, "Aspectos sobre la inmigración jamaicana," 81.

20. The role of kinship ties and social networks among Chinese immigrants is described at length by León Azofeifa, "Chinese Immigrants on the Atlantic Coast," 141–64.

21. Koch, "Ethnicity and Livelihoods," 68–70; Meléndez Chaverri, "Aspectos sobre la inmigración jamaicana," 76.

22. Carl Bovallius, "Estadía en Costa Rica (Julio a Octubre de 1882)," in *Viajes por la República de Costa Rica*, vol. 1, comp. Elías Zeledón Cartín (San José: Ministerio de Cultura, Juventud y Deportes, 1997), 118–19.

23. Ibid., 122.

24. Koch, "Ethnicity and Livelihoods," 136; Costa Rica, Dirección General de Estadística y Censos, *Censo General de la República de Costa Rica . . . de 1892*, facsimile ed. (San José: Ministerio de Economía, Industria y Comercio, Dirección General de Estadística y Censos, 1974), 56–57.

25. LAU 1678 (desahucio, 1882).

26. ANCR, Jurídico (Limón) 876 (violación, 1882).

27. David McCullough, *The Path between the Seas: The Creation of the Panama Canal, 1870-1914* (New York: Simon and Schuster, 1977), 191–235.

28. *Governor's Report on the Blue Book*, 1883–84, as cited in George W. Roberts, *The Population of Jamaica* (Cambridge: Cambridge University Press, 1957), 133.

29. Petras, *Jamaican Labor Migration*, 97–100; Jaén Suárez, *Población del istmo*, 453; McCullough, *Path between the Seas*, 161.

30. McCullough, *Path between the Seas*, 174–81; Petras, *Jamaican Labor Migration*, 115; Roberts, *Population of Jamaica*, 134.

31. "Informe del gobernador de la Comarca de Limón," in MGP (1885, 1886, 1887). See also Jeffrey Casey Gaspar, *Limón, 1880-1940: Un estudio de la industria bananera en Costa Rica* (San José: Editorial Costa Rica, 1979), 236–37. In 1886–87 Jamaican officials tallied 10,400 departures for Panama and 7,100 returns (a ratio of 1.5:1). The same source noted 1,200 departures for Costa Rica and only 60 returns from that site (a ratio of 20:1). Roberts, *Population of Jamaica*, 134.

32. Eisner, *Jamaica*, 149. Estimates of the number of stranded workers range from 6,000 to 20,000. See Michael Conniff, *Black Labor on a White Canal: West Indians in Panama, 1904-1980* (Pittsburgh: University of Pittsburgh Press, 1985), 20, and Petras, *Jamaican Labor Migration*, 117.

33. Koch, "Ethnicity and Livelihoods," 70–72, 109–11, 126–40.

34. Palmer, *"Wa'apin man,"* 44–71. Quote is from Costa Rica, Departamento Nacional de Estadística, "Banana Culture," *Monthly Bulletin of the American Republics Bureau* 3 (1896): 391, as cited in Koch, "Ethnicity and Livelihoods," 123–24, n. 2.

35. Koch, "Ethnicity and Livelihoods," 146–54.

36. Brunilda Hilje Quirós, *La colonización agrícola de Costa Rica (1840-1940)* (San José: Editorial Universidad Estatal a Distancia, 1995), 32–33; Mario Samper Kutschbach, "Café, trabajo y sociedad en Centroamérica, 1870–1930: Una historia común y divergente," in *Las repúblicas agroexportadoras*, ed. Víctor Hugo Acuña Ortega, vol. 4 of *Historia general de Centroamérica*, coordinated by Edelberto Torres Rivas (Madrid: Sociedad Estatal Quinto Centenario and FLACSO, 1993), 61–62; Orlando Salazar Mora, *El apogeo de la república liberal en Costa Rica, 1870-1914* (San José: Editorial Universidad de Costa Rica, 1990), 101–4.

37. George Earl Church, *Report upon the Costa Rican Railway* (London, 1895), as cited in Stewart, *Keith y Costa Rica*, 162.

38. MGP (1883), 27; Aviva Chomsky, *West Indian Workers and the United Fruit Company in Costa Rica, 1870-1940* (Baton Rouge: Louisiana State University Press, 1996), 27–28.

39. LAU 2654 (desahucio, 1902); LAU 2655 (desahucio, 1902); LAU 2650 (desahucio, 1902).

40. Casey Gaspar, *Limón*, 97; Koch, "Ethnicity and Livelihoods," 128–32; Chomsky, *West Indian Workers*, chap. 3.

41. See, for instance, LAU 1660 (desahucio, 1891); LAU 1827 (desahucio, 1897); LAU 1828 (desahucio, 1897); LAU 1824 (desahucio, 1897); LAU 1703 (desahucio, 1895); LAU 1832 (desahucio, 1897); LAU 1831 (desahucio, 1897); LAU 1919 (desahucio, 1897); LAU 2052 (daños, 1901); LAU 1065 (daños, 1900).

42. See, for example, LJCyC 660 (desahucio, 1906); LJCyC 658 (desahucio, 1907); LAU 1660 (desahucio, 1891). Two-fifths of defendants in eviction cases that progressed beyond a single notification employed lawyers.

43. Under the sponsorship of the Centro de Investigaciones Históricas of the Universidad de Costa Rica (CIHAC) a systematic one-in-ten sample was created from the original tally sheets of the 1927 census. It can be downloaded from the Centro Centroamericano de Población at http://pcp1.eest.fce.ucr.ac.cr. English-speaking immigrants who remained in Limón in 1927 and appear in this sample include 826 born in Jamaica, 53 born "elsewhere in the Caribbean," 38 born in Panama, 21 in Nicaragua, 5 in Colombia, 3 in Cuba, 3 in Honduras, and 1 in Guatemala. The sample also includes 17 French speakers born "elsewhere in the Caribbean," most of them probably from St. Lucia.

44. In the 1911 Jamaican census, own-account farmers outnumbered agricultural laborers in Portland, St. Ann, Clarendon, and St. Catherine and did so by especially large margins in St. Elizabeth (2.8 to 1) and Manchester (4.4 to 1). Richard A. Lobdell, "Women in the Jamaican Labour Force, 1881–1921" *Social and Economic Studies* 37, nos. 1 and 2 (1988): tables 10 and 11.

45. Roberts, *Population of Jamaica*, 282.

46. LJCyC 381 (homicidio, 1901).

47. LAU 2148 (daños, 1903); LAU 2069 (daños, 1903); LJCyC 97 (tentativa de violación, 1899); LAU 3466 (calumnia, 1907). See also Trevor W. Purcell, *Banana Fallout: Class, Color and Culture among West Indians in Costa Rica* (Los Angeles: Center for Afro-American Studies, University of California, 1993), 137.

48. See León Azofeifa, "Chinese Immigrants on the Atlantic Coast," 106, 111.

49. LAU 472 (injurias, 1899); LJCrimen 1119 (incendio, 1906).

50. LJCyC 27 (estupro, 1898). See also LAU 1605 (deuda, 1898); LAU 254 (embargo, 1899); LJCyC 669 (deuda, 1901); LAU 2599 (deuda, 1902); LAU 2463 (deuda, 1902); LAU 2462 (deuda, 1902); LAU 2461 (deuda, 1902); LAU 2459 (deuda, 1902); LAU 2460 (deuda, 1902).

51. Over half of the twenty-nine West Indian girls who appear as injured parties in deflowering or rape cases from this era resided with an aunt or godmother and had neither mother nor father living in Limón.

52. LJCrimen 266 (violación, 1901). See also LJCrimen 41 (violación, 1902).

53. LJCyC 394 (homicidio, 1899). See also LAU 2490 (daños, 1902).

54. LJCrimen 417 (incendio, 1913). See also LJCrimen 596 (homicidio, 1910).

55. LJCivil 103 (separación de cuerpos, 1902). It is unclear whether either of them actually cleared and cultivated the land themselves, or whether they hired others to do so.

56. LJCyC 662 (separación de cuerpos, 1898). In fact their joint property was rather more than subsistence level. In the final separation agreement Vargas received the five-hectare (12.4-acre) banana farm in Moín and a small boat, while Pardo kept nine cows, one mare, sixteen calves, three boats, a six-hectare farm on Río Blanco, and a 200-hectare farm planted in pasture, bananas, and fruit trees that included "one house for the family and one for the *peones*."

57. LAU 2052 (daños, 1901); LAU 201 (daños 1901).

58. At the wealthy end of the spectrum, two published lists of local planters, from 1886 and 1894, include two women and fifty-four men (and seven individuals cited by first initial alone whom I have not been able to identify conclusively). Eviction cases suggest a similar pattern among a sample that includes the poor and indebted. I surveyed 110 eviction (*desahucio*) cases from Limón (out of a total 160 preserved cases) dating from the years 1882–1907. Including actors, defendants, subletters, and prior owners, 318 individuals are named in these suits; the ratio of male to female named parties is 4.4:1. Only twenty-one of the cases deal with agricultural holdings, and in this subset of cases the ratio of male to female named parties is 12:1.

59. Trevor Purcell describes one of his informants as "Mrs. Lewin, a field hand who began working for the Company as early as 1910." Purcell, *Banana Fallout*, 37. Almost certainly she worked on a cocoa plantation, where women's and children's labor was routinely employed in later years. See Chapter 4, note 44.

60. TPP 427, 78.

61. ANCR, Policía 61 (causa, 24 June 1904).

62. ANCR, Policía 61 (decreto, 8 Aug. 1904).

63. Costa Rica, Dirección de Estadística y Censos, "Movimiento marítimo del Puerto de Limón," *Censo de 1892*, 206–17. For official Jamaican statistics on travel to and from Costa Rica and Panama see Malcolm J. Proudfoot, *Population Movements in the Caribbean* (Caribbean Commission Central Secretariat: Port-of-Spain, Trinidad, 1950), 77–80.

64. A. Hyatt Verrill, *Thirty Years in the Jungle* (London: John Lane, 1929), 182–83.

65. LAU 399 (injurias, 1898). Cases referring to connections between Colón and Port Limón include LAU 413 (injurias, 1899), LAU 540 (injurias, 1901), LJCrimen 69 (violación, 1904), LJCrimen 72 (estupro, 1906).

66. LJCrimen 343 (estupro, 1913).

67. LJCrimen 359 (homicidio, 1895).

68. LJCrimen 753 (homicidio, 1898).

69. See 1927 census figures discussed below. The 90 percent estimates are given by E. B. Branson, "Some Observations of the Geography and Geology of Middle Eastern Costa Rica," *University of Missouri Studies* 3, no. 1 (1928): 42, and A. Grenfell Price, *White*

Settlers in the Tropics, Special Publication no. 23 (New York: American Geographical Society, 1939), 128, both cited in Koch, "Ethnicity and Livelihoods," 268, n. 1. It was "a matter of general comment," wrote one visitor in 1939, that "[a]t Turrialba there is a most striking line of racial cleavage: below the town more than 90 percent of the inhabitants are black, above more than 95 percent are white." Leo Waibel, "White Settlement in Costa Rica," *Geographical Review* 29, no. 4 (1939): 548, n. 20.

70. Wallace Thompson, *The Rainbow Countries of Central America* (New York: E. P. Dutton, 1926), 19–20.

71. Mario Posas, "La plantación bananera en Centroamérica (1870-1929)," in Acuña Ortega, *Repúblicas agroexportadoras*, 141; Chomsky, *West Indian Workers*, 60.

72. The estimate is based on a productivity estimate of ten to fifteen acres per field worker, a rule-of-thumb figure derived from the number of men employed on banana farms in the 1927 CIHAC census sample and acreage in cultivation in that year (Koch, "Ethnicity and Livelihoods," 155). The productivity estimate is consistent with contemporary estimates of employees needed for clearing, cultivation, and harvest. See Koch, "Ethnicity and Livelihoods," 95, 131, and Charles Kepner, *Social Aspects of the Banana Industry* (New York: Columbia University Press, 1936), 96.

73. Casey Gaspar, *Limón*, 96–102.

74. See UFCo Medical Department, *Annual Reports*, as compiled by Chomsky, *West Indian Workers*, 48–49. Testimony from 114 homicide cases originated in Limón between 1890 and 1915 suggests that Costa Rican and Central American work crews predominated along the Old Line from the late 1890s onward and in the Estrella Valley from the 1900s on, and that both all-Hispanic and ethnically mixed workforces were common around Siquirres throughout the era. In contrast, nearly all participants in cases from the Main Line and southern coast are West Indian. Participants in cases from Port Limón are of every origin.

75. Jaén Suárez, *Población del istmo*, 458–61; Petras, *Jamaican Labor Migration*, 119–25, 142–45; McCullough, *Path between the Seas*, 476.

76. Roberts, *Population of Jamaica*, 135–36; Eisner, *Jamaica*, 379; Conniff, *Black Labor on a White Canal*, 31.

77. Winifred James, *The Mulberry Tree* (London: Chapman and Hall, 1913), 190.

78. Petras, *Jamaican Labor Migration*, 148–49; Costa Rica, Dirección General de Estadística y Censos, *Anuario estadístico* (1913); Koch, "Ethnicity and Livelihoods," 263; MGP (1911), lxxii–lxxiv.

79. ANCR, Policía 1484 (letter, 16 Mar. 1906); Policía 1567 (letter, 20 Apr. 1907); Policía 1120 (letter, 9 July 1908); Policía 1249 (telegram, 17 Apr. 1908); Policía 1593 (telegram, 14 Oct. 1909); Policía 1594 (telegram, 21 Aug. 1909).

80. Figure 2.2 presents the year of arrival reported by foreign-born respondents residing in Limón at the time of the 1927 census. Jamaicans make up 84 percent of those classed as West Indians on this graph; those born in Nicaragua make up 71 percent of Hispanics. This data is far from ideal for measuring the relative volume of arrivals over time. Obviously deaths and outmigration have diminished reported arrivals for

the earliest years more than later ones, but variations within that general trend are impossible to assess. The CIHAC database includes an expansion factor for each entry derived from the proportion of entries sampled in that individual's canton of residence. The expansion factors are 10.40557 for Central Limón, 9.15077 for Pococí, and 15.67198 for Siquirres. The distribution of plantation agriculture meant that the sex ratio and ethnic breakdown varied markedly by canton. To avoid understating the numbers of Hispanic men in the province I have used the expanded figures throughout my analysis.

81. Both contemporary statistics and later census data suggest that the rate of West Indian arrivals in Limón slowed between 1903 and 1906. Koch, "Ethnicity and Livelihoods," 262–63.

82. TPP 425 (interview with David Buchanan), 31. See also TPP 428 (interview with Cyril Gray), 1–2.

83. Roberts, *Population of Jamaica*, 139. See Eisner, *Jamaica*, 148–51; Conniff, *Black Labor on a White Canal*, 47–49; Petras, *Jamaican Labor Migration*, 211–13.

84. British Public Records Office, CO 137 690 3729 (report by Governor Sydney Olivier, 1911), 4. I am grateful to Ronald Harpelle for providing me with his transcription of this citation.

85. Petras, *Jamaican Labor Migration*, 210; *Annual Report of the Isthmian Canal Commission* (1913-14), as cited in Roberts, *Population of Jamaica*, 136.

86. Koch, "Ethnicity and Livelihoods," 152–53; George Palmer Putnam, *The Southland of North America: Rambles and Observations in Central America during the Year 1912* (New York: G. P. Putnam and Sons, 1914), 111.

87. LJCrimen 925 (incendio,1914); LJCrimen 181 (incendio, 1910); LJCrimen 295 (incendio, 1911); LJCrimen 30 (incendio, 1910); LJCrimen 1118 (incendio, 1915). See also Chomsky, *West Indian Workers*, 66–67.

88. Koch, "Ethnicity and Livelihoods," 152; Kepner, *Social Aspects*, 64.

89. Casey Gaspar, *Limón*, 40-43, 113.

90. On labor activism in this era, see Chapter 6, notes 33 and 34, below.

91. According to the CIHAC sample only 6 percent of the province's population— 1,900-odd souls—were Spanish speakers of any nationality born in Limón before 1920.

92. Philippe Bourgois, *Ethnicity at Work: Divided Labor on a Central American Banana Plantation* (Baltimore: Johns Hopkins University Press, 1989), 54–58. Quote is from British Colonial Office 318-350-2946 (29 May 1919), as cited in ibid., 57.

93. Vladimir De la Cruz, *Las luchas sociales en Costa Rica* (San José: Editorial Universidad de Costa Rica, 1980), 114–19; Elisavinda Echeverri-Gent, "Forgotten Workers: British West Indians and the Early Days of the Banana Industry in Costa Rica and Honduras," *Journal of Latin American Studies* 24, no. 2 (1992): 293–97.

94. Koch, "Ethnicity and Livelihoods," 265.

95. Reinaldo Carcanholo, "Sobre la evolución de las actividades bananeras en Costa Rica," *Anuario de Estudios Centroamericanos* 19 (1978): 150.

96. UFCo Medical Department, *Annual Report* 9 (1920), as cited in Chomsky, *West Indian Workers*, 47, n. 36. See also Kepner, *Social Aspects*, 162–63.

97. LJCrimen 765 (homicidio, 1911).

98. Costa Rica, Dirección General de Estadística y Censos, *Censo de Población de 1927* (San José, 1960), 90. The groups that contradict this basic alignment of race and language are a few French-speaking blacks from the Caribbean, a few English-speaking whites (Jamaican and U.S.), and a few more Spanish-speaking blacks (mostly from Nicaragua, Panama, and Colombia). None of these groups totals more than 1 percent of the census sample.

99. Casey Gaspar, *Limón*, chap. 4; Ronny José Viales Hurtado, *Después del enclave: Un estudio de la región atlántica costarricense, 1927–1950* (San José: Editorial Universidad de Costa Rica, 1998), 55.

100. See Table A.1.

101. Among West Indian immigrants living in Limón in 1927, the sex ratio was 234:100 for those who had arrived before 1899 and 191:100 for those who had arrived between 1900 and 1906. Disproportionate numbers of male migrants had died in the intervening years, so the male bias among incoming migrants was likely even greater. In contrast, the sex ratio among West Indians who had arrived between 1907 and 1914 was only 140:100.

102. Over 113,000 laborers traveled directly from Jamaica to Cuba in the first four decades of this century, but by 1940 cumulative returns of Jamaicans *from* Cuba exceeded cumulative departures *to* Cuba by more than 6,000, evidence of the numbers of Costa Rica– and Panama-born West Indians among Jamaicans exiting Cuba in the 1930s. Proudfoot, *Population Movements in the Caribbean*, 77–80.

103. Fifty-eight percent of children under fifteen and 64 percent of adults thirty and over were black. Sixty-three percent of men fifteen to twenty-nine were white, as were only 39 percent of their female peers.

104. The census sample includes 199 English-speaking women between the ages of fifteen and twenty-nine. Only one of them resided in a household that included a Spanish-speaking man, and he was a black man from Nicaragua. Of these women, 13 percent were married and lived with their husbands, 24 percent were living in free unions with male partners, 31 percent were single and living with their mothers or fathers, 14 percent were single and living in other households, and 8 percent were single heads of household. Husbands or male partners were on average ten years older than their wives or female partners.

105. Carlos Luís Fallas, *Mamita Yunai*, 2d ed. (1941; reprint, San José: Editorial Costa Rica, 1995), 131.

106. Figures refer to those reporting arrival between 1920 and 1927.

107. The following is based on forty life history interviews conducted by Peace Corps volunteer Paula Palmer in Cahuita and Puerto Viejo in 1976–77 and subsequently donated to the ANCR. A selection was published in Paula Palmer, *"What Happen": A*

Folk-History of Costa Rica's Talamanca Coast (San José: Ecodesarrollos, 1977), and a Spanish translation incorporating additional material followed in Palmer, *"Wa'apin man."*

108. TPP 425, 37–41.

109. TPP 425, 106.

110. See occupation and property ownership data in Lara Putnam, "Public Women and One-Pant Men: Labor Migration and the Politics of Gender in Caribbean Costa Rica, 1870–1960" (Ph.D. diss., University of Michigan, 2000), 175–82.

111. TPP 427, 208; TPP 428, 12. Similarly, see TPP 427, 86, and TPP 427, 163–64.

112. AC, vol. 26, pt. 1, "Autobiografía de R.G.C." (interview), 227–49; AC, vol. 26, pt. 3, "Autobiografía de I.P.R.," 86–89. In 1977 hundreds of self-identified "campesinos" submitted autobiographies to a national contest sponsored by the School of Social Planning of the Universidad Nacional. Several dozen of the submissions were published in a five-volume series: Escuela de Planificación y Promoción Social, *Autobiografías campesinas* (Heredia, Costa Rica: Editorial de la Universidad Nacional, 1979). All submissions were transcribed and are available to researchers at the Biblioteca Central of the Universidad Nacional. For this project I surveyed fifty-five autobiographies, covering 1,120 typescript pages, which include all those submitted from Limón by men ages fifty-one and over in 1977 (thirty-nine) and all those submitted from Limón by women ages thirty-one and over (sixteen).

113. AC, vol. 26, pt. 2, "Autobiografía de M.M. (escrita por él)" (13th in vol.), 1–2. See also AC, vol. 26, pt. 3, "Autobiografía de R.Q.P." (interview), 92–102.

114. AC, vol. 26, pt. 1, "Autobiografía de A.H.Ch.," 258. See also MGP (1942), 126–27.

115. AC, vol. 26, pt. 1, "Autobiografía de A.H.Ch.," 251–73.

116. The two exceptions were the Guanacaste ranch and the cocoa grove in Cahuita.

117. See especially Aviva Chomsky, "West Indian Workers in Costa Rican Radical and Nationalist Ideology: 1900–1950," *The Americas* 51, no. 1 (1994): 25–37.

118. Costa Rica, Dirección General de Estadística y Censos, *Censo de 1927*, 91.

119. Under the constitution of 1871 locally born children of foreign parents could only acquire Costa Rican citizenship through a costly petitioning procedure. See Ronald N. Harpelle, "The Social and Political Integration of West Indians in Costa Rica: 1930–50," *Journal of Latin American Studies* 25 (1993): 103–20.

120. Casey Gaspar, *Limón*, 214–15. The census tally sheets were discovered in 1985, dispersed among unclassified documents in the National Archives.

121. José Guerrero, "¿Cómo se quiere que sea Costa Rica, blanca o negra? El problema racial del negro y las actuales contrataciones bananeras," *La Tribuna*, 13 Aug. 1930, reprinted in the San José literary review *Repertorio Americano* 21, no. 10 (1930): 149.

122. See, for instance, Rodrigo Facio Brenes, *Estudio sobre la economía costarricense*, 4th ed. (San José: Editorial Costa Rica, 1990), 79–80.

123. See, for example, Casey Gaspar, *Limón*, 202–3, and Héctor Pérez Brignoli, *Breve historia de Centroamérica*, 2d ed. (Mexico City: Alianza Editorial Mexicana, 1989), 111–12.

124. Chomsky, *West Indian Workers*, 235–53; Koch, "Ethnicity and Livelihoods," 289–90.

125. Harpelle, "Social and Political Integration," 107; Ronald Harpelle, "Racism and Nationalism in the Creation of Costa Rica's Pacific Coast Banana Enclave," *The Americas* 56, no. 3 (2000): 29–51.

126. *Searchlight*, 12 Mar. 1930, 3. Spelling as in original. A 1926 law in Panama had declared all "Negroes whose native language is not Spanish" as "undesirables" and placed limitations on their citizenship. Bourgois, *Ethnicity at Work*, 89–91. The English-language press in Limón covered these developments at length.

127. Fully half of the thirty Hispanic *campesinos* and *campesinas* who submitted autobiographies as Limón residents in 1977 had worked in the Pacific coast banana zone in their youth. See AC, vols. 23 and 26.

128. Decreto no. 4 del 26 de abril de 1942, Art. 41, in Costa Rica, *Colección de leyes y decretos* (San José: Imprenta Nacional, 1942), 176.

129. TPP 427, 41–48.

130. TPP 427, 49–64.

131. The Calderón regime began to facilitate naturalizations after 1942, reversing former policies. Still, emigration removed some 45 percent of the potential black population of Limón between 1927 and 1950. Koch, "Ethnicity and Livelihoods," 251, 293–99.

Chapter Three

1. Joaquín Gutiérrez, *Puerto Limón*, 7th ed. (1950; reprint, San José: Editorial de la Universidad de Costa Rica, 1991), 13–14.

2. Carlos Luís Fallas, *Mamita Yunai*, 2d ed. (1941; reprint, San José: Editorial Costa Rica, 1995), 111. See Marielos Aguilar Hernández, *Carlos Luís Fallas: Su época y sus lucha* (San José: Editorial Porvenir, 1983).

3. UFCo Medical Department, *Annual Report* 14 (1925), 18, as cited in Aviva Chomsky, "Plantation Society, Land and Labor on Costa Rica's Atlantic Coast, 1870–1940" (Ph.D. diss., University of California, Berkeley, 1990), 161.

4. U.S. Department of State, American Foreign Service Report 818.504/3 (18 Mar. 1925; prepared by John James Meily, American consul). I am indebted to Ronald Harpelle for supplying me with this citation. Bourgois describes a similarly central role played by two company-sanctioned brothels on the Bocas del Toro banana plantation today. Philippe Bourgois, *Ethnicity at Work: Divided Labor on a Central American Banana Plantation* (Baltimore: Johns Hopkins University Press, 1989), 5, 141–42.

5. British Public Records Office, CO 137 690 3729 (Report of Governor Sydney Olivier, 1911), 23–24. I am indebted to Ronald Harpelle for supplying me with this citation.

6. See Eileen J. Suárez Findlay, *Imposing Decency: The Politics of Sexuality and Race in Puerto Rico, 1870–1920* (Durham: Duke University Press, 1999), chap. 6, and Rebecca

Lord, "Quarantine in the Fort Ozama Dungeon: The Control of Prostitution and Venereal Disease in the Dominican Republic, 1923–1924," unpublished paper, University of
Maryland, 1999.

7. Charles Kepner, *Social Aspects of the Banana Industry* (New York: Columbia University Press, 1936), 96; Clarence F. Jones and Paul C. Morrison, "Evolution of the Banana
Industry in Costa Rica," *Economic Geography* 28, no. 1 (1952): 7.

8. John Soluri, "Landscape and Livelihood: An Agroecological History of Export
Banana-Growing in Honduras, 1870–1975" (Ph.D. diss., University of Michigan, 1998),
esp. chap. 3.

9. Thomas Miller Klubock, *Contested Communities: Class, Gender, and Politics in Chile's
El Teniente Copper Mine, 1904–1951* (Durham: Duke University Press, 1998), esp. chap. 2.
All quotes are from the mine's company paper, from 1920 and 1922, and are cited on
pages 66–67.

10. Aviva Chomsky, *West Indian Workers and the United Fruit Company in Costa Rica,
1870–1940* (Baton Rouge: Louisiana State University Press, 1996), chaps. 4 and 5, esp.
96–100.

11. UFCo Medical Department, *Annual Report* 18 (1929), 101–2, as cited in Chomsky,
"Plantation Society," 162.

12. UFCo Medical Department, *Annual Report* 7 (1918), 54, as cited in Chomsky, *West
Indian Workers*, 116.

13. In Hispanic *peones bananeros'* households taken as a whole, adult men outnumbered adult women by more than 6 to 1, and only 7 percent of household residents
were children under fifteen. In the homes of West Indian *peones bananeros*, in contrast,
men outnumbered women by less than 2 to 1, and over a third of household members were children. Three-fourths of *peones bananeros* in the 1927 census sample are
Hispanics; one-quarter are West Indian.

14. My analysis of the role of prostitution in the daily social reproduction of the
migrant workforce is particularly indebted to Luise White, *The Comforts of Home: Prostitution in Colonial Nairobi* (Chicago: University of Chicago Press, 1990).

15. Sueann Caulfield, "Women of Vice, Virtue, and Rebellion: New Studies of the
Representation of the Female in Latin America," *Latin American Research Review* 28,
no. 2 (1993): 171; T. Dunbar Moodie, "Migrancy and Male Sexuality on the South African Gold Mines," *Journal of Southern African Studies* 14, no. 2 (1988): 228–56.

16. José León Sánchez, *La isla de los hombres solos*, 10th ed. (Barcelona: Organización
Editorial Novaro, 1976), 56–57.

17. ANCR, Gobernación 2123 (tax table, Oct. 1909).

18. ANCR, Gobernación 23396 (letter, 29 Sept. 1925). El Rincón Bellaco, El Arca de
Noé, and La Casa Azúl are mentioned repeatedly in judicial cases involving prostitutes
during the first boom years.

19. LJCyC 97 (tentativa de violación, 1899). Henriques was charged with attempted
rape, a charge that was dropped the following day after Zelaya's testimony had been

taken. The officer's decisive action in defense of the virtue of a solitary, drunken woman was unusual. I suspect that if she had not been white, or Henriques had not been black, the response would have been different.

20. ANCR, Policía 2146 (causa, 1896).

21. MGP (1911), 448. See also MGP (1913), 543.

22. LAU 370 (daños, 1892).

23. LAU 3466 (calumnia, 1907).

24. ANCR, Policía 4270 (letter, 3 Oct. 1912).

25. SJA1 7664 (daños, 1914).

26. LAU 369 (abuso de autoridad, 1912).

27. ANCR, Gobernación 23396 (testimony, 30 July 1925).

28. ANCR, Gobernación 23396 (letter, 5 Aug. 1925).

29. Fallas, *Mamita Yunai*, 157–58.

30. See Flora Ovares, Margarita Rojas, Carlos Santander, and María Elena Carballo, *La casa paterna: Escritura y nación en Costa Rica* (San José: Editorial de la Universidad de Costa Rica, 1993), 245–54.

31. Fallas, *Mamita Yunai*, 158. For wages and exchange rates, see 137, 148.

32. LJCrimen 955 (estupro, 1914).

33. LJCrimen 770 (violación, 1913). As with almost all sex crime cases, participants offered conflicting versions of who did what with or to whom. Mary's mother reported that her daughter had been deflowered by McKay by force, while Mary gave several conflicting accounts of what happened. In this case, as opposed to many others, the men's accounts have a certain verisimilitude. At a minimum the story of the girl's multiple sex exchanges was one the witnesses thought would be believed.

34. LJPenal 1231 (estupro, 1922).

35. See, for instance, SJJCrimen 4661 (amenazas de atentado, 1895); SJA1 7664 (daños, 1914).

36. Sixteen women born before 1945 submitted personal narratives to the "Autobiografías campesinas" project from Limón in 1977. Most describe incidents in which they gave in against their will to boyfriends' pressure to have sex. Quite apart from this, five of them recount frankly violent sexual assaults: two by employers (O.C.C., born 1916; Dalia, born 1945), one by her godmother's husband (E.G. de L., born 1914), and two by male peers (V.P., born ca. 1922; L.R.A., born 1921). Other autobiographies confirm the weight of coerced sex within women's fears and lore, as when E.Z.S.'s mother warned her to avoid their *patrón*'s son, who was known for attacking female workers in the fields. See AC, vol. 23.

37. A total of forty-one *violación* cases were filed in Limón from 1907 to 1926, according to figures published in Costa Rica, Dirección General de Estadística y Censos, *Anuario estadístico* (1907–26). Twenty-seven *violación* investigations from turn-of-the-century Limón are preserved in the ANCR. The victims' median age is twelve. Only six cases ended in conviction. *Violación* was defined as sexual intercourse or "the begin-

ning of the act" with a girl under twelve under any circumstances, or sexual intercourse with any woman "by force or intimidation." *Código Penal de la República de Costa Rica* (San José, Imprenta Nacional, n.d. [1880]), book 2, title 7, chapter 5.

38. LAU 3461 (estupro, 1910). Ana Luísa insisted that she had left home to escape the sexual advances of her mother's consensual partner. Her accusations against Víctor Araya and her mother's partner may have been intended to derail the lawsuit against her boyfriend (although the medical exam, which found her "long sexually active," had already made prosecution highly unlikely). At the very least, these were stories Ana Luísa thought would be believed.

39. See LAU 502 (injurias, 1902), LJCrimen 407 (estupro, 1911), LJCrimen 335 (violación, 1912); see also SJJCrimen 7193 (hurto, 1877).

40. This point was emphasized by women in prostitution in Guápiles (the center of contemporary banana production) interviewed by public health researchers in 1995. One explained, "It's relative: when things are going bad, when you think about what your kids and your family are going to think, when you're sick, you wish you'd win the lottery and get out of there. But when things are good—I'd rather be here than giving it away in the street." The speaker framed prostitution not against alternative female occupations, but against alternative forms of unwanted sex. Tatiana Picado Le-Frank, "La situación de salud de las mujeres en prostitución en Guápiles: Una propuesta de abordaje con enfoque integral," unpublished thesis, Programa de Estudios de Posgrado en Salud Pública, Universidad de Costa Rica, 1995, 57.

41. MGP (1890), 20.

42. Decreto no. 24 del 28 de julio de 1894, in Costa Rica, *Colección de leyes y decretos*, vol. 2 (San José: Tipografía Nacional, 1894), 60-66.

43. See, for instance, ANCR, Policía 1453 (letter, 28 Sept. 1898); Policía 1484 (letter, 25 June 1906); Policía 1250 (letter, 7 Dec. 1908).

44. MGP (1899), xxvii, 150; ANCR, Policía 3687 (1895).

45. Juan José Marín Hernández, "Prostitución y pecado en la bella y próspera ciudad de San José (1850-1930)," in *El paso del cometa: Estado, política social y culturas populares en Costa Rica (1800/1950)*, ed. Iván Molina Jiménez and Steven Palmer (San José: Editorial Porvenir/Plumsock Mesoamerican Studies, 1994), 70.

46. David McCreery, "'This Life of Misery and Shame': Female Prostitution in Guatemala City, 1880-1920," *Journal of Latin American Studies* 18 (1993): 341.

47. Ibid., 347-49.

48. Douglas W. Trefzger, "Making West Indians Unwelcome: Race, Gender and the National Question in Guatemala's Banana Belt, 1914-1920" (paper prepared for the 23d Annual Meeting of the Latin American Studies Association, Washington, D.C., 6-8 Sept. 2001).

49. ANCR, Policía 3687 (letter, 3 Jan. 1895).

50. ANCR, Policía 3687 (letter, 12 Jan. 1895); Policía 1820 (1897).

51. ANCR, Policía 1486 (1906). No evidence exists as to whether any of these foreigners were ever actually expelled.

52. ANCR, Policía 1484 (letter, 19 July 1906); Policía 1566 (letter, 11 July 1907).

53. ANCR, Gobernación 8101 (letter, 6 Nov. 1924).

54. ANCR, Gobernación 8258 (letter, 2 Jan. 1925).

55. MGP (1897), 201. Statistics here and below are from MGP (1898), "Memoria de la campaña anti-venerea," 201–4. See also Jeffrey Casey Gaspar, *Limón, 1880–1940: Un estudio de la industria bananera en Costa Rica* (San José: Editorial Costa Rica, 1979), 230–32.

56. It is likely that most of the ten women listed as French were from St. Lucia or Martinique. See Casey Gaspar, *Limón*, 231.

57. MGP (1910), 396. See also ANCR, Policía 1120 (letter, 11 Aug. 1908); MGP (1911), 451; MGP (1913), 536; *El Limonense*, 21 Dec. 1914.

58. MGP (1913), 539.

59. MGP (1911), 448. See also MGP (1913), 524, 539, 543.

60. MGP (1913), 534.

61. MGP (1913), 537. See also MGP (1910), 396; MGP (1922), 142. On the sexualization of black women in elite writings at this time, see Lara Putnam, "Ideología racial, práctica social, y estado liberal en Costa Rica," *Revista de Historia* (San José, Costa Rica) 39 (1999): 139–86.

62. ANCR, Policía 1250 (letter, 7 Dec. 1908).

63. MGP (1921), 164, 167. The canton of Pococí was created in 1911 and encompassed the town of Guápiles and the upper Old Line region.

64. MGP (1922), 142.

65. Kepner, *Social Aspects*, 162–63.

66. See also ANCR, Gobernación 8258 (letter, 1 Nov 1925); MGP (1926), 399.

67. See, for instance, ANCR, Heredia Juzgado del Crimen 1511 (estupro, 1902); ANCR, Policía 2006 (información, 1902); SJA3 8116 (injurias, 1905); ANCR, Puntarenas Juzgado Civil y del Crimen 492 (hurto, 1907).

68. *Prensa Libre*, 25 Apr. 1914.

69. MGP (1913), 524; see also ANCR, Policía 3687 (comunicación, 1895).

70. The ambiguities surrounding the role of *querido* or *preferido* are discussed below.

71. SJJ1Crimen 1144 (robo, 1906); LJCrimen 234 (hurto, 1906); ANCR, Puntarenas Juzgado Civil y del Crimen 492 (hurto, 1907); SJJ1Crimen 1701 (hurto, 1908).

72. SJJ2Crimen 4785 (estafa, 1932).

73. In addition to the cases involving Pacífica Bermúdez, discussed below, see ANCR, Policía 3016 (información, 1893); ANCR, Cartago Alcaldía Segunda 295 (desahucio, 1900); SJJ1Crimen 1701 (hurto, 1908); LJCrimen 596 (homicidio, 1910); ANCR, Policía 4270 (apelación, 1912); and many more.

74. SJJ1Crimen 956 (hurto, 1906).

75. SJA1 19 (injurias, 1890); ANCR, Juzgado de lo Contencioso Administrativo 5589 (denuncia, 1893); Juzgado de lo Contencioso Administrativo 1539 (denuncia, 1893); Juzgado de lo Contencioso Administrativo 5591 (denuncia, 1894).

76. LAU 1422 (deuda, 1899); LAU 1420 (deuda, 1899); ANCR, Cartago Alcaldía Se-

gunda 102 (otorgamiento de escritura, 1900); ANCR, Policía 2973 (información, 1901); SJJ2Civil 11098 (embargo, 1901); SJA3 2468 (deuda, 1901); SJJ1Civil 11301 (reivindicación, 1901); SJA3 2964 (injurias, 1902); SJA2 1917 (deuda, 1902); LAU 2035 (embargo, 1902); LAU 2368 (confesión judicial, 1902); LAU 2034 (deuda, 1903); SJJ1Civil 10277 (deuda, 1904); ANCR, Cartago Alcaldía Primera 3364 (deuda, 1904); SJA1 445 (deuda, 1904); LJCivil 5 (reivindicación, 1904); LJCyC 494 (deslinde, 1904); LJCyC 507 (varios, 1904); LAU 2811 (desahucio, 1907); ANCR, Cartago Alcaldía Segunda 850 (reivindicación, 1907); LJCrimen 434 (violación, 1909); LJCrimen 656 (homicidio, 1912).

77. Antonia Bermúdez Solano was still residing in Limón in 1927, living as the consensual partner of a Colombian man who worked as banana receiver for the United Fruit Company. Next door to the couple within the same building lived a male *cantina* owner, and in the adjacent rooms lived four women who gave their occupation as *meretriz*, or prostitute. It is possible that Antonia was still involved in the commercial sex business, perhaps supervising these young *meretrices* (ages fourteen to twenty-four) and profiting from their labor. Judging by earlier records Antonia Bermúdez must have been closer to fifty than forty, the age she reported to census takers, but the discrepancy is not surprising: the ages she declared in turn-of-the-century court cases already showed her aging more slowly than the passing years would have indicated. See SJJCrimen 3524 (amenazas de atentado, 1895); SJJCrimen 4661 (amenazas de atentado, 1895); SJJCrimen 3540 (lesiones, 1895); SJA3 1954 (confesión judicial, 1896); SJJ1Crimen 4 (lesiones, 1899); SJA2 1722 (reconocimiento de documento, 1899); SJA3 1983 (embargo, 1900); SJA3 3402 (embargo, 1900); SJA1 5928 (deuda, 1900); ANCR, Policia 2973 (información, 1901); SJJ2Civil 11098 (embargo, 1901); SJA3 1728 (confesión judicial, 1901); SJA3 600 (daños, 1901); SJJ1Civil 11301 (reivindicación de bienes, 1901); ANCR, Policía 2006 (información, 1902); SJA1 555 (embargo, 1902); SJA3 3675 (embargo, 1903); SJA3 7660 (deuda, 1904); SJA1 1850 (injurias, 1905); ANCR, Juzgado de lo Contencioso Administrativo 8294 (expendio clandestino de licor, 1905); LAU 2924 (confesión judicial, 1908); LAU 2939 (confesión judicial, 1908); LAU 2952 (confesión judicial, 1908); LJCrimen 1022 (homicidio, 1915); ANCR, Censos 281 (Limón, 1927), folio 1B.

78. SJJCrimen 4661 (amenazas de atentado, 1895). In a typical example of police support for the public women whose social space they shared day after day, when Bermúdez and San José artisan Ramón Mendoza threatened each other with knives in this incident, it was Mendoza and not Bermúdez whom police decided to arrest. Another example of a Costa Rican public woman relocating temporarily to Colón is found in LJCrimen 656 (homicidio, 1912).

79. British Public Records Office, FO 288 125 153 (letter to C. C. Mallet). I am grateful to Ronald Harpelle for providing me with this citation.

80. Rosa María Sánchez de Isaza, "La prostitución y su reglamentación en la República de Panama," unpublished thesis, Facultad de Derecho y Ciencias Políticas, Universidad de Panama, 1986, chap. 1. See also Gil Blas Tejeira, *Pueblos Perdidos*, 4th ed. (Panama City: Editorial Universitaria, 1995), 8.

81. Surveying three dozen criminal cases from the Archivo Nacional de Panamá originated in Colón, Panama City, and Bocas del Toro between 1905 and 1930, I found fourteen women who described themselves or were unequivocally described by others as prostitutes. Five had been born in Panama, two in Costa Rica, and one each in the other countries cited above. One of the women from Panama and one of the Costa Ricans had Anglo names, though they testified in Spanish; it is likely that both were second- or third-generation West Indians. In the late 1930s the Third Locks expansion and a surge in U.S. Navy traffic intensified demand for commercial sex along the canal. In these years the "white slavery" of Costa Rican women duped into prostitution in Panama became, briefly, a matter of government concern. See MGP (1937), 60.

82. LJCrimen 520 (homicidio, 1912).

83. Carlos Luís Fallas Monge, *El movimiento obrero en Costa Rica, 1830-1902* (San José: Editorial Universidad Estatal a Distancia, 1983), 113.

84. See SJJ1Crimen 1701 (hurto, 1908).

85. ANCR, Alajuela Alcaldía Primera 1785 (allanamiento, 1898).

86. LJCrimen 878 (incendio, 1914).

87. LJCrimen 234 (hurto, 1906).

88. LJCrimen 694 (homicidio, 1912); LJCrimen 689 (homicidio, 1911). On each of these occasions, however, the women in question were shot to death later the same evening, in both cases by resentful lovers. One should not overestimate the amount of protection fellow prostitutes' interventions provided.

89. ANCR, Alajuela Alcaldía Primera 1803 (retención indebida de bienes, 1900).

90. ANCR, Policía 1909 (información, 1897); Policía 1820 (información, 1897).

91. *Hoja Obrera*, 27 Feb. 1910, "A los obreros y obreras."

92. Juan José Marín Hernández, "Las causas de la prostitución josefina, 1939-1949: Entre lo imaginario y el estigma," *Revista de Historia* (San José, Costa Rica) 27 (1993): 92.

93. My sample is not a representative one, particularly in this aspect. The structure of the ANCR card catalog facilitates finding patrilineal family ties in general, and siblings in particular, since it is alphabetical by individuals' two last names. It is impossible to estimate the prevalence of such family networks in the sex business as a whole. However, to find multiple hits at all is rare, and to find multiple clusters of them is remarkable.

94. SJA1 1770 (injurias, 1906); LJCrimen 694 (homicidio, 1912); LJCrimen 656 (homicidio, 1912).

95. SJJCrimen 723 (amenazas, 1891); ANCR, Policía 591 (revisión, 1895); ANCR, Policía 2622 (causa, 1895); SJJCrimen 1765 (estupro, 1895); ANCR, Puntarenas Alcaldía Única 2055 (injurias, 1897); LAU 389 (injurias, 1897); ANCR, Alajuela Alcaldía Primera 1785 (allanamiento, 1898); ANCR, Alajuela Alcaldía Primera 1803 (retención indebida de bienes, 1900); ANCR, Policía 2006 (información, 1902); SJA1 3458 (injurias, 1903); LJCrimen 924 (homicidio, 1904); SJA2 5058 (injurias, 1907); ANCR, Policía 154 (comunicaciones, 1910); SJA1 7664 (daños, 1914).

96. LJCrimen 855 (estupro, 1913).

97. Lowell Gudmundson, "Peasant, Farmer, Proletarian: Class Formation in a Small-holder Coffee Economy, 1850–1950," in *Coffee, Society and Power in Latin America*, ed. William Roseberry, Lowell Gudmundson, and Mario Samper Kutschbach (Baltimore: Johns Hopkins University Press, 1995), 126.

98. ANCR, Alajuela Juzgado Civil 2027 (depósito de menores, 1904).

99. ANCR, Heredia Juzgado Crimen 1447 (hurto, 1910); see also ANCR, Alajuela Juzgado del Crimen 2346 (hurto, 1910).

100. LJCrimen 878 (incendio, 1914).

101. LAU 3398 (injurias, 1906). This is my translation of the court interpreter's Spanish rendering of the original testimony, which was in English.

102. LAU 3495 (injurias, 1908); LAU 3485 (injurias, 1907).

103. LAU 916 (hurto, 1914).

104. See, for instance, Fallas, *Mamita Yunai*, 126–29.

105. Ministerio de Cultura, Juventud y Deportes, Centro de Investigación y Conservación, Departamento de Antropología, Proyecto Historias Orales, interview conducted by Fernando González in Hone Creek, 5 Mar. 1980. No date of birth was recorded for this informant. Most subjects interviewed for this project were between seventy and ninety years of age at the time. I am grateful to Moji Anderson for sharing this source with me.

106. Bourgois, *Ethnicity at Work*, 141.

107. Roughly 3 percent of prostitutes Marín Hernández found in San José police documents from 1868 to 1923 were Jamaican. Marín Hernández, "Prostitución y pecado," 54–56.

108. SJJCrimen 11207 (amenazas, 1857); SJJCrimen 9946 (lesiones, 1869); SJJCrimen 8890 (corrupción de menores, 1873); SJJCrimen 7705 (lesiones, 1875); SJA3 5152 (injurias, 1881); SJA1 28 (injurias, 1882); SJA3 5020 (injurias, 1888); SJJCrimen 7568 (lesiones, 1891); SJJCrimen 4022 (sustracción de menores, 1893).

109. SJJ2Crimen 670 (violación, 1898); SJJ2Crimen 565 (tentativa de violación, 1900); SJJ1Crimen 927 (amenazas de atentado, 1905).

110. LJCrimen 657 (homicidio, 1912). Both the local judge and the court of appeals refused to consider infidelity as an extenuating circumstance in this case, and the accused was sentenced to twenty years deportation to San Lucas, the maximum sentence for homicide at the time.

111. LJCrimen 694 (homicidio, 1912).

112. Ibid.

113. LJCrimen 234 (hurto, 1906); SJJ1Crimen 1144 (robo, 1906).

114. LJCrimen 520 (homicidio, 1912).

115. Of the 100-plus homicide inquiries from the years before 1920 that have been preserved from Limón, in only three cases were women accused of murdering adult men, and in each of these the charges were dismissed for lack of evidence. See Chapter 7, below. Twenty-eight cases involving women who died by violence in Limón during the first decades of the twentieth century are preserved in the ANCR. In six of these

cases the victims were working prostitutes, each killed in her own rented room by a *querido* or former *querido*. (This does not include Eva Barrantes, who seems indeed to have died by her own hand rather than that of Rafael Bonilla.)

116. Chapter 5 discusses patterns in insults cases at length.

117. SJA1 1770 (injurias, 1906).

118. LAU 522 (injurias, 1901).

119. SJJCrimen 8411 (atentado a la autoridad, 1881).

120. ANCR, Policía 2973 (información, 1901).

121. ANCR, Policía 2841 (causa, 1897).

122. LAU 3495 (injurias, 1908).

123. SJJCrimen 3540 (lesiones, 1895).

124. Alexandre Dumas, *La Dame aux Camélias*, trans. David Coward (Oxford: Oxford University Press, 1986), 202.

125. MGP (1890), unpaged.

126. ANCR, Censos 281 (Limón, 1927), folio 2B, lines 90–93.

Chapter Four

1. Here the age and gender breakdown by ethnic group, the overall age structure, the portion of the population involved in agriculture, and the relative weight of cocoa and bananas within agricultural employment all coincide with census data for the province.

2. See Table A.2.

3. ANCR, Censos 281 (Limón, 1927), folio 2A, lines 15–21.

4. While other inconsistencies in family status designations were altered by the census sheets' subsequent reviewer, the many cases of *hijos* who were clearly *not* the sons and daughters of named household heads were left unamended. This understanding of children's social identity was shared common sense.

5. This is clear in the multiple corrections to entries for men living in consensual unions with prostitutes, for instance. ANCR, Censos 281 (Limón, 1927), folio 2B, lines 90–93.

6. This is the portion of male household heads residing in a home with a woman whose relationship to them is listed as *alojada* and whose civil status is listed as S.S.L. Elsewhere in Latin America, the phrase *sin sanción legal* (no legal sanction) was used in censuses to designate consensual unions. It is possible that the Costa Rican S.S.L. originated in the same phrase. However, it is clear that by 1927 the letters were understood to stand for *soltera sin ligamen*.

7. See Nancie L. González, "Toward a Definition of Matrifocality," in *Afro-American Anthropology: Contemporary Perspectives*, ed. Norman E. Whitten Jr. and John F. Szwed (New York: Free Press, 1970), 231–44, and "Rethinking the Consanguineal Household and Matrifocality," *Ethnology* 23 (1984): 1–12. For data on conjugal and domestic pat-

terns see Lara Putnam, "Public Women and One-Pant Men: Labor Migration and the Politics of Gender in Caribbean Costa Rica, 1870–1960" (Ph.D. diss., University of Michigan, 2000), 432–34.

8. Of West Indian female heads of households that included children, 48 percent were single, 23 percent married, and 24 percent widowed; their average age was thirty-seven. Of Hispanic female heads of households with children, 71 percent were single, 14 percent married, and 15 percent widowed; their average age was thirty-three.

9. See Table A.3. In 1943 10 percent of Jamaican men aged twenty to twenty-four and 40 percent of those aged thirty-five to forty-four had married. The equivalent figures for Costa Rica excluding Limón in 1927 were much higher: 23 percent and 74 percent. One-quarter of Jamaican men married for the first time late in life, so the portion of men ever married rose to 67 percent among those forty-five and over. In Costa Rica 82 percent of men forty-five and over had married. See George W. Roberts, *The Population of Jamaica* (Cambridge: Cambridge University Press, 1957), 267.

10. More than half of the indigenous population tallied in the census lived in households of ten members or more. See Lara Putnam, "Public Women and One-Pant Men," 434.

11. AC, vol. 26, pt. 3, "Autobiografía de El Compositor Cariareño, E.S.C.," 223–67.

12. AC, vol. 26, pt. 1, "Autobiografía de M.G.L.," 165.

13. AC, vol. 26, pt. 1, "Autobiografía de M.F.A.," 71–73.

14. AC, vol. 26, pt. 1, "Autobiografía de A.H.Ch.," 251–71.

15. AC, vol. 26, pt. 3, "Autobiografía de S.T.," 183–84. S.T. is describing his experience in the Estrella Valley circa 1918–22.

16. AC, vol. 26, pt. 3, "Autobiografía de J.V.O.G.," 32.

17. AC, vol. 26, pt. 1, "Autobiografía de M.G.L.," 120.

18. AC, vol. 26, pt. 3, "Autobiografía de L.O.M.," 83–84.

19. AC, vol. 26, pt. 1, "Autobiografía de M.G.L.," 122–39.

20. Ibid., 133.

21. Ibid., 108–9.

22. AC, vol. 26, pt. 2, "Autobiografía de Chonsito M.J." (15th in vol.), 9–10. The Spanish original is composed in rhyming couplets; no translation can do it justice.

23. AC, vol. 26, pt. 3, "Autobiografía de S.T.," 186. S.T. was interviewed in Spanish; this is my translation. See also AC, vol. 26, pt. 2, "Autobiografía de E.N.B." (18th in vol.), 1–2.

24. AC, vol. 26, pt. 3, "Autobiografía de J.V.O.G.," 74. "Llegue a tener varias mujeres tengo dies y seis hijos regados estube para casarme seis veces y siempre me adelante."

25. AC, vol. 26, pt. 3, "Autobiografía de C.S.W.," 220.

26. AC, vol. 26, pt. 3, "Autobiografía de I.P.R.," 87–89. "[T]engo 82 años si me mero queda el orgullo para mis ijos í e ijas Que su padre murio en la bida luchando lo como chonbre eparsado i de efuerso material i personal estube preso una bes porque el chonbre ti em que defender onrra bida i capital defendia mi bida."

27. This was the experience of five of the ten women in this age group who sub-

mitted testimonials to the AC project. Of the others, one was raised by her father and grandmother after her mother's death and worked as a domestic from the age of fifteen, one was sent to an orphanage by her father after her mother's death, and one sought agricultural wage work to help support her mother and younger brother after her father died when she was ten.

28. AC, vol. 23, "Autobiografía de J.M.L.," 354.

29. AC, vol. 23, "Autobiografía de H.C.A." (born Cartago, ca. 1914), 311; "Autobiografía de E.G. de L." (born San José, 1914), 346; "Autobiografía de O.C.C." (born Alajuela[?], 1916), 315; "Autobiografía de R.R.A." (born Alajuela, ca. 1919), 422; "Autobiografía de V.P." (born Port Limón, ca. 1922), 361; "Autobiografía de A.Mc.K." (born San Juan del Norte, 1928), 264; "Autobiografía de E.Z.S." (born Turrialba, 1933), 290; "Autobiografía de A.C.C. de G." (born Turrialba, 1936), 64; "Autobiografía de M.A.H.R." (born Cartago, 1942), 98; "Autobiografía de J.S.A." (born Puerto Limón, 1942), 280; "Autobiografía de Dalia" (born Siquirres, 1945), 267.

30. AC, vol. 23, "Autobiografía de O.C.C.," 331.

31. Ibid.

32. AC, vol. 23, "Autobiografía de E.G. de L.," 351.

33. AC, vol. 23, "Autobiografía de O.C.C.," 331.

34. AC, vol. 23, "Autobiografía de J.S.A.," 281. *Tepezcuintle* is *Dasyprocta punctata*, *guatuza* is *Agouti paca*, and *león* is likely *Felis onca*, a now-endangered jaguar once common in the coastal mangrove swamps.

35. This is true of both Hispanic and West Indian women who submitted autobiographies but not of indigenous women, who describe working as own-account farmers only, either with their husbands or with their brothers.

36. AC, vol. 23, "Autobiografía de E.G. de L.," 346–52.

37. Mario Samper Kutschbach, "Café, trabajo y sociedad en Centroamérica, 1870–1930: Una historia común y divergente," in *Las repúblicas agroexportadoras*, ed. Víctor Hugo Acuña Ortega, vol. 4 of *Historia general de Centroamérica* (Madrid: Sociedad Estatal Quinto Centenario and FLACSO, 1993), 84–96, and *Generations of Settlers: Rural Households and Markets on the Costa Rican Frontier, 1850–1935* (Boulder, Colo.: Westview Press, 1990), 213–16.

38. Lowell Gudmundson, "Peasant, Farmer, Proletarian: Class Formation in a Smallholder Coffee Economy, 1850–1950," in *Coffee, Society, and Power in Latin America*, ed. William Roseberry, Lowell Gudmundson, and Mario Samper Kutschbach (Baltimore: Johns Hopkins University Press, 1995), 128–41.

39. AC, vol. 23, "Autobiografía de L.R.A.," 369, 385–88. Similarly, see AC, vol. 23, "Autobiografía de E.Z.S.," 290–95. A decade later 15 percent of field workers on one Turrialba plantation were women. William Solano Pérez, "El día de trabajo en la Hacienda Aragón, Turrialba, 1943," *Revista de Historia* 32 (1995): 167–70.

40. AC, vol. 23, "Autobiografía de L.R.A.," 388–89.

41. Ibid., 390.

42. Ibid., 392–93.

43. See Lara Putnam, "Migración y género en la organización de la producción: Una comparación de la industria bananera en Costa Rica y Jamaica (1880–1935)" (paper presented at the 4th Simposio Panamericano de Historia of the Instituto Panamericano de Geografía e Historia, Universidad de Costa Rica, San José, Costa Rica, 10–13 Aug. 1999).

44. I have found no secondary sources that describe employment patterns on cocoa plantations in these years. This description is based on the AC sources cited. In 1925 United Fruit had more than 10,000 hectares planted in cocoa in Limón, about half of the provincial total. Production fell drastically as international prices dropped over the next decade but then rebounded after World War II. Juan Rafael Quesada Camacho, "Algunos aspectos de la historia económica del cocoa en Costa Rica, 1880–1930," pt. 1, *Revista de Historia* (Heredia, Costa Rica) 3, no. 5 (1977): 65–100.

45. AC, vol. 23, "Autobiografía de A.C.C. de G.," 67, 80. Likewise A.A.C.C., born in Santa Rosa de Bufalo (near Zent) around 1922, reports that when he was ten his mother took him out of school and put him to work on Finca Santa Rosa tending and cutting cocoa. AC, vol. 26, pt. 1, "Autobiografía de A.A.C.C." (dictated), 29.

46. AC, vol. 23, "Autobiografía de Dalia," 271.

47. AC, vol. 26, pt. 3, "Autobiografía de J.V.O.G.," 5.

48. AC, vol. 26, pt. 3, "Autobiografía de El Compositor Cariareño, E.S.C.," 229. "Vengando un jornal / Muere uno en la Carestía."

49. AC, vol. 26, pt. 2, "Autobiografía de A.M.R." (12th in vol.), 2.

50. AC, vol. 26, pt. 3, "Autobiografía de L. Campesino," 129–30.

51. AC, vol. 26, pt. 1, "Autobiografía de R.J.G.," 286–88.

52. AC, vol. 26, pt. 1, "Autobiografía de M.F.A.," 65.

53. AC, vol. 26, pt. 1, "Autobiografía de A.H.Ch.," 266.

54. AC, vol. 26, pt. 2, "Autobiografía de Chonsito M.J." (15th in vol.), 12.

55. Ibid., 20.

56. AC, vol. 23, "Autobiografía de H.C.A." (dictated), 313.

57. AC, vol. 23, "Autobiografía de E.G. de L.," 352.

58. AC, vol. 23, "Autobiografía de O.C.C.," 315; "Autobiografía de A.C.C. de G.," 64; "Autobiografía de E.M.J.," 278; and "Autobiografía de E.Z.S.," 290, all include very similar descriptions of the isolation and dependency of homesteading.

59. See the description of one such village, based on research carried out in the 1960s, in Roy Simon Bryce-Laporte, "Family, Household, and Intergenerational Relations in a 'Jamaican' Village in Limón, Costa Rica," in *The Family in the Caribbean: Proceedings of the Second Conference on the Family in the Caribbean*, ed. Stanford N. Gerber (Rio Piedras: University of Puerto Rico Institute of Caribbean Studies, 1973), 65–93.

60. TPP 427, 64–65.

61. TPP 425, 112.

62. Paula Palmer, *"Wa'apin man": La historia de la costa talamanqueña de Costa Rica, según sus protagonistas*, trans. Quince Duncan and Paula Palmer, 2d ed. (San José: Editorial de la Universidad de Costa Rica, 1994), 206–7. My translation. Additional infor-

mation provided by Moji Anderson from interview with Daisy Lewis, Puerto Viejo, 27 Apr. 2000.

63. On settlement patterns see Pierre Stouse, "Cambios en el uso de la tierra en las regiones ex-bananeras de Costa Rica," unpublished report, San José, Costa Rica, 1967; Charles W. Koch, "Ethnicity and Livelihoods: A Social Geography of Costa Rica's Atlantic Zone" (Ph.D. diss., University of Kansas, 1975), 225–43.

64. AC, vol. 23, "Autobiografía de A.C.C. de G.," 78–79.

65. Ibid., 79.

66. Ibid., 80–83.

67. AC, vol 23, "Autobiografía de V.P." (dictated), 361.

68. LJCyC 394 (homicidio, 1899) For instances of indigenous Talamancans who took in Hispanic children or were taken in by West Indian or Hispanic foster parents, see AC, vol. 26, pt. 2, "Autobiografía de S.L.L." (dictated, 3d in vol.), 23, and AC, vol. 26, pt. 3, "Autobiografía de L. Campesino," 128.

Chapter Five

1. Costa Rica, Dirección General de Estadística y Censos, *Anuario estadístico* (1913), 15.

2. MGP (1912), 570.

3. LAU 443 (injurias, 1899).

4. ANCR, Policía 449 (telegram, 21 June 1902).

5. See Michel-Rolph Trouillot, "The Caribbean Region: An Open Frontier in Anthropological Theory," *Annual Review of Anthropology* 21 (1992): 19–42. In part due to the efficiency of gatekeeper concepts like "honor and shame" and "legacy of slavery," scholarship on the Hispanic Caribbean has never managed to unseat the perceived dichotomy between the two regions.

6. Overviews include Steve J. Stern, *The Secret History of Gender: Women, Men, and Power in Late Colonial Mexico* (Chapel Hill: University of North Carolina Press, 1995), chap. 2, and Lyman L. Johnson and Sonya Lipsett-Rivera, introduction to *The Faces of Honor: Sex, Shame, and Violence in Colonial Latin America* (Albuquerque: University of New Mexico Press, 1998).

7. For an overview of this research and sampling of key texts see Christine Barrow, *Family in the Caribbean: Themes and Perspectives* (Kingston: Ian Randle, 1996).

8. Peter J. Wilson, *Crab Antics: The Social Anthropology of English-Speaking Negro Societies of the Caribbean* (New Haven: Yale University Press, 1973).

9. To lime is to participate in street-corner and rum-shop sociability, or as Gussler puts it, to "do nothing, but with a certain amount of style." Judith D. Gussler, "Adaptive Strategies and Social Networks of Women in St. Kitts," in *A World of Women: Anthropological Studies of Women in Societies of the World*, ed. Erika Bourguignon (New York: Praeger, 1980), 206.

10. See Jean Besson, "Reputation and Respectability Reconsidered: A New Perspective on Afro-Caribbean Peasant Women," in *Women and Change in the Caribbean: A Pan-Caribbean Perspective*, ed. Janet Momsen (Bloomington: Indiana University Press, 1993), 15–37, and Carolyn Cooper, *Noises in the Blood: Orality, Gender, and the "Vulgar" Body of Jamaican Popular Culture* (Durham: Duke University Press, 1995). Purcell's sociology of Limón draws on Wilson's formulation; see Trevor W. Purcell, *Banana Fallout: Class, Color, and Culture among West Indians in Costa Rica* (Los Angeles: Center for Afro-American Studies, University of California, 1993), esp. chaps. 5 and 9.

11. Calculated from provincial totals published in Costa Rica, Dirección General de Estadística y Censos, *Anuario estadístico* (1907–26). In Limón, insults suits were the most common of all "crimes against persons" established by the 1880 Penal Code.

12. *Código Penal de la República de Costa Rica* (San José: Imprenta Nacional, n.d. [1880]), title 8, chapter 5, article 437.

13. See Table A.4.

14. Lila Abu-Lughod, *Veiled Sentiments: Honor and Poetry in a Bedouin Society* (Berkeley: University of California Press, 1986), 90, citing Pierre Bourdieu on the Kabyle bedouins.

15. See Jane Schneider, "Of Vigilance and Virgins: Honor, Shame, and Access to Resources in Mediterranean Societies," *Ethnology* 10, no. 1 (1971): 1–24, and Julian Pitt-Rivers, "Honour and Social Status," in *Honour and Shame: The Values of Mediterranean Society*, ed. J. G. Péristiany (Chicago: Chicago University Press, 1966), 19–77.

16. LAU 3498 (injurias, 1908).

17. By law, if a woman's honor was impugned she was the injured party, and no one else could sue on her behalf unless she was a minor. (The case between Powell and Lloyd foundered on this very point.) But very few cases include any suggestion that a husband or male partner took an active role in urging the female plaintiff to sue. The exceptions are LAU 535 (injurias, 1901), LAU 467 (injurias, 1900), and LAU 470 (injurias, 1901).

18. Although the words "hijo de puta" or "son of a bitch" were frequently cited in insults suits, it seems clear the phrase was a formulaic humiliation whose link to one's actual mother's sex life was beside the point.

19. LAU 3411 (injurias, 1907). The threat to have Jamieson deported as a prostitute was not necessarily an empty one. Six months earlier the governor of Limón had reported to his superiors that he was "gathering information" on forty-eight foreign women, doubtless Jamaican in their majority, whom he was planning to deport for illegal prostitution. In practice, "gathering information" against "clandestine prostitutes" meant finding neighbors willing to denounce the moral character of the woman in question. ANCR, Policía 1486 (letter, 8 Aug. 1906).

20. LJCyC 730 (injurias, 1903).

21. LAU 510 (injurias, 1902). Davis himself is identified as "un negro" in other court cases. See note 72, below.

22. LAU 3406 (injurias, 1906).

23. LAU 399 (injurias, 1898); LAU 472 (injurias, 1899).

24. LAU 3481 (injurias, 1908).

25. LAU 508 (injurias, 1902). Franklin was from the United States. According to him, Forbes had prompted his retort by making comments about his "bastard daughter," to whom the clothes belonged. Franklin may well have been African American.

26. See, for instance, LAU 466 (injurias, 1900), LAU 476 (injurias, 1900).

27. LAU 3441 (injurias, 1909). For more on the 1909 elections in Limón see note 62, below. The life story of Juan José León is recounted by Moisés León Azofeifa, "Chinese Immigrants on the Atlantic Coast of Costa Rica: The Economic Adaptation of an Asian Minority in a Pluralistic Society" (Ph.D. diss., Tulane University, 1987), 169–81.

28. I selected seventy-four cases by blind sampling for detailed review. Of these, forty were not pursued beyond the initial complaint or first round of testimony and twelve were ended by the parties through extrajudicial accord. For two-thirds of the cases settled out of court there is no record of a monetary accord. The other four settled for costs so far: nine *colones* in one case, and between thirty-one and seventy-seven *colones* in the others. Twelve cases were carried through to *enjuiciamiento* and dismissed by the judge for lack of evidence or because the insults had been "reciprocal and thus compensated." Only ten cases actually reached judgment. In at least five of these the accused was absolved (for two of the other cases the outcome is unclear). By law the maximum sentence for *injurias graves* was two months in jail or a 100-*colón* fine, plus costs. In the two cases for which cost claims are preserved, plaintiffs' lawyers charged 100 and 200 *colones* for their honoraria, sums that surely suggest the cases had been taken on spec. LAU 529 (injurias, 1901); LAU 549 (injurias, 1901). Laborers in these years earned 1.50 to 4 *colones* per day, and boardinghouse rooms rented for around 10 *colones* per month.

29. LAU 3470 (injurias, 1908).

30. Louis Mennereck, "A Study of Puerto Limon, Costa Rica" (San José, Costa Rica: Associated Colleges of the Midwest Central American Field Program, 1964, mimeographed), 36.

31. MGP (1910), 595. See also ANCR, Policía 2123 (letter, 10 Sept. 1909).

32. ANCR, Policía 1486 (letter, 2 Oct. 1906). ". . . a mejorar sus infectos barracones que les produce en la negrada hasta el dos por ciento mensual."

33. LAU 3487 (injurias, 1908).

34. LAU 3494 (injurias, 1908).

35. See list of tenants owing back rent in LJCyC 659 (desahucio, 1905). Witnesses called to testify to a specific verbal conflict tended to be of the same regional origin, as did the parties to such conflicts. However, witnesses to crises that affected entire buildings (arson, for instance) were more diverse. This suggests both the social separation and the residential integration of city life. See LJCyC 53 (incendio, 1910), LJCrimen 137 (incendio, 1910), LJCrimen 1122 (incendio, 1915).

36. LAU 460 (injurias, 1900); LAU 447 (injurias, 1900). Despite *don* Lucas's efforts to minimize the issue, discrepancies over which language MacPherson had issued the in-

sults in were cited by the Sala de Casación as grounds for overturning the lower court, which had ordered her to pay 101 *colones* in damages, plus costs.

37. See LAU 522 (injurias, 1901), LAU 409 (injurias, 1898), LAU 426 (injurias, 1899), LAU 460 (injurias, 1900), LAU 447 (injurias, 1900).

38. LAU 3417 (injurias, 1907).

39. LAU 426 (injurias, 1899). According to the *Código Penal*, evidence that the content of insults was true could only be used as a defense if the plaintiff "habitually and publicly" engaged in the behavior of which he or she had been accused (fornication, fraud, etc.). Even if the objectionable insults were proven to be both accurate and common knowledge, the effect was not to exonerate the defendant but to decrease the fine by two-thirds. In the Levi case, the threat of publicity was surely more significant than the legal impact of the promised evidence.

40. See references in Chapter 3.

41. LAU 3487 (injurias, 1908).

42. LAU 408 (injurias, 1898).

43. LAU 539 (injurias, 1901). This case was one of the few in which a husband took an active role in defending his wife's honor against sexual insult. The suit Barnes filed was annulled because he could not legally sue on his wife's behalf, and she appeared at the *alcalde*'s office to file suit herself the following day.

44. LAU 537 (injurias, 1901).

45. See Roger D. Abrahams, *The Man-of-Words in the West Indies: Performance and the Emergence of Creole Culture* (Baltimore: Johns Hopkins University Press, 1983).

46. LAU 3472 (injurias, 1907); LAU 3471 (injurias, 1908).

47. See ANCR, Policía 2198 (causa, 1897); LAU 422 (injurias, 1899); LAU 522 (injurias, 1901); ANCR, Policía 2973 (información, 1901); SJA1 1770 (injurias, 1906); LAU 3467 (injurias, 1908). I suspect this reflects Chinese men's role in small-scale retail across the country. For many working people the "pulpería del chino" was a site of unending petty debt.

48. The *Dictionary of Caribbean English Usage* defines "facety" as "bold and barefaced; brazen; impudent" and illustrates usage with Louise Bennet's poem on the occasion of Jamaican independence: "Matty say it mean we facety / Stan up pon we dignity / An we don't allow nobody / Fe teck liberty wid we." Richard Allsopp, ed., *Dictionary of Caribbean English Usage* (Oxford: Oxford University Press, 1996).

49. David Warren Sabean, *Power in the Blood: Popular Culture and Village Discourse in Early Modern Germany* (London: Cambridge University Press, 1984). See also Stern, *Secret History of Gender*, 386–87.

50. MacPherson's lawyer in fact had tried to make cultural difference the basis of his defense. He called on four West Indian men (one originally from Belize, two from Barbados, one from Jamaica—all long-time residents of Limón) to testify that "the word 'bitch' or 'puta' is very common among Jamaicans and among them, it is a grave offense when directed at a married woman, but not when it refers to a woman who, not

being married, lives or has lived maritally with some man." Three out of four of his hand-picked witnesses disagreed with this statement. LAU 460 (injurias, 1900).

51. LAU 3406 (injurias, 1906). On the other hand, several early-twentieth-century travelers commented on the relative freedom of upper-class women in Costa Rica. See Frederick Palmer, *Central America and Its Problems* (New York: Moffat, Yard, 1913), 206, and L. E. Elliott, *Central America: New Paths in Ancient Lands* (New York: Dodd, Mead, 1925), 223.

52. SJJCrimen 1621 (lesiones, 1892).

53. See, for instance, the many scores of cases from San José's police courts against women for slander, brawling, and scandal (ANCR, Serie Policía). As Steven Palmer has shown, the sharp division between social undesirables like prostitutes and the "honorable poor" was more an official fantasy (or policy goal) than a reality. Steven Palmer, "Confinement, Policing, and the Emergence of Social Policy in Costa Rica," in *The Birth of the Penitentiary in Latin America: Essays on Criminology, Prison Reform, and Social Control, 1840–1940*, ed. Carlos Aguirre and Ricardo Salvatore (Austin: University of Texas Press, 1996), 224–53. In court testimony neither police agents nor bystanders expressed much surprise at women's actions, and the most common defense was not "I didn't do it" but "She started it."

54. Harry A. Franck, *Roaming through the West Indies* (New York: Century, 1923), 405.

55. Cited in Cooper, *Noises in the Blood*, 41. Translation: "Spread yourself out, Liza, it looks like that 'one-dress woman' has seen a little space next to us and wants to force herself in there." The Jamaicanism "one-dress woman" suggests that the object of scorn is a sham: the woman may be wearing an expensive-looking dress, but it is her only one. In this poem the phrase, which usually deflates the pretensions of the poor, is used by the market women to belittle the middle-class passenger who does not know her place. The same figure occurs in Limón Creole, as in the "one-pant man" in the calypso quoted in the epigraph at the beginning of this book.

56. Franck, *Roaming through the West Indies*, 405. Carolyn Cooper writes of contemporary Jamaican dance hall culture: "Slackness is not just sexual looseness—though it certainly is that. Slackness is a metaphorical revolt against law and order; an undermining of the consensual standards of decency." Cooper, *Noises in the Blood*, 141.

57. George Palmer Putnam, *The Southland of North America: Rambles and Observations in Central America during the Year 1912* (New York: G. P. Putnam and Sons, 1914), 109.

58. Wallace Thompson, *The Rainbow Countries of Central America* (New York: E. P. Dutton, 1926), 15.

59. Frederick Upham Adams, *Conquest of the Tropics: The Story of the Creative Enterprises Conducted by the United Fruit Company* (New York: Doubleday, 1914), 192. Winifred James describes black longshoremen "singing the bananas into the holds and talking religion in between the loads" in Bocas del Toro. Winifred James, *The Mulberry Tree* (London: Chapman and Hall, 1913), 277.

60. George Palmer Putnam, *Southland of North America*, 108.

61. ANCR, Policía 1567 (letter, 11 Mar. 1907).

62. For example, in the 1909 presidential election campaign Minor Keith gave financial and other support to Rafael Iglesias, candidate of the Partido Civil, because as a congressman several years earlier Partido Republicano candidate Ricardo Jiménez had denounced the most recent government contract with United Fruit. Some of the nature of the "other support" Keith provided is indicated by the election results for that year. While Iglesias won only 29 percent of the popular vote nationally, he won 74 percent of the vote in Limón. Limón, the province with the smallest number of electors (33, as opposed to 288 for the province of San José), accounted for over a third of the *civilistas'* eighty-one electoral votes nationwide. Orlando Salazar Mora, *El apogeo de la república liberal en Costa Rica, 1870-1914* (San José: Editorial de la Universidad de Costa Rica, 1990), 155, 230-31. Not surprisingly, there were widespread accusations of fraud (see telegrams from Sept. and Oct. 1909 in ANCR, Policía 1594 and Gobernación 2123). On the systematic role of fraud in Costa Rican elections see Mario Samper Kutschbach, "Fuerzas sociopolíticas y procesos electorales en Costa Rica, 1921-1936," *Revista de Historia* (San José, Costa Rica) Número Especial (1988), 157-222, and Iván Molina Jiménez and Fabrice Lehoucq, *Urnas de lo inesperado: Fraude electoral y lucha política en Costa Rica (1901-1948)* (San José: Editorial de la Universidad de Costa Rica, 1999).

63. ANCR, Policía 1550 (letter, 1 Mar. 1905); Policía 1120 (letter, 2 July 1908); Policía 06196 (1911); Gobernación 3419 (letter, 15 Nov. 1912); Policía 1567 (letter, 11 Mar. 1907). The links between United Fruit, local politics, and elites' personal conflicts are many and complex. For example, Lucas Alvarado, former *alcalde* and omnipresent Limón lawyer, was local counsel for United Fruit and its subsidiary Northern Railway Company. He was a prominent *civilista* and several times elected president of the *municipalidad*. He also feuded with almost every significantly powerful local man at one time or other. See LAU 395 (injurias, 1898); LAU 546 (injurias, 1901); LJCrimen 308 (homicidio, 1903); ANCR, Policía 1565 (letter, 12 Sept. 1907); and the caning incident at the beginning of this chapter.

64. ANCR, Gobernación 2084 (letter, 31 Jan. 1906). See also ANCR, Gobernación 3419 (letters, 28 Mar. and 15 Nov. 1912); ANCR, Policía 1565 (letter, 12 Sept. 1907).

65. The "Blue Book" of influential Costa Ricans described *regidor* Carlos Saborío in 1916 as "one of the most intelligent and progressive agriculturists and ranchers in the country." The profile of Alvarado begins, "In the city of Limon, beautifully situated on the Atlantic Coast of Costa Rica, don Lucas Daniel Alvarado, has for many years followed his profession as lawyer with so great a success that he seems to have been born with a legal gift just as others are born gifted as poets. . . . His decision in a law case is as infallible as the compass that points out a ship's course. In Knowledge other men might have the advantage at times, but never in Judgement." Latin American Publicity Bureau, *Costa Rica, 1916* (San José: Imprenta Alsina, 1916), 236, 434.

66. LJCrimen 70 (homicidio, 1904).

67. Stern, *Secret History of Gender*, 320.

68. See, for instance, Lyman L. Johnson, "Dangerous Words, Provocative Gestures, and Violent Acts," in Johnson and Lipsett, *Faces of Honor*, 129. Wilson's earliest work on male "reputation" described it as a Caribbean-wide phenomenon and cited research on Puerto Rico (including Oscar Lewis's work), which would be fundamental to scholarship on Latin American "machismo." Peter J. Wilson, "Reputation and Respectability: A Suggestion for Caribbean Historians," *Man*, n.s., 4 (1969): 73, 75, 82–83.

69. LAU 546 (injurias, 1901).

70. LAU 463 (injurias, 1900).

71. On culture as "serious play" see Sherry B. Ortner, *Making Gender: The Politics and Erotics of Culture* (Boston: Beacon Press, 1996).

72. LAU 3414 (injurias, 1906). The preceding insults were "You are a goddamned ashy-faced son-of-a-bitch, you killed your mother and a curse is upon you, you're a damned thief and the sack of money you've stolen will not make you prosper, you were going after a bitch when you fornicated with Mary Jane, all you do is smell [like] a bucket of shit." This is the same Frederick Davis whom Jerome Bright accused of being "a thief in Jamaica, a thief in Colón, and a thief here," above. Davis was a particularly enthusiastic student of the possibilities of judicial redress. Over the course of two decades in Limón he filed more than a dozen cases (that have been preserved—he may have filed many more), including several for insults, many for debt, and multiple suits for evictions from properties he sublet. He also sued three Chinese merchants for deflowering his daughter—except that from evidence presented, it seems clear that she was neither his daughter nor had she been deflowered on the occasion in question. LJPenal 1231 (estupro, 1922).

73. LAU 3414 (injurias, 1906). It is still the case in Costa Rica that women avoid going outside after ironing until they have waited several hours to cool down. The belief is that ironing raises one's body temperature, in which state exposure to a cool breeze can cause facial paralysis and other illness. References in court testimony and autobiographies bear witness to the currency of this belief early in the century among Costa Ricans, Nicaraguans, and Jamaicans alike in Limón.

74. AC, vol. 23, "Autobiografía de O.C.C.," 336. Original reads in part: "Dios te sabe María a puta chancho saquelo de hay y llena eres de gracia perro putón ya se chó adentro, el señor es contigo con todos diblos muchacha espantá esas gallinas me van a dejar sin masa, vendita tu eres entre todas las mujeres, a desgracia con estas hifueputas güilas, bullistos, callense cabrones."

75. See Donna J. Guy, *Sex and Danger in Buenos Aires: Prostitution, Family, and Nation in Argentina* (Lincoln: University of Nebraska Press, 1991); Jean Franco, *Plotting Women: Gender and Representation in Mexico* (New York: Columbia University Press, 1989), chaps. 4 and 5; and Teresa A. Meade, *"Civilizing" Rio: Reform and Resistance in a Brazilian City, 1889–1930* (University Park: Pennsylvania State University Press, 1997).

76. León Azofeifa, "Chinese Immigrants on the Atlantic Coast," 109.

77. Recent scholarship in legal anthropology highlights the contradictory role of the law as a tool of both rule and resistance. See Mindie Lazarus-Black and Susan F. Hirsch,

eds., *Contested States: Law, Hegemony, and Resistance* (New York: Routledge, 1994), and Mindie Lazarus-Black, *Legitimate Acts and Illegal Encounters: Law and Society in Antigua and Barbuda* (Washington, D.C.: Smithsonian Institution Press, 1994), esp. chap. 8.

78. See, for instance, ANCR, Policía 890 (1903); Policía 1310 (1903); Policía 1484 (telegram, 18 May 1906); Policía 1484 (letter, 8 June 1906); LJCrimen 821 (abuso de autoridad, 1908); ANCR, Policía 1120 (letter, 17 July 1908). Complaints about "how unjustly some people, particularly the coloured people[,] are treated" by local officials were common in the English-language press. *Searchlight*, 26 July 1930, 2; 26 Dec. 1931, 3. On the use of police to combat labor activism by West Indian workers, see Aviva Chomsky, "Afro-Jamaican Traditions and Labor Organizing on United Fruit Company Plantations in Costa Rica, 1910," *Journal of Social History* 28, no. 4 (1995): 840–41, and Carlos Hernández, "Los inmigrantes de St. Kitts: 1910, un capítulo en la historia de los conflictos bananeros costarricenses," *Revista de Historia* (San José, Costa Rica) 23 (1991): 191–240.

79. Carlos Luís Fallas, *Mamita Yunai*, 2d ed. (1941; reprint, San José: Editorial Costa Rica, 1995), 157.

80. *Atlantic Voice*, 11 May 1935, 7. The *Atlantic Voice/La Voz del Atlántico* was a bilingual newspaper published in Port Limón from 1934 to 1946. Articles cited here as from the *Atlantic Voice* appeared in English in the original, while those cited as from *La Voz del Atlántico* are my translations of Spanish originals.

81. LAU 3479 (injurias, 1907); LAU 3472 (injurias, 1907); LAU 3453 (injurias, 1909).

82. Calculated from Costa Rica, Dirección General de Estadística y Censos, *Anuario estadístico* (1907–26). Prior to 1910 *injurias* accusations took two distinct legal forms. An informal complaint to police would be handled as a *falta de policía*, investigated and sentenced at the discretion of the police captain within guidelines set by the *Reglamentación de Policía*. In contrast, a formal accusation before the *alcalde* would result in an investigation of the incident as a *delito*, or crime, in accordance with the 1880 Penal Code. All cases preserved in the ANCR are *delito* prosecutions. A new law in 1910 eliminated *injurias* as a *delito*, and from then on all insults cases were handled as *faltas de policía*. Figures given here are for *injurias* as *faltas de policía*.

83. According to the 1927 census sample, two-fifths of young West Indian men lived in a parent's home, as opposed to one-tenth of young white men. Sixty-one percent of young West Indian men lived in Port Limón, by far the highest portion of any adult male cohort in the province. Literacy rates are discussed below.

84. Charles W. Koch, "Jamaican Blacks and Their Descendants in Costa Rica," *Social and Economic Studies* 26, no. 3 (1977): 339–61.

85. All of these phrases are from the English-language press in Limón, as cited in Ronald Harpelle, "West Indians in Costa Rica: Class and Ethnicity in the Transformation of a Community" (Ph.D. diss., University of Toronto, 1992), 158, 160, 165, 177–78.

86. See Aviva Chomsky, "West Indian Workers in Costa Rican Radical and Nationalist Ideology: 1900–1950," *The Americas* 51, no. 1 (1994): 25–37.

87. ANCR, Congreso 15400 ("Exposición sobre el problema bananera: Iniciativa de la Sociedad Económica de Amigos del País," 1927).

88. "No es posible llegar a convivir con ellos, porque sus malas costumbres no lo permiten:—para ellos no existe la familia, ni el honor de la mujer, y de allí que viven en un hacinamiento y una promiscuidad que resulta peligrosa para nuestros hogares, fundados de acuerdo con los preceptos de la religión y las buenas costumbres de los costarricenses." ANCR, Congreso 16753 ("Prohibir la entrada de negros al país," July 1933).

89. Aviva Chomsky, *West Indian Workers and the United Fruit Company in Costa Rica, 1870-1940* (Baton Rouge: Louisiana State University Press, 1996), 235-54. Chomsky also uses the phrase "lowest common denominator," to refer to the rise of anticommunism among Costa Rican planters.

90. Ronald N. Harpelle, "The Social and Political Integration of West Indians in Costa Rica: 1930-50," *Journal of Latin American Studies* 25 (1993): 110-11; Koch, "Jamaican Blacks," 348-49; Harpelle, "West Indians in Costa Rica," 75-79. On the social distinction between "Coloreds" and "Blacks" in Limón in these years see Purcell, *Banana Fallout*, 32-35.

91. *Atlantic Voice*, 7 Sept. 1935, 5.

92. *Atlantic Voice*, 14 Sept. 1935, 6.

93. Ronald N. Harpelle, "Ethnicity, Religion and Repression: The Denial of African Heritage in Costa Rica," *Canadian Journal of History* 29 (1994): 95-112. On Pocomia, see Chapter 6, below.

94. *Searchlight*, 9 Nov. 1929, 4. All spelling as in original.

95. *Searchlight*, 4 Jan. 1930, 2.

96. *Searchlight*, 1 Feb. 1930, 1.

97. *Atlantic Voice*, 8 Dec. 1934, 1. Likewise see *Searchlight*, 3 May 1930, 2, and *La Voz del Atlántico*, 10 Aug. 1935, 1; 25 Aug. 1934, 7; and 1 Sept. 1934, 3, 5.

98. An account of an *injurias* suit between three women that stemmed from insults proffered from the podium at a Universal Negro Improvement Association meeting appears in the *Atlantic Voice*, 31 Aug. 1935, 6.

99. "What a vulgar little nigger."

100. *Searchlight*, 26 Dec. 1931, 1. All spelling as in original.

101. *Searchlight*, 4 Oct. 1930, 5.

102. *Searchlight*, 6 June 1931, 4; see also *Searchlight*, 13 Dec. 1930, 5. Shortly thereafter the club dissolved, apparently due to conflicts arising from internal class divisions. *Searchlight*, 12 Dec. 1931, 3.

103. *Searchlight*, 1 Nov. 1930, 1.

104. *Searchlight*, 22 Nov. 1930, 5. Emphasis in original.

105. Author's analysis of CIHAC 1927 census sample. Among those over thirty, literacy was 81 percent for West Indian men, 77 percent for West Indian women, 80 percent for Hispanic men, and 63 percent for Hispanic women. For both men and women, and

for both Spanish and English speakers, literacy rates were slightly higher among those born abroad than among the Costa Rican-born.

106. West India Royal Commission, "Report," in Great Britain, *Parliamentary Papers*, 1944/45, 6:35–36, 221. See also Thomas C. Holt, *The Problem of Freedom: Race, Labor, and Politics in Jamaica and Britain, 1832–1938* (Baltimore: Johns Hopkins University Press, 1992), 381–90.

107. For example, see Carlos Meléndez Chaverri and Quince Duncan, *El negro en Costa Rica*, 8th ed. (San José: Editorial Costa Rica, 1981). On the ideological shift see Purcell, *Banana Fallout*, 48, and Philippe Bourgois, *Ethnicity at Work: Divided Labor on a Central American Banana Plantation* (Baltimore: Johns Hopkins University Press, 1989), chap. 7.

108. See Flora Ovares, Margarita Rojas, Carlos Santander, and María Elena Carballo, *La casa paterna: Escritura y nación en Costa Rica* (San José: Editorial de la Universidad de Costa Rica, 1993).

Chapter Six

1. AC, vol. 26, pt. 1, "Autobiografía de A.H.Ch.," 253. "Cachirulasos" is today a slang term for shots of alcohol. This may be a misspelling or a mistranscription.

2. Carlos Luís Fallas, *Mamita Yunai*, 2d ed. (1941; reprint, San José: Editorial Costa Rica, 1995), 157.

3. This point is also made by Charles W. Koch, "Ethnicity and Livelihoods: A Social Geography of Costa Rica's Atlantic Zone" (Ph.D. diss., University of Kansas, 1975), 314, and Philippe Bourgois, *Ethnicity at Work: Divided Labor on a Central American Banana Plantation* (Baltimore: Johns Hopkins University Press, 1989), 182.

4. "Informe del gobernador de la comarca de Limón," in MGP (1891), unpaged.

5. MGP (1911), 443. Similar claims are made in "Informe del gobernador de la comarca de Limón," MGP (1902), unpaged.

6. Riots by West Indians are mentioned in ANCR, Policía 1486 (telegram, 23 Sept. 1906); LJCrimen 720 (homicidio frustrado, 1909); LJCrimen 181 (incendio, 1910); LJCyC 449 (tentativa de incendio, 1898); and elsewhere.

7. LJCrimen 145 (homicidio, 1897). "Que bien podía hacerlo como quisiera porque yo no era mas que un hijo de puta, sinvergüenza, baboso, cochino, que lo que yo trataba de hostilizar a los jamaicanos honrados y que algún día lo vería." Throughout the case Moodie gave testimony in Spanish, and it seems likely that this exchange between Moodie and the police commander took place in Spanish as well.

8. LJCrimen 145 (homicidio, 1897). Similarly, see LJCrimen 217 (homicidio, 1902).

9. MGP (1910), unpaged. See also ANCR, Policía 1564 (letter, 30 Sept. 1907); Policía 1484 (letter, 16 Mar. 1906); Policía 1486 (letter, 24 Nov. 1906); Policía 1567 (letter, 20 Apr. 1907); Policía 1120 (letter, 9 July 1908); Policía 1249 (telegram, 17 Apr. 1908).

10. LJCrimen 49 (homicidio, 1902). It was extremely rare for an *agente fiscal* to refer

to parties' nationalities in the text of his sentencing recommendations, as he did here. On the demonization of Nicaraguan *huleros* in Costa Rican nationalist rhetoric at the turn of the century, see Marc Edelman, "A Central American Genocide: Rubber, Slavery, Nationalism, and the Destruction of the Guatusos-Malekus," *Comparative Studies in Society and History* 40, no. 2 (1998): 356–90.

11. Bourgois, *Ethnicity at Work*, 182.

12. AC, vol. 26, pt. 2, "Autobiografía de E.N.B." (18th in vol.), 6. Chontales, just west of Lake Nicaragua, is the area of Spanish-speaking mestizo settlement located closest to the traditionally Creole/Miskitu Caribbean lowlands.

13. AC, vol. 26, pt. 1, "Autobiografía de M.G.L.," 148.

14. LJCrimen 748 (homicidio, 1913).

15. AC, vol. 26, pt. 1, "Autobiografía de A.H.Ch.," 259. See also Fallas, *Mamita Yunai*, 154–55; Bourgois, *Ethnicity at Work*, 209–10.

16. MGP (1890), unpaged.

17. Ibid.

18. See Lara Putnam, "Ideología racial, práctica social y estado liberal en Costa Rica," *Revista de Historia* (San José, Costa Rica) 39 (1999): 139–86.

19. Trevor W. Purcell, *Banana Fallout: Class, Color, and Culture among West Indians in Costa Rica* (Los Angeles: Center for Afro-American Studies, University of California, 1993), 37.

20. Paula Palmer, *"Wa'apin man": La historia de la costa talamanqueña de Costa Rica, según sus protagonistas*, trans. Quince Duncan and Paula Palmer, 2d ed. (San José: Editorial de la Universidad de Costa Rica, 1994), 150. My translation.

21. Ronald N. Harpelle, "Ethnicity, Religion, and Repression: The Denial of African Heritage in Costa Rica," *Canadian Journal of History* 29 (1994): 101, n. 25. "Cocomia" was a misspelling or mishearing of Pocomia, the local term for what in Jamaica is more commonly called Pukumina.

22. Diane J. Austin-Broos, *Jamaica Genesis: Religion and the Politics of Moral Orders* (Kingston: Ian Randle, 1997), chap. 4.

23. Harpelle, "Ethnicity, Religion, and Repression," 103, 105.

24. AC, vol. 23, "Autobiografía de E.Z.S.," 304.

25. LJCrimen 626 (homicidio frustrado, 1899). Bosses also killed subordinates in the course of challenges and disputes in LJCyC 96 (homicidio, 1900); LJCrimen 912 (homicidio, 1906); LJCrimen 158 (homicidio, 1907).

26. LJCrimen 906 (homicidio, 1914). Similarly, see LJCyC 115 (homicidio, 1898).

27. LJCrimen 950 (homicidio, 1915). The case contains no reference to Thurgood's race. I am tempted to think he was African American, because I find it hard to believe UFCo officials would support a Jamaican worker who punched a white American boss no matter what the circumstances.

28. LJCrimen 1182 (homicidio, 1904).

29. See also LJCrimen 44 (homicidio frustrado, 1907); LJCrimen 748 (homicidio, 1913).

30. ANCR, Policía 1567 (letter, 18 Apr. 1907). "[S]i llegamos a discutir vervalmente tengo que torcerle el pescuezo y eso seria el escandalo mas feo siendo yo autoridad." The recent creation of the Estrada police agency had taken jurisdiction and revenue from the agency at Matina, and the previous Matina police agent had transferred out after a similar feud with Estrada police.

31. ANCR, LJCrimen 720 (homicidio frustrado, 1909). Solís insisted that he had fired in self-defense, and that he had earned Arias's enmity through his fervent defense of the rights of the people of Matina, his native town. Other witnesses explained that "Solís's political color was *civilista*," linking the conflict to the electoral battle between Ricardo Jiménez and Rafael Iglesias (see Chapter 5, note 62, above). Solís was defended in court by UFCo retainer and *civilista* leader Lucas Daniel Alvarado. Nevertheless, he was sentenced to seven years on San Lucas.

32. ANCR, Policía 1552 (telegram, 28 Oct. 1905).

33. Carlos Hernández, "Los inmigrantes de St. Kitts: 1910, un capítulo en la historia de los conflictos bananeros costarricenses," *Revista de Historia* (San José, Costa Rica) 23 (1991): 198–204; Aviva Chomsky, "Afro-Jamaican Traditions and Labor Organizing on United Fruit Company Plantations in Costa Rica, 1910," *Journal of Social History* 28, no. 4 (1995): 837–55; LJPenal 1085 (homicidio, 1910).

34. Workers on Barmouth struck in December 1911 and again in June 1912, and in March 1912 shots were fired at the home of the UFCo superintendent in Zent. Aviva Chomsky, *West Indian Workers and the United Fruit Company in Costa Rica, 1870–1940* (Baton Rouge: Louisiana State University Press, 1996), 153–72; ANCR, Gobernación 3419 (telegram, 25 Mar. 1912).

35. See Bourgois, *Ethnicity at Work*, 54–58.

36. In 1927 one-quarter of banana plantation laborers were English speakers. Their median age was forty, as opposed to twenty-seven for Spanish speakers. Over the following seven years the median age of Hispanic workers would have been kept low by the constant infusion of incoming youths. The same was not true of West Indians.

37. Víctor Hugo Acuña Ortega, *La huelga bananera de 1934* (San José: CENAP-CEPAS, 1984), 29–42; Marielos Aguilar Hernández, "Algunas consideraciones sobre la huelga bananera de 1934," *Estudios* (Escuela de Estudios Generales de la Universidad de Costa Rica) 9 (1991): 123–37. On the limited participation of West Indian workers see Bourgois, *Ethnicity at Work*, 105–9, and Ronald Harpelle, "West Indians in Costa Rica: Class and Ethnicity in the Transformation of a Community" (Ph.D. diss., University of Toronto, 1992), 54–63.

38. Acuña Ortega, *Huelga bananera*, 47.

39. See "The Outlaw," by Limón poet Alderman Johnson Roden, reproduced in Harpelle, "Ethnicity, Religion, and Oppression," 96, and Quince Duncan, "La leyenda de José Gordon," in *Las mejores historias de Quince Duncan*, trans. and comp. Dellita Martin-Ogunsola (San José: Editorial Costa Rica, 1995), 214–49.

40. Thirty-seven of the 200 *lesiones* cases from Limón preserved in the ANCR involve female victims. In eleven of these cases the assailants were women as well.

41. See, for instance, Fallas, *Mamita Yunai*, 149, 156.

42. LJCyC 113 (homicidio, 1897); LJCrimen 520 (homicidio, 1912).

43. They were, for instance, far more likely than their *josefina* counterparts to be arrested for disruptive public behavior. From 1907 to 1926, women made up 20 percent of those charged with *faltas de policía* in Limón, where they comprised a mere third of the population, but only 13 percent of those so charged in San José, where they comprised well over half the population. Furthermore, the overall rate of *falta* arrests was nearly twice as high in Limón as in San José in these years. Costa Rica, Dirección General de Estadística y Censos, *Anuario estadístico* (1907–26). The sex ratio of those arrested in Limón in earlier years was likely similar. On an August 1894 police blotter from Port Limón exactly one-third of arrestees were women, nearly all of them Jamaicans. The great majority were charged with insults, scandal, or disrespect to police. ANCR, Gobernación 26723.

44. See Table A.5.

45. My discussion here is based on a close reading of all extant homicide investigations that originated in Limón before 1925 (111 cases, preserved in the ANCR). At the turn of the century roughly 60 percent of Limón's residents were Jamaicans or other West Indians, 30 percent were Costa Ricans or other Central Americans, and 10 percent hailed from farther abroad (see Chapter 2). Of men accused of homicide, 42 percent were West Indian, 46 percent Hispanic. Of female victims, 39 percent were West Indian, 43 percent Hispanic. See Tables A.6 and A.7. Women were accused of deadly violence in only four cases preserved from turn-of-the-century Limón. In two of the cases charges were dismissed. In another the female accused was bound over to trial but ultimately absolved. The only woman found guilty of homicide in early Limón was Felicitas Montealegre, an aging procurer convicted of killing her eight-year-old foster son through abuse and neglect. LJCrimen 596 (homicidio, 1910).

46. Overall, 26 percent of male victims were West Indian, 57 percent Hispanic.

47. Three cases were exceptions to this rule. One Costa Rican policeman was briefly charged with responsibility for the death of a drunken French engineer; one Costa Rican man was charged with killing his former lover's grandson, an indigenous youth; and one Nicaraguan, reputedly insane, was charged with killing a Jamaican coworker.

48. LJPenal 1244 (homicidio, 1922).

49. Richard D. E. Burton, *Afro-Creole: Power, Opposition, and Play in the Caribbean* (Ithaca: Cornell University Press, 1997), 159.

50. Fallas, *Mamita Yunai*, 126.

51. LJCrimen 720 (homicidio frustrado, 1909).

52. LJCrimen 109 (homicidio, 1903). In four other cases unrelated men attempted to stop conjugal violence and ended up killing or being killed.

53. There are only two partial exceptions. In one case the woman killed was the mother of the accused's former lover. The former lover herself was also shot but survived. In another case a woman was killed when the accused fired at her friend, his former lover. Three of the twenty-nine female victims were killed by accidental firearm

discharge, and a fourth died from malaria, rather than witchcraft, as local rumor had claimed. The death of Eva Barrantes, one of thirteen cases in which Hispanic former lovers stood accused, seems to have been a suicide (see Chapter 3).

54. LJCrimen 6 (homicidio, 1903).

55. LJCyC 433 (homicidio, 1900).

56. LJCrimen 924 (homicidio, 1904).

57. LJCrimen 648 (homicidio, 1907).

58. LJCrimen 681 (homicidio, 1909).

59. LJCrimen 140 (tentativa de homicidio, 1906).

60. LJCrimen 689 (homicidio, 1911).

61. LJCrimen 988 (homicidio, 1915).

62. LJCrimen 1022 (homicidio, 1915). Emphasis in original.

63. *Código Penal de la República de Costa Rica* (San José: Imprenta Nacional, n.d. [1880]), title 8, chapter 2, article 10.

64. Ibid., title 8, chapter 3, article 11.

65. Other cases in which defense lawyers rearranged chronologies, ignored their defendant's prior testimony, or misidentified those present at the time of a homicide in order to present a tale of proximate sexual betrayal include LJCrimen 47 (homicidio, 1902); LJCrimen 409 (homicidio, 1911); LJCrimen 657 (homicidio, 1912).

66. LJCyC 433 (homicidio, 1900).

67. LJCrimen 694 (homicidio, 1912). Other cases in which judges refused to consider jealousy an irresistible force include LJCrimen 657 (homicidio, 1912) and LJCrimen 731 (homicidio, 1911).

68. LJCrimen 656 (homicidio, 1912).

69. Ibid.

70. LJCrimen 304 (homicidio, 1913); LJCrimen 694 (homicidio, 1912); LJCrimen 140 (tentativa de homicidio, 1906).

71. LJCrimen 694 (homicidio, 1912); LJCrimen 656 (homicidio, 1912).

72. See LJCrimen 252 (homicidio, 1912); LJCrimen 802 (homicidio, 1913).

73. Sidney Chaloub, "Interpreting Machado de Assis: Paternalism, Slavery, and the Free Womb Law," paper presented at the conference "Honor, Status, and Law in Modern Latin America," University of Michigan, 4–6 Dec. 1998.

74. Barbara Jeanne Fields, "Slavery, Race and Ideology in the United States of America," *New Left Review* 181 (1990), 112–13.

75. The ethnic breakdown of Limón's population in 1950 was roughly as follows: 57 percent Hispanic born in Costa Rica, 25 percent West Indian born in Costa Rica, 9 percent West Indian born abroad, 6 percent Hispanic born in Nicaragua, and 3 percent indigenous. Costa Rica, Dirección General de Estadística y Censos, *Censo de Población de Costa Rica, 22 de mayo de 1950* (San José, 1953), 165–66, 181.

76. Between 1948 and 1959, homicide convictions averaged 10.9 per 100,000 residents in Limón, 10.5 in Puntarenas (site of the Pacific coast banana plantations), 3.4 in

San José, and 4.2 nationwide. Costa Rica, Dirección General de Estadística y Censos, *Anuario estadístico* (1948–59).

77. See David T. Courtwright, *Violent Land: Single Men and Social Disorder from the Frontier to the Inner City* (Cambridge: Harvard University Press, 1996). Courtwright's otherwise nuanced development of this hypothesis does not discuss how women's risk varied by time and place.

78. In 1950 the male-female ratio among black adults was 109:100; among white adults, 123:100. Costa Rica, Dirección General de Estadística y Censos, *Censo de 1950*, 181. My discussion here is based on a close reading of all preserved homicide investigations with female parties originated between 1925 and 1959, and a one-in-three sample of male-male cases from the same era, all located in the Archivo Judicial of the Costa Rican Supreme Court. See Tables A.8, A.9, and A.10. Hispanic women made up 73 percent of female victims, although they made up only 63 percent of the female population of the province. Hispanic men made up 73 percent of male victims in the sample, but only 64 percent of the male population. West Indian women comprised 20 percent of female victims, but 34 percent of the female population as a whole. West Indian men made up 24 percent of male victims, but 33 percent of the male population overall.

79. The sex ratio of victims in the 158 homicide cases from Limón from before 1959 preserved in the Archivo Judicial (median year 1949) is 953:100.

80. Disputes between bosses and subordinates accounted for one-eighth of turn-of-the-century homicides between men, but only one-twentieth of midcentury cases. Another two cases pitted plantation watchmen against men accused of stealing green cocoa.

81. Of the thirty-seven cases, four involved long-standing feuds over land; three were robberies (not including the cocoa cases mentioned above); three involved jailers or army officers accused of the murder of prisoners or subordinates; three stemmed from accusations of sexual betrayal by female partners; and in three cases no evidence of motive or perpetrator was ever uncovered.

82. AJ, remesa 161, archivo 0119 (homicidio, 1937). *Pendejo* actually means female pubic hair, but "asshole" is a rough equivalent in frequency of use and degree of offensiveness.

83. AJ, remesa 161, archivo 0613 (homicidio, 1948).

84. AJ, remesa 659, archivo 0917 (homicidio, 1958).

85. West Indian men made up less than one-fifth of participants in such cases; they comprised more than one-third of the total male population.

86. AJ, remesa 659, archivo 0035 (homicidio, 1949). The police commander and *subteniente* who shot the prisoners were sentenced to thirty years in prison, but they escaped the country with official connivance while out on bail and never served time. Marielos Aguilar Hernández, *Carlos Luís Fallas: Su época y sus luchas* (San José: Editorial Porvenir, 1983), 210–11.

87. AJ, remesa 659, archivo 0176 (homicidio, 1954).

88. Ibid. "Hoy es el dia que te mato gran puta, estás pensando que conmigo vas a jugar."

89. See AJ, remesa 659, archivo 0061 (homicidio, 1953), among many others.

90. AC, vol. 26, pt. 1, "Autobiografía de M.F.A.," 55.

91. Ibid., 63.

92. Ibid., 65.

93. Ibid., 68. "Emilse se rio de mi pero a ella le va a pesar: porque yo cuando me case yo se lo dije a Emilse que nunca intentara ninguna mala jugada porque le pesaria."

94. Ibid., 70-71.

95. AC, vol. 26, pt. 3, "Autobiografía de J.V.O.G.," 39.

96. LJCrimen 657 (homicidio, 1912).

97. AC, vol. 26, pt. 3, "Autobiografía de J.V.O.G.," 57.

98. AC, vol. 26, pt. 1, "Autobiografía de M.G.L.," 162.

99. Ibid., 105.

100. AC, vol. 26, pt. 3, "Autobiografía de I.P.R.," 88.

101. AC, vol. 23, "Autobiografía de O.C.C.," 335.

102. AC, vol. 26, pt. 1, "Autobiografía de A.H.Ch.," 251.

103. AC, vol. 26, pt. 1, "Autobiografía de M.G.L.," 84.

104. AC, vol. 26, pt. 3, "Autobiografía de F.R.S.," 145.

105. AC, vol. 26, pt. 1, "Autobiografía de R.J.G.," 284.

106. AC, vol. 26, pt. 2, "Autobiografía de Chonsito M.J." (15th in vol.), 4-5. Men report this organization of fieldwork on both cocoa and *abacá* plantations in Limón, as well as on rice and other farms in Nicaragua and Guanacaste. See AC, vol. 26, pt. 3, "Autobiografía de J.V.O.G.," 19. As far as I know, it was never practiced on banana plantations.

107. AC, vol. 26, pt. 3, "Autobiografía de J.V.O.G.," 67.

108. AC, vol. 26, pt. 1, "Autobiografía de J.A.B.B." (interview), 5.

109. AC, vol. 26, pt. 3, "Autobiografía de C.Q.D.H.D.," 118.

110. The use of the word "macho" to mean a North American man was common at least as early as 1911. See LJCrimen 689 (homicidio, 1911); George Palmer Putnam, *The Southland of North America: Rambles and Observations in Central America during the Year 1912* (New York: G. P. Putnam and Sons, 1914), 94.

111. Lowell Gudmundson, "Peasant, Farmer, Proletarian: Class Formation in a Smallholder Coffee Economy, 1850-1950," in *Coffee, Society, and Power in Latin America*, ed. William Roseberry, Lowell Gudmundson, and Mario Samper Kutschbach (Baltimore: Johns Hopkins University Press, 1995), 128.

112. LJCrimen 145 (homicidio, 1897); ANCR, Policía 06129 (14 Feb. 1910).

113. Cited in Bourgois, *Ethnicity at Work*, 85.

114. Ken Post, *Arise Ye Starvelings: The Jamaican Labour Rebellion of 1938 and Its Aftermath* (The Hague: Martinus Nijhoff, 1978), 164, 176, 243; Burton, *Afro-Creole*, 122-38; Barry Chevannes, *Rastafari: Roots and Ideology* (Syracuse: Syracuse University Press,

1994). The three returnees were Leonard Howell, Joseph Hibbert, and Archibald Dunkley. Post reports Howell had lived in Costa Rica since 1911 and had become a banana planter there.

115. Aguilar Hernández, *Carlos Luís Fallas*, 197–98.

116. Jacobo Schifter, *La fase oculta de la guerra civil en Costa Rica*, 4th ed. (San José: EDUCA, 1985), 102–7; John Patrick Bell, *Guerra civil en Costa Rica: Los sucesos políticos de 1948*, 4th ed. (San José: EDUCA, 1986), 190–93.

Conclusion

1. On recent years, see Philippe Bourgois, *Ethnicity at Work: Divided Labor on a Central American Banana Plantation* (Baltimore: Johns Hopkins University Press, 1989).

2. Charles W. Koch, "Ethnicity and Livelihoods: A Social Geography of Costa Rica's Atlantic Zone" (Ph.D. diss., University of Kansas, 1975), 155.

3. For a careful discussion of what is and is not radically new about transnational migrants today see Peggy Levitt, *The Transnational Villagers* (Berkeley: University of California Press, 2001).

4. See José Moya, *Cousins and Strangers: Spanish Immigrants in Buenos Aires, 1850–1930* (Berkeley: University of California Press, 1998).

5. AC, vol. 26, pt. 3, "Autobiografía de J.V.O.G.," 3–78.

6. Thomas Miller Klubock, *Contested Communities: Class, Gender, and Politics in Chile's El Teniente Copper Mine, 1904–1951* (Durham: Duke University Press, 1998).

7. Ann Farnsworth-Alvear, *Dulcinea in the Factory: Myths, Morals, Men, and Women in Colombia's Industrial Experiment, 1905–1960* (Durham: Duke University Press, 2000).

8. Steve Striffler, *In the Shadows of State and Capital: The United Fruit Company, Popular Struggle, and Agrarian Restructuring in Ecuador, 1900–1995* (Durham: Duke University Press, 2002). O'Brien also emphasizes the role of the civilizing mission in guiding UFCo enterprises in Honduras. Thomas F. O'Brien, *The Revolutionary Mission: American Enterprise in Latin America, 1900–1945* (Cambridge: Cambridge University Press, 1996).

9. Catherine LeGrand, "Living in Macondo: Economy and Culture in a United Fruit Company Enclave in Colombia," in *Close Encounters of Empire: Writing the Cultural History of U.S.-Latin American Relations*, ed. Gilbert M. Joseph, Catherine C. LeGrand, and Ricardo D. Salvatore, 348–52.

10. This is consistent with Marquardt's argument that the new agroecological strategy attempted on UFCo Pacific coast plantations was accompanied by tightened social control of the plantation workforce. Steve Marquardt, "'Green Havoc': Panama Disease, Environmental Change, and Labor Process in the Central American Banana Industry," *American Historical Review* 106, no. 1 (2001): 49–80. UFCo officials themselves described the shifting plantation strategy they pursued in the Western Caribbean as incompatible with attempts to engineer domestic life. Company boosters May and Plaza wrote in 1958 that United Fruit had considered a homeownership plan for workers

"as a means of increasing their stake and sense of pride in the community. However, so long as Panama disease forces the periodic abandonment of farms and moving of workers to new locations, any such plan seems to be impracticable." Stacy May and Galo Plaza, *The United Fruit Company in Latin America* (New York: National Planning Association, 1958), 210.

11. Similarly, it was local bureaucrats and "the colored ministers," rather than UFCo officials, who actively promoted the Rockefeller Foundation's anti-hookworm campaign in Limón. Steven Palmer, "Central American Encounters with Rockefeller Public Health, 1914-1921," in Joseph, LeGrand, and Salvatore, *Close Encounters of Empire*, 322.

12. Ronald N. Harpelle, *The West Indians of Costa Rica: Race, Class, and the Integration of an Ethnic Minority* (Kingston: Ian Randle and McGill-Queen's University Press, 2001), 125-29; Iván Molina Jiménez and Steven Palmer, *The History of Costa Rica* (San José: Editorial de la Universidad de Costa Rica, 1998).

13. See especially ANCR, INCOFER 45 (correspondence, 1943-45). The means of manipulation show marked similarities to those described in Paul Dosal, *Doing Business with the Dictators: A Political History of United Fruit in Guatemala, 1899-1944* (Wilmington, Del.: Scholarly Resources, 1993).

14. My findings here coincide with the suggestions made by LeGrand, "Living in Macondo," 355-56.

15. Recent analyses of domestic violence in other Latin American contexts include Roger Lancaster, *Life Is Hard: Machismo, Danger, and the Intimacy of Power in Nicaragua* (Berkeley: University of California Press, 1992); Olivia Harris, "Condor and Bull: The Ambiguities of Masculinity in Northern Potosí," in *Sex and Violence: Issues in Representation and Experience*, ed. Penelope Harvey and Peter Gow (London: Routledge, 1994), 40-65; Peter Wade, "Man the Hunter: Gender and Violence in Music and Drinking Contexts in Colombia," in Harvey and Gow, *Sex and Violence*, 115-37; and Heidi Tinsmann, "Household *Patrones*: Wife-Beating and Sexual Control in Rural Chile, 1964-1988," in *The Gendered Worlds of Latin American Women Workers: From Household and Factory to the Union Hall and Ballot Box*, ed. John French and Daniel James (Durham: Duke University Press, 1997), 264-96.

16. The use of the courts by mothers to enforce marriage promises by men who had sex with the complainants' daughters showed a similar popular appropriation of the judicial arena. Convictions depended on stringent (and highly subjective) proofs of the girl's prior chastity. But the accusation itself might work as a bargaining chip to the advantage of the mother or daughter in question, while still not equalizing the power relations involved. See Lara Putnam, "Intimacy, Entitlement, and Enforcement in Caribbean Costa Rica (1890-1920)," unpublished manuscript.

17. See vagrancy cases from 1950s profiled in Lara Putnam, "Beneficencia, pobreza, y racismo en Costa Rica, 1920-1960" (paper presented at the conference "Culturas Populares y Políticas Públicas en México y Centroamérica (siglos XIX y XX)," Alajuela, Costa Rica, 20-22 Sept. 2000).

18. William Roseberry, "Hegemony and the Language of Contention," in *Everyday*

Forms of State Formation: Revolution and the Negotiation of Rule in Modern Mexico, ed. Gilbert M. Joseph and Daniel Nugent (Durham: Duke University Press, 1994), 365.

19. As I argued in Chapter 1, it was by shaping this terrain through property laws, immigration policy, and so forth that the state impacted popular practices of kinship and gender—in largely unforeseen and unintended ways.

20. See Jean Besson, "Freedom and Community: The British West Indies," in *The Meaning of Freedom: Economics, Politics, and Culture after Slavery*, ed. Frank McGlynn and Seymour Drescher (Pittsburgh: University of Pittsburgh Press, 1992), 183–220. A letter to the editor of the Limón *Times* in 1912 argued, "Tis true that the Company provides camps for the laborers; but there are a good many respectable men with their wives and children, who can't live in camps." *Times* (Limón), 13 June 1913, as cited in Aviva Chomsky, *West Indian Workers and the United Fruit Company in Costa Rica, 1870–1940* (Baton Rouge: Louisiana State University Press, 1996), 116.

21. According to the CIHAC 1927 census sample projection, the households of the 2,800 Hispanic *peones bananeros* in Limón contained 149 wives, 258 *compañeras*, and 276 children under fifteen. The households of the 1,030 West Indian *peones bananeros* contained 537 wives, 276 *compañeras*, and 976 children.

Bibliography

Archival Sources

Archivo Judicial de la Corte Suprema de Justicia, San Pablo de Heredia, Costa Rica
Juzgado Penal de Limón
    Remesa 5-228-161
    Remesa 6-229-161
    Remesa 6-261-659
    Remesa 6-263-659
    Remesa 8-352-738
Archivo Nacional de Costa Rica, San José, Costa Rica
  Fondo Fotografías
  Fondo Grabaciones
    Transcripciones de entrevistas de Paula Palmer. 4 vols.
  Fondo INCOFER
  Serie Censos
  Serie Congreso
  Serie Gobernación
  Serie Jurídica
    Alajuela Alcaldía Primera
    Alajuela Juzgado del Crimen
    Cartago Alcaldía Primera
    Cartago Alcaldía Segunda
    Heredia Juzgado del Crimen
    Juzgado de lo Contencioso
      Administrativo
    Juzgado Penal de Limón
    Limón Alcaldía Única
    Limón Juzgado Civil
    Limón Juzgado Civil y del
      Crimen
  Serie Policía
    Limón Juzgado del Crimen
    Puntarenas Alcaldía Única
    Puntarenas Juzgado Civil y
      del Crimen
    San José Alcaldía Primera
    San José Alcaldía Segunda
    San José Alcaldía Tercera
    San José Juzgado del Crimen
    San José Juzgado Primero Civil
    San José Juzgado Primero del Crimen
    San José Juzgado Segundo Civil
    San José Juzgado Segundo del Crimen

Government Documents

Census of Jamaica, 25th of April, 1921. Kingston, 1922.
Census of Jamaica, 4th of January, 1943. Population Bulletins 1–6; Agriculture Bulletin 1–3. Kingston, 1944.
Código Penal de la República de Costa Rica. San José: Imprenta Nacional, n.d. [1880].
Costa Rica. *Colección de leyes y decretos.* (Annual. Exact title and publisher vary.)
Costa Rica. Dirección General de Estadística y Censos. *Anuario estadístico.* 1907–59. (Exact title varies.)
————. *Censo de Población de Costa Rica, 22 de mayo de 1950.* San José, 1953.
————. *Censo de Población de 1927.* San José, 1960.
————. *Censo General de la República de Costa Rica . . . de 1892.* Facsimile ed. San José: Ministerio de Economía, Industria y Comercio, Dirección General de Estadística y Censos, 1974.
Costa Rica. Ministerio de Gobernación y Policía. *Memoria.* 1883–1945. (Exact title of issuing agency varies.)
Costa Rica. Secretaría de Salubridad Pública. *Memoria.* 1930–36.

Newspapers

Atlantic Voice/La Voz del Atlántico (Limón), 1934–46
Hoja Obrera (San José), 1910
El Limonense, 1914
La Prensa Libre (San José), 1914
Searchlight (Limón), 1929–31

Published Sources

Abrahams, Roger D. *The Man-of-Words in the West Indies: Performance and the Emergence of Creole Culture.* Baltimore: Johns Hopkins University Press, 1983.
Abu-Lughod, Lila. *Veiled Sentiments: Honor and Poetry in a Bedouin Society.* Berkeley: University of California Press, 1988.
————. "Writing against Culture." In *Recapturing Anthropology,* edited by Richard Fox, 137–62. Santa Fe, N.M.: School of American Research Press, 1991.
————. *Writing Women's Worlds: Bedouin Stories.* Berkeley: University of California Press, 1993.
Acuña León, María de los Angeles, and Doriam Chavarría López. "Endogamia y exogamia en la sociedad colonial cartaginesa (1738-1821)." *Revista de Historia* (San José, Costa Rica) 23 (1991): 107–44.
Acuña Ortega, Víctor Hugo. *Conflicto y Reforma (1940-1949).* San José: Editorial Universidad Estatal a Distancia, 1995.
————. *La huelga bananera de 1934.* San José: CENAP-CEPAS, 1984.

———. "Nación y clase obrera en Centroamérica durante la época liberal (1870–1930)." In *El paso del cometa: Estado, política social y culturas populares en Costa Rica (1800/1950),* edited by Iván Molina Jiménez and Steven Palmer, 145–66. San José: Editorial Porvenir/Plumsock Mesoamerican Studies, 1994.

———, ed. *Las repúblicas agroexportadoras (1870–1945).* Vol. 4 of *Historia general de Centroamérica,* coordinated by Edelberto Torres Rivas. Madrid: Sociedad Estatal Quinto Centenario and FLACSO, 1993.

Acuña Ortega, Víctor Hugo, and Iván Molina Jiménez. *Historia económica y social de Costa Rica (1750–1950).* San José: Editorial Porvenir, 1991.

Adams, Frederick Upham. *Conquest of the Tropics: The Story of the Creative Enterprises Conducted by the United Fruit Company.* New York: Doubleday, 1914.

Aguilar Hernández, Marielos. "Algunas consideraciones sobre la huelga bananera de 1934." *Estudios* (Escuela de Estudios Generales de la Universidad de Costa Rica) 9 (1991): 123–37.

———. *Carlos Luís Fallas: Su época y sus luchas.* San José: Editorial Porvenir, 1983.

Alexander, Jack L. "Love, Race, Slavery, and Sexuality in Jamaican Images of the Family." In *Kinship Ideology and Practice in Latin America,* edited by Raymond T. Smith, 147–80. Chapel Hill: University of North Carolina Press, 1984.

Alleyne, Mervyn C. *Roots of Jamaican Culture.* London: Pluto Press, 1988.

Allsopp, Richard, ed. *Dictionary of Caribbean English Usage.* Oxford: Oxford University Press, 1996.

Augelli, John P. "The Rimland-Mainland Concept of Culture Areas in Middle America." *Annals of the Association of American Geographers* 52, no. 2 (1962): 119–29.

Austin Broos, Diane J. *Jamaica Genesis: Religion and the Politics of Moral Orders.* Kingston: Ian Randle, 1997

———. "Redefining the Moral Order: Interpretations of Christianity in Postemancipation Jamaica." In *The Meaning of Freedom: Economics, Politics, and Culture after Slavery,* edited by Frank McGlynn and Seymour Drescher, 221–43. Pittsburgh: University of Pittsburgh Press, 1992.

Badilla, Patricia. "Ideología y derecho: El espíritu mesiánico de la reforma jurídica costarricense (1882–1888)." *Revista de Historia* (San José, Costa Rica) 18 (1988): 187–201.

Barriatti, Rita. "Inmigrantes italianos en Costa Rica: Estudio de su integración mediante fuentes orales." *Revista de Historia* (San José, Costa Rica) 20 (1989): 105–31.

Barrow, Christine. *Family in the Caribbean: Themes and Perspectives.* Kingston: Ian Randle, 1996.

———, ed. *Caribbean Portraits: Essays on Gender Ideologies and Identities.* Kingston: Ian Randle, 1998.

Beals, Carleton. *Banana Gold.* Philadelphia: J. B. Lippincott, 1932.

Beckles, Hilary M. "Centreing Woman: The Political Economy of Gender in West African and Caribbean Slavery." In *Caribbean Portraits: Essays on Gender Ideologies and Identities,* edited by Christine Barrow, 93–114. Kingston: Ian Randle, 1998.

Beckles, Hilary, and Verene Shepherd, eds. *Caribbean Freedom: Economy and Society from Emancipation to the Present.* Princeton: Markus Weiner, 1996.

———, eds. *Caribbean Slave Society and Economy.* New York: W. W. Norton, 1991.

Behar, Ruth. *Translated Woman: Crossing the Border with Esperanza's Story.* Boston: Beacon Press, 1993.

Bell, John Patrick. *Guerra civil en Costa Rica: Los sucesos políticos de 1948.* 4th ed. San José: EDUCA, 1986.

Berlin, Ira, and Philip D. Morgan, eds. *Cultivation and Culture: Labor and the Shaping of Slave Life in the Americas.* Charlottesville: University Press of Virginia, 1993.

Besson, Jean. "Freedom and Community: The British West Indies." In *The Meaning of Freedom: Economics, Politics, and Culture after Slavery,* edited by Frank McGlynn and Seymour Drescher, 183–220. Pittsburgh: University of Pittsburgh Press, 1992.

———. "Reputation and Respectability Reconsidered: A New Perspective on Afro-Caribbean Peasant Women." In *Women and Change in the Caribbean: A Pan-Caribbean Perspective,* edited by Janet Momsen, 15–37. Bloomington: Indiana University Press, 1993.

Bliss, Katherine Elaine. "'Guided by an Imperious, Moral Need': Prostitutes, Motherhood, and Nationalism in Revolutionary Mexico." In *Reconstructing Criminality in Latin America,* edited by Carlos A. Aguirre and Robert Buffington, 167–94. Wilmington, Del: Scholarly Resources, 2000.

Bourgois, Philippe. *Ethnicity at Work: Divided Labor on a Central American Banana Plantation.* Baltimore: Johns Hopkins University Press, 1989.

———. *In Search of Respect: Selling Crack in El Barrio.* Cambridge: Cambridge University Press, 1995.

Bovallius, Carl. "Estadía en Costa Rica (Julio a Octubre de 1882)." In *Viajes por la República de Costa Rica,* vol. 1, comp. Elías Zeledón Cartín, 89–158. San José: Ministerio de Cultura, Juventud y Deportes, 1997.

Brettell, Caroline B., and James F. Hollifield, eds. *Migration Theory: Talking across Disciplines.* New York: Routledge, 2000.

Brodber, Erna. "Afro-Jamaican Women at the Turn of the Century." *Social and Economic Studies* 35 (1986): 23–50.

Bryce-Laporte, Roy Simon. "Crisis, Contraculture and Religion among West Indians in the Panama Canal Zone." In *Blackness in Latin America and the Caribbean,* vol. 1, edited by Norman E. Whitten Jr. and Arlene Torres, 100–118. Bloomington: Indiana University Press, 1998. First published in *Afro-American Anthropology: Contemporary Perspectives,* edited by Norman E. Whitten Jr. and John F. Szwed (New York: Free Press, 1970).

———. "Family, Household and Intergenerational Relations in a 'Jamaican' Village in Limón, Costa Rica." In *The Family in the Caribbean: Proceedings of the Second Conference on the Family in the Caribbean,* edited by Stanford N. Gerber, 65–93. Rio Piedras: University of Puerto Rico Institute of Caribbean Studies, 1973.

Bryce-Laporte, Roy Simon, and Trevor Purcell. "A Lesser-Known Chapter of the African Diaspora: West Indians in Costa Rica, Central America." In *Global*

Dimensions of the African Diaspora, edited by Joseph E. Harris, 137–57. Washington, D.C.: Howard University Press, 1993.

Buffington, Robert, and Pablo Piccato. "Tales of Two Women: The Narrative Construal of Porfirian Reality." *The Americas* 55, no. 3 (1999): 391–424.

Bulmer-Thomas, Victor. *The Economic History of Latin America since Independence.* Cambridge: Cambridge University Press, 1994.

Burton, Richard D. E. *Afro-Creole: Power, Opposition and Play in the Caribbean.* Ithaca: Cornell University Press, 1997.

Bush, Barbara. *Slave Women in Caribbean Society, 1650–1838.* Bloomington: Indiana University Press, 1990.

Butler, Judith. *Gender Trouble: Feminism and the Subversion of Identity.* New York: Routledge, 1990.

Calvo, Joaquín B. *The Republic of Costa Rica.* Chicago: Rand McNally, 1890.

Carcanholo, Reinaldo. "Sobre la evolución de las actividades bananeras en Costa Rica." *Anuario de Estudios Centroamericanos* 19 (1978): 145–203.

Carmack, Robert M. "Perspectivas sobre la historia antigua de Centroamérica." In *Historia antigua*, edited by Robert M. Carmack, 283–326. Vol. 1 of *Historia general de Centroamérica*, coordinated by Edelberto Torres Rivas. Madrid: Sociedad Estatal Quinto Centenario and FLACSO, 1993.

Carr, A. "*Chelonia mydas* (Tortuga, Tortuga Blanca, Green Turtle)." In *Costa Rican Natural History*, edited by Daniel Janzen, 390–92. Chicago: University of Chicago Press, 1983.

Casey Gaspar, Jeffrey. "El Ferrocarril al Atlántico en Costa Rica, 1871–1874." *Anuario de Estudios Centroamericanos* 2 (1976): 291–344.

———. *Limón, 1880–1940: Un estudio de la industria bananera en Costa Rica.* San José: Editorial Costa Rica, 1979.

Caulfield, Sueann. "Getting into Trouble: Dishonest Women, Modern Girls, and Women-Men in the Conceptual Language of *Vida Policial*, 1925–1927." *Signs* 19, no. 1 (1993): 146–76.

———. *In Defense of Honor: Morality, Modernity, and Nation in Rio de Janeiro, Brazil, 1920–1940.* Durham: Duke University Press, 2000.

———. "Women of Vice, Virtue, and Rebellion: New Studies of the Representation of the Female in Latin America." *Latin American Research Review* 28, no. 2 (1993): 163–74.

Cerdas, Ana Luisa. "El surgimiento del enclave bananera en el Pacífico Sur." *Revista de Historia* (San José, Costa Rica) 28 (1993): 117–62.

Cerdas Bokhan, Dorita. "Matrimonio y vida cotidiana en el graven central costarricense, 1851–1890." *Revista de Historia* (San José, Costa Rica) 26 (1992): 69–96.

Céspedes, Benjamín de. *La prostitución en la ciudad de la Habana.* Havana, 1888.

Chauncey, George, Jr. "The Locus of Reproduction: Women's Labour in the Zambian Copperbelt, 1927–1953." *Journal of South African Studies* 7, no. 2 (1981): 135–64.

Chevannes, Barry. *Rastafari: Roots and Ideology.* Syracuse: Syracuse University Press, 1994.

Chomsky, Aviva. "Afro-Jamaican Traditions and Labor Organizing on United Fruit Company Plantations in Costa Rica, 1910." *Journal of Social History* 28, no. 4 (1995): 837–55.

———. "Laborers and Smallholders in Costa Rica's Mining Communities, 1900–1940." In *Identity and Struggle at the Margins of the Nation-State: The Laboring Peoples of Central America and the Hispanic Caribbean*, edited by Aviva Chomsky and Aldo Lauria-Santiago, 169–95. Durham: Duke University Press, 1998.

———. *West Indian Workers and the United Fruit Company in Costa Rica, 1870–1940*. Baton Rouge: Louisiana State University Press, 1996.

———. "West Indian Workers in Costa Rican Radical and Nationalist Ideology: 1900–1950." *The Americas* 51, no. 1 (1994): 11–40.

Chomsky, Aviva, and Aldo Lauria-Santiago, eds. *Identity and Struggle at the Margins of the Nation-State: The Laboring Peoples of Central America and the Hispanic Caribbean*. Durham: Duke University Press, 1998.

Collazos, Sharon Phillips. "The Cities of Panama: Sixty Years of Development." In *Cities of Hope: People, Protests, and Progress in Urbanizing Latin America, 1870–1930*, edited by Ronn Pineo and James A. Baer, 240–57. Boulder, Colo.: Westview Press, 1998.

Comaroff, John L. "Of Totemism and Ethnicity; Consciousness, Practice, and the Signs of Inequality." *Ethnos* 52 (1987): 301–23.

Conniff, Michael. *Black Labor on a White Canal: West Indians in Panama, 1904–1980*. Pittsburgh: University of Pittsburgh Press, 1985.

Cooper, Carolyn. *Noises in the Blood: Orality, Gender, and the "Vulgar" Body of Jamaican Popular Culture*. Durham: Duke University Press, 1995.

Courtwright, David T. *Violent Land: Single Men and Social Disorder from the Frontier to the Inner City*. Cambridge: Harvard University Press, 1996.

Craton, Michael. "Changing Patterns of Slave Families in the British West Indies." In *Caribbean Slave Society and Economy*, edited by Hilary Beckles and Verene Shepherd, 228–49. New York: W. W. Norton, 1991. First published in *Journal of Interdisciplinary History* 10, no. 1 (1979): 1–35.

Crowther, Samuel. *The Romance and Rise of the American Tropics*. Garden City, N.Y.: Doubleday, Doran, 1929.

Cumper, G. E. "Population Movements in Jamaica, 1830–1950." *Social and Economic Studies* 5 (1956): 261–80.

da Costa, Emilia Viotti. "Experience versus Structures: New Tendencies in the History of Labor and the Working Class in Latin America—What Do We Gain? What Do We Lose?" *International Labor and Working Class History* 36 (1989): 3–23.

Davis, Richard Harding. *Three Gringos in Venezuela and Central America*. Cambridge: Harvard University Press, 1896.

De la Cruz, Vladimir. *Las luchas sociales en Costa Rica*. San José: Editorial Universidad de Costa Rica, 1980.

di Leonardo, Micaela. "Introduction: Gender, Culture, and Political Economy: Feminist Anthropology in Historical Perspective." In *Gender at the Crossroads of*

Knowledge: Feminist Anthropology in the Postmodern Era, edited by Micaela di Leonardo, 1–47. Berkeley: University of California Press, 1991.

Dore, Elizabeth, ed. *Gender Politics in Latin America: Debates in Theory and Practice.* New York: Monthly Review Press, 1997.

Dore, Elizabeth, and Maxine Molyneux, eds. *Hidden Histories of Gender and the State in Latin America.* Durham: Duke University Press, 2000.

Dosal, Paul J. *Doing Business with the Dictators: A Political History of United Fruit in Guatemala, 1899–1944.* Wilmington, Del.: Scholarly Resources, 1993.

Dumas, Alexandre. *La Dame aux Camélias.* Translated by David Coward. Oxford: Oxford University Press, 1986.

Duncan, Quince. *Las mejores historias de Quince Duncan/The Best Short Stories of Quince Duncan.* Translated by Dellita Martin-Ogunsola. San José: Editorial Costa Rica, 1995.

Dunn, Richard S. "Sugar Production and Slave Women in Jamaica." In *Cultivation and Culture: Labor and the Shaping of Slave Life in the Americas,* edited by Ira Berlin and Philip D. Morgan, 49–72. Charlottesville: University Press of Virginia, 1993.

Echeverri-Gent, Elisavinda. "Forgotten Workers: British West Indians and the Early Days of the Banana Industry in Costa Rica and Honduras." *Journal of Latin American Studies* 24, no. 2 (1992): 275–308.

Edelman, Marc. "A Central American Genocide: Rubber, Slavery, Nationalism, and the Destruction of the Guatusos-Malekus." *Comparative Studies in Society and History* 40, no. 2 (1998): 356–90.

———. *The Logic of the Latifundio: The Large Estates of Northwestern Costa Rica since the Late Nineteenth Century.* Stanford: Stanford University Press, 1992.

Eisner, Gisela. *Jamaica, 1830–1930: A Study in Economic Growth.* Manchester: Manchester University Press, 1961.

Elliott, L. E. *Central America: New Paths in Ancient Lands.* New York: Dodd, Mead, 1925.

Euraque, Darío. "The Banana Enclave, Nationalism, and Mestizaje in Honduras, 1910s–1930s." In *Identity and Struggle at the Margins of the Nation-State: The Laboring Peoples of Central America and the Hispanic Caribbean,* edited by Aviva Chomsky and Aldo Lauria-Santiago, 151–68. Durham: Duke University Press, 1998.

———. *Reinterpreting the Banana Republic: Region and State in Honduras, 1870–1972.* Chapel Hill: University of North Carolina Press, 1996.

Facio Brenes, Rodrigo. *Estudio sobre la economía costarricense.* 4th ed. San José: Editorial Costa Rica, 1990.

Fallas, Carlos Luís. *Mamita Yunai.* 2d ed. San José: Editorial Costa Rica, 1995.

Fallas Monge, Carlos Luís. *El movimiento obrero en Costa Rica, 1830–1902.* San José: Editorial Universidad Estatal a Distancia, 1983.

Farnsworth-Alvear, Ann. *Dulcinea in the Factory: Myths, Morals, Men, and Women in Colombia's Industrial Experiment, 1905–1960.* Durham: Duke University Press, 2000.

Fernández Guardia, Ricardo. *Reseña histórica de Talamanca.* San José: Alsina, 1918.

Fields, Barbara Jeanne. "Slavery, Race, and Ideology in the United States of America." *New Left Review* 181 (1990): 95–118.

Findlay, Eileen J. Suárez. *Imposing Decency: The Politics of Sexuality and Race in Puerto Rico, 1870–1920*. Durham: Duke University Press, 1999.

Fonseca Corrales, Elizabeth. *Costa Rica colonial: La tierra y el hombre*. 3d ed. San José: EDUCA, 1986.

Fournier, Eduardo. "Aproximación a un estudio histórico del matrimonio en Costa Rica (siglos XVIII y XIX)." *Revista Senderos* (San José, Costa Rica) 35 (1989): 5–26.

Franck, Harry A. *Roaming through the West Indies*. New York: Century, 1923.

Franco, Jean. *Plotting Women: Gender and Representation in Mexico*. New York: Columbia University Press, 1989.

French, John D., and Daniel James, eds. *The Gendered Worlds of Latin American Women Workers: From Household and Factory to the Union Hall and Ballot Box*. Durham: Duke University Press, 1997.

French, William E. "Prostitutes and Guardian Angels: Women, Work, and the Family in Porfirian Mexico." *Hispanic American Historical Review* 72, no. 4 (1992): 529–53.

Gallant, Thomas W. "Honor, Masculinity, and Ritual Knife Fighting in Nineteenth-Century Greece." *American Historical Review* 105, no. 2 (2000): 359–82.

García Buchard, Ethel. *Poder político, interés bananero, e identidad nacional en Centro América*. Tegucigalpa: Editorial Universitaria, 1997.

Gilfoyle, Timothy J. "Prostitutes in History: From Parables of Pornography to Metaphors of Modernity." *American Historical Review* 104, no. 1 (1999): 117–41.

González, Nancie L. Solien. "Rethinking the Consanguineal Household and Matrifocality." *Ethnology* 23 (1984): 1–12.

———. "Toward a Definition of Matrifocality." In *Afro-American Anthropology: Contemporary Perspectives*, edited by Norman E. Whitten Jr. and John F. Szwed, 231–44. New York: Free Press, 1970.

González Salas, Edwin. *Evolución histórica de la población de Costa Rica (1840–1940)*. San José: Editorial Universidad Estatal a Distancia, 1995.

González Vásquez, Fernando, and Elías Zeledón Cartín, comp. *Crónicas y relatos para la historia de Puerto Limón*. San José: Ministerio de Cultura, Juventud y Deportes, Centro de Investigación y Conservación del Patrimonio Cultural, 1999.

Gordon, Linda. *Heroes of Their Own Lives: The Politics and History of Family Violence*. New York: Penguin Books, 1988.

Gordon, Sally W. "I Go to 'Tanties': The Economic Significance of Child-Shifting in Antigua, West Indies." *Journal of Comparative Family Studies* 18, no. 3 (1987): 427–43.

Gould, Jeffrey L. *To Lead as Equals: Rural Protest and Political Consciousness in Chinandega, Nicaragua, 1912–1979*. Chapel Hill: University of North Carolina Press, 1990.

Graham, Richard. *Patronage and Politics in Nineteenth-Century Brazil*. Stanford: Stanford University Press, 1990.

Gudmundson, Lowell. "Aspectos socioeconómicos del delito en Costa Rica, 1725–1850." *Revista de Historia* (Heredia, Costa Rica) 3, no. 5 (1977): 101–48.

————. "Black into White in Nineteenth-Century Spanish America: Afro-American Assimilation in Argentina and Costa Rica." *Slavery and Abolition* 5 (1984): 34–49.

————. *Costa Rica before Coffee: Society and Economy on the Eve of the Export Boom.* Baton Rouge: Louisiana State University Press, 1986.

————. *Estratificación socio-racial y económica de Costa Rica, 1700–1850.* San José: Editorial Universidad Estatal a Distancia, 1978.

————. "Peasant, Farmer, Proletarian: Class Formation in a Smallholder Coffee Economy, 1850–1950." In *Coffee, Society, and Power in Latin America,* edited by William Roseberry, Lowell Gudmundson, and Mario Samper Kutschbach, 112–50. Baltimore: Johns Hopkins University Press, 1995.

Gudmundson, Lowell, and Héctor Lindo-Fuentes. *Central America, 1821–1871: Liberalism before Liberal Reform.* Tuscaloosa: University of Alabama Press, 1995.

Gussler, Judith D. "Adaptive Strategies and Social Networks of Women in St. Kitts." In *A World of Women: Anthropological Studies of Women in the Societies of the World,* edited by Erika Bourguignon, 185–209. New York: Praeger, 1980.

Gutiérrez, Joaquín. *Puerto Limón.* 7th ed. San José: Editorial de la Universidad de Costa Rica, 1991.

Gutiérrez, Ramón. *When Jesus Came, the Corn Mothers Went Away: Marriage, Sexuality, and Power in New Mexico, 1500–1846.* Stanford: Stanford University Press, 1991.

Guy, Donna J. *Sex and Danger in Buenos Aires: Prostitution, Family, and Nation in Argentina.* Lincoln: University of Nebraska Press, 1991.

Hall, Carolyn. *El café y el desarrollo histórico-geográfico de Costa Rica.* 2d ed. San José: Editorial Costa Rica, 1991.

Hall, Douglas. "The Flight from the Estates Reconsidered: The British West Indies, 1838–1842." In *Caribbean Freedom: Economy and Society from Emancipation to the Present,* edited by Hilary Beckles and Verene Shepherd, 55–63. Princeton: Markus Wiener, 1996. First published in *Journal of Caribbean History* 10/11 (1978): 7–24.

————. *Free Jamaica, 1838–1865: An Economic History.* New Haven: Yale University Press, 1959.

Haraway, Donna. *Primate Visions: Gender, Race, and Nature in the World of Modern Science.* New York: Routledge, 1989.

————. *Simians, Cyborgs, and Women: The Reinvention of Nature.* New York: Routledge, 1991.

Hareven, Tamara K. "The History of the Family and the Complexity of Social Change." *American Historical Review* 96, no. 1 (1991): 95–124.

Harpelle, Ronald N. "Ethnicity, Religion, and Repression: The Denial of African Heritage in Costa Rica." *Canadian Journal of History* 29 (1994): 95–112.

————. "Racism and Nationalism in the Creation of Costa Rica's Pacific Coast Banana Enclave." *The Americas* 56, no. 3 (2000): 29–51.

————. "The Social and Political Integration of West Indians in Costa Rica: 1930–50." *Journal of Latin American Studies* 25 (1993): 103–20.

————. *The West Indians of Costa Rica: Race, Class and the Integration of an Ethnic Minority.* Montreal: McGill-Queen's University Press, 2001.

Harris, Olivia. "Condor and Bull: The Ambiguities of Masculinity in Northern

Potosí." In *Sex and Violence: Issues in Representation and Experience*, edited by
Penelope Harvey and Peter Gow, 40–65. London: Routledge, 1994.

Harvey, Penelope, and Peter Gow, eds. *Sex and Violence: Issues in Representation and Experience*. London: Routledge, 1994.

Helms, Mary W. "Miskito Slaving and Culture Contact: Ethnicity and Opportunity in an Expanding Population." *Journal of Anthropological Research* 39 (1983): 179–97.

Hernández, Carlos. "Los inmigrantes de St. Kitts: 1910, un capítulo en la historia de los conflictos bananeros costarricenses." *Revista de Historia* (San José, Costa Rica) 23 (1991): 191–242.

Higman, B. W. *Slave Population and Economy in Jamaica, 1807–1834*. Cambridge: Cambridge University Press, 1976.

Hilje Quirós, Brunilda. *La colonización agrícola de Costa Rica (1840–1940)*. San José: Editorial Universidad Estatal a Distancia, 1995.

Hine, Darlene Clark, and Jacqueline McLeod, eds. *Crossing Boundaries: Comparative History of Black People in Diaspora*. Bloomington: Indiana University Press, 1999.

Holt, Thomas C. "Marking: Race, Race-Making, and the Writing of History." *American Historical Review* 100, no. 1 (1995): 1–20.

———. *The Problem of Freedom: Race, Labor, and Politics in Jamaica and Britain, 1832–1938*. Baltimore: Johns Hopkins University Press, 1992.

Jaén Suárez, Omar. *La población del istmo de Panamá del siglo XVI al siglo XX*. Panama City: n.p., 1979.

James, Winifred. *The Mulberry Tree*. London: Chapman and Hall, 1913.

James, Winston. *Holding Aloft the Banner of Ethiopia: Caribbean Radicalism in Early Twentieth-Century America*. New York: Verso, 1998.

Janzen, Daniel H., ed. *Costa Rican Natural History*. Chicago: University of Chicago Press, 1983.

Johnson, Lyman L. "Dangerous Words, Provocative Gestures, and Violent Acts: The Disputed Hierarchies of Plebeian Life in Colonial Buenos Aires." In *The Faces of Honor: Sex, Shame, and Violence in Colonial Latin America*, edited by Lyman L. Johnson and Sonya Lipsett-Rivera, 127–51. Albuquerque: University of New Mexico Press, 1998.

Johnson, Lyman L., and Sonya Lipsett-Rivera. *The Faces of Honor: Sex, Shame, and Violence in Colonial Latin America*. Albuquerque: University of New Mexico Press, 1998.

Jones, Clarence F., and Paul C. Morrison. "Evolution of the Banana Industry in Costa Rica." *Economic Geography* 28, no. 1 (1952): 1–19.

Joseph, Gilbert M., Catherine C. LeGrand, and Ricardo D. Salvatore, eds. *Close Encounters of Empire: Writing the Cultural History of U.S.-Latin American Relations*. Durham: Duke University Press, 1998.

Kepner, Charles. *Social Aspects of the Banana Industry*. New York: Columbia University Press, 1936.

Kepner, Charles, and Jay Soothill. *The Banana Empire: A Case Study of Economic Imperialism*. New York: Vanguard Press, 1935.

Klubock, Thomas Miller. *Contested Communities: Class, Gender, and Politics in Chile's El Teniente Copper Mine, 1904-1951.* Durham: Duke University Press, 1998.

Knight, Franklin. *The Caribbean: The Genesis of a Fragmented Nationalism.* 2d ed. New York: Oxford University Press, 1990.

Koch, Charles W. "Jamaican Blacks and Their Descendants in Costa Rica." *Social and Economic Studies* 26, no. 3 (1977): 339-61.

Kramer, Wendy, W. George Lovell, and Christopher H. Lutz, "La conquista española de Centroamérica." In *El régimen colonial,* edited by Julio César Pinto Soria, 21-94. Vol. 2 of *Historia general de Centroamérica,* coordinated by Edelberto Torres Rivas. Madrid: Sociedad Estatal Quinto Centenario and FLACSO, 1993.

Lancaster, Roger N. "Guto's Performance: Notes on the Transvestitism of Everyday Life." In *Sex and Sexuality in Latin America,* edited by Daniel Balderston and Donna J. Guy, 9-32. New York: New York University Press, 1997.

———. *Life Is Hard: Machismo, Danger, and the Intimacy of Power in Nicaragua,* Berkeley: University of California Press, 1992.

Langley, Lester D., and Thomas Schoonover. *The Banana Men: American Mercenaries and Entrepreneurs in Central America, 1880-1930.* Lexington: University of Kentucky Press, 1995.

Latin American Publicity Bureau. *Costa Rica, 1916* ["Blue Book"]. San José: Imprenta Alsina, 1916.

Lauria-Santiago, Aldo. *An Agrarian Republic: Commercial Agriculture and the Politics of Peasant Communities in El Salvador, 1823-1914.* Pittsburgh: University of Pittsburgh Press, 1999.

Lazarus-Black, Mindie. *Legitimate Acts and Illegal Encounters: Law and Society in Antigua and Barbuda.* Washington: Smithsonian Institution Press, 1994.

Lazarus Black, Mindie, and Susan F. Hirsch, eds., *Contested States: Law, Hegemony, and Resistance.* New York: Routledge, 1994.

Lefever, Harry G. *Turtle Bogue: Afro-Caribbean Life and Culture in a Costa Rican Village.* Cranbury, N.J.: Associated University Presses, 1992.

LeGrand, Catherine. "Colombian Transformations: Peasants and Wage Laborers in the Santa Marta Banana Zone." *Journal of Peasant Studies* 2, no. 4 (1984): 178-200.

———. "Living in Macondo: Economy and Culture in a United Fruit Banana Enclave in Colombia." In *Close Encounters of Empire: Writing the Cultural History of U.S.-Latin American Relations,* edited by Gilbert M. Joseph, Catherine C. LeGrand, and Ricardo D. Salvatore, 333-68. Durham: Duke University Press, 1998.

León Sáenz, Jorge. *Evolución del comercio exterior y del transporte marítimo de Costa Rica, 1821-1900.* San José: Editorial de la Universidad de Costa Rica, 1997.

León Sánchez, José. *La isla de los hombres solos.* 10th ed. Barcelona: Organización Editorial Novaro, 1976.

Lesser, Jeffrey. *Negotiating National Identity: Immigrants, Minorities, and the Struggle for Ethnicity in Brazil.* Durham: Duke University Press, 1999.

Levi, Giovanni. "On Microhistory." In *New Perspectives on Historical Writing,* edited by Peter Burke, 93-113. University Park: Pennsylvania State University Press, 1992.

Levitt, Peggy. *The Transnational Villagers*. Berkeley: University of California Press, 2001.

Lindo Fuentes, Héctor. "Economía y sociedad (1810–1870)." In *De la ilustración al liberalismo*, edited by Héctor Pérez Brignoli, 141–202. Vol. 3 of *Historia general de Centroamérica*, coordinated by Edelberto Torres Rivas. Madrid: Sociedad Estatal Quinto Centenario and FLACSO, 1993.

Linger, Daniel Touro. *Dangerous Encounters: Meanings of Violence in a Brazilian City*. Stanford: Stanford University Press, 1992.

Lobdell, Richard A. "Women in the Jamaican Labour Force, 1881–1921." *Social and Economic Studies* 37, nos. 1 and 2 (1988): 203–40.

Lobo Wiehoff, Tatiana, and Mauricio Meléndez Obando. *Negros y blancos todo mezclado*. San José: Editorial de la Universidad de Costa Rica, 1997.

Look Lai, Walton. *Indentured Labor, Caribbean Sugar: Chinese and Indian Migrants to the British West Indies, 1838–1918*. Baltimore: Johns Hopkins University Press, 1993.

Lovejoy, Paul. *Transformations in Slavery*. Cambridge: Cambridge University Press, 1983.

Lüdtke, Alf. "Polymorphous Synchrony: German Industrial Workers and the Politics of Everyday Life." *International Review of Social History* 38 (1993): 39–84.

Lund Drolet, Patricia. *El ritual congo del noroeste de Panamá: Una estructura afro-americana expresiva de adaptación cultural*. Panama City: Instituto Nacional de Cultura, n.d.

McCreery, David. "'This Life of Misery and Shame': Female Prostitution in Guatemala City, 1880–1920." *Journal of Latin American Studies* 18 (1993): 333–53.

McCullough, David. *The Path between the Seas: The Creation of the Panama Canal, 1870–1914*. New York: Simon and Schuster, 1977.

Marín Hernández, Juan José. "Las causas de la prostitución josefina, 1939–1949: Entre lo imaginario y el estigma." *Revista de Historia* (San José, Costa Rica) 27 (1993): 87–108.

———. "Prostitución y pecado en la bella y próspera ciudad de San José (1850–1930)." In *El paso del cometa: Estado, política social y culturas populares en Costa Rica (1800/1950)*, edited by Iván Molina Jiménez and Steven Palmer, 47–80. San José: Editorial Porvenir/Plumsock Mesoamerican Studies, 1994.

Marquardt, Steve. "'Green Havoc': Panama Disease, Environmental Change, and Labor Process in the Central American Banana Industry." *American Historical Review* 106, no. 1 (2001): 49–80.

Martínez-Alier, Verena. *Marriage, Class, and Colour in Nineteenth-Century Cuba: A Study of Racial Attitudes and Sexual Values in a Slave Society*. 2d ed. Ann Arbor: University of Michigan Press, 1989.

May, Stacy, and Galo Plaza. *The United Fruit Company in Latin America*. New York: National Planning Association, 1958.

Meade, Teresa A. *"Civilizing" Rio: Reform and Resistance in a Brazilian City, 1889–1930*. University Park: Pennsylvania State University Press, 1997.

Meléndez Chaverri, Carlos, and Quince Duncan. *El negro en Costa Rica*. 8th ed. San José: Editorial Costa Rica, 1981.

Meléndez Obando, Mauricio. "Los últimos esclavos en Costa Rica." *Revista de Historia* (San José, Costa Rica) 39 (1999): 51–138.

Melhuus, Marit, and Kristi Anne Stølen, eds. *Machos, Mistresses, Madonnas: Contesting the Power of Latin American Gender Imagery.* London: Verso, 1996.

Mintz, Sidney W. *Caribbean Transformations.* 2d ed. New York: Columbia University Press, 1989.

Molina Jiménez, Iván. *Costa Rica (1800-1850): El legado colonial y la génesis del capitalismo.* San José: Editorial de la Universidad de Costa Rica, 1991.

Molina Jiménez, Iván, and Fabrice Lehoucq. *Urnas de lo inesperado: Fraude electoral y lucha política en Costa Rica (1901-1948).* San José: Editorial de la Universidad de Costa Rica, Colección Identidad Cultural, 1999.

Molina Jiménez, Iván, and Steven Palmer. *The History of Costa Rica.* San José: Editorial de la Universidad de Costa Rica, 1998.

———, eds. *El paso del cometa: Estado, política social y culturas populares en Costa Rica (1800/1950).* San José: Editorial Porvenir/Plumsock Mesoamerican Studies, 1994.

———, eds. *Héroes al gusto y libros de moda: Sociedad y cambio cultural en Costa Rica (1750-1900).* San José: Editorial Porvenir/Plumsock Mesoamerican Studies, 1992.

Momsen, Janet Henshall. "Gender Ideology and Land." In *Caribbean Portraits: Essays on Gender Ideologies and Identities,* edited by Christine Barrow, 115–32. Kingston: Ian Randle, 1998.

———, ed. *Women and Change in the Caribbean: A Pan-Caribbean Perspective.* Bloomington: Indiana University Press, 1993.

Montes, Luis. *Bananas!* New York: John Reed Club of New York, 1933.

Moodie, T. Dunbar. "Migrancy and Male Sexuality on the South African Gold Mines." *Journal of Southern African Studies* 14, no. 2 (1988): 228–56.

Moya, José C. *Cousins and Strangers: Spanish Immigrants in Buenos Aires, 1850-1930.* Berkeley: University of California Press, 1998.

Murillo Chaverri, Carmen. *Identidades de hierro y humo: La construcción del Ferrocarril al Atlántico, 1870-1890.* San José: Editorial Porvenir, 1995.

Naranjo, Carlos, and Mayela Solano. "El delito en San José, 1870–1900." *Revista de Historia* (San José, Costa Rica) 20 (1989): 81–104.

Nash, June. *We Eat the Mines and the Mines Eat Us: Dependency and Exploitation in Bolivian Tin Mines.* New York: Columbia University Press, 1979.

Newton, Velma. *The Silver Men: West Indian Labour Migration to Panama, 1850-1914.* Mona, Jamaica: Institute for Social and Economic Research, 1984.

O'Brien, Thomas F. *The Century of U.S. Capitalism in Latin America.* Albuquerque: University of New Mexico Press, 1999.

———. *The Revolutionary Mission: American Enterprise in Latin America, 1900-1945.* Cambridge: Cambridge University Press, 1996.

Olien, Michael D. "The Adaptation of West Indian Blacks to North American and Hispanic Culture in Costa Rica." In *Old Roots in New Lands: Historical and Anthropological Perspectives on Black Experiences in the Americas,* edited by Ann M. Pescatello, 132–56. Westport, Conn.: Greenwood Press, 1977.

Olivier, Lord Sydney. *Jamaica: The Blessed Island.* London: Faber and Faber, 1936.

Ortner, Sherry B. *Making Gender: The Politics and Erotics of Culture*. Boston: Beacon Press, 1996.

———. "Theory in Anthropology since the Sixties." In *Culture/Power/History: A Reader in Contemporary Social Theory*, edited by Nicholas B. Dirks, Geoff Eley, and Sherry B. Ortner, 372–411. Princeton: Princeton University Press, 1994. First published in *Comparative Studies in Society and History* 26, no. 1 (1984): 126–66.

Ovares, Flora, Margarita Rojas, Carlos Santander, and María Elena Carballo. *La casa paterna: Escritura y nación en Costa Rica*. San José: Editorial Universidad de Costa Rica, 1993.

Overall, Christine. "What's Wrong with Prostitution? Evaluating Sex Work." *Signs* 17 (1992): 705–24.

Pakkasvirta, Jussi. *¿Un continente, una nación? Intelectuales latinoamericanos, comunidad política y las revistas culturales en Costa Rica y Perú (1919-1930)*. Helsinki: Academia Scientarum Fennica, 1997.

Palma Murga, Gustavo. "Economía y sociedad en Centroamérica (1680-1750)." In *El régimen colonial*, edited by Julio Pinto Soria, 219–306. Vol. 2 of *Historia general de Centroamérica*, coordinated by Edelberto Torres Rivas. Madrid: Sociedad Estatal Quinto Centenario and FLACSO, 1993.

Palmer, Frederick. *Central America and Its Problems*. New York: Moffat, Yard, 1913.

Palmer, Paula. *"Wa'apin man": La historia de la costa talamanqueña de Costa Rica, según sus protagonistas*. Translated by Quince Duncan and Paula Palmer. 2d ed. San José: Editorial de la Universidad de Costa Rica, 1994.

———. *"What Happen": A Folk-History of Costa Rica's Talamanca Coast*. San José: Ecodesarrollos, 1977.

Palmer, Steven. "Adiós 'laissez-faire': La política social en Costa Rica, 1880–1940." *Revista de Historia de América* 124 (1999): 99–117.

———. "Central American Encounters with Rockefeller Public Health, 1914–1921." In *Close Encounters of Empire: Writing the Cultural History of U.S.-Latin American Relations*, edited by Gilbert M. Joseph, Catherine C. LeGrand, and Ricardo D. Salvatore, 311–32. Durham: Duke University Press, 1998.

———. "Confinement, Policing, and the Emergence of Social Policy in Costa Rica." In *The Birth of the Penitentiary in Latin America: Essays on Criminology, Prison Reform, and Social Control, 1840-1940*, edited by Carlos Aguirre and Ricardo Salvatore, 224–53. Austin: University of Texas Press, 1996.

———. "Hacia la auto-inmigración: El nacionalismo oficial en Costa Rica (1870–1930)." In *Identidades nacionales y estado moderno en Centroamérica*, edited by Arturo Taracena and Jean Piel, 75–85. San José: Editorial Universidad de Costa Rica, 1995.

———. "Racismo intelectual en Costa Rica y Guatemala, 1870–1920." *Mesoamérica* 17, no. 31 (1996): 99–121.

Palmer, Steven, and Gladys Rojas. "Educating Señorita: Teacher Training, Social Mobility, and the Birth of Costa Rican Feminism, 1885–1925." *Hispanic American Historical Review* 78, no. 1 (1998): 45–82.

Parpart, Jane. "Class and Gender on the Copperbelt: Women in Northern Rhodesian

Copper Mining Areas." Working Paper no. 53. Boston: Boston University African Studies Center, 1982.

Parsons, James J. "English-Speaking Settlements of the Western Caribbean." *Yearbook of the Association of Pacific Coast Geographers* 16 (1954): 3–16.

———. "San Andrés and Providencia." *University of California Publications in Geography* 12, no. 1 (1956): 1–84.

Pérez, Louis A., Jr. *Cuba between Reform and Revolution.* New York: Oxford University Press, 1988.

Pérez Brignoli, Héctor. *Breve historia contemporánea de Costa Rica.* Mexico City: Fondo de Cultura Económica, 1997.

———. *Breve historia de Centroamérica.* 2d ed. Mexico City: Alianza Editorial Mexicana, 1989.

———. "Deux siècles d'illégitimité au Costa Rica, 1770–1974." In *Marriage and Remarriage in Populations of the Past,* edited by J. Dupaquier, E. Hélin, P. Laslett, M. Livi-Bacci, and S. Sogner, 481–93. London: Academic Press/Harcourt Brace Jovanovich, 1981.

———, ed. *De la ilustración al liberalismo.* Vol. 3 of *Historia general de Centroamérica,* coordinated by Edelberto Torres Rivas. Madrid: Sociedad Estatal Quinto Centenario and FLACSO, 1993.

Petras, Elizabeth MacLean. *Jamaican Labor Migration: White Capital and Black Labor, 1850–1930.* Boulder, Colo.: Westview Press, 1988.

Pinto Soria, Julio César, ed. *El régimen colonial.* Vol. 2 of *Historia general de Centroamérica,* coordinated by Edelberto Torres Rivas. Madrid: Sociedad Estatal Quinto Centenario and FLACSO, 1993.

Pitt-Rivers, Julian. "Honour and Social Status." In *Honour and Shame: The Values of Mediterranean Society,* edited by J. G. Péristiany, 19–77. Chicago: University of Chicago Press, 1966.

Posas, Mario. "La plantación bananera en Centroamérica (1870–1929)." In *Las repúblicas agroexportadoras,* edited by Víctor Hugo Acuña Ortega, 111–66. Vol. 4 of *Historia general de Centroamérica,* coordinated by Edelberto Torres Rivas. Madrid: Sociedad Estatal Quinto Centenario and FLACSO, 1993.

Post, Ken. *Arise Ye Starvelings: The Jamaican Labour Rebellion of 1938 and Its Aftermath.* The Hague: Martinus Nijhoff, 1978.

Pulpisher, Lydia Mihelic. "Changing Roles in the Life Cycles of Women in Traditional West Indian Houseyards." In *Women and Change in the Caribbean: A Pan-Caribbean Perspective,* edited by Janet H. Momsen, 50–64. Bloomington: Indiana University Press, 1993.

Purcell, Trevor W. *Banana Fallout: Class, Color, and Culture among West Indians in Costa Rica.* Los Angeles: Center for Afro-American Studies, University of California, 1993.

Putnam, George Palmer. *The Southland of North America: Rambles and Observations in Central America during the Year 1912.* New York: G. P. Putnam and Sons, 1914.

Putnam, Lara. "Ideología racial, práctica social y estado liberal en Costa Rica." *Revista de Historia* (San José, Costa Rica) 39 (1999): 139–86.

Quesada Avendaño, Florencia. "'Los del Barrio Amón': Marco habitacional, familiar y arquitectónico del primer barrio residencial de la burguesía josefina (1900–1930)." *Mesoamérica* 31 (1989): 215–41.

Quesada Camacho, Juan Rafael. "Algunos aspectos de la historia económica del cacao en Costa Rica, 1880–1930." Pt. 1. *Revista de Historia* (Heredia, Costa Rica) 3, no. 5 (1977): 65–100.

———. "Comercialización y movimiento coyuntural del cacao." *Revista de Historia* (Heredia, Costa Rica) 3, no. 6 (1978): 69–110.

Quesada Monge, Rodrigo. *Recuerdos del imperio: Los ingleses en América Central (1821–1915)*. Heredia, Costa Rica: Editorial de la Universidad Nacional, 1998.

Quirós Vargas, Claudia, and Margarita Bolaños Arquín. "El mestizaje en el siglo XVII: Consideraciones para comprender la génesis del campesinado criollo del Valle Central." In *Costa Rica colonial*, edited by Luis Fernando Sibaja, 61–78. San José: Ediciones Guayacán, 1989.

Reddock, Rhoda. "Indian Women and Indentureship in Trinidad and Tobago, 1845–1917: Freedom Denied." In *Caribbean Freedom: Economy and Society from Emancipation to the Present*, edited by Hilary Beckles and Verene Shepherd, 225–37. Princeton: Markus Wiener, 1996.

Richardson, Bonham C. "Caribbean Migrations, 1838–1985." In *The Modern Caribbean*, edited by Franklin W. Knight and Colin A. Palmer, 203–28. Chapel Hill: University of North Carolina Press, 1989.

———. *Panama Money in Barbados, 1900–1920*. Knoxville: University of Tennessee Press, 1985.

Roberts, George W. *The Population of Jamaica*. Cambridge: Cambridge University Press, 1957.

Robles Soto, Arodys. "Patrones de población en Costa Rica, 1860–1930." *Avances de Investigación*, no. 14. San José: Centro de Investigaciones Históricas de la Universidad de Costa Rica, 1986.

Robotham, Don. "'The Notorious Riot': The Socio-economic and Political Bases of Paul Bogle's Revolt." Working Paper no. 28. Mona, Jamaica: Institute of Social and Economic Research, University of the West Indies, 1981.

Rodríguez Sáenz, Eugenia. "Civilizando la vida doméstica en el Valle Central de Costa Rica (1750–1850)." In *Entre silencios y voces: Género e historia en América Central*, edited by Eugenia Rodríguez Sáenz, 41–79. San José: Editorial Porvenir/Centro Nacional para el Desarrollo de la Mujer y la Familia, 1998.

———. *Hijas, novias y esposas: Familia, matrimonio y violencia doméstica en el Valle Central de Costa Rica (1750–1850)*. Heredia, Costa Rica: Editorial de la Universidad Nacional, 2000.

———. "'Matrimonios Felices': Cambios y continuidades en las percepciones y en las actitudes hacia la violencia doméstica en el Valle Central de Costa Rica (1750–1930)." In *Violencia doméstica en Costa Rica: Más allá de los mitos*, edited by Eugenia Rodríguez Sáenz, 9–30. Cuadernos de Ciencias Sociales, no. 105. San José: FLACSO, 1998.

———. "Padres e Hijos: Familia y mercado matrimonial en el Valle Central de Costa

Rica (1821–1850)." In *Héroes al gusto y libros de moda: Sociedad y cambio cultural en Costa Rica (1750–1900)*, edited by Iván Molina Jiménez and Steven Palmer, 45–76. San José: Editorial Porvenir/Plumsock Mesoamerican Studies, 1992.

———, ed. *Entre silencios y voces: Género e historia en América Central*. San José: Editorial Porvenir/Centro Nacional para el Desarrollo de la Mujer y la Familia, 1998.

Roseberry, William. "Hegemony and the Language of Contention." In *Everyday Forms of State Formation: Revolution and the Negotiation of Rule in Modern Mexico*, edited by Gilbert M. Joseph and Daniel Nugent, 355–66. Durham: Duke University Press, 1994.

Salazar Mora, Orlando. *El apogeo de la república liberal en Costa Rica, 1870–1914*. San José: Editorial Universidad de Costa Rica, 1990.

Samper Kutschbach, Mario. "Café, trabajo y sociedad en Centroamérica, 1870–1930: Una historia común y divergente." In *Las repúblicas agroexportadoras*, edited by Víctor Hugo Acuña Ortega, 11–110. Vol. 4 of *Historia general de Centroamérica*, coordinated by Edelberto Torres Rivas. Madrid: Sociedad Estatal Quinto Centenario and FLACSO, 1993.

———. "Fuerzas sociopolíticas y procesos electorales en Costa Rica, 1921–1936." *Revista de Historia* (San José, Costa Rica), Número Especial (1988): 157–222.

———. *Generations of Settlers: Rural Households and Markets on the Costa Rican Frontier, 1850–1935*. Boulder, Colo.: Westview Press, 1990.

———. "Metodología y procedimientos para la utilización del Censo de población de 1927 como base nominal." In *El censo de población de 1927: Creación de una base nominal computarizada*, edited by Mario Samper Kutschbach, 45–56. Trabajos de Metodología, no. 2. San José: Centro de Investigaciones Históricas, Universidad de Costa Rica, 1991.

Schifter, Jacobo. *La fase oculta de la guerra civil en Costa Rica*. 4th ed. San José: EDUCA, 1985.

Schneider, Jane. "Of Vigilance and Virgins: Honor, Shame, and Access to Resources in Mediterranean Societies." *Ethnology* 10, no. 1 (1971): 1–24.

Schoonover, Thomas. *The United States in Central America, 1860–1911: Episodes of Social Imperialism and Imperial Rivalry in the World System*. Durham: Duke University Press, 1991.

Scott, Joan Wallace. *Gender and the Politics of History*. New York: Columbia University Press, 1988.

Scott, Rebecca J. "Small-Scale Dynamics of Large-Scale Processes." *American Historical Review* 105, no. 2 (2000): 472–79.

Seed, Patricia. *To Love, Honor, and Obey in Colonial Mexico: Conflicts over Marriage Choice, 1574–1821*. Stanford: Stanford University Press, 1988.

Shepherd, Verene. "Gender, Migration, and Settlement: The Indentureship and Post-Indentureship Experience of Indian Females in Jamaica, 1845–1943." In *Engendering History: Caribbean Women in Historical Perspective*, edited by Verene Shepherd, Bridget Brereton, and Barbara Bailey, 233–57. Kingston: Ian Randle, 1995.

Shepherd, Verene, Bridget Brereton, and Barbara Bailey, eds. *Engendering History: Caribbean Women in Historical Perspective*. Kingston: Ian Randle, 1995.

Smith, Raymond T. "Hierarchy and the Dual Marriage System in West Indian Society." In *Gender and Kinship: Essays toward a Unified Analysis*, edited by Jane Fishburne Collier and Sylvia Junko Yanagisako, 163–96. Stanford: Stanford University Press, 1987.

———. *Kinship and Class in the West Indies: A Genealogical Study of Jamaica and Guyana*. Cambridge: Cambridge University Press, 1988.

Solano Pérez, William. "El día de trabajo en la Hacienda Aragón, Turrialba, 1943." *Revista de Historia* (San José, Costa Rica) 32 (1995): 133–73.

Solórzano Fonseca, Juan Carlos. "Los años finales de la dominación española (1750–1821)." In *De la ilustración al liberalismo*, edited by Héctor Pérez Brignoli, 13–72. Vol. 3 of *Historia general de Centroamérica*, coordinated by Edelberto Torres Rivas. Madrid: Sociedad Estatal Quinto Centenario and FLACSO, 1993.

———. "Los indígenas en las áreas fronterizas de Costa Rica durante el siglo XIX." *Avances de Investigación*, no. 78. San José: Centro de Investigaciones Históricas de América Central, Universidad de Costa Rica, 2000.

Soluri, John. "People, Plants, and Pathogens: The Eco-social Dynamics of Export Banana Production in Honduras, 1875–1950." *Hispanic American Historical Review* 80, no. 3 (2000): 463–502.

Soto, Isa María. "West Indian Child Fostering: Its Role in Migrant Exchanges." In *Caribbean Life in New York City: Sociocultural Dimensions*, edited by Constance R. Sutton and Elsa M. Chaney, 121–37. New York: Center for Migration Studies of New York, 1992.

Squier, E. G. *The States of Central America*. New York: Harper and Brothers, 1858.

Stansell, Christine. *City of Women: Sex and Class in New York, 1789-1860*. Urbana: University of Illinois Press, 1987.

Starr, June, and Jane Collier, eds., *History and Power in the Study of Law: New Directions in Legal Anthropology*. Ithaca: Cornell University Press, 1989.

Steedman, Carolyn Kay. *Landscape for a Good Woman*. New Brunswick, N.J.: Rutgers University Press, 1987.

Stern, Steve J. *The Secret History of Gender: Women, Men and Power in Late Colonial Mexico*. Chapel Hill: University of North Carolina Press, 1995.

Stewart, Watt. *Keith and Costa Rica: A Biographical Study of Minor Cooper Keith*. Albuquerque: University of New Mexico Press, 1964.

———. *Keith y Costa Rica*. Translated by José B. Acuña. San José: Editorial Costa Rica, 1991.

Stoler, Ann L. *Capitalism and Confrontation in Sumatra's Plantation Belt, 1870-1979*. 2d ed. Ann Arbor: University of Michigan Press, 1995.

———. "Carnal Knowledge and Imperial Power: Gender, Race, and Morality in Colonial Asia." In *Gender at the Crossroads of Knowledge: Feminist Anthropology in the Postmodern Era*, edited by Micaela di Leonardo, 51–101. Berkeley: University of California Press, 1991.

————. "'In Cold Blood': Hierarchies of Credibility and the Politics of Colonial Narratives." *Representations* 37 (1992): 151–89.

————. "Sexual Affronts and Racial Frontiers: European Identities and the Cultural Politics of Exclusion in Colonial Southeast Asia," *Comparative Studies in Society and History* 34, no. 3 (1992): 514–51.

Striffler, Steve. *In the Shadows of State and Capital: The United Fruit Company, Popular Struggle, and Agrarian Restructuring in Ecuador, 1900–1995.* Durham: Duke University Press, 2002.

Tejeira, Gil Blas. *Pueblos Perdidos.* 4th ed. Panama City: Editorial Universitaria, 1995.

Thomas-Hope, Elizabeth M. "The Establishment of a Migration Tradition: British West Indian Movements to the Hispanic Caribbean in the Century after Emancipation." *International Migration* 24 (1986): 559–71.

Thompson, Wallace. *The Rainbow Countries of Central America.* New York: E. P. Dutton, 1926.

Tinsmann, Heidi. "Household *Patrones*: Wife-Beating and Sexual Control in Rural Chile, 1964–1988." In *The Gendered Worlds of Latin American Women Workers: From Household and Factory to the Union Hall and Ballot Box,* edited by John D. French and Daniel James, 264–96. Durham: Duke University Press, 1997.

Trouillot, Michel-Rolph. "The Caribbean Region: An Open Frontier in Anthropological Theory." *Annual Review of Anthropology* 21 (1992): 19–42.

Twinam, Ann. *Public Lives, Private Secrets: Gender, Honor, Sexuality, and Illegitimacy in Colonial Spanish America.* Stanford: Stanford University Press, 1999.

Van Young, Eric. "The New Cultural History Comes to Old Mexico." *Hispanic American Historical Review* 79, no. 2 (1999): 211–48.

Verrill, A. Hyatt. *Thirty Years in the Jungle.* London: John Lane, 1929.

Viales Hurtado, Ronny José. *Después del enclave: Un estudio de la región atlántica costarricense, 1927–1950.* San José: Editorial Universidad de Costa Rica, 1998.

Wade, Peter. *Blackness and Race Mixture: The Dynamics of Racial Identity in Colombia.* Baltimore: Johns Hopkins University Press, 1993.

————. "Man the Hunter: Gender and Violence in Music and Drinking Contexts in Colombia." In *Sex and Violence: Issues in Representation and Experience,* edited by Penelope Harvey and Peter Gow, 115–37. London: Routledge, 1994.

Waibel, Leo. "White Settlement in Costa Rica." *Geographical Review* 29, no. 4 (1939): 529–60.

White, Luise. *The Comforts of Home: Prostitution in Colonial Nairobi.* Chicago: University of Chicago Press, 1990.

Wilmot, Swithin. "'Females of Abandoned Character'? Women and Protest in Jamaica, 1838–65." In *Engendering History: Caribbean Women in Historical Perspective,* edited by Verene Shepherd, Bridget Brereton, and Barbara Bailey, 279–95. Kingston: Ian Randle, 1995.

Wilson, Charles. *Empire in Green and Gold.* New York: Henry Holt, 1947.

Wilson, Peter J. *Crab Antics: The Social Anthropology of English-Speaking Negro Societies of the Caribbean.* New Haven: Yale University Press, 1973.

———. "Reputation and Respectability: A Suggestion for Caribbean Historians," *Man*, n.s., 4 (1969): 70–84.

Wood, Betty, and Roy Clayton. "Jamaica's Struggle for a Self-Perpetuating Slave Population: Demographic, Social, and Religious Changes on Golden Grove Plantation, 1812–1832." *Journal of Caribbean Studies* 6, no. 3 (1988): 287–308.

Woodward, Ralph Lee, Jr. *Central America: A Nation Divided*. 2d ed. New York: Oxford University Press, 1985.

Zeledón Cartín, Elías, comp. *Viajes por la República de Costa Rica*. 3 vols. San José: Ministerio de Cultura, Juventud y Deportes, 1997.

Unpublished Sources

Chaloub, Sidney. "Interpreting Machado de Assis: Paternalism, Slavery, and the Free Womb Law." Paper presented at the conference "Honor, Status, and Law in Modern Latin America," University of Michigan, 4–6 Dec. 1998.

Chomsky, Aviva. "Plantation Society, Land, and Labor on Costa Rica's Atlantic Coast, 1870–1940." Ph.D. diss., University of California, Berkeley, 1990.

Desanti Henderson, Javier. "Aspectos socio-legales de la prostitución en Puntarenas." Licenciatura thesis, Escuela de Derecho, Universidad de Costa Rica, 1985.

Escuela de Planificación Social. "Autobiografías Campesinas." 30 vols. Biblioteca Central, Universidad Nacional Autónoma, Heredia, Costa Rica, 1977. Mimeographed.

Harpelle, Ronald. "West Indians in Costa Rica: Class and Ethnicity in the Transformation of a Community." Ph.D. diss., University of Toronto, 1992.

Koch, Charles W. "Ethnicity and Livelihoods: A Social Geography of Costa Rica's Atlantic Zone." Ph.D. diss., University of Kansas, 1975.

León Azofeifa, Moisés Guillermo. "Chinese Immigrants on the Atlantic Coast of Costa Rica: The Economic Adaptation of an Asian Minority in a Pluralistic Society." Ph.D. diss., Tulane University, 1987.

Lord, Rebecca. "Quarantine in the Fort Ozama Dungeon: The Control of Prostitution and Venereal Disease in the Dominican Republic, 1923–1924." Unpublished paper, University of Maryland, 1999.

McGuinness, Aims C. "In the Path of Empire: Popular Politics and U.S. Imperialism in Panama, 1848–1860." Ph.D. diss., University of Michigan, 2001.

Mennereck, Louis. "A Study of Puerto Limon, Costa Rica." Associated Colleges of the Midwest Central American Field Program, San José, Costa Rica, 1964. Mimeographed.

Palmer, Steven. "A Liberal Discipline: Inventing Nations in Guatemala and Costa Rica, 1870–1900." Ph.D. diss., Columbia University, 1990.

Picado Le-Frank, Tatiana. "La situación de salud de las mujeres en prostitución en Guápiles: Una propuesta de abordaje con enfoque integral." Master's thesis, Programa de Estudios de Posgrado en Salud Pública, Universidad de Costa Rica, 1995.

Putnam, Lara. "Beneficencia, pobreza, y racismo en Costa Rica, 1920-1960." Paper presented at the conference "Culturas Populares y Políticas Públicas en México y Centroamérica (siglos XIX y XX)," Alajuela, Costa Rica, 20-22 Sept. 2000.

———. "La construcción social de las categorías raciales: El caso de la Costa Rica colonial." Paper presented at the Reunión Internacional: Ruta del Esclavo en Hispanoamérica, San José, Costa Rica, 23-26 Feb. 1999.

———. "Intimacy, Entitlement, and Enforcement in Caribbean Costa Rica (1890-1920)." Unpublished manuscript.

———. "Migración y género en la organización de la producción: Una comparación de la industria bananera en Costa Rica y Jamaica (1880-1935)." Paper presented at the 4th Simposio Panamericano de Historia of the Instituto Panamericano de Geografía e Historia, San José, Costa Rica, 10-13 Aug. 1999.

———. "Public Women and One Pant Men: Labor Migration and the Politics of Gender in Caribbean Costa Rica, 1870-1960." Ph.D. diss., University of Michigan, 2000.

Salas, José Antonio. "Liberalismo y legislación agraria: Apuntes introductorios para el estudio de la colonización agrícola de Costa Rica durante el siglo XIX." Unpublished research report, Escuela de Historia, Universidad Nacional, Heredia, Costa Rica, 1983.

Sánchez de Isaza, Rosa María. "La prostitución y su reglamentación en la República de Panamá." Unpublished thesis, Facultad de Derecho y Ciencias Sociales, Universidad de Panamá, 1986.

Soluri, John. "Landscape and Livelihood: An Agroecological History of Export Banana-Growing in Honduras, 1870-1975." Ph.D. diss., University of Michigan, 1998.

Stouse, Pierre. "Cambios en el uso de la tierra en las regiones ex-bananeras de Costa Rica." Unpublished report, San José, Costa Rica, 1967.

Trefzger, Douglas W. "Making West Indians Unwelcome: Race, Gender, and the National Question in Guatemala's Banana Belt, 1914-1920." Paper prepared for the 23d Annual Meeting of the Latin American Studies Association, Washington, D.C., 6-8 Sept. 2001.

Viales Hurtado, Ronny J. "Los liberales y la colonización de las áreas de frontera no cafetaleras: El caso de la región Atlántica (Caribe) costarricense entre 1870 y 1930." Ph.D. diss., Universitat Autónoma de Barcelona, 2000.

Index

China: migrants from, 39, 40, 41, 51, 53, 74, 100, 146, 149, 152, 158, 186, 235 (nn. 15, 20), 258 (n. 47)
Chiriquí Land Company, 48
Cieneguita, 43
Citizenship, 12, 35, 71–75, 212, 242 (n. 119), 243 (n. 126)
Civilizing mission, 8–10, 78–79, 177–78, 208–10, 215, 271 (n. 8)
Clarendon parish (Jamaica), 51
Cocoa, 6, 7, 18, 23, 24, 49, 55, 73, 118, 121, 122, 128, 131, 165, 194, 205, 206, 254 (n. 44), 270 (n. 106)
Coconuts, 37, 45, 49, 55, 58
Código Civil, 49, 50
Código Fiscal, 49
Código Penal, 141, 190–91, 256 (n. 11), 258 (n. 39)
Coffee cultivation, 29, 30–32, 49, 128, 131, 233 (n. 40)
Colombia, 21, 36–37, 44–45, 60, 206; migrants from, 6, 43, 49, 51, 149, 157, 194
Colón, 3, 10, 11, 43, 44, 45, 53, 56, 57, 58, 60, 61, 95, 206, 249 (n. 81)
Coloured group: among West Indians, 29, 167
Communist Party, Costa Rican, 77, 183, 197, 203
Community, 12, 137–38, 213
Compagnie Universelle du Canal Interocéanique de Panama, 44, 45
Compañeros (work companions), 11, 18, 113, 117–24, 132–33, 137, 207, 214
Confederación General de Trabajadores, 64
Conjugal practice, 124–27, 133–36, 208, 214, 219; role of violence in, 185, 187–88, 192–94, 197–200, 211, 272 (n. 15). See also Consensual union; Households; Kinship; Marriage
Consensual union, 11, 115, 116, 127, 137. See also Conjugal practice
Cooper, Carolyn, 141
Corruption, 158–59, 163–64
Costa Rica: pre-Colombian, 21–22; colonial, 22–23, 25–26; Central Valley, 30–34, 58, 59, 62, 128, 209; migrants from, in Limón, 91, 149, 152, 157, 158, 165, 194, 204, 214
Costa Rican state: role in Limón, 12, 42, 158, 162–64, 177–78, 209–10, 212; and cof-

fee elites, 31, 33–34, 38; legal reforms, 48, 54
Courts. See Judicial system
Cuba, 3, 11, 26, 29, 36, 68–69, 179, 203, 206; migration to, 10, 35, 64, 66, 91, 205, 241 (n. 102); migrants from, 51, 157
Culture: as concept, 153, 160, 213–15
Curaçao, 40; migrants from, 51

Deflowering, 3, 84, 85, 100
Demerara: migrants from, 51
Demography: impact of, 15, 17, 19, 212
Denuncias de terrenos baldíos, 43, 48–49
Dependency theory, 4
Domestic violence. See Conjugal practice: role of violence in
Dominica: migrants from, 51
Dos Novillos, 54
Dumas, Alexandre, 109

East Indians, 9
Ecosystems: damage to, 37, 45, 78
Ecuador, 56
El Salvador: migrants from, 51
Emancipation, 17, 27, 28, 37
Enclave economy, 4, 11, 12, 73
England: migrants from, 51
Estrada, 182
Estrella River, 45
Estrella Valley, 51, 64, 79, 165, 177, 181, 239 (n. 74)
Estupro. See Deflowering

Fallas, Carlos Luís, 77, 84, 163, 173, 183, 187, 203
Family. See Kinship
Family labor system, 128–31
Family land, 28, 29
Farnsworth-Alvear, Ann, 209
Ferrocarril al Atlántico, 6, 38–40, 42, 43, 44, 45
Fields, Barbara, 193
Figueres, José, 203
Fostering, informal, 7, 11, 53–54, 137–38
France: migrants from, 51
Franck, Harry, 155
Fusarium oxysporum, 6, 45

Garantías Sociales, 203
Garvey, Marcus, 171, 202

Gender, 19, 214–15; and division of labor, 7, 23, 29, 51–53, 55, 128–31; and race, 8, 15–17; and the state, 12, 13–15, 210–12; roles in intimate life, 21, 32–33, 124, 126, 161, 172, 197–200, 208–9. *See also* Conjugal practice; Honor; Masculinity; Men; Women
Germany: migrants from, 42, 51
Gran Chiriquí, 21, 27
Gran Nicoya, 21, 22
Grenada: migrants from, 51
Greytown. *See* San Juan del Norte
Guácimo, 90, 198
Guadeloupe: migrants from, 51
Guanacaste, 65, 172, 186; migrants from, 118, 177, 183
Guápiles, 90, 118, 122, 165, 175, 247 (n. 63)
Guardia, Tomás, 38, 39
Guatemala, 6, 25, 88, 206
Gudmundson, Lowell, 100, 202
Guerrero, José, 72, 73
Gutiérrez, Joaquín, 76, 124
Guyana, 9; migrants from, 51

Heredia, 100, 206
Higglers, 28, 33, 53
Homesteading, 128, 131–37, 194, 206, 211
Homicide statistics, 14, 185–87, 194–95, 221–25, 267 (n. 45), 268–69 (nn. 76, 78). *See also* Violence
Homosexuality. *See* Same-sex intimacy
Honduras, 6, 24, 40, 62; migrants from, 51, 177
Hone Creek, 120, 196
Honor, 106–7, 109–10, 140–41, 144, 151, 154, 157, 159–60, 163, 166, 187, 190, 202, 212, 214, 215
Hospital de Profilaxis Venérea, 87, 96, 97
Households, 4; composition of, 24, 28, 113–17, 137, 241 (n. 104), 252 (n. 8), 273 (n. 21)
Hygiene officials. *See* Prostitution: regulation of; Venereal disease

Iglesias, Rafael, 260 (n. 62), 266 (n. 31)
Illegitimacy, 29, 32, 34, 66, 137, 169–70
Imperialism, 8
Indentured labor, 9, 30, 40
Indigenous groups in Costa Rica, 8, 23, 25, 37, 42, 48, 65, 117, 177

Indigo, 24
Informal fostering. *See* Fostering, informal
Injurias. *See* Insults suits
Insults suits: trends in, 14, 18, 164–65, 256 (n. 11); profile of participants, 141–43, 211, 220; contents of, 143–51; reasons for use of courts, 151–52, 163
Isthmian Canal Commission, 60
Italy: migrants from, 45, 51

Jamaica, 4, 6, 9, 11, 17, 21, 23–24, 25, 27–30, 33–34, 49, 77–78, 141, 152, 155, 171; migrants from, 40–41, 44–45, 51, 55–59, 60, 61, 62, 68, 101–2, 112, 149, 152, 174–75, 194, 214; returnees in, 66, 203, 241 (n. 102). *See also* Migration: from British West Indies; Western Caribbean
Jealousy, 187, 189–92, 200, 208
Jiménez, 90
Jiménez, Ricardo, 146, 147, 183, 260 (n. 62), 266 (n. 31)
Judicial system: popular use of, 12, 33, 151–54, 163–64, 272 (n. 16); and land conflicts, 50; handling of insults suits, 146, 151–52, 257 (n. 28), 262 (n. 82); handling of homicide cases, 184–85, 189–94, 196; and gender relations, 211–13

Keith, Henry Meiggs, 38, 40, 45
Keith, Minor Cooper, 6, 20, 38, 43, 45, 48, 56, 57, 94, 147, 208, 260 (n. 62)
Kingston, 7, 10, 11, 30, 35, 36, 44, 51, 58, 155–56, 206
Kinship: role in structuring labor, 4, 7, 8, 51, 79, 207; role in structuring access to resources, 11, 124; impact of state policy on, 12, 13–15, 17, 20–21, 32–33, 34, 212–13; in Limón, 18, 117, 210–12, 214–15; in British West Indies, 20–21, 23, 28, 29, 112, 214; legal systems of, 28, 32, 34, 116; in highland Costa Rica, 32, 112, 214; as categorized by census takers, 113–15; and community, 137–38; scholarship on, in Caribbean, 140–41, 159, 170–71. *See also* Conjugal practice; Gender; Households
Klubbock, Thomas, 209

Labor activism, 9, 64, 183–84, 201, 208, 262 (n. 78). *See also* Strikes
Lake Nicaragua, 21

Land tenure: in Jamaica, 28, 29, 33; in highland Costa Rica, 31, 32, 33–34; concessions in Limón, 38, 42, 43, 48–49; disputes over, 50, 135
Lara, Gerardo, 174
Laws. *See* Judicial system
Lebanon: immigrants from, 53
Leeward Islands, 23
Legal system. *See* Judicial system
LeGrand, Catherine, 209
León, Juan José, 146, 158, 257 (n. 27)
León Sánchez, José, 65, 80
Liberals, 34, 48, 54, 86, 162, 233–34 (n. 46)
Limón: demographic profile of, 65–68, 112, 118, 119, 194, 218, 268 (n. 75)
Limón Workers' Federation, 64
Lindo, Cecil Vernor, 142
Literacy, 170, 263–64 (n. 105)
Logging, 122
London, 38

Machismo. *See* Masculinity
Main Line, 45, 46, 62, 79, 91, 134, 183, 211, 239 (n. 74)
Mamita Yunai, 77, 84, 163, 173
Manchester parish (Jamaica), 51
Manila hemp. See *Abacá*
Marín Hernández, Juan José, 87–88
Marriage, 25–26, 28, 29, 32, 34, 66, 115, 117, 127, 137, 153, 172, 192, 212, 252 (n. 9). *See also* Conjugal practice
Martinique: migrants from, 51
Masaya, 207
Masculinity, 11, 19, 126, 159–60, 172, 184, 186–87, 200–203, 211, 215
Matina, 23, 24, 37, 53, 54, 58, 118, 182, 199, 266 (n. 31)
Matina River, 45
Matrifocality, 113, 116, 140
Men, 211; and prostitution, 80, 84; views on conjugal life, 124–26; patterns of participation in insults suits, 142, 155, 159–60; violence between, 173–74, 180–84, 186–87, 195–96, 214–15; laboring life cycle, 207. *See also* Banana workers; *Compañeros*; Gender; Masculinity
Mestizos, 25, 26
Mexico, 21, 44; migrants from, 51
Microhistory, 10
Migration: and the enclave economy, 4,

6, 204–7; from British West Indies, 6, 7, 10–11, 35–37, 43–45, 51, 60–62, 204, 234 (n. 1); and social networks, 11, 207; and worker mobility, 17, 35–36, 43, 55–58, 118; via recruiters or contracts, 30, 36, 44, 45, 51, 56–57, 60, 62; legal constraints on, 36, 39, 49, 73–75, 167, 206; male and female patterns, 66, 68; transnational, 207. *See also* Indentured labor; Western Caribbean: migratory circuits
Miskitu, 24, 27
Moín, 37, 54, 238 (n. 56)
Montego Bay (Jamaica), 51
Montserrat: migrants from, 51
Mora, Manuel, 74, 183
Mora, Ricardo, 158, 183
Moral reform, 14, 15, 162–63, 208–10, 212, 213, 215
Mosquitia, 24
Moyne Commission Report, 140–41, 171
Mulatos y pardos, 23, 25, 38

Nassau: migrants from, 51
Networks. *See* Social networks
Nevis, 23; migrants from, 51
New Granada, 36. *See also* Colombia; Panama
Newspapers, English-language: in Limón, 16, 167–71, 262 (n. 80)
New York City, 66
Nicaragua, 11, 21, 35; migrants from, 43, 45, 51, 54, 62, 70, 91, 118, 149, 152, 183, 186, 204; stereotypes of migrants from, 171, 175–77, 265 (n. 10)
Northern Railway, 164, 202, 204, 205, 210, 260 (n. 63)

Old Harbour. *See* Puerto Viejo
Old Line, 45, 62, 64, 79, 90, 91, 239 (n. 74), 247 (n. 63)
Olimpos, 48
Olivier, Sydney, Lord, 77–78

Pacific coast banana zone, 73, 118, 120, 167, 203, 206, 271 (n. 10)
Pacuarito, 53
Panama, 6, 7, 10, 11, 35, 36, 40, 44, 45, 51, 60, 62, 64, 66, 71, 118, 206
Panama Canal: as French project, 3, 6, 43–45, 51; need for workers after comple-

tion, 36, 69, 74–75; construction under U.S. control, 60–62; and racial segregation, 74–75, 83; and prostitution, 78, 95, 248 (n. 78), 249 (n. 81)
Panama City, 95, 249 (n. 81)
Panama disease, 6, 45
Panama Railroad Company, 36–37
Pardo, Rogelio, 55
Pardo y Figueroa, Amelia, 54, 238 (n. 56)
Parismina, 37, 54
Parismina River, 45
Partido Civil, 146, 147, 158, 260 (n. 62), 266 (n. 31)
Partido Republicano, 146, 147, 158, 260 (n. 62)
Partido Vanguardia Popular. See Communist Party, Costa Rican
Patriarchal households, 113, 116, 140, 143, 185, 202
Patron-client ties, 51, 158
Penal Code. See Código Penal
Peones bananeros. See Banana workers
Pococí, 135, 247 (n. 63)
Pocomia, 167, 179–80, 265 (n. 21)
Police: role in Limón, 163–64, 174, 183, 184, 196–97, 212, 213, 262 (n. 78). See also Prostitution: regulation of
Politics: in Limón, 146–47, 157–59, 182–83, 196–97, 260 (n. 62), 266 (n. 31)
Port Antonio, 206
Port Limón, 3, 43, 50, 139, 156–57, 206, 239 (n. 74); travel to, 10, 35–36, 56, 57, 61; prostitution in, 82–84, 91, 92; built environment of, 147–49, 152–53
Postcolonial studies, 8
Prostitutes: use of courts by, 14, 87, 107, 150–51, 154, 211; mobility of, 81, 90, 92–95; mutual support among, 85, 86, 96–98, 110, 136; physical violence against, 85, 103, 104, 106, 110, 136, 184, 189, 192–94, 249 (n. 88), 250–51 (n. 115); earnings of, 93–95, 98; family ties among, 98–101; romantic love among, 103–6, 109, 111; insults among, 106–11; public deportment of, 109–10, 168. See also Prostitution
Prostitution, 18, 207; and race, 3, 30, 82, 101–3; and other sexual exchanges, 8, 84–93; regulation of, 14, 86–93, 96, 110, 163, 212, 256 (n. 19); and migrant labor force, 76–80, 208, 243 (n. 4), 244 (n. 14);

organization of, in Limón, 81–84. See also Prostitutes
Providencia, 141, 152; migrants from, 51
Public space, 139, 148, 149, 153, 155–57, 160, 168–70, 211
Puerto Barrios, 207
Puerto Cortés, 199
Puerto Limón (novel), 76, 124
Puerto Rico: migrants from, 51
Puerto Viejo, 37, 134, 197
Puntarenas, 31, 93, 186, 206
Punta Uva, 122
Purcell, Trevor, 179
Putnam, George Palmer, 156

Race: and perceptions of women, 4, 91; ideologies of, 8, 18–19, 38–39, 41, 138; and citizenship, 12, 35, 71–75, 212, 242 (n. 119), 243 (n. 126); social construction of, 15–16, 83, 215, 229 (n. 17); heightened racism in 1930s, 16, 71–75, 153, 165–71, 174, 179–80; within Spanish colonial system, 24–25; and immigration policy, 36, 39, 49, 73–75, 167, 206; and perceptions of Limón, 58–59, 73, 163, 205, 238–39 (n. 69); classification of, in census, 65; in insults suits, 107, 144, 146–47, 149, 150, 152; violence and stereotypes in Limón, 174–78
Rape, 86, 245–46 (n. 37)
Rastafarianism, 203
Religion: missionaries, 27, 28; Afro-Jamaican, 29, 167, 179; popular piety, 161–62
Reproductive labor, 4, 7–8, 51–53. See also Gender; Kinship; Sex
Respectability, 19, 140–41, 159, 167–71
Reventazón River, 45
Rodman, Paul, 179
Roseberry, William, 213
Royal Pragmatic, 25, 26
Rubber (hule), 42, 49, 118, 121, 122, 194, 201
Russia: migrants from, 51

Sabean, David Warren, 153
Saborío, Carlos, 158, 260 (n. 65)
St. Andrew parish (Jamaica), 44
St. Ann parish (Jamaica), 51
St. Elizabeth parish (Jamaica), 51
St. James parish (Jamaica), 51, 207

174, 180–84, 195; against women, 174, 184–200, 211, 215; and racial stereotypes, 174–80; and public authority, 182–84, 196–97. *See also* Homicide statistics

Víquez, Daniel, 147

Virginity, loss of, 3–4. *See also* Deflowering

Wages, 30, 31, 53, 60, 81, 124, 125, 126, 146, 201

Welfare state, 12, 209, 212–13

Western Caribbean, 4, 6; migratory circuits, 10, 17, 35–36, 40, 43, 44, 57–58, 68–69, 73–74, 206–8

West Indians in Limón: upward mobility of, 69–70, 164–65, 166; role of leaders, 139, 164, 165–71, 179, 209, 272 (n. 11). *See also* Migration: from British West Indies

Wilson, Peter, 141, 256 (n. 10), 261 (n. 68)

Women: as plantation laborers, 9, 131, 206; use of courts by, 12, 211–12, 214, 253 (n. 39), 272 (n. 16); and service economy, 43, 52–53, 128, 148, 165, 205, 207, 215; patterns of participation in insults suits, 142, 154, 155; violence against, 174, 184–200, 211, 215; laboring life cycle, 207–8. *See also* Gender; Kinship; Sex

Work companions. See *Compañeros*

World War I, 6, 10, 64

Xirinach, Miguel, 144, 159

Yucatán, 44

Zambos, 25

Zent, 45, 53, 56, 57, 131, 156, 175, 199